Dictionary *of* Business Terms

by

Jae K. Shim, MBA, Ph.D.

Professor of Business Administration
California State University, Long Beach

and

President
Delta Consulting Company

THOMSON

Australia · Brazil · Canada · Mexico · Singapore · Spain · United Kingdom · United States

THOMSON

TM

Dictionary of Business Terms
Jae K. Shim, MBA, Ph.D.

Composed by:
Chip Butzko

Printed in the United States of America by RR Donnelley, Crawfordsville

1 2 3 4 5 09 08 07 06
This book is printed on acid-free paper.

ISBN 0-324-20545-7

A CIP Library of Congress Cataloging in Publication Data Requested.

For more information about our products, contact us at:
Thomson Learning
Academic Resource Center
1-800-423-0563

Thomson Higher Education
5191 Natorp Boulevard
Mason, Ohio 45040
USA

About Dr. Jae K. Shim

Dr. Jae K. Shim, MBA, Ph.D. is Professor of Business Administration at California State University, Long Beach, and CEO of Delta Consulting Company, a management consulting and training firm. Dr. Shim received his M.B.A. and Ph.D. degrees from the University of California at Berkeley (Haas School of Business). Dr. Shim has been a consultant to commercial and nonprofit organizations over 25 years.

Dr. Shim has over 50 college and professional books to his credit, including *2006-2007 Corporate Controller's Handbook of Financial Management, Barron's Accounting Handbook, Dictionary of Accounting Terms, Investment Sourcebook, Dictionary of Real Estate, Dictionary of Economics, Dictionary of International Investment Terms, Dictionary of Personal Finance, Encyclopedic Dictionary of Accounting and Finance, Dictionary of International Business Terms, Encyclopedic Dictionary of International Finance and Banking, U.S Master Finance Guide, The Vest-Pocket CPA, The Vest-Pocket CFO,* and the best-selling *Vest-Pocket MBA.*

His books have been published by Penguin Portfolio, Prentice-Hall, McGraw-Hill, Barron's, Commercial Clearing House (CCH), Southwestern, Aspen, John Wiley, American Management Association (Amacom), Fitzroy Dearborn, CRC Press, and the American Institute of CPAs (AICPA). Nineteen of his publications have been translated into foreign languages such as Spanish, Chinese, Russian, Italian, Japanese, and Korean.

Dr. Shim has been frequently quoted by such media as the *Los Angeles Times, Orange County Register, Business Start-ups, Personal Finance,* and *Money Radio.* Dr. Shim has also published numerous articles in professional and academic journals. He was the recipient of the *Credit Research Foundation Award* for his article on cash flow forecasting and financial modeling.

What This Book Will Do for You

This dictionary is directed toward the public at large. The idea behind the *Dictionary of Business Terms* is for the layperson, consumer, and professional to be able to read and comprehend terms and concepts continuously appearing in daily newspapers (e.g., *Wall Street Journal, New York Times, Financial Times, USA Today)* and business magazines (e.g., *Business Week, Fortune, Money, The Economist*) dealing with business and management, law, investments, personal finance, and consumer economics.

The dictionary will cover all the areas and terms of business and management. The topics include accounting, finance, investments, banking, personal finance and money management, taxation, real estate, organization and management, marketing and advertising, operations/production management, computers and information technology (IT), economics, insurance, business law, real estate and housing, international business and finance, government, statistics, quantitative methods, and any other related field. The dictionary includes the latest terminology, thinking, and Internet.

The Dictionary of Business Terms contains a host of practical applications, examples, illustrations, tables, graphs, and checklists to aid reader comprehension and use. Acronyms and abbreviations are provided in the Appendix.

Some unique features that separate this dictionary from the competition are as follows:
1. It is practical and user friendly, rather than cut, dry and theoretical.
2. It is full of practical examples, applications, and use of information technology (IT) and Internet.
3. It is packed with charts, diagrams, and tables that facilitate an increased understanding on the part of users.
4. It includes the latest terms and slangs reflecting a growing trend and new developments.
5. Detailed discussions are presented on economic statistics and indicators released by governments and private sources.

This dictionary can also be used as a supplement by students taking business-related courses in adult education programs, extension centers, and colleges and universities, individuals contemplating business start-ups, or business managers.

Table of Contents

Numbers

802.11 a family of specifications developed by the US Institute of Electrical and Electronics Engineers (IEEE). There are currently three specifications in the family (802.11a, 802.11b and 802.11g), with more being developed. The 802.11b standard often referred to as Wi-Fi is currently more widespread. However, hardware manufacturers are increasingly offering multi-standard equipment that can work with various standards.

8K form filed by corporations with the SEC to report corporate changes or material events that are important to investors and not previously disclosed in any other form.

10-K annual filing with the Securities and Exchange Commission (SEC) for publicly traded companies. Financial statements and supporting details are provided. Form 10-K typically contains more financial information than the annual report to stockholders. Audited basic financial statements are included. Examples of disclosures are sales, operating income, segmental sales by major line of business for the last five years, and general business information.

10-Q quarterly filing with the Securities and Exchange Commission (SEC) by publicly traded companies. It contains interim financial statements and related disclosures and may cover one particular quarter or be cumulative. It should present comparative figures for the same period of the prior year. The statements may or may not be audited. Form 10-Q is less comprehensive than Form 10-K.

12b-1 Fees fees of a mutual fund that cover advertising and marketing costs, but do nothing to improve the performance of the fund. Their main purpose is to bring new customers to the fund, and ultimately more money for the fund's management to invest.

30-year Treasury Bond a U.S. Treasury debt obligation that has a maturity of 30 years. The 30-year Treasury used to be the bellwether U.S. bond, but now most consider the 10-year to be the benchmark.

401 (k) Plan a company-sponsored retirement plan; also called 401(k) salary reduction plan. The amount withheld may be invested in stocks, bonds, or money market funds. The employee's contributions and all earnings arising therefrom go tax free until withdrawn at the request of the employee or until the employee retires. Usually, the employer provides a choice of investment vehicles into which the funds may be placed while earning tax-deferred returns. Furthermore, many employers offer matching contributions. These contributions, plus the current reduction in income taxes, typically make 401(k) salary reduction plans an excellent long-term investment. *See also* 403(k) plans; 457 plans.

403(B) Plans employer-sponsored retirement plans that are equivalent to 401(k) but for nonprofit employers. *See also* 401(k) plans; 457 plans.

407 Plans employer-sponsored retirement plans that are equivalent to 401(k) but for for state or local government employees. *See also* 401(k) plans; 403 (b) plans.

80-20 Rule *see* pareto rule.

Aa

AAA, AA, A Ratings bond ratings given by Standard & Poor's as well as Moody's. These ratings refer to the financial stability of the bond issuer. *See also* Bond Ratings.

Abatement
In General:
> 1. to decrease in amount or value.
> 2. reduction or rebate on service charges.

Taxation: a complete or partial cancellation of a levy imposed by a governmental unit. Abatements usually apply to tax levies, special assessments, and service charges.

Law: a temporary suspension or termination in a lawsuit.

ABC Inventory Analysis or Management, ABC Method, ABC Analysis
inventory control system that divides the inventory into three classes. A (high value), B (medium value), and C (low value) depending on the value and importance of the item. It gives the most attention to A inventory, then B, then C. The figure is an illustration of the ABC inventory control system.

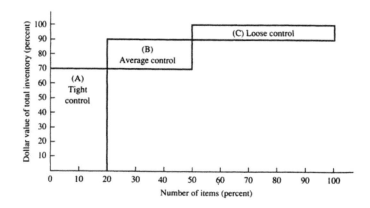

Ability to Pay

Business: a customer's ability to make payments to the vendor.

Banking: a borrower's financial ability to service the interest and principal requirements of a loan agreement. Normally the ability to pay is determined by future earnings prospects. Those having a higher ability to pay would have a higher credit rating.

Labor relations: the ability of an employer to meet a union's financial demands.

Bonds: the source of revenue pledged to service the bonds. In the case of a corporate bond, the source of revenue would be the earnings of the corporation. In the case of governmental bonds, tax revenues would determine the ability of the governmental unit to service the interest and principal needs.

Absenteeism habitual failure of employees to appear, especially for work or other regular duty. It also refers to the rate of occurrence of habitual absence from work or duty. One formula for computing absenteeism rates, suggested by the U.S. Department of Labor, is as follows:

$$\frac{\textbf{Number of person days lost through job absence during period}}{\textbf{(Average number of employees) x (Number of work days)}} \times 100$$

Absolute Advantage

1. ability to produce a good with fewer resources per unit than that of its trading partners.
2. an advantage held by a particular company because of patents, ownership of natural resources, skills of its people, or some other factor; often called *absolute cost advantage.*

Absolute Value the numerical, or positive, value of a real number without regard to its sign; also called numerical value. For example, the absolute value of -4 (written |-4|) is 4.

Absorption Costing a costing method whereby all manufacturing costs, variable and fixed, are treated as product costs, while nonmanufacturing costs (e.g., selling and administrative expenses) are treated as period expenses. Absorption costing for inventory valuation is required for external reporting; also called *Full Costing.*

Accelerated Cost Recovery System (ACRS) a system of depreciation for tax purposes mandated by the Tax Reform Act of 1986. The type of property determines its class. Instead of providing statutory tables, prescribed methods of depreciation are assigned to each class of property. For 3,5,7, and 10-year classes, the relevant depreciation method is the 200% declining balance method. For 15- and 20-year property, the appropriate method is the 150% declining balance method switching to the straight-line method when it will yield a larger allowance. For residential rental property (27.5 years) and nonresidential real property (31.5 years), the applicable method is the straight-line method. A taxpayer may make an irrevocable election to treat all property in one of the classes under the straight-line method. Property is statutorily placed in one of the classes. The purpose of

ACRS is to encourage more capital investment by businesses. It permits a faster recovery of the asset's cost and thus provides larger tax benefits in the earlier years.

Accelerated Depreciation depreciation system that results in expense recognition of greater amounts in the earliest years. The greatest tax benefits from depreciation are enjoyed in the earlier years. Accelerated depreciation methods include double declining balance, 150% declining balance, sum-of-the-years-digits, and others. *See also* Accelerated Cost Recovery System; Double-Declining-Balance Depreciation; Sum-of-the-Year's Digits (SYD) Method.

Accelerator Principle a proposition that net investment in capital goods depends upon changes in the level of GDP. If aggregate demand increases, the economy, operating at full capacity, will have to undertake additional investment in order to produce an increase in GDP.

Acceptable Quality Level (AQL) quality standard that allows for a prespecified number of defects.

Access Code a password containing numbers, characters, or both used to gain access to computer systems, internet, or files.

Access Time the length of time that a data storage device, associated with a computer, takes to process and return data from the time of the original request for the data. This can occur as fast as seventy nanoseconds in the latest computers. A nanosecond is one billionth of a second.

Accidental Death and Dismemberment (AD&D) a type of health insurance that pays a lump sum if the insured is accidentally killed in an auto accident or if he/she is hit by another car. The policy also pays a portion of the insured amount if he/she loses part of his/her body such as a leg, an arm or an eye. It may also pay disability income should he/she become totally disabled.

Accommotive Monetary Policy Federal Reserve System policy to increase the amount of money available to banks for lending.

Account
1. a record of the relationship and transactions between an individual and another party. The other party may be providing products or services. Examples are an individual's checking account at a bank and credit account at a retail store.
2. a record of the changes in an accounting item, such as cash, inventory, or revenues.

Accountability
1. the liability of a board of directors to shareholders and stakeholders for corporate performance and actions of the corporation.
2. an organization system of delegating responsibility.

Accountant one trained in one or more fields of accounting. Accountants prepare financial statements and tax returns, audit financial records, and develop financial plans. A bookkeeper is distinguished from an accountant as one who employs lesser professional skills. The bookkeeping function is primarily one of recording transactions in the accounting books.

Accounting Equation an expression of the equivalency in dollar amounts of assets and liabilities and equity in double-entry accounting, often stated as:

Assets = Liabilities + Owners' Equity.

Accounting Principles Board (APB) former body of AICPA that used to determine accounting procedures and principles for the accounting field. The APB was replaced by the Financial Accounting Standards Board (FASB).

Accounting System a system or procedure that processes financial transactions to provide scorekeeping, attention-directing, and decision-making information to management. Accounting is concerned with these two kinds of management information (1) financial information, and (2) information generated from the processing of transaction data. The system is responsible for the preparation of financial information and the information obtained from transaction data for the purposes of (1) internal reporting to managers for use in planning and controlling current and future operations and for nonroutine decision making, as well as for (2) external reporting to outside parties such as stockholders, creditors, and government.

Accounts Payable obligations to pay for goods or services that have been acquired on open account from suppliers.

Accounts Receivable amounts due the company on account from customers who have bought merchandise or received services.

Accretion
1. growth in assets in acquisitions, mergers, multiplication, or internal expansion. Examples are aging of wine, nursery stock, and livestock. It increases the economic value of an asset, usually due to natural causes.
2. the process of land build-up because of the gradual accumulation of waterborne rock, sand, and soil.
3. an increase in value derived from an intended accumulation. An example is the increased value in a pension fund due to accumulated contributions, income from the contributed principal, or both.
4. adjustment of the difference between the face value of a bond and the price of the bond bought at an original discount.

Accrual Accounting recognizing revenue when earned and expenses when incurred regardless of when cash is received or paid. This differs from cash basis accounting, which records revenues and expenses only when cash is received or paid.

Accrued Expense a financial obligation, debt, claim, or potential loss is recorded when incurred at the end of the reporting period buy not yet paid; also called accrued liability.

Accrued Liability *see* Accrued Expense.

Accumulated Depreciation sum of depreciation charges taken to date since its date of acquisition on a fixed asset such as plant and equipment.

Accumulated Dividend an unpaid dividend due, typically to owners of cumulative preferred shares; also known as cumulative dividends and dividends in arrears.

Acid Test a stringent measure of a company's ability to meet current obligations; also called *Quick Ratio*. The ratio is found by dividing the most liquid current assets (quick assets) by current liabilities.

Acquisition
1. the purchase of an item such as an asset or good.
2. the process of obtaining a controlling interest.
3. takeover of one business by another business.

Acre a two dimensional land measurement equivalent to: 4.046856E+07 square centimeters, 4046.856 square meters, 4.046856E-03 square kilometers, 627,2640 square inches, 43, 560 square feet, 4,840 square yards, .0015625 square miles, or 10 square chains. For example, a survey of Smith's property shows that it is 5.2018 acres of land.

Across the Board including all, or almost, all, of everything within a group or category. Examples are all employees receiving the same percentage raise from the employer, or almost all stocks rising in price on the same day.

Act of God an unpreventable action occurring without the intervention of man. Acts of God are normally associated with violent natural occurrences such as droughts, earthquakes, floods, hurricanes, lightning, monsoons, pestilence, tornadoes, and wind storms. An Act of God is a physical occurrence, usually accidental in nature, and is an outcome of the natural universe having no relationship to the actions of man. For example, an individual files an insurance claim to indemnify the damages caused to his roof by the effects of a hurricane, which was an Act of God.

Action
Legal: a suit brought before a court of law, in the form of a complaint, demanding from another party a legal right. It has all the procedures accompanying any judicial action including court adjudication and its enforcement or denial.
Real estate: a procedure brought before the court to repossess or regain specific properties or hereditaments. There are two basic types of real actions. Those based upon the right of property are termed *droitural* and those based upon the right of possession are termed *possessory*.

Active Financial Planning Software new-breed, Web-enabled software that includes applications and the new level of functionality that combine budgeting, forecasting analytics, business intelligence, and collaboration.

Activity Analysis the process of identifying, describing, and evaluating the activities an organization performs.

Activity-Based Costing (ABC) system that accumulates costs on the basis of production or service activities at a firm. Basically it assigns costs by activity and links them to specific products

Activity-Based Management (ABM) a systemwide, integrated approach that focuses management's attention on activities with the objectives of improving customer value and the profit achieved by providing this value. Activity-based costing (ABC) is the major source of information for activity-based management.

Actual Cash Value (ACV) the replacement cost of an item less accumulated depreciation.

Actuarial Equivalent a mathematical equivalent, such as a lump-sum distribution from a pension plan that is equivalent to an annuity distribution. It is equivalent because the present value of both are identical.

Actuary the expert involved in mathematical computations and analyses of risks and premiums for insurance considering probability estimates.

ADB *see* Asian Development Bank.

Add-On Loan
1. a second loan taken out for a larger amount before the first loan is repaid. Taking out add-on loans is called *flipping*. For example, assume that one's original loan of $10,000 has been repaid down to $5,000. He/she may decide to refinance the debt balance of $5,000 and borrow an additional $4,000 from the same lender. It may be a wise decision to increase an existing note at a lower interest rate.
2. a loan in which the interest is added to the original loan balance to determine the monthly payments.

Adhesion Contract a legally enforceable standardized contract offered by a business for a product or service to consumers essentially on a "take it or leave it" basis. Under its terms, the consumer has no opportunity to negotiate the terms or conditions of the agreement and can only be satisfied by accepting it. An adhesion contract puts the consumer at a serious disadvantage. An example would be a real estate lease agreement where the terms are non-negotiable.

ADR *see* American Depository Receipt.

Advertising Agency a firm specializing in the planning, monitoring, and placing of advertising in a variety of media for its client company. The firm oversees its client account to help determine what message the company wants to communicate and how, and then implements the strategy through specific art and layout of advertising pages or production of radio, television, and Internet spots.

Advertising Elasticity of Demand the percentage change in the quantity sold (or market share) that is associated with a percentage change in the advertising expenditures of that product. It is used as a measure of short-run advertising effectiveness. This elasticity may be affected by a number of factors such as the stage of the product's market development, the extent to which competitors react to the firm's advertising, either by further advertising or by increased promotional efforts, the importance of other marketing factors (e.g., prices, incomes, tastes, etc.), and the quality and quantity of the firm's past and present advertising. *See also* Elasticity of Demand.

Ad Valorem a literal translation is "according to value." *See also* Ad Valorem Tax.

Ad Valorem Tax taxes imposed on the value of property. The more common ad valorem tax is that imposed by states, counties, and cities on real estate. Ad valorem taxes can, however, be imposed on personal property.

Advertising-to-Sales Ratio the ratio of advertising expenses to sales (in the same period or in one future period). The ratio is of interest to business economists and marketing managers when comparing advertising activity to competitors. Generally, the advertising-to-sales ratio of companies in the industry is usually higher with a lack of price competition.

Adapted Marketing Mix an international marketing strategy for adjusting the marketing-mix elements to each international target market, bearing more cost but hoping for a larger market share and return.

Address
1. e-mail address
2. uniform resource locator (URL)
3. street address

Adjudication determination of a final judgment in a legal action.

Adjustable Life Insurance insurance coverage that may be changed by the policyholder as necessary depending upon changing circumstances. The policy owner may change the plan of insurance, premiums, and face value. For example, the insured may decide for financial reasons to modify the time period and amount of premiums to be paid.

Adjustable Rate Mortgage (ARM) or, variable or flexible rate mortgage. A mortgage where the interest rate is not fixed but changes over the life of the loan. ARMs often feature attractive starting interest rates and monthly payments. An adjustable rate often uses the basis such as the one-year Treasury bill average, three-month certificate of deposit (CD) rate, 11th District cost of funds, London Inter-Bank Offering Rate (LIBOR), or prime rate.

Adjustable-Morgages Indexes Benchmark indexes that determine the rate for an adjustable-rate mortgage. When borrowers get this type of mortgage two main factors determine how payments will change:
• The benchmark indexes set by market forces and published by a neutral third party.
• The margin—an agreed-upon number of percentage points—added to the index to determine your rate.

Below is a look at some popular indexes for adjustable mortgages and how these benchmarks work:

- **11th District Cost of Funds:** This index represents the cost of funds for banks in the 11th district of the Federal Home Loan Bank system (Arizona, California, and Nevada) The index averages the interest banks pay on money they borrow, mostly on customers' savings accounts. Anyone who has had an interest-bearing savings account knows that those rates are low and move tortoise-like. COFI (pronounced "coffee") lags the overall market and benefits borrowers when rates are rising.

- **12-Month Treasury Average:** Average yields of the one-year Treasury bill are usually called the "12 MAT" or "12 MTA." Every month, the U.S. Treasury publishes the average yield on a constant-maturity 1-year Treasury bill for the previous month. The 12 MAT index takes the average of the last 12 averages. This index moves slowly

- **London Interbank Offered Rate Indexes:** "LIBOR" (pronounced LIE-bore) tracks rates at which London banks pay to borrow one another's reserves. There are various LIBOR maturities. Most common are one-month, six-month and 12-month. Lenders like LIBOR because it moves quickly.

- **Constant-Maturity Treasury Indexes:** These benchmarks follow weekly or monthly fluctuations in yields for 1-year Treasury bills. CMT rates move up and down rather quickly. Most CMT-indexed mortgages adjust once a year.

Adjusted Capitalized Cost in a lease, capitalized cost reduced by factory rebates, a down payment, a capitalized cost reduction, or other amounts; also called net capitalized cost. It might also reflect amounts added to the capitalized cost, such as a loan balance from a trade-in. *See also* Capitalized Cost.

Adjusted Gross Income (AGI) a federal tax term applying to the difference between a tax payer's gross income and adjustments to income. These adjustments include deductions for IRA and Keogh pension plans, alimony payments, and penalty on early withdrawal of savings. AGI is the taxpayer's income before taking wither the standard deduction or itemized deductions, such as medical expenses, state and local taxes, interest expenses, and contributions.

Adjuster an insurance term referring to an employee of an insurance company or an outside consultant who ascertains the reason for loss and estimates the amount of the insurable loss, if any. The adjuster may decide that the insured is not covered under the policy. The insured may retain his or her own representative, called a public adjuster.

Administrative Budget a formal and comprehensive financial plan through which management of an nonprofit organization (NPO) may control day-to-day affairs and activities.

Administrator

1. performer of executive duties of an organization.
2. court-appointed individual to settle an estate when an executor is not qualified or not available to do so or there is no will and the court has to appoint someone.

Adverse Possession acquisition of land through prolonged and unauthorized occupation under an evident claim or right, in denial or opposition to the title of another claimant. Adverse possession is a statue of limitations that prevents a legal owner from claiming title to the land when the owner has done nothing to evict an adverse occupant during the statutory period. The courts are quite demanding of proof before they permit adverse possession. For example, the claimant must show proof that he or she has maintained actual, visible, continuous, exclusive, hostile, and notorious possession and be publicly claiming ownership to the property.

Advertising any paid form of nonpersonal communication, by paid announcements in the print, broadcast, or electronic media, designed to gain acceptance of the advertiser's message.

Advertising Agency an independent business organization composed of creative and business people who develop, prepare, and place advertising in the media for sellers seeking to find buyers for their goods and services.

Advertising Triad a group composed of advertisers (who sponsor and pay for advertisements), agencies (who create, execute, and place advertisements), and media (who deliver advertisements).

Affidavit a statement or declaration in writing, made under an oath before some officer (such as a notary public) who has the authority to administer the oath or affirmation. For example, in the case of affidavit of title, the seller (the affiant) identifies himself or herself and his or her marital status certifying that since the examination of title on the contract date there are no judgments, divorces, or bankruptcies, or unrecorded deeds, unpaid repairs or defects of title known to him or her and that he or she is in possession of the property.

Affiliate a partly or fully owned unit of a multinational company. Affiliates include wholly owned branches, foreign-incorporated subsidiaries, joint ventures, and any other legal foreign operation.

Affirm to confirm, ratify, verify, and accept a transaction that can be canceled.

Affirmative Action federal and state programs prohibiting any form of preferential treatment or discrimination based on age, national origin, race, religion, sex or other personal characteristics, using devices such as deception and quotas, to prevent equal access to employment and other societal opportunities including voting and housing. Beginning with several Federal civil rights acts, most particularly the Civil Rights Act of 1964, and subsequent state legislation affirmative action programs encourage equal opportunities and open access for all.

Age Discrimination in Employment Act (ADEA) the 1967 legislation that prohibits job discrimination against people age 40 and older. It prohibits discrimination in pay, benefits, and continued employment. ADEA outlaws almost all mandatory retirement. It awards double unpaid wages for willful violations, and grants a broad set of private lawsuit remedies.

Agency

1. the relationship between two individuals in which one is a PRINCIPAL and the other is his or her agent representing the principal in transactions with other parties. This relationship arises out of a contract, either expressed or implied, written or oral, wherein the agent is employed by the principal to do certain acts dealing with a third party.
2. a governmental unit, such as a department, committee, or council.
3. the capacity of buying and selling a security or property for a client.

Agency Costs reduction in the value of the organization when an agent (a subunit manager) pursues his/her interest to the detriment of the principal's (the organization's) interest.

Agency for International Development (AID) an agency (*www.usaid.gov/*) of the U.S. government founded by President Kennedy in 1961 whose mission is to foster social and economic development in the Third World. Its initiatives are the following: assisting transition to market-based economies in Eastern Europe; establishment of a regulatory framework for securities markets in Indonesia, Jordan, and Sri Lanka; road construction and maintenance in Latin America and Southern Asia; and agricultural research and farm credits worldwide.

Agency Fund the assets held in a fund under an agency relationship for another entity. For example, it consists of resources retained by ABC agency as an agent for DEF governmental unit.

Agency Problem the problem that interferes with the implementation of a firm's goal of maximization of shareholder wealth. The agency problem is the result of a separation of ownership from control (or management). For example, a large firm may be run by professional managers who have little or no ownership position in the firm. As a result of this separation between the decision makers and owners (shareholders), managers may make decisions that are not in line with the goal of maximization of shareholder wealth. They may attempt to benefit themselves in terms of salary and perquisites at the expense of owners. *See also* Agency Costs.

Agent a person authorized by another, the principal, to perform or transact a service involving a third party. An agent generally performs a business-related service either for the private or public sector. Agents have three basic characteristics: (1) they act on behalf of and are subject to the control of a principal, (2) they are not the principal, and (3) they must follow the principal's instructions.
co-agent: agents who share the principal's authorization to perform his or her best instructions.
exclusive agent: the only agent permitted to act for the principal in a particular territory or matter although the principal may act for himself.
general agent: one who is authorized to act for a principal in all matters concerning a particular nature.
independent agent: an independent business person contracting with a principal to achieve a particular outcome.
mercantile agent: individuals employed for the sale of goods or merchandise.

The two principal classes of mercantile agents are brokers and factors. Factors are sometimes referred to as *commission agents* or *commission merchants*.

private agent: an individual acting solely for an individual in the conduct of his or her private affairs.

public agent: a person appointed by a unit of the government or state for the purpose of representing the public on matters pertaining to the administration of public business affairs.

real estate agent: an individual primarily engaged in the sale or rent of real estate for others. Real estate includes all types of property including vacant land, businesses, houses, and apartments.

Aggregate Concentration Ratios ratios that measure the percentage market share held by an industry's leading firms. Leading firm market shares are calculated using sales data typically for the top four or top eight firms in an industry. When these ratios are low, competition will be keen; high ratios suggest that leading firms may have the potential for both pricing flexibility and abnormal (or excess) profits. Concentration ratios are published periodically in the *Census of Manufacturers*.

Aggregate Demand/Supply an economic term for the total goods and services supplied to the market at alternative price levels in a given period of time; also referred to as total output. Aggregate demand is the total amount of goods and services demanded in the economy at alternative income levels in a given period including both consumer and producer's goods, also referred to as total spending.

Aggressive Growth Fund or, Maximum Capital Gain, Capital Appreciation, or Small-Company Growth Fund. A type of mutual fund taking greater risk in order to yield maximum appreciation (instead of current dividend income). It typically invests in the stocks of upstart, and high-tech oriented companies. Return can be great but so can risk. Aggressive investment strategies include leverage purchases, options, short sales, and even the purchase of high-risk stock.

Aggregate Production Planning establishment of aggregate production and inventory levels over a medium range time horizon. There are two types: level plan and chase plan.

Level Plan aggregate production plan that maintains a uniform output rate.

Chase Plan aggregate production plan that adjusts capacity in response to seasonal demand.

Aging Schedule a list of outstanding accounts receivable, usually grouped by length of time payments are overdue.

Agreement of Sale a written agreement between seller and purchaser in which the purchaser agrees to buy certain property and the seller agrees to sell them upon terms of the agreement; also called *offer and acceptance*, *contract of sale*, or *earnest money contract*. Example: Jeannette's broker prepared an agreement of sale to sell a home to David. Both principals signed it. The agreement states that the price of $100,000 is to be paid in cash at closing, subject to David's ability to arrange an $80,000 loan at a 10% interest rate.

AICPA *see* American Institute of Certified Public Accountants.

AID *see* Agency for International Development.

Air Rights rights to the use of open air space over property, including commercial aircraft flight paths, the erection of signs, buildings, railroad rights of way, and the rights to preserve an open view by preventing the building of obstructions. Condominium owners retain the air space within their individual units.

Airway Bill a document corresponding to the bill of lading in land surface transport or of a marine bill of lading in water transport. It is used for goods shipped by air (air transport).

A.K.A. "also known as." In a contract or other document, an individual may be referred to as AKA. For example, a married woman may customarily use her maiden name interchangeably. Therefore, a contract stipulates her maiden name as AKA.

Algorithm a step-by-step, reiterative mathematical or problem-solving procedure.

All Inclusive Trust Deed (AITD) *see* Wraparound Mortgage (Trust Deed).

All Risk/All Peril Policy a feature in a property insurance policy that covers each and every loss except for those specifically excluded by the policy. This is the broadest type of insurance that can be bought. For example, if an insurance policy does not specifically exclude losses from flood damage, the insured is covered automatically for such losses.

Alliance The collaboration of two or more companies to provide a wider range of products or services to customers than anyone can offer separately. *See also* Strategic Alliance.

Allocation to spread costs systematically to different objects such as products, accounts, services, departments, and the like.

Allotment the part of an appropriation that may be encumbered or expended during an allotment period, which is usually a period of time less than one fiscal year. Bi-monthly and quarterly allotment periods are most common.

Allowance
1. the number of withholding allowances on the W-4 form. A company computes how much taxes to withhold from your paycheck based on this number.
2. promotional money paid by manufacturers to retailers in return for an agreement to feature the manufacture's products in some way

Alpha the excess return that the portfolio manager is able to earn above an unmanaged portfolio (or market portfolio) that has the same risk. In the context of a mutual fund, an alpha value is the value representing the difference between the return on a fund and a point on the market line, where the market line describes the relationship between excess returns and the portfolio beta. Alpha = beta x (market return–risk-free return)

Morningstar Inc. (800) 876-5005 offers alpha values of major funds, as does its website at *www.morningstar.net*.

Example 1: If the market return is 8% and the risk-free rate (such as a rate on a T-bill) is 5%, the market excess return equals 3%. A portfolio with a beta of 1 should expect to earn the market rate of excess returns, or alpha, equal to 3% (1 x 3%). A fund with a beta of 1.5 should provide excess returns of 4.5% (1.5 x 3%). Alpha value is used to evaluate the performance of mutual funds. Generally, a positive alpha (excess return) indicates superior performance while a negative value leads to the opposite conclusion.

Example 2: The fund in Example 1 has a beta of 1.5, which indicates an expected excess return of 4.5% along the market line. Assume that the fund had an actual excess return of only 4.1%. That means the fund has a negative alpha of .4% (4.1% - 4.5%). The fund's performance is therefore inferior to that of the market. The following presents alphas for some selected mutual funds:

Alphas For Some Selected Mutual Funds

Company	Ticker Symbol	Alpha
Harbor International	HAINX	2.18
Fidelity Overseas	FOSFX	-3.58
Templeton International A	TEGEX	-1.35
Vanguard International Growth	VWIGX	-0.89

Source: MSN Money Central Investor *(http://moneycentral.msn.com/investor/ partsub/funds/portfolio.asp)*, February, 2006.

Note: A fund's alpha is only reliable when its R-squared is relatively high.

Alphanumeric consisting of both characters and numbers.

Alternative Minimum Tax (AMT) an IRS mechanism created to ensure that high-income individuals, corporations, trusts, and estates pay at least some minimum amount of tax, regardless of deductions, credits, or exemptions. It operates by adding certain tax-preference items back into adjusted gross income. It is taxed based in part on the taxpayer's tax preferences that are levied when it exceeds the regular tax. The idea behind the AMT is that everyone should pay a fair share of taxes.

Alternative Mortgage Instrument (AMI) an alternative mortgage that is different from a standard fixed-rate, level-payment mortgage.

Alternative Work Arrangements work schedules that are given to employees that are not the typical "9 A.M. to 5 P.M." schedules.

Amended Tax Return changes in income, deductions, or credits that must be made to an individual tax return, Form 1040, after it has been filed. Form 1040X, Amended U.S. Individual Income Tax Return, must be used to report these changes. The amended tax return must be filed within three years after the date the original return was filed, or within two years after the date the tax was paid, whichever is greater. A return filed early is considered filed on the date it was due.

America Online the largest commercial online service or Internet Service Provider (ISP).

American Accounting Association (AAA) *(aaahq.org)* organization primarily of accounting academicians emphasizing the development of a theoretical foundation for accounting. Its research with respect to education and theory is distributed through committee report and a quarterly journal, *The Accounting Review*.

American Depository Receipt (ADR) a certificate of ownership, issued by a U.S. bank, representing a claim on underlying foreign stocks. ADRs let U.S. residents buy and sell foreign stocks without the hassle of actually owning them. Banks issue ADRs, not the corporation's stock certificate, to an American investor who buys shares of that corporation. The stock certificate is kept at the bank. The Bank of New York maintains indexes of how ADRS listed in the United States perform. This information can be retrieved at the Bank of New York Internet site *(www.bankofny.com)*. J.P.Morgan also maintains an Internet site providing ADR market performance *(adr.com)*. The Bank of New York *(www.bankofny.com/ htmlpages/index.htm)* and Stock City provide the name, exchange and Ticker Symbol for ADRs. You can download *The Complete Depository Receipt (DR) Directory* from the Bank of New York Website *(see* Figure 1)

Figure 1
The Bank Of New York Website

See also The Bank Of New York Adr Indexes.

American Federation of Labor-Congress of Industrial Organizations (AFL-CIO) American federation of autonomous labor unions formed in 1955 by the merger of the AFL (founded 1886), which originally organized workers in craft unions, and the CIO (founded 1935), which organized workers by industries. AFL-CIO is the voluntary federation of America's labor unions, representing more than 13 million working women and men.

American Institute of Certified Public Accountants (AICPA) the professional association of Certified Public Accountants (CPAs). It is a group of accountants who issue pronouncements that make up Generally Accepted Accounting Principles (GAAP). The AICPA also issues Statements on Auditing Standards, which set forth the requirements to be followed by independent CPAs when conducting audits of their clients' financial statements.

American Management Association (AMA) *(www.amanet.org/)* an association of executives, managers, and supervisors in industry, commerce, government, and nonprofit organizations. It is a global not-for-profit, membership-based association that provides a full range of management development and educational services to individuals, companies and government agencies worldwide, including 486 of the Fortune 500 companies. Each year, thousands of business professionals acquire the latest business know-how, valuable insights and increased confidence at AMA seminars, conferences, current issues forums and briefings, as well as through AMA books and publications, research and print and online self-study courses.

American Marketing Association (AMA) *(www.marketingpower.com)* an international professional organization for people involved in the practice, study and teaching of marketing. Its principal roles are (1) to always understand and satisfy the needs of marketers so as to provide them with products and services that will help them be better marketers, (2) to empower marketers through information, education, (3) provide relationships and resources that will enrich their professional development and careers, and (4) to advance the thought, application, and ethical practice of marketing.

American Production and Inventory Control Society (APICS) *(www.apics.org)* an international, not-for-profit organization serving the manufacturing, materials management, resource management, and service industries. Established in 1957, American Production and Inventory Control Society (APICS) is designed to meet the needs of professionals in all areas of resource management, including inventory, materials, information systems, accounting/finance, supply chain, and all other functional areas that contribute to the overall efficiency and productivity of an organization.

American Society of Real Estate Counselors (ASREC) founded in 1953 and located in Chicago, IL, ASREC has 850 members. ASREC is a society of real estate professionals providing a counseling service on real estate purchase and investment decisions through a negotiated fee rather than charging a commission. Members have the CRE (Counselor of Real Estate) title. The society maintains a speaker's bureau and conducts educational campaigns. It publishes a directory and the semiannual *Real Estate Issues*.

American Stock Exchange (AMEX) the second-oldest stock exchange in the United States and was founded in 1842.

American Terms foreign exchange quotations for the U.S. dollar, expressed as the number of U.S. dollars per unit of non-U.S. currency.

Americans with Disabilities Act (ADA) the 1990 legislation that forbids employment discrimination against *qualified* individuals with mental or physical impairments limiting a major life activity (e.g., blindness, cancer, AIDS, and learning disabilities), records of such impairments, or perception—albeit false—of such impairments.

Amortization
1. payment of a loan on an installment basis. The term is usually associated with a mortgage payment schedule. As a loan is amortized, the equity in the associated property is increased. However, in the early years of a mortgage, the majority of the payments are for interest rather than principal.
2. to write off gradually and systematically over time. For instance, a CPA amortizes the cost of an asset through depreciation.

Amortized Loan a loan paid off in periodic equal installments and includes varying portions of principal and interest during its term. Examples include mortgage loans and most commercial loans.

Amount of $1 The decimal ratio of the future value of an accumulation at compound interest to each dollar of the original sum. The future value (compound amount) and present value tables are available for the amount of $1. Also available are the future value and present value tables for an annuity of $1.

Analog representation of data in a form other than digits as opposed to binary digital that represents the same information with switches that are either on (1) or off (0). Analog transmission uses analog representation by analog signals. For example, a telephone conversation can be transmitted in analog representation and use analog transmission.

Analyst a research analyst that has expertise in assessing and analyzing investments, and typically is employed by investment banks, brokerage firms, investment advisors, or mutual fund companies; also called a *financial analyst* or *security analyst*. They make buy, sell and hold recommendations on securities. Most specialize in specific sectors in the economy or specific countries to allow for more thorough research. An analyst will often be a key component in selecting an underwriter since analyst coverage of the company after the public offering helps to generate interest in the company's securities.

Analysts' Estimates Forecasts by investment analysts at securities companies and banks of the future financial performance of companies, in particular forthcoming earnings reports. Consensus estimates are compiled by such organizations as Multex Global Estimates.

Angel
1. a person or entity that provides financing to companies that have progressed beyond the start-up phase but are not yet ready for venture financing.
2. a bond of an investment grade.
3. an opposite of a fallen angel.

Annual Benefit Statement an annual statement detailing all benefits received for the entire year.

Annual Debt Service the required total annual interest and principal loan payments. For example, the monthly payments on a 30 year $94,999.75 mortgage are $869.00. The first year's total interest payment is $9,952.52 and the total principal payment is $475.48 for a total annual debt service of $10,428.

Annual (General) Meeting AGM for short, a company gathering, usually held at the end of each fiscal year, at which shareholders and management discuss the previous year and the outlook for the future. Directors are elected and other shareholder concerns are addressed.

Annual Percentage Rate (APR)

1. a true measure of the effective cost of credit. It is the ratio of the finance charge to the average amount of credit in use during the life of the loan, and is expressed as a percentage rate per year.
2. a true measure of the effective annual rate of return on investments. Different types of investments use different compounding periods. For example, most bonds pay interest semiannually. Some banks pay interest quarterly. If an investor wishes to compare investments with different compounding periods, he needs to put them on a common basis. The annual percentage rate (APR), or effective annual rate, is used for this purpose and is computed as follows:

$$APR = (1 + r/m)^m - 1.0$$

where r = the stated, nominal or quoted rate

m = the number of compounding periods per year.

Example: Assume that a bank offers 6 percent interest, compounded quarterly, then the APR is:

$(1 + .06/4)^4 - 1.0 = (1.015)^4 - 1.0 = 1.0614 - 1.0 = .0614 = .0614 = 6.14\%$

This means that if one bank offered 6 percent with quarterly compounding, while another offered 6.14 percent with annual compounding, they would both be paying the same effective rate of interest.

Annual Report evaluation prepared by companies at the end of the reporting year, which might be either on a calendar or fiscal basis. Contained in the annual report are the company's financial statements including footnotes, supplementary schedules, management discussion and analysis of earnings, president's letter, audit report, and other explanatory data (e.g., research and marketing efforts) helpful in evaluating the entity's financial position and operating performance. The annual report is read by stockholders, potential investors, creditors, employees, regulatory bodies, and other interested financial statement users. *See also* 10-Q; 10-K.

Annualized Returns investment returns converted to an annual (yearly) basis. For example, a fund returning 0.5% a month returns 6% on an annualized (yearly) basis. Most mutual funds must show average annual returns for one, three, five, and 10 year periods (when applicable).

Annuitant one who receives or is qualified to receive the benefits of an annuity.

Annuity

1. a series of equal payments or receipts. With an ordinary annuity, payments or

receipts are at the end of the year. With an annuity due, payments or receipts are at the beginning of the year.

2. in retirement planning, a savings account with an insurance company or other investment company. The annuitant makes either a lump-sum deposit or periodic payments to the company and at retirement, he/she "annuitizes," receives regular payments for a specified time period (usually a certain number of years or for the rest of his/her life). All of the payments build up tax-free and are only taxed when withdrawn at retirement, a time when he/she is usually in a lower tax bracket. Although mostly sold by life insurance companies, annuities are really the opposite of life insurance: annuities pay off at retirement; life insurance pays off at death.

Anti a prefix having several different uses and meanings:
1. opposed or against something as in antitrust or antisemitism.
2. opposite as in anticyclical or anticlimax.
3. imputing strife as in antiking or anti manifesto.
4. neutralizing or restorative as in anticorrosive, or anti-friction.

Anticipatory Breach breach of contract committed prior to the time of required performance.

Antidumping Law statute that sets a minimum price on an import. If the import enters the country at a price below the minimum, the law prompts a government probe of possible dumping.

Antitrust Laws government laws designed to improve market efficiency, encourage competition, and curtail unfair trade practices, by reducing barriers to entry, breaking up monopolies, and preventing conspiracies to restrict production or raise prices in the real estate industry. There are three major antitrust laws: the Sherman Antitrust Act of 1890, Clayton Antitrust Act of 1914, and Federal Trade Commission Act of 1914.

Appellate Court a court whose only function is to review cases of lower courts.

APICS *see* American Production and Inventory Control Society.

Application another term for a type of program.

Application Server server running application programs. It is a network server performing applications requested by a client.

Applications Software computer software, including word processing, presentation, spreadsheet, database, statistical, and communications applications. It performs tasks and solves problems applicable to a manager's work.

Applied Economics economic tools and methodology applied to solving real economic problems. It utilizes a variety of techniques beyond economics, including finance and decision sciences.

Apportionment the allocation of state or federal aid, district taxes, or other monies among nonprofit organizations.

Appraisal an opinion or estimate of the value of an asset. An asset may be a piece of property, a collectible or precious metal. In the case of property, for example, an appraisal is made for the purposes of (1) allocating the purchase price to the assets acquired (e.g., land, building, equipment); (2) determining the amount of hazard insurance to carry; (3) determining the value at death for estate tax purposes; and (4) determining a reasonable asking price in a sale.

Appraisal Costs the costs associated with measuring, evaluating, or auditing products or services to assure conformance to quality standards and performance requirements. These include the costs of incoming and source inspection/test of purchased material, in process and final inspection/test, product, process, or service audits, calibration of measuring and test equipment, and the costs of associated supplies and materials.

Appraisal Fee a fee required for a professionally prepared estimate of the value of an asset (e.g., property, a collectible, or precious metal) by an independent expert.

Appraisal Institute *(www.appraisalinstitute.org/),* formerly American Institute of Real Estate Appraisers (AIREA), an international membership association of professional real estate appraisers, with more than 18,000 members and 99 chapters throughout the United States, Canada and abroad. Its mission is to support and advance its members as the choice for real estate solutions and uphold professional credentials, standards of professional practice and ethics consistent with the public good.

Appreciation

1. an increase in the value of an asset. The asset may be real estate or a security. For example, an individual sold 100 shares of X company's stock for $105 per share that he bought 10 years ago for $25 per share. During that time the amount of appreciation was $8,000 = ($105 - $25) x 100 shares.
2. recognition given such as an employer bonus to an employee for good performance.
3. an increase in the value of a currency.

Appreciation of the Dollar a rise in the foreign exchange value of the dollar relative to other currencies; also called *strong dollar, strengthening dollar,* or *revaluation of a dollar.* The opposite of appreciation is weakening, deteriorating, or depreciation of the dollar. Strictly speaking, revaluation refers to a rise in the value of a currency that is pegged to gold or to another currency. A strong dollar makes Americans' cash go further overseas and reduces import prices—generally good for U.S. consumers. If the dollar is overvalued, U.S. products are harder to sell abroad and at home, where they compete with low-cost imports. This helps give the U.S. its huge trade deficit. A weak dollar can restore competitiveness to American products by making foreign goods comparatively more expensive. But too weak a dollar can spawn inflation, first through higher import prices and then through spiraling prices for all goods. Even worse, a falling dollar can drive foreign investors away from U.S. securities, which lose value along with the dollar. A strong dollar can be induced by raising U.S. interest rates. The figure below summarizes the impacts of changes in foreign exchange rates on the multinational company's products, services, and foreign investments.

The Impact Of Changes In Foreign Exchange Rates		
	Weak Currency (Depreciation/devaluation)	**Strong Currency (Appreciation /revaluation)**
Imports	More expensive	Cheaper
Exports	Cheaper	More expensive
Payables	More expensive	Cheaper
Receivables	Cheaper	More expensive
Inflation	Fuel inflation by making imports more costly	Low inflation
Foreign investment	Discourage foreign investment. Lower return on investments by international investors.	High interest rates could attract foreign investors.
The effect	Raising interest rates could slow down the economy.	Reduced exports could trigger a trade deficit.

Appropriation the authorization of a governmental unit to spend money within specified restrictions such as amount, time period, and objective. There must be prior approval for such expenditure through agreements or legislation.

Appropriate Technology the technology—whether advanced, intermediate, undeveloped, or whether labor intensive, intermediate, or capital intensive— that is most fit for the distribution of the factors of production for the country using it. For example, in countries where labor is relatively cheap and abundant, appropriate technology would be labor intensive.

Appurtenance; Appurtenant Structures something outside the property itself but considered a part of the property and adds to its greater enjoyment, such as the right to cross another's land (i.e., easement or right-of-way).

Arbitrator impartial third party used to settle disputes. An arbitrator has become very popular in labor disputes in recent years.

Arbitrageur one who engages in arbitrage.

Arbitration a process where a grievance or contract dispute is referred to an impartial arbitrator or a panel of arbitrators for the purpose of arriving at a mutually acceptable solution avoiding the necessity of a judicial settlement. The arbitrator(s) hear the evidence and arrive at a decision. It is faster and less expensive than having a court action.

Arbitrage profiting from price differences when the same asset is traded in different markets. For example, an arbitrageur simultaneously buys one contract of silver in the Chicago market and sells one contract of silver in the New York market, locking in a profit since at that moment the price on the two markets is different, provided the selling price is higher than the buying price. It is also the process of selling overvalued and buying undervalued assets so as to bring about an equilibrium where all assets are properly valued.

Arbitrage Pricing Model (APM) a theory that relates stock returns and risk. The theory maintains that security returns vary from their expected amounts when there are unanticipated changes in basic economic forces. Such forces would include unexpected changes in industrial production, inflation rates, term structure of interest rates, and the difference between interest rates of high- and low-risk bonds.

Archive a place or collection containing records, documents, or other materials of historical interest. It is often used in the plural.
Computers:
1. a long-term storage area, often on magnetic tape, for backup copies of files or for files that are no longer in active use.
2. a file containing one or more files in compressed format for more efficient storage and transfer.
3. a single file containing one or (usually) more separate files plus information to allow them to be extracted (separated) by a suitable program.

Arithmetic Mean *see* Mean.

Arithmetic Progression a sequence in which each term after the first is formed by adding a constant to the preceding term.
Example
"1-3-5-7-" is the start of an arithmetic progression.

Arm's Length Transaction a transaction entered into by unrelated parties, each acting in their own best interest. It is assumed that in this type of transaction the prices used are the fair market values of the property or services being transferred in the transaction.

Arrears
1. at the end of a term. For example, interest on mortgage loans is paid at the end of a month.
2. past due payments or other liabilities, such as cumulative preferred stock dividends that have been declared but have not been paid following their payment dates (common dividends cannot be paid as long as cumulative preferred dividends are in arrears).

Articles of Incorporation formal documents prepared by individuals wishing to establish a corporation in the United States. They must file these documents with the authorities in the state in which the corporation wishes to reside. One copy is returned, after being reviewed, and, together with the Certificate of Incorporation, becomes the corporation's charter that formally recognizes the corporation as a business entity entitled to begin business operations. Rules governing the company's internal management are set forth in its bylaws.

Articles of Partnership a formal document drawn up by partners indicating significant and important aspects of the partnership. Items included are capital contributions, profit and loss ratios, name of the enterprise, duration of relationship, and individual duties.

Artificial Intelligence (AI) the umbrella terminology for several main categories of research, which include natural language systems, visual and voice recognition systems, robotic systems, and expert systems. Artificial intelligence generally is the attempt to build machines that think, that is the study of mental faculties through the use of computational models. A reasoning process is involved with self-correction. Significant data are evaluated and relevant relationships, such as the determination of a warranty reserve, uncovered. The computer learns which kind of answers are reasonable and which are not. Artificial intelligence performs complicated strategies that compute the best or worst way to achieve a task or avoid an undesirable result. An example of an application is in tax planning involving tax shelter options given the client's financial position. *See also* Expert Systems.

As If

1. speculation, most commonly associated with insurance, to demonstrate what the underwriting or reinsurance treaty results would have been in prior years if a new premium calculation had been in effect. A term referring to loss experience.
2. to examine what the financial results would have been if an alternative course of action had been taken.

As Is

1. a term for secondhand or damaged goods sold without either an express or implied warranty by the seller. That is, the buyer shall accept delivery of goods in the condition found on inspection before purchase, even if they are defective or damaged. The term in effect warns the buyer to inspect the items carefully, since the burden of determining their condition falls on him/her.
2. without guarantee as the condition of real estate.

ASAP as soon as possible.

Asian Development Bank (ADB) a financial institution for supporting economic development in Asia, created in the late 1960s. Asian Development Bank (ADB) operates on similar lines as the World Bank. Member countries range from Iran to the United States of America. *See also* International Monetary Fund (IMF), and World Bank.

Asian Dollars dollar-denominated deposits held in Asian-based banks.

Ask *see* Asked Price.

Ask Price *see* Asked Price.

Asked Price also called *Offering Price, Ask Price, Asking Price,*
1. the price at which an investment (such as a security, commodity, or real estate) is offered for sale. It is usually the lowest price at which one can purchase the investment.
2. for mutual funds, the current net asset value per share plus sales charges, if any.

Assembler Language an intermediate-level computer language that is less complex to use than a machine language. Assembly languages use abbreviations or mnemonic codes to replace 0s and 1s of machine language (A for "add", C for "compare", and MP for "multiply"). A translator is required to convert the assembly language program into machine languages that can be executed by the computer. This translator is the assembly program. Every command in assembly language has a corresponding command in machine language. The assembly language differs among computers and thus these programs are not easily transferable to machines of a different type from the one on which they were written.

Assessed Value the value established for real estate or other property by a government as a basis for levying taxes. For example, an individual receives a statement that, in the judgment of the local tax assessor, the individual's property is worth $50,000. If by law, properties in this jurisdiction are assessed at 80% of market value, the individual's assessed value then is $40,000 (80% of $50,000) and property taxes will be based on this assessed value.

Assessment 1. the process of making an official valuation of property for purposes of taxation. 2. the valuation placed upon property as a result of this process. For example, an individual owns a parcel of land assessed on the tax roll for $50,000. The tax rate is $1.00 per $100 of value. The tax assessment for the land is $500.

Assets economic resources that are owned by an organization and are expected to benefit future operations. Assets may have definite physical form such as buildings, machinery, or supplies. On the other hand, some assets exist not in physical or tangible form, but in the form of valuable legal claims or rights, such as accounts receivables from customers and notes receivables from debtors.

Asset Allocation
1. apportionment of money invested among different asset classes such as cash, stocks, bonds, precious metals, collectibles, commodities, and real estate. The way assets are allocated will have an effect on expected return and risk.
2. apportionment of funds invested in different instruments within a particular class. An example is buying stocks within 20 different industry groupings. Another example is buying different kinds of stock such as blue chips, growth stocks, income stocks, and defensive stocks. Another example is buying different kinds of bonds including U.S. bonds, municipal bonds of states and cities, and corporate bonds.
3. a mutual fund manager switching funds among different investment types based

on changing market conditions. For example, if the fund manager believes stocks will rise, he or she will switch from money market funds to stocks. If the fund manager believes the U.S. stock market is excessively overvalued, he or she may sell U.S. stocks and buy stocks of foreign companies.

Asset Turnover net sales divided by total assets; also called *Total Asset Turnover.* It measures how well assets are being used to generate sales revenue.

Asset-Backed Bond a bond that is secured against a specific asset of the issuing company; also called *Mortgage Bond.*

Assets economic resources that are owned by an organization and are expected to benefit future operations. Assets may have definite physical form such as buildings, machinery, or supplies. On the other hand, some assets exist not in physical or tangible form, but in the form of valuable legal claims or rights, such as accounts receivables from customers and notes receivables from debtors.

Assignment
1. the conveying of any type of property by one party to another. An assignor conveys his or her title to property to the assignee. The assignability of property relates to it being free of all claims and capable of being exchanged.
2. transfer of the right to collect wages from the wage earner to the creditor; a form of garnishment governed by a statute that provides relief for creditors. Before such wage assignment occurs, a judgment must be entered at which time the affected individual has the right of reply.
3. an agreement to transfer monies to a third party. For example, an agreement may provide that an insurance company will pay a party other than the insured for a reimbursable loss.
4. the right of a party, the assignor, to allocate the benefits of particular insurance policies to a third party, the assignee.
5. Bankruptcy: in the case of bankruptcy, an assignment of assets can occur where all the assets are assigned to the creditors for their disposal.
6. Stock options: in the event a put or call option is exercised, the Options Clearing Corporation will notify the stockbroker that the holder's option has been exercised and the underlying stock is assigned by the broker.
7. Stock and bond securities: stocks and registered bonds are commonly assigned by simply filling out and signing the form on the back of the certificate. It is also possible to complete a separate stock or bond assignment certificate to fulfill the assignment.

Assumable Mortgage a mortgage that can be transferred from the seller of a property directly to the buyer whereby the buyer continues the payments. The buyer takes ownership to real estate encumbered by an existing mortgage and assumes responsibility as the guarantor for the unpaid balance of the mortgage.

Assumpsit
1. an agreement or promise made orally or in writing where one party was not certified to perform the work.
2. a legal action to enforce or recover damages for a breach of such an agreement.

Assumption of risk the act of performing certain duties that are deemed to be risky.

Assumption

1. a hypothesis constructed in a mathematical or statistical argument.
2. an obligation taken on by a person who did not obtain it originally, but agrees to honor the terms of the existing obligation as a condition for the transaction. By assuming the loan, rather than taking subject to the loan, the buyer becomes personally liable on the debt.

Asterisk (*) a commonly used symbol for multiplication, especially in electronic spreadsheets.

Asymmetric Information one party's having more information than the other in negotiations or in deal making.

ATAR Model *see* Awareness-Trial-Availability-Repeat (ATAR) Model

At Risk a term indicating that the money is exposed to the possibility of loss. Thus, money invested is at risk. Speculative stocks are an extreme example of "at risk" investments.

At-the-Money the term used when the exercise (strike) price of an option is equal or virtually equal to the current market price of the underlying stock.

ATM (Automated Teller Machine) you need an ATM card linked to one or more bank accounts to use an ATM. These machines allow you to do many of the things like inside a bank, including withdraw money, deposit money, transfer funds from one account to another, etc.

Attachment

1. a legal term of the writ authorizing the taking of property of rights due to a legal action. It is designed to safeguard the property possibly to satisfy a judgment in favor of the plaintiff in the action.
2. a file enclosed in an electronic mail

Attitude a person's consistently favorable or unfavorable evaluations, feelings, and tendencies toward an object or ideas.

Attorney term indicating an attorney who has been admitted to practice law in his or her respective state and is authorized to perform both civil and criminal legal functions for clients. An attorney-at-law can perform the full range of legal functions including drafting legal documents, giving legal advice, and representing clients before courts, administrative agencies, boards, and other entitles. In English law an attorney-at-law is referred to as a solicitor.

Attorney in Fact a power of attorney giving permission for a lawyer to represent a client.

Attorney of Record an attorney whose name officially appears in permanent records of a case or an appeal thereto, or on the appearance docket. It gives public notice of the attorney who is handling the case.

Attributes

1. a quality or characteristic inherent in or ascribed to someone or something.
2. a data file's special features.

Audit

1. inspection of the accounting records, books, financial statements, and operations of a business, governmental unit, or individual by a trained accountant for the purpose of verifying the accuracy and completeness of all transactions and operations. The accuracy of transactions is tested and samples are verified to determine if generally accepted accounting principles (GAAP) were followed.
2. an examination of books, vouchers, and records of a taxpayer conducted by agents of the IRS.

Compliance audit: a determination of the firm's compliance with specified organizational rules and regulations.

Desk audit: a term normally used in connection with civil service procedures involving a review of the activities of a particular person filling a particular position to determine whether these activities fulfill the job classification responsibilities.

Financial audit: examination of a client's accounting records by an independent certified public accountant to formulate an audit opinion. The auditor must follow generally accepted auditing standards. A careful evaluation of the internal control structure is necessary.

Independent audit: an audit performed on an organization's records and procedures by an outside accounting firm.

Internal audit: investigation of an organization's procedures and operations by an internal auditor to assure that they conform to the organization's accounting and operating policies.

Management audit: an evaluation of the efficiency and effectiveness of management.

Correspondence audit: an audit conducted by the IRS through the use of the mail. Normally, the IRS requests verification of a particular deduction of exemption through the completion of a form or the remittance of copies of records or other supporting materials.

Field audit: an audit by the IRS conducted on the business premises of the taxpayer or in the office of the attorney or accountant representing the taxpayer.

Audit Trail

1. in computers, a series of records or information regarding any additions, deletions, or modifications to the system providing evidence concerning transactions. An effective audit trail allows the data to be retrieved and certified. Audit trails will give information regarding the date and time of the transaction, who processed it and at which terminal.
2. in accounting, a sequence of records or documentation that shows the series of details back to the origin of the transaction. For example, the audit trail of selling expenses can show the account balances back through the journal entries and back to paid checks or payments by check. The goal of the audit

trail is to allow the auditors to substantiate transactions and to capture any errors.

Auditor an accountant who performs an audit of a portion or the entirety of a company's books. The auditor may be internal or independent. The independent accountant is a certified public accountant (CPA) in public practice who has no financial or other interest in the client whose financial statements are being examined.

Auditor's Opinion, Auditor's Report the report by a CPA that the company's financial statements were examined and the expression of an opinion of the fairness of those statements. An unqualified opinion means the CPA is satisfied that the company's financial statements present fairly its financial position and results of operations and gives the financial manager confidence that the financial statements are an accurate reflection of the company's financial health and operating performance. However, an auditor can give a qualified opinion that contains phrases such as "except for" or "subject to."

Authentication mechanism used to ascertain if a user is who he or she purports to be.

Authority
1. one possessing power over others, such as a company manager who has the right to hire and fire.
2. one having the right to act, such as an attorney having the right to represent clients and make decisions on their behalf.

Auto Sales the number of domestic and foreign cars and trucks that automakers have sold. It is used as a sign of consumer confidence; upswings are good news and declines are bad news. Auto sales affect millions of workers at manufacturers, parts suppliers, and dealers, not to mention the labor force of the related industries.

Automated Teller Machine (ATM) a computerized electronic device allowing customers to make specific transactions by the use of a plastic card that has account information recorded on it.

Automatic Extension the routine granting of additional time needed by an individual to do something. For example, taxpayers are granted an automatic extension of four months for filing tax returns (but not for payment of tax). This requires the filing of Form 4868, accompanied by the remaining estimated tax payment for the year. The application must be filed by the due date of the return.

Automatic Investment Plan an investment plan that allows you to contribute as little as $20 a month. The funds are automatically deducted from your checking/ savings account or off of your paycheck and invested in a retirement account or mutual fund.

Automatic Stabilizer structural features of the economy that automatically mitigate recession by helping to create a budget deficit and check inflation by helping to create a budget surplus, without the need for discretionary fiscal or monetary action; also called *built-in stabilizers* or *nondiscretionary fiscal policy*. Examples are unemployment insurance payments, farm aid programs, and personal and corporate income taxes.

Average

1. for a set of numbers, the total of all number values divided by the number of items in the set; also called arithmetic mean.
2. a measure of central tendency. Three common measures are the (arithmetic) mean, median, and mode.
3. number used to measure the general behavior of security prices by reflecting the arithmetic average price behavior of a representative group of securities at a given point in time and comparing it with the arithmetic average price of the same group at a different time.

Average Age of Inventory the number of days an average inventory item takes to sell. Average age of inventory = Cost of goods sold x 365 days. For example, assume that average inventory is $47,500 and cost of goods sold is $500,000. The average age of inventory is ($47,500/$500,000) x 365 days = 34.8 days.

Average Tax Rate the tax rate applicable to all taxable income; also called *effective tax rate*. It is total tax liability divided by taxable income. *See also* Marginal Tax Rate.

Avoidance rendering null and void, refusing to honor, or avoiding the recognition of the terms of a contract. If an individual violates a warranty agreement by not servicing at the proper intervals, then a company may render the warranty null and void and consider itself exempt from any liability.

Awareness-Trial-Availability-Repeat (ATAR) Model a model that projects future sales growth without data. The ATAR model originates from what is called *diffusion of innovation*, explained this way: for a person or a firm to become a regular buyer/user of an innovation, there must first be awareness that it exists, then there must be a decision to try that innovation, then the person must find the item available to them, and finally there must be the type of happiness with it that leads to adoption, or repeat usage.

Axis a straight line that intersects with another straight line with right angles at a point, the origin, in an xy-coordinate graph. The vertical axis is called the *y-axis*, and the horizontal axis, the *x-axis*.

Bb

B2B (Business-to-Business) E-Commerce the online selling of goods and services between businesses. Using B2B trading networks, auction sites, spot exchanges, online product catalogs, barter sites, and other online resources to reach new customers, this online business serves current business customers more effectively, and obtains buying efficiencies and better prices.

B2C (Business-to-Consumer) E-Commerce the online selling of goods and services to final customers.

Baby Boomers; Baby Boom Generation a term referring to those Americans born between the end of World War II and the 1960s when the veterans of World War II were in the family formation stage of their lives. The result was a tremendous surge in the birthrate: the intrinsic rate of natural increase went from 4.6 in the 1940-1944 period to a high of 21.1 in 1955-1959, declining to 8.2 by 1965-1969. The baby boomer generation created tremendous consumer demand in the economy, beginning with housing, as popularized in Levittown, New York, and including all types of consumer goods.

Back Charge an item previously charged to an account but unpaid. The current invoice requests payment of the previous charge as well as of current charges.

Back Taxes taxes owed but not paid when due or were under reported or omitted unknowingly or intentionally from a prior year. The taxing authority will demand the back taxes, including possible fines, penalties, and interest.

Back-End Load (Deferred Sales Charge) deferred charges assessed when funds are withdrawn from the fund. These charges are intended to discourage frequent trading in the fund. Deferred sales charges are typically on a scale, which reduces them yearly until it disappears after a predetermined time period. For example, if a holder of a mutual fund exits after being in the fund for one year, the fee might be 4%, after two years 3%, after three years 2%, after 4 years 1%, and thereafter no exit fee. The back-end load charge is subtracted from the selling price to arrive at the net proceeds to be received.

Backlog
1. an accumulation, especially of unfinished work.
2. the monetary value of any orders that have yet to be filled.

Back Up making a duplicate copy of original data or files usually stored on a separate data storage medium. Backup insures the recoverability of files in the event of loss of the original data.

Back-Up Plan a secondary plan, or plan B, in case the primary plan, or plan A, doesn't work out.

Bad Debt
1. an accounts receivable that is uncollectible due to the customer's inability to pay.
2. a debt that is unlikely to be repaid.

Bail security, usually a sum of money, exchanged for the release of a defendant as a guarantee of that person's appearance for trial.

Bail Out
1. action of an individual when he or she has financial difficulty that prompts him or her to sell a stock irrespective of price.
2. when the collateral for a loan is used as the basis for payment.
3. one entity giving financial aid to another. For example, the federal government gave a financial guarantee for loans to New York City.

Bailment transfer of possession of personal property without transfer of title. Bailments are common in the business world and include such activities as leaving a car at a repair shop or a parking garage, or leaving clothes at the cleaners.

Bait and Switch an unethical and often illegal practice by which a good or service is advertised at a low price with the intention of attracting customers and then switching them over to higher-priced items. The seller may have no intention of selling the "bait item." The customer is often told the bait item is out-of-stock or inferior.

Balance
1. a portfolio concept implying that risk needs to be weighted against return in order to pick the right kind of investment.
2. difference between total debits and credits in an account.
3. balance of a loan or a bank account

Balance of International Indebtedness a schedule that measures a nation's foreign assets and liabilities at a point in time.

Balance of Payments (BOP) a systematic record of a country's receipts from, or payments to, other countries. In a way, it is like the balance sheets for businesses, only on a national level. The reference you see in the media to the balance of trade usually refers to goods within the goods and services category of the current account. It is also known as merchandise or "visible" trade because it consists of tangibles like foods, manufactured goods, and raw materials. "Services," the other part of the category, is known as "invisible" trade and consists of intangibles such as interest or dividends, technology transfers, and others (like insurance, transportation, and financial). When the net result of both the current account and the capital account yields more credits than debits, the country is said to have a surplus in its balance of payments. Figures are reported in seasonally adjusted volumes and dollar amounts. It is the only non-survey, non-judgmental report that appears in *Survey of Current Business* produced by the Department of Commerce.

Balance of Trade the balance of trade is merchandise exports minus imports; also called *merchandise trade balance* or *visible trade*. Thus if exports of goods exceed imports the trade balance is said to be 'favorable,' or to have a trade surplus, while an excess of imports over exports yields an 'unfavorable' trade balance or a trade deficit. Visit a website such as *www.economy.com* for its statistical data. The balance of trade is an important item in calculating balance of payments. *See also* Balance of Payments.

Balance Sheet a condensed financial statement showing the nature and amount of a company's assets, liabilities, and stockholders' equity as of a given date; also called *financial position statement*. A financial snapshot of what the company owns, what it owes, and the ownership stake.

Assets		Liabilities and Stockholders' Equity	
Current assets:		Current liabilities:	
Cash	$10,000	Accounts payable	$2,200
Accounts receivable	9,500	Income tax payable	4,000
Material inventory	474	Total current liabilities	6,200
Finished goods inventory	3,280	Stockholders' equity:	
Total current assets	23,254	Common stock, no-par	70,000
Fixed assets:		Retained earnings	37,054
Land	50,000		
Buildings and equipment	100,000		
Accumulated depreciation	(60,000)		
Total fixed asset	90,000		
Total assets	113,254	Total liabilities and stockholders' equity	113,254

Balanced Budget a budget in which total expenditures equal total revenue. An entity has a budget surplus if expenditures are less than tax revenues. It has a budget deficit if expenditures are greater than tax revenues. The constitutional amendment has an important provision. It essentially requires a balanced budget. It thus limits the government's ability to have deficits.

Balanced Scorecard approach using multiple measures to evaluate managerial performance. These measures may be financial or nonfinancial, internal or external, and short-term or long-term. The scorecard allows a determination as to whether a manager is achieving certain objectives at the expense of others that may be equally or more important.

There are four different perspectives: (1) the financial perspective, (2) the customer perspective, (3) the process perspective, and (4) the learning and growth perspective. A variety of potential measures for each perspective of a Balanced Scorecard are indicated in the figure below.

Perspective	Issue	Measures
Financial	Is the company achieving its financial goals?	Operating income Return on assets Sales growth Cash flow from operations Reduction of administrative expense
Customer	Is the company meeting customer expectations?	Customer satisfaction Customer retention New customer acquisition Market share On-time delivery Time to fill orders
Processes	Is the company improving critical internal processes?	Defect rate Lead time Number of suppliers Material turnover Percent of practical capacity
Learning and Growth	Is the company improving its ability to innovate?	Amount spent on employee training Employee satisfaction Employee retention Number of new products New product sales as a percent of total sales Number of patents

Balanced (Mutual) Fund a mutual fund that combines investments in common stocks and bonds and often preferred stocks, and attempts to provide income and some capital appreciation. Balanced funds tend to underperform all-stock funds in strong bull markets.

Balloon Clause provision in a mortgage that requires the final payment to be substantially more than all other payments.

Balloon Loan a loan having the last payment either (1) more than twice the amount of any other payment, or (2) a payment arising from the lender's "call" provision. The term loan (or straight loan) is a form of balloon loan.

Balloon Payment the last payment to be abnormally large, as compared to the other installment payments.

Bandwidth the range of frequencies available in any communication channel. The transmission capacity (stated in bits per second) is largely dependent on its bandwidth. Broadband has the highest capacity, used by microwave, cable, and fiber-optic lines.

Bank Balance an amount in a bank deposit account, such as a checking or savings account, as of a certain specified time or date indicated on a bank statement. Bank charges, deposits in transit, and outstanding checks usually are primary factors in reconciling an individual's or organization's books and the bank's statement, as of a particular date.

Bank Failure the bankruptcy of a bank.

Banker's Acceptance a time draft drawn by a business firm whose payment is guaranteed by the bank's "acceptance" of it. It is especially important in foreign trade when the seller of goods can be certain that the buyer's draft will actually have funds behind it. Banker's acceptances are money market instruments actively traded in the secondary market.

Bankruptcy (Business) situation in which a business' debt exceeds the fair market value of its assets. It is also a court action under which a debtor may be discharged for unpaid debts, in whole or in part, and in which creditors receive distributions of assets from the debtor's property under the supervision of the court. Chapter 11 of the Bankruptcy Law provides for reorganization in which the debtor remains in possession of the business and in control of its operation while the debtor and creditors are allowed to work together. *See also* Bankruptcy (Personal).

Bankruptcy (Personal) legal process that is available for an individual who is overextended financially and is unable to pay his/her debts. The individual can file for bankruptcy in order to legally seek to eliminate some or all of his/her debts. Under Chapter 7 of the Bankruptcy Law, often called *straight bankruptcy*, the intent is to liquidate assets to pay the debts. Should this method be elected, the bankrupt can claim certain property as "exempt" and this property can be retained to preserve the basic necessities of life (such as a certain amount of equity in the home, economical car, and personal clothing and effects.) Once a person has declared bankruptcy, he/she cannot be discharged from debts again for six years. *Note*: The Bankruptcy Abuse Prevention and Consumer Protection Act of 2005 (Public Law 109–8) makes the most sweeping changes in a generation, affecting both consumer and business bankruptcies. Under the law, debtors who earn at least the median income in their state may be refused Chapter 7. Instead, they will have to file under Chapter 13, in which you have to use some of future income to repay a portion of your credit card bills and other unsecured debt over five years. Debtors with car loans would have to repay the loan in full, if they want to keep the car. Under Chapter 13, often called *wage-earner plans*, the assets are not liquidated. Instead, interest and late charges are eliminated and arrangements are made to pay off some or all of the debts over several years. Note that bankruptcy will not discharge all the debts. Debts that cannot be eliminated through bankruptcy proceedings include income taxes, child support, alimony, student loans, and debts incurred under false pretenses. Bankruptcy should not be taken lightly. One should be sure to consult an attorney on various decisions surrounding the issue and on how to get the greatest benefit from the new financial start. *See also* Bankruptcy (Business).

Banner Advertising one popular form of online advertising. It is a graphical web advertising unit, typically measuring 468 pixels wide and 60 pixels tall (i.e. 468x60). Banner ads are graphic images on web pages that are often animated and can include small pieces of software code to allow further interaction. Most importantly, they are "clickable," and take a viewer to another web location when chosen.

Bar Code lines and numbers that appear on just about every product in the world, as shown below. A computer terminal at the point of sale scans a bar code for data such as price and inventory information. The bar-code is a read-only technology.

Bar Graph, Chart, or **Histogram**. Graphical representations of statistical data using rectangular shapes showing frequency distributions. There is a vertical axis, y, and a horizontal axis, x, which are labeled to illustrate basic concepts. The method allows comparison of concepts along a graduated basis of various concepts.

Barometric Forecasting use of economic indicators such as leading indicators to predict turning points in economic activity. It is used primarily to identify potential future changes in general business conditions or conditions of a specific industry rather than conditions for a specific firm. The series chosen serve as barometers of economic change. Types of indicators frequently used are coincident indicator, lagging indicator, and leading indicators.

Barrier to Competition any factor or industry characteristic that hinders fair competition. Barriers include legal rights such as patents and business licenses, substantial economies of scale, large capital requirements, and customer loyalty.

Barriers to Entry any economic and technical factor or industry characteristic that creates a cost advantage for existing firms in the industry over new rivals. These factors include (1) economies of scale in production and distribution, (2) exclusive control of essential factors of production such as raw materials and technology, (3) legal rights such as patents and licenses, (3) large capital requirements, and (4) ties of customer loyalty through product differentiation activities.

Barron's weekly publication by Dow Jones; the second-most popular source of financial news behind *The Wall Street Journal*.

Barter the trading of goods or services instead of actual dollars; no cash is involved. For tax purposes, each party has to recognize income based on the fair market value of the product or service received. For example, a barter takes place when an electrician renders services to a retail store in exchange for furniture.

Base Period a selected period of time that serves as a basis for a comparison, a standard, or a mathematical construct to aid in financial computations. The base period selected should be the one that is the most typical of the business. For example, in financial statement analysis, an index-number trend series may be prepared. Assume the base year is 20x1 when cash is $14,000. The cash balances are $17,000 in 20x2 and $18,000 in 20x3. The index numbers are:

20x1	20x2	20x3
1.0	1.214	1.286

The term *base period* also applies to economic statistics such as Consumer Price Index and certain stock indexes.

Basel II, Basel Agreement or Accord a new set of regulations designed by the Basel Committee on Banking Supervision to cover operational risk as well as financial risk for global financial institutions. Set up in 1974, the Basel Committee on Banking Supervision is an international regulatory body for the world's financial institutions. In 1988, it introduced capital adequacy rules for banks in member countries, which required them to implement a financial risk measurement framework. The committee is currently creating a new set of regulations to replace the original rules that would cover operational risk as well as financial risk. The new framework, usually called *Basel II*, is based around three "pillars": the first determines minimum capital requirements, the second stipulates an effective supervisory review process, and the third sets out to strengthen market discipline by greater disclosure of banks' financial status.

Basic (Beginner's All-Purpose Instruction Code) a popular and easy to learn programming language.

Basis
1. a figure or value that is the starting point in computing gain or loss, depreciation, depletion and amortization. For example, in an asset sale, "gain" is proceeds minus basis, where "basis" is the amount on which depreciation is calculated.
2. a figure or value that is the starting point in computing capital gain or loss. If you bought a stock for $500 a year ago and sold it today for $1,500, the basis is $500 and the profit of $1,000 ($1,500 - $500) is a capital gain.
3. the difference between the futures (or forward) price of an asset and its spot (or cash) price. Expressed as a value or as a percentage of the spot price.

4. a bond's yield to maturity at a given price. A 10% bond selling at 100 has a 10% basis.

Basis Point a unit of measure for the change in interest rates for bonds and notes. One basis point is equal to 1/100 of a percentage point, that is, 0.01 percent. Thus 100 basis points = 1 percent. For example, if you hear that something is down 50 basis points, that means it is down half a percentage point.

Baud serial information transfer speed with which a modem receives and sends data. It is a unit of data transmission speed equal to one bit per second.

Baud rate the bits per second that can speed through a phone line.

Baumol Model a mathematical model to determine the optimum amount of transaction cash under conditions of certainty. The objective is to minimize the sum of the fixed costs associated with transactions and the opportunity cost of holding cash balances.

Bayesian Probability revised prior estimates of probabilities, based on additional experience and information. An example of Bayesian probability applied to business is when the estimated bad debt percentage has to be revised because of such considerations as recent uncollectibility experience of customer defaults, sales to marginal customers, or poor economic conditions.

Bayesian Techniques a statistical method under which prior information is revised based on sample data to produce estimates to test hypotheses. *See also* Bayesian Probability.

BCG Matrix a strategy tool, developed by the Boston Consulting Group, to guide resource allocation decisions on the basis of growth and market share of a company's strategic business units (SBUs). The BCG Matrix defines four business groups:
• Cash cows (low growth, high market share)
• Stars (high growth, high market share)
• Question marks (high growth, low market share)
• Dogs (low growth, low market share)

Bear; Bear Market a market declining about 20% or more after reaching a peak. Such a situation may occur when there is an expectation of declining economic activity or higher interest rates. A bear market may last six months to several years, during which stock prices continue declining. Any upward movement in price is brief.

Bearer Bond an unregistered bond where the holder is entitled to payments of both principal and interest; also called a *coupon bond*, because whoever presents the coupon is entitled to the interest. With respect to transfers, bond endorsement is not a requirement.

Beige Book the economic report released about every six weeks by the Federal Reserve Board. It provides the most recent assessment of the nation's economy, with a regional emphasis. It is used to help the Fed decide on its monetary policy such as changes in interest rates.

Bell-Shaped Curve *see* **Normal Curve; Normal Distribution**.

Bellwether, Bellwether Stock stock that indicates the direction of the security market. General Electric is an example because much of it is owned by institutional investors whose trading actions have a pronounced affect on the market price of securities. Further, actions by institutional investors usually influence smaller investors. Bellwether stocks exist for each industry to reflect its performance and directions such as Microsoft as an indicator of the technology sector. A bellwether in the bond market is the 10- or 30-year U.S. Treasury bond, which indicates the direction other bonds are apt to go.

Benchmark
1. a standard, norm, or yardstick to judge one's performance as an individual or company.
2. a standard measurement or metric used to evaluate the performance of a portfolio. For example, an appropriate stock or bond index can be used to gauge the performance of an investment such as a mutual fund. An example is the Europe, Australia, and Far East (EAFE) Index, a value-weighted index of the equity performance of major foreign markets, which is often used to evaluate the performance of international mutual funds.

Benchmark Bond a bond that provides a standard against which the performance of other bonds can be measured; also called *Benchmark Issue* or *Bellwether Issue*. Government bonds are almost always used as benchmark bonds.

Benchmark Rates interest or loan rates that other rates are pegged to. An example is the U.S. prime rate on which other loan rates are based.

Benchmarking (Best Practices) the process of searching for new and better procedures by comparing your own procedures with that of the very best. The objective is to measure the key outputs of a business process or function against the best and to analyze the reasons for the performance difference. Benchmarking applies to services and practices as well as to products and is an ongoing systematic process. It entails both quantitative and qualitative measurements that allow both an internal and an external assessment. Process benchmarking is the process of assessing the quality of key internal processes by comparing them with those of other firms. In results benchmarking, a firm examines the end product or service of another company, focusing on product/service specifications and performance results.

Beneficiary individual who will receive an inheritance upon the death of another. The proceeds of an insurance policy may be in the form of a lump-sum annuity. Real estate also passes to the beneficiary.

Bernoulli Trial a sampling process credited with the theoretical work on the binomial distribution; also called *Bernoulli process*. It is characterized as (1) only two mutually exclusive possible outcomes are possible in each trial: success or failure, (2) the outcomes in the series of trials constitute independent events, and (3) the probability of success remains constant from trial to trial.

Best Insurance Report ratings of health and life insurance companies.

Best Practices *see* Benchmarking.

Best-Practice Benchmarking the measurement and implementation of the most successful operational standard or strategy available in an industry. This can be one of the most effective tools for increasing a corporation's efficiency, productivity, and ultimately, earnings.

Beta *see* Beta Coefficient.

Beta Coefficient the second letter of the Greek alphabet, used as a statistical measure of risk relative to its benchmark; also simply called *beta*. For equity funds, the market benchmark is the S&P 500 index. For fixed-income funds, it is Treasury bills. Beta measures volatility. Put another way, it is a measure of a security's return over time to that of the overall market. For example, if ABC's beta is 1.5, it means that if the stock market goes up 10%, ABC's common stock goes up 15%; if the market goes down 10%, ABC goes down 15%. The following presents betas for some selected companies:

Betas for selected corporations		
Company	Ticker Symbol	Beta
IBM	IBM	1.56
Wal-Mart	WMT	0.63
Microsoft	MSFT	1.16
McDonald's	MCD	1.11
Honda	HMC	0.46
Pfizer	PFE	0.54
Nokia	NOK	2.00

Source: AOL Personal Finance Channel and MSN Money Central Investor *(http://moneycentral.msn.com/investor/contents.asp)*, February 27, 2006.

Beta Test the actual testing of an almost final software program before its official release.

Better Business Bureau (BBB) local business-supported organization designed to promote good business practices, assist the public in dealing with complaints, and provide useful consumer information. The Better Business Bureau, which is loosely affiliated with the National Better Business Bureau, maintains information about local business firms and coordinates complaints and information with them.

Bid the highest price a buyer will pay for a security at a given time.

Bid and Asked a term used in the over-the-counter market to describe unlisted securities. "Bid" is the highest price an investor is willing to pay while "Asked" is the lowest price a seller is willing to take. Together, the two prices represent a quotation in a security or commodity. A spread is the difference between the bid price and the asked price for the security or commodity. For example, if a stock has a bid and asked price of $5.50 and $6.00, the spread is $0.50 per share.

Bid Price

1. the price a buyer is willing to pay, or "bid," for a particular security. It is the highest price offered by a dealer to buy a given security traded in the over-the-counter market.
2. the price per share that shareholders receive when they cash in (redeem) their shares.

Big 4 Accounting Firms four major public accounting firms, from the original eight, with many regional and local firms as well. The four in the order of revenue in 2003 are PricewaterhouseCoopers, Deloitte & Touche, KPMG, and Ernest & Young. The second-tier firms include BDO Seidman, Grant Thornton, and McGladrey & Pullen.

Big Bang

1. the deregulation that allowed foreign firms to operate in London's financial markets on Big Bang Day (October 27, 1986).
2. supporting drastic changes in the foreign or economic policies of a country.

Big Board term used for the New York Stock Exchange.

Bilateral Contract a legal agreement between individuals (or entities) who both agree to do or not to do some act.

Bill of Lading a written document issued by a carrier that specifies contractual conditions and terms (such as time, place, person named for receipt) for delivery of goods. It also evidences receipt of goods. Upon transfer of the bill, title is passed to the receiver.

Bill of Sale a formal document for the transfer of title to personal property and chattels. It states that the property has been paid for and that no outstanding liens exist on it. This is the buyer's receipt that gives him or her the right to sell the property at a later date. There is usually a need to register it.

Billing Cycle the time period between periodic billings for merchandise or services rendered, typically one month.

Bimodal Distribution a probability distribution in which there are two modes of data.

Binary a number system that uses only two digits, 0 and 1.

Binder

1. a temporary and symbolic payment evidencing good faith and obligating two or more individuals until a final transaction takes place. The binder is typically returned if the final agreement is not consummated.
2. a deposit paid to secure the right to buy a house based on the agreed terms. It is a temporary deposit until there is a contract.

3. a written memorandum of the contract terms of insurance that provides temporary protection to the insured pending final approval by the insurance company.

Binding Arbitration a term used in a contract dispute in which an independent third party arbitrates by listening to the arguments of both parties and issues a judgment to which the parties agree. Binding arbitration may be voluntary or compulsory. It is voluntary if the parties have agreed to it, but is compulsory if a government authority requires it.

Binomial Distribution a discrete probability distribution describing the results of an experiment known as a Bernoulli trial. It calculates the probability of obtaining x successes in n independent trials when each trial results in success or failure. Binomial distribution can be approximated by normal distributions when the number of trials is relatively large.

Biometric Authentication users approved for access based on voice, palm prints, retinal patterns, fingerprints, or other physical attributes.

Biometrics a technique that identifies people based on their unique physical characteristics or behavioral traits.

Bit a shorthand term for binary digits. There are only two possible binary digits: 0 and 1. A bit is the smallest unit of memory.

Bit Map, Bitmap the arrangement of bits representing an image for display on a computer monitor or a paper printout. A set of dots, or bits, on a screen that represents an image.

Bits Per Second (BPS) the measurement of the capacity (or transmission rate) of a communications channel.

Bi-Weekly (Mortgage) Loan a bi-weekly accelerated mortgage reduction payment plan that will help a borrower payoff his/her current 30-year mortgage in approximately 20 years. It is a fixed interest rate loan in which the payments are made every two weeks, but the payment is one-half the amount of a regular monthly fixed-rate mortgage with the same amortization schedule. These payment plans provide a dramatic build-up of equity, saving the borrower thousands of dollars in interest. Bi-weekly payment plans are offered by several firms that are retained to serve as money managers to aid the owner. Once in the program, everything is automatic. Each 14 days, an electronic wire transfer of half of his/her monthly payment is sent from his/her local bank. After the second monthly half-payment, the funds are combined and the entire payment is transferred to the lender.

Black Markets illegal markets in foreign exchange. Developing nations generally do not permit free markets in foreign exchange and impose many restrictions on foreign currency transactions. These restrictions take many forms, such as limiting the amounts of foreign currency to be purchased or government licensing requirements. As a result, illegal markets in foreign exchange develop to satisfy trader demand. In many countries such illegal markets exist openly, with little government interventions.

Black-Scholes Option Pricing Model (OPM) formula for valuing stock options designed in 1973 by Nobel Laureates Fischer Black and Myron Scholes. A model is used to determine the value of option securities prices based on the relationship between six variables—the current underlying asset price, the option strike price, the option time-to-expiration, the riskless return, the underlying asset payout return, and the underlying asset volatility.

Blanket Mortgage A single mortgage or other encumbrance that covers more than one piece of real estate. It is usually released only after the mortgage loan is fully repaid. A partial release clause can be included. However, the original mortgage agreement must specify how much of the loan must be repaid before a piece of property can be released.

Blanket Rate the same rate for transportation charges for a delivery of household items to a homeowner within a particular locality.

Blind Pool a limited partnership in which limited partners rely on the general partner to choose specific properties after the funds are available. For example, each of 1,000 investors contributes $25,000 into a limited partnership. The general partner has not yet selected the property to be bought, so the investment money is considered a blind pool.

Blind Trust a person gives approval to a third party, e.g., fiduciary, to manage his/her finances. This arrangement may exist when there is a possible conflict of interest.

Block
1. a voluminous number of shares, bonds or dollar amounts attributed thereto owned or traded. An example is the purchase or sale of 10,000 or more shares. Another example is the buying or selling of $100 million bonds.
2. in word processing software, a whole section of text that will be cut, copied, deleted, have a special font, or some other operation.
3. a rectangular area bounded on all sides by consecutive streets. It is part of a platted area.
4. a substantial amount of real estate properties to be sold together.
5. a group of houses, apartments, or businesses in one area such as on Foster Avenue between Charles Street and Blake Street.

Blockbusting the illegal practice of inducing panic selling in a neighborhood for financial gain. Such selling may arise because of a threatened move to the area by a specific racial or ethnic group.

Block Pricing is one way a firm with market power can increase profits. An example is the purchase of toilet paper in packages of three rolls or cans of soft drink in a six pack. By packaging units of a product and selling them as one package, the firm earns more than by posting a simple per unit price. Block pricing enhances profits by forcing consumers to make all-or-none decisions to purchase units of a good.

Block Trade a large size transaction, usually involving at least 10,000 or more shares of stock or $200,000 or more worth of bonds.

Blocked Rates the type of price discrimination that involves the setting of prices on the basis of quantity purchased. Prices are blocked with a high price set for the first block of units bought by each consumer and lower prices set for successive blocks of units. Utility companies frequently use this type of pricing.

Blog short for web log, frequently updated web site content, usually posted in reverse chronological order. It is a web page that serves as a publicly accessible personal journal for an individual. Chatty, frequently updated web logs provide marketing benefits.

Blow Off the climax of a substantial stock market advance marked by extremely high volume often followed by a sharp price decline as traders take profits.

Blowout the quick sale of all shares of a new stock offering because of strong demand for it.

Blue Chip
1. common stock of high quality that has a long record of earnings and dividend payments. They are known for excellent management, goods and services, and personnel. They have an excellent reputation. Blue chip stocks are often viewed as long-term investment instruments. They have low risk and provide modest but dependable return. Examples are General Electric and Merck. Blue chip stocks usually have high prices and moderate ratios of dividends to market price per share. They are less vulnerable to cyclical market changes than other stocks. Note: The term originates from the blue chips used in poker—always the most valuable chips.
2. high-quality bonds that are secure and stable in price and interest payments.

Blue Chip Economic Indicators economic consensus forecasts constructed by Eggert Economic Enterprises, Inc., Sedona, Arizona, based on a poll of 50 business economists working for investment houses, banks, and businesses. Forecasts include real Gross Domestic Product (GDP), GDP Deflator, Consumer Price Index (CPI), unemployment rate, industrial production, housing starts, and auto sales.

Blue Chip Stock *see* Blue Chip.

Blue Laws laws prohibiting the use of certain products due to local custom or belief. Sales of alcoholic beverages or limits of alcoholic content on Sunday is a common example of a "blue law."

Blue Sky Law U.S. State regulations to protect investors against securities fraud. Blue Sky Laws require sellers of new issues to register their offerings and provide financial details so investors can base judgments on trustworthy data.

BMI *see* Body Mass Index (BMI).

Board of Equalization (BOE) a governmental body that reviews property tax assessment procedures.

Board of Directors the collective group of individuals elected by the shareholders of a corporation to oversee the management of the corporation.

Board of Trustees a group of people responsible for the oversight of a non-profit organization.

Body Mass Index (BMI) a measure of body weight relative to height. BMI can be used to determine if people are at a healthy weight, overweight, or obese. A BMI of 18.5 up to 25 refers to a health weight, a BMI of 25 up to 30 refers to overweight, and a BMI of 30 or higher refers to obese. To get your BMI number go to ww.nibisupport.com/bmi/bmicalc.htm.

Boiler Room a place having high-pressure brokers calling typically uninformed investors to make unsuitable or even fraudulent speculative investments. Such activities, if not against the law, do violate fair practice rules of the National Association of Securities Dealers (NASD).

Boilerplate Standard language found in contracts, indentures, prospectuses, and the like. It typically appears in fine print.

Bona Fide in law, a Latin term meaning "in good faith," without fraud.

Bona Fide Sale an arm's length transaction in which both buyer and seller are acting in good faith, without fraud.

Bond an IOU or promissory note of a corporation, municipal, government debt, expressed in a stipulated face value, and a date at which the issuer–U.S. or foreign–will pay the holder the face value of the bond. Investors essentially lend money to these organizations in exchange of IOUs, represented by bond certificates. The borrowers promise to repay the loan by a certain date and to pay interest regularly to the investors in the interim.

Bond ETFs fixed income ETFs. Bond ETFs have several advantages: (1) it is a well diversified basket of bonds with different maturities, (2) their expense ratio is low (15 basis points) compared with an average of 39 for bond mutual funds, and (3) their greater transparency over individual bonds further lowers costs. Also, with bonds individual investors can't get good prices, while institutions can.

Bond (Mutual) Fund a mutual fund that emphasizes safety and invests in bonds. The portfolio may consist of various levels of quality of bonds depending on the particular objectives of the specific mutual fund. For example, there may be high-grade bonds, medium-grade bonds, or low-grade bonds (e.g., junk bonds).

Bond Ratings calculations of the probability that a bond issue will go into default. They measure risk, and therefore have an impact on the interest rate. Bond investors tend to place more emphasis on independent analysis of quality than do common stock investors. Bond analysis and ratings are done, notably, by Moody's Investors Service, Standard & Poor's, Duff & Phelps/MCM, and Fitch Investors Service. For examples of these see the following figure. Bond investors pay careful attention to ratings since they can affect not only potential market behavior but relative yields as well. Specifically, the higher the rating, the lower the yield of a bond, other things being equal. It should be noted that the ratings do change over time and the rating agencies have "credit watch lists" of various types.

Description Of Bond Ratings		
Moody's	Standard & Poor's	Quality Indication
Aaa	AAA	Highest quality
Aa	AA	High quality
A	A	Upper medium grade
Baa	BBB	Medium grade
Ba	BB	Contains speculative elements
B	B	Outright speculative
Caa	CCC & CC	Default, definitely possible
Ca	C	Default, only partial recovery likely
C	D	Default, little recovery likely Risky, applied to derivatives

Bond Yields effective rate of return on a bond. Bonds are evaluated on many different types of returns, including current yield and yield to maturity.

Bonus additional consideration, premium, or gratuity to which the recipient has no right to make a demand.

Athletics: an additional incentive given to a professional athlete for agreeing to sign on with a particular team.

Business: an addition to salary or wages often given at the end of the year without expectation of a direct return, such as Christmas bonus or end-of-the-year profit bonus. It services as a token of appreciation for a job well done and to provide a continuing incentive for future effort.

Insurance: a life insurance payment made by the insurance company to the insured arising from the amount accrued in the form of investment returns.

Book

1. used as a noun (usually plural); refers to journals or ledgers.
2. used as a verb; refers to the recording of an entry.

Book Value the difference between total tangible assets and total liabilities, less the value of the preferred stock. This gives the book value of the common stockholders' equity. Book value of the net assets of a company may have little or no significant relationship to their market value. It was once used as a proxy for a company's intrinsic value. Especially with the new economy, book value is a less relevant measure for a company's fair value for investors. For example, many new economy companies have assets that do not register significantly on their balance sheet, such as intellectual property, employees, strong brand name, and market share.

Book Value Per Share the value of each share of stock on the books of a company based on historical cost. Book value per share is usually less than the current market price per share. Book value per share equals:

$$\frac{\text{Total Stockholders' Equity}}{\text{Outstanding Shares}}$$

Book-to-Bill Ratio a ratio comparing new orders against shipments of specific goods. As an example, the Semiconductor Industry Association's book-to-bill ratio monthly movements are an indication of strengths or weaknesses in the computer business because they show the current demand for computer chips. For example, a ratio of 1.4 means that there are 1.4 orders outstanding to be filled for each order received.

Boolean Algebra or Logic the algebra of logic; often called *symbolic logic*. It is based on two elements, 1 and 0, or true and false, and the operations and, or, and not. It provides the theoretical concepts for computer design. It is not used to solve managerial problems directly.

Boomerang Effect
1. a situation where technology sold to firms in one nation is used against the seller of the technology. This is one reason why firms often fear to sell their technology abroad and face the competition later.
2. taking steps to reduce the effect of product dumping.

Boot
1. any net cash or net mortgage relief a participant in an exchange might receive in addition to the actual "like kind" property. For example, in a 1031 tax-free exchange, John exchanges his apartment complex worth $500,000 and receives Brian's land worth $550,000. John pays $300,000 cash and jewelry worth $200,000 to balance the values of properties exchanged. The cash and jewelry are boot.
2. in computers, the process of starting up a computer.

Bottleneck an activity for which the work equals or exceeds the capacity of the activity.

Bottom Line
1. a term referring to the last line in an income statement that reflects a firm's net profit or earnings. A good bottom line allows a company to reward its investors for risking their capital. Companies can research and develop new and better products or services, add jobs to employ more people, reward employees, allow opportunities for employer growth and development, and take pride in efficient performance. *See also* Top Line.
2. "net" rather than "gross."

Bottom Up achieving company goals by asking for suggestions from the bottom up versus the top down approach.

Bounced Check a check that has been returned for insufficient funds.

Bounded Rationality a principle stating that economic agents (i.e., consumers and producers) are rational up to a limit because of their limited capacity for computation and information processing.

Bracket Creep moving into higher tax brackets as taxable income increases to adjust for inflation. Current tax law adjusts the brackets for inflation.

Brady Bonds U.S. dollar denominated bonds of developing nations, such as Argentina, exchanged because of a restructuring of defaulted bank loans. The bonds are named after Nicholas Brady who served as treasury secretary when George Bush (Senior) was president. There was a pledging of U.S. Treasury zero-coupon bonds to guarantee principal. Details on Brady Bonds and other emerging market bonds are covered in BradyNet.com (*www.bradynet.com*).

Brainstorming a group decision-making technique operating under the rules that no one's idea should be criticized no matter how outrageous it may appear. The basic purpose of the technique is to generate ideas and original thinking. Now managers can use computer software to encourage brainstorming.

Brand a name term, sign, symbol, design, or a combination of them all, intended to distinguish products of one seller from those of competitors.

Brand Loyalty repeated purchases made by consumers on the basis of brand name. Consumers with bran royalty tend to prefer national brands because the brands give good value and save shoppers time and energy by eliminating the need to search for alternatives.

Brand Name has a narrower meaning than brand. It is a word, letter, or a group of words or letters that can be spoken.

Breach violating a law, commitment, duty, or obligation through commission or omission. The responsibilities of an agreement or guarantee are not met.

Breach of Contract failure, without just cause, for one or both parties to carry out the terms of a contract. For a breach of contract to occur, there must be an unequivocal, decisive, and absolute refusal to perform the agreement. When a breach of contract occurs, including the assured anticipation of a breach, the aggrieved party or parties may recover damages by entering a suit for such purpose. In these cases it is also possible to sue for performance when simple damage recovery is insufficient.

Break a significant and usually unexpected decline in the price of a particular security. If, for example, on the opening of its trading, a stock is several points lower than the previous day's close, then it has suffered a break. It is also said to have gapped. Another term for a stock experiencing a break in prices is *it has fallen out of bed*. A break may occur when it is announced prior to trading that a company is under investigation by a governmental agency for accounting irregularities or fraudulent activities.

Break-Even Analysis the analysis of a company's costs and revenues to determine the level of sales where total costs equal total revenue; the analysis of profits by determining the relationship between the costs and the revenues.

Break-Even Chart a graphical representation of break-even analysis.

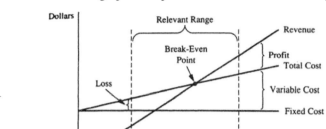

Break-Even Sales (Point) the sales result in there being no profit or loss, also called *break-even point*. It is the sales volume, in units or in dollars where total sales revenue equals total costs. Thus, zero profit results. *See also* Break-Even Analysis.

Break-Up Value the estimated value of company assets if the company was liquidated; also called *Liquidating Value*.

Bretton Woods Agreement An agreement made in 1944 at an international conference in Bretton Woods, New Hampshire, that established the international monetary system in effect from 1945 to 1971. Each member government pledged to maintain a fixed, or pegged, exchange rate for its currency vs. the dollar or gold. These fixed exchange rates were designed to reduce the riskiness of international transactions, thus promoting growth in global trade. The agreement created the International Monetary Fund (IMF) and the World Bank.

Brick and Mortar having a physical location, a conventional "street-side" business that deals with its customers face-to-face in an office or storefront. It is often compared with web-based businesses that commonly have lower costs and greater flexibility than brick-and-mortar operations.

Bridge Loan a short-term loan that is made in expectation of intermediate-or long-term loans, also called a swing loan. The interest rate on the bridge loan is generally higher than on longer term loans. An example would be a temporary loan to finance the purchase of a building where its purpose would be to permit a closing on the purchase prior to a closing on long-term mortgage financing.

Broadband high-speed digital communication, sometimes defined as at least 200 kbps. T1, Cable modem, and DSL provide broadband. A general term for very fast data transmission, such as fiber optics.

Broker

1. an agent who handles the public's orders to buy and sell securities or commodities. A commission is charged for this service. Depending on where you do business, a broker may be called by any other name. Examples are a financial consultant, intuitional salesperson, securities salesperson, account

executive, investment executive, or portfolio salesperson.

2. real estate broker.

Broker-Dealer a securities brokerage firm, usually registered with the SEC, the NASD, and the NYSE, acting as a broker and dealer. It acts as a broker when it buys and sells for its customers and as a dealer when it buys for its own inventory with the likelihood of later sales to clients. Broker-dealers are required to state how they are serving in consummating a transaction.

Browse (or Surf) to search the web for specific sites and retrieve information.

Browser special software designed to search the web for specific sites and retrieve information in the form of text, pictures, sound, and animation.

Bubble a speculative market or stock in which the values rise very rapidly and then fall sharply. A bubble is a situation where stock prices are excessively overvalued.

Bucket Shop an illegal operation in which the bucket shop operator accepted a client's money without ever actually buying or selling securities the client ordered. Instead, the operator held the money, gambling that the customer was wrong. When too many customers were right, the bucket shop operator closed its doors and opened a new office.

Budget

1. a quantitative plan of activities and programs expressed in terms of the assets, equities, revenues, and expenses that will be involved in carrying out the plans, or in other quantitative terms, such as units of product or service. The budget expresses the organizational goals in terms of specific financial and operating objectives. Advantages of budget preparation are planning, communicating company-wide goals to subunits, fostering cooperation between departments, control by evaluating actual figures to budget figures, and revealing the interrelationship of one function to another.

2. a financial plan of activities expressed in monetary terms of the assets, debts, net worth, revenue and expenses that will be involved in carrying out an individual's plans. Simply put, it is a set of projected or planned personal financial statements. A budget is used as a tool for planning and control. At the beginning of the period, the budget is a plan. At the end of a period, it serves as a control device to monitor the individual's income and spending.

Budget Control budgetary actions carried out according to a budget plan. Through the use of a budget as a standard, an organization ensures that managers are implementing its plans and objectives and their activities are appraised by comparing their actual performance against budgeted performance. Budgets are used as a basis for rewarding or punishing them, or perhaps for modifying future budgets and plans.

Budget Deficit/Surplus an excess of expenditure over income in a budget. The budget surplus (or deficit) in a particular year depends not only on the level of expenditures and the rates set for various taxes and transfers, but also on the rate of GDP during the year.

Budget Estimates the planned or projected figures of incomes and expenditures in a budget during a certain period of time.

Budget Exceptions the deviations of the actual expenses or income compared with the budget figures of expenses or income. A detailed listing of exceptions may be made for each major item of expense or income.

Budget Summary a condensation of a budget document in which the major expenditure and revenue categories for the forthcoming budget are summarized. A budget summary is usually accompanied by a narrative explaining the major changes in the budget from the previous year as well as the overall rationale guiding the budget.

Budget Surplus an excess of income over expenditure in a budget.

Budgetary Accountability the process of recording budgetary amounts in the accounts of a fund. Recording the balances has a dual effect. The control aspect of the budgetary function is stressed and recognition is given to the legal foundations of the budget.

Budgetary Slack intentional underestimation of revenues and/or overestimation of expenses; also called *Budget Slack*. This must be avoided if a budget is to have its desired effects. Misstating projections of costs and revenues for this purpose is behavior that is both dysfunctional and unethical.

Budgeting
1. a process of estimating all income and expenses for specified period.
2. a process of financial forecasting, planning and controlling. It involves using a budget to set and achieve short-term goals and ensuring that actual goals are in harmony with budgeted goals. *See also* Budget.

Buffer area of a computer's memory set aside to hold information temporarily.

Bug an error in a computer program.

Bull an individual or institution that believes a given stock, particular industry, or the stock market in general, will experience a price rise. An investor can also be bullish (optimistic) about bonds or commodities.

Bull Market a prolonged advancing market that experiences a period of rising prices in securities or commodities; the bull's horns thrust upward. There is a high trading volume. Bull markets are favorable markets normally associated with investor optimism, economic recovery, and government stimulus.

Bulldogs foreign bonds sold in the United Kingdom.

Bulletin Board System (BBS)
1. a collection of message boards and files devoted to a particular topic.
2. properly known as the *OTC Bulletin Board*, an electronic quotation service that lists the prices of stocks that don't meet the minimum requirements for listing on a stock exchange or the NASDAQ stock-listing system.

Bullion Coins any coins minted from pure gold or silver bullion. American gold and silver dollars are highly prized bullion coins. Many other nations mint gold bullion coins that are traded on a bullion exchange. The advantage of a bullion coin is that it is extremely liquid for trading purposes and easily verified.

Bundesbank the German central bank equivalent to the Federal Reserve Bank of the U.S. Its primary goals are to (1) set the discount rate, known as the Lombard rate, (2) monitor the money supply, and (3) assist economic policies.

Bundle Of Rights the various legal rights or interests that owners have in their property. They include title of property, such as the right to occupy and use, sell, rent or lease, build, grant easements, and mortgage on the property.

Bus the set of wires or soldered conductors in the computer through which the different components (such as CPU and RAM) communicate.

Bus Line an electrical pathway through which bits are transmitted between the CPU and other devices. There are different types of buses. The bus between the CPU and the expansion slots is called a local bus. The bus between RAM and the expansion slots is called an expansion bus. The old 8 bit bus can only transfer 8 bits at a time, while a 32 bit bus can transmit 32 bits at one time.

Business Conditions Digest the business conditions report, published monthly by the Bureau of Economic Analysis of the U.S. Department of Commerce that provides the information that differs from the other publications previously discussed in that its primary emphasis is on cyclical indicators of economic activity. The National Bureau of Economic Research (NBER) analyzes and selects the time series data based on each series' ability to be identified as a leading, coincident, or lagging indicator over several decades of aggregate economic activity. Over the years, the NBER has identified the approximate dates when aggregate economic activity reached its cyclical high or low point. Each time series is related to the business cycle. Leading indicators move prior to the business cycle, coincident indicators move with the cycle, and lagging indicators follow directional changes in the business cycle. Note: This publication can be very helpful in understanding past economic behavior and in forecasting future economic activity with a higher degree of success.

Business Continuity Plan a plan that aims at safeguarding business disruptions, disaster recovery, risk and crisis management, and protection of reputations and brands. The reasons for the plan include supply chain disruption, communications failure, the loss of staffing, the protection of buildings, and preparation for the rising threat of terrorism.

Business Cycle the regular pattern of expansion (recovery) and contraction (recession) in aggregate economic activity around the path of trend growth, with effects on growth, employment, and inflation. At the peak of the cycle, economic activity is high relative to trend, while at the trough (valley) of the cycle, the low point in economic activity is reached. The business cycle tends to have an impact on corporate earnings, cash flow, and expansion.

Business Intelligence a business strategy that integrates and analyzes operational data from an array of internal sources to improve decision making and competitiveness.

Business Inventories stock of unsold goods on hand. A change in business inventories is used as a signal for economic outlook. For example, a decrease in business inventories means more production and hiring ahead.

Business Model the matter in which businesses generate income.

Business Performance Management (BPM) the use of business intelligence-derived operational metrics, ranging from ad hoc yardsticks to Six Sigma or Balanced Scorecard, to measure company performance.

Business Plan a road map to guide in detail a new business venture. It serves as a written guide for its future operations and covers its short- and long-term goals, details about the business, management strategy, method of operation, and timetables. It also includes the description of the new business products or services, the analysis of the customers and opportunities, the projected financial revenues and expenses, and timetables for the business to become a success.

Business Process Reengineering (BPR) an approach aiming at making revolutionary changes as opposed to evolutionary changes by eliminating non-value added steps in a business process and computerizing the remaining steps to achieve desired outcomes. *See also* Total Quality Management (TQM)

Business Risk the risk caused by fluctuations in a firm's earnings. This may be due to operating difficulties, such as strikes and technological obsolescence. Business risk depends on variability in demand, sales price, input prices, and amount of operating leverage.

Business Unit a part of a company that is a business unto itself. *See also* Strategic Business Unit (SBU).

Business Week a major weekly business magazine.

Buy In

Securities: a transaction made when a security purchase fails because of a delivery failure and the purchaser or purchasing broker can obtain the securities elsewhere, charging the additional expense to the seller who failed to make delivery.

Option: a method for terminating the responsibility to accept delivery of stock in which the option writer buys an option identical to the one he or she previously sold. This is also known as a closing purchase.

Real estate: purchase of property at an auction or tax or mortgage foreclosure sale by the original owner, or one with a previous interest in the property.

Government contracts: a strategy for obtaining future government work by submitting a low bid for a contract in the expectation that future modifications and other opportunities will more than compensate any short-term loss. It is a way of getting one's foot in the government contract door.

Buy Order an order entered by the security dealer with the investor's approval for the purpose of purchasing a security.

Buy Limit Order: a buy order entered with a specific price to purchase a particular security. The investor is not obligated to pay more than the price limit, although he or she could actually pay less if the market conditions favored a lower price.

Buy Stop Order: a customer's instruction that if the market price reaches or exceeds the buy stop limit, the broker is authorized to execute a market buy order at the best obtainable price. Reaching or exceeding the stated price triggers the buy stop order, converting it into a marker buy order.

Buy the Book: the buyer's instruction to buy all the shares available on the floor trader's book as well as any that can be obtained from the crowd at the same price.

Market Buy Order: instruction to the broker by the customer to purchase a security at whatever price can be obtained in the open market.

Buy-and-Hold Strategy a long-term stock purchase strategy in which the investor makes purchases in quality companies over the years and ignores short-term trading patterns. The basic assumption is that a well-managed company will weather the storms and grow over the years. It is a rather passive strategy that does not require day-to-day stock management.

Buyback

Stock: the repurchase of stock by a corporation. Also called *stock buyback*, it suggests that the company thinks its stock is undervalued and inexpensive enough to buy. Many firms have announced or executed stock buybacks in recent years. Buying back shares is also a way for a company to reward its shareholders.

Short Sale: after a short sale (in which shares are borrowed and then sold), the purchase of an identical amount in order to repay the loan.

Reverse Transactions: an agreement to sell an item with a pre-arranged reverse buy at a set price. This is illegal in some cases, and any short-term losses will be disallowed by the IRS under such and arrangement.

Insurance: an agreement to rescind certain policy limitations on the insured if additional coverage is purchased from the insurer.

Production Agreement: an agreement between two manufacturers by which the first gains control over the second's manufacturing output by agreeing to buy it first and then sell it back. Often, this is merely a paper agreement to implement control by the purchasing company over the units produced by the second company.

International Trade: an agreement by "X" trading country to buy merchandise from the "Y" trading country in return for Y's agreement to purchase X's products.

Buy-Back

1. an agreement to sell real estate with a pre-arranged reverse buy at an established price. This may not be legal in some instances, and any resulting losses may not be tax deductible.
2. an arrangement to rescind specified policy limitations on the insured if further coverage is bought from the insurer.

Buyback Agreement any clause in a contrast that guarantees that the seller will buy the item back from the buyer within a certain time frame.

Buydown a cash payment to a lender so as to reduce a rate of interest on a loan a borrower must pay. The reduced rate may apply for all or a portion of the loan term. For example, a builder has a tract of homes for sale. In order to accomplish a sale of a house, the builder arranged for a buy down loan with a lender to pay discount points so that the lender can offer a loan at a lower interest to the buyer.

Buyers' Market a market condition in a specific industry, such as the housing industry, in which a buyer is in a more commanding position. This is the market with few buyers and many sellers. This means a buyer can negotiate prices and terms, such as quality assurance and closing dates, more to his or her liking and a seller, who wishes to sell, must accept them.

Buying on Margin buying bonds, commodities, or stock through credit extended by the broker to the customer in a qualified margin account. Margin rules set by the federal reserve board and the participating exchanges for securities generally require a ratio of 50% collateral to cover stock purchases. Margin rules for bonds and commodities vary considerably.

Buying Power
Personal: the amount of money an individual has or has control of, enabling purchases to be made. In this sense, buying power refers to liquid assets.
Goods or Services: the number of products or services that can be purchased by an individual.
Money: the relative purchasing power of various currencies when compared with each other. Rating one currency based on its value with another international currency.
Securities: the amount of credit available for additional security purchases or short sales for an investor maintaining a margin buying account with a brokerage firm.

Buying Power Index a market index of a geographic area's market characteristics that indicate marketing opportunities. It is composed of:
• percent of effective buying income
• percent of retail sales
• percent of population

Buyout the acquisition of a controlling interest of a company's stock. A buyout can be previously negotiated or accomplished by a hostile tender offer, resulting in the hot pursuit of the company in the security markets.

Buzzwords new or existing words that take on a very specific meaning when used in a particular context. They are usually business-type words that are in vogue such as TQM, ABC, and JIT. Buzzwords are used to impress someone with new jargons or to promote a product, service, or idea.

Bylaws

1. a document stating the rules of internal governance for a corporation as adopted by its board of directors.
2. the rules for running a company that were documented at the time of incorporation, or have been added to them since then.

Bypass Trust an estate tax strategy that allows a surviving spouse to receive income from certain assets, the principal of which will not be taxed in the spouse's estate. An irrevocable trust created by parents to protect their assets from outside claims, excepting estate taxes, in order to bequeath the largest amount possible of their estate. In this type of a trust, it is possible for the parents or parent to receive income from the assets placed in the trust during their lifetimes. The trust bypasses probate upon the death of the parents.

By-Product any output of a joint process that is designed for another product. It is useful in its own right but has limited market value, as compared with a joint product.

Byte the number of bits (usually 8) that stand for one character; bytes are used as a measure of your computer's capacity, usually in the past as kilobytes, now as megabytes and gigabytes. Characters may be letters, numbers, or symbols. One kilobyte (1 KB) is equivalent to 1,024 bytes. A byte is the smallest unit of memory containing one character of data.

Cc

C2B (Consumer-to-Business) E-Commerce online exchanges in which consumers search out sellers, learn about their offers, initiate purchases, and sometimes even driving transactions terms.

C2C (Consumer-to-consumer) E-commerce Refers to web-based transactions between two consumers via the servers of a company, such as a auctions and sales. eBay is an example of a C2C site.

C Corporation a regular corporation as opposed to an S corporation that has elected an S corporation status.

C Language, C++ a high-level programming language used by professional software programmers.

Cache a part of RAM devoted to the most frequently used instructions and data of a program for faster retrieval; pronounced "cash," from French. It is a special high speed memory area that the CPU can access quickly. Most frequently used routines are stored in the cache memory to improve performance.

CAD *see* **Computer-Aided Design (CAD).**

Cafeteria Employee Benefit Plan a benefit plan permitting employees to choose from a variety of fringe benefits, like retirement plans, insurance, day care, and just like a cafeteria, the employees are allowed those options they wish to pay for. The money taken out of their paycheck reduces their taxable income.

Calculated Risk a knowingly risky action taken with the aim of a favorable outcome.

Calculus a branch of mathematics concerned with the determination of the derivative of a function and the problem of finding a maximum or minimum point of the function; also called *differential calculus*, or *classical optimization technique*.

Call

1. an option to buy (or "call") an asset at a specified price within a specified period.
2. the right to buy 100 shares of stock at a specified price within a specified period. *See also* Options.
3. the process of redeeming a bond or preferred stock issue before its normal maturity. A security with a call provision typically is issued at an interest rate higher than one without a call provision. This is because investors demand it; they look at yield-to-call rather than yield-to-maturity.

Call Provision (Feature) a provision of some bond indentures allowing the issuing company to redeem bonds prior to maturity by paying holders a premium above face value. An issuing company typically wishes to retire a callable bond when interest rates decline.

Callable Bond a bond issue with a call provision. *See also* Callable Security.

Callable Security a bond or preferred stock issue with a call provision. The provision in the indenture or preferred stock agreement allows an issuing company to redeem the security early. When interest rates are anticipated to decline, a call provision in the bond issue is desirable from an issuer's standpoint. Such a provision enables the firm to buy back the high-interest security and issue a lower-interest one. *See also* Call.

CAM *see* **Computer-Aided Manufacturing (CAM).**

Canada Awards for Business Excellence a medal given annually to Canadian companies that demonstrated outstandingly high levels of quality. *See also* Deming Prize; Malcolm Baldrige National Quality Award.

Cancel

1. to make null and void; to revoke or destroy; to rescind or set aside.
2. to abandon; abolish; repeal; surrender; waive; terminate.

Securities Trading: to void a buy or sell order, price, or quantity. Cancel orders are normally executed very rapidly. They may or may not be accompanied by new instructions.

Insurance: the termination of any insurance policy.

Cancelable Agreement a contractual clause allowing one or both parties to terminate the agreement if a specified occurrence takes place. This is a cancellation clause, which allows the agreement to become null and void thereby allowing the parties to end their duties. The cancellation stipulation protects the interests of each participant if one is damaged.

Cancellation

In General: voiding a negotiable instrument by nullifying or paying it.

Insurance: prematurely terminating an insurance policy.

Securities:

1. void an order to buy or sell.
2. prematurely terminating a bond contract.

Cancellation Clause contractual provision describing the terms under which coverage may be terminated. An insured or insurer may cancel a policy (such as a property and casualty insurance policy) before its expiration date. However, a written notice of cancellation must be sent. The insurance company then should refund a part of the premium as stipulated in the insurance contract.

Cap
1. a contract on an interest rate, whereby at periodic payment dates, the writer of the cap pays the difference between the market interest rate and a specified cap rate if, and only if, this difference is positive. This is equivalent to a stream of call options on the interest rate.
2. also used in bonds and mortgages as abbreviations for capitalization, small cap, large cap, etc.
3. a limit on charges.

Capacity
1. the ability to produce during a given time period, with an upper limit imposed by the availability of space, machinery, labor, materials, or capital. It may be expressed in units, weight, size, dollars, man hours, labor costs, etc.
2. the number of bytes that can be used or stored in the memory, or hard drive. This number is expressed as kilobytes, megabytes, and gigabytes.
3. the ability to grasp the facts and charges brought against a defendant.

Capacity Requirements Planning (CRP) system for determining if a planned production schedule can be accomplished with available capacity and, if not, making adjustments as necessary.

Capacity Utilization Rate the ratio of actual production to potential production. This can be measured for firms, industries, or whole economies. *See also* Capacity Utilization.

Capital
1. net assets of an individual or business entity (owners' equity).
2. the amount invested in a business (proprietorship, partnership, and corporation) by its owners.
3. working capital, which is the difference between current assets and current liabilities.

Capital Asset
In general: any asset purchased for use in production over long periods of time rather than for resale. It includes (a) land, buildings, plant and equipment, mineral deposits, and timber reserves; (b) patents, goodwill, trademarks, and leaseholds; and (c) investments in affiliated companies.
Economics: a productive asset employed to create wealth that is consumed over time.
Taxation: assets to include most property one owns and uses for personal purposes, pleasure, or investments; for example, a house, furniture, car, stocks, and bonds.
Real estate: income-producing assets.

Capital Asset Pricing Model (CAPM) a theory of asset pricing in which the return of an asset or security is the risk-free return, plus a risk premium based on the excess of the return on the market, over the risk-free rate multiplied by the asset's systematic risk (which cannot be eliminated by diversification). The model, also called the *security market line* (SML), is given as follows: $r = r_f + b$ $(r_m - r_f)$ where r = the expected (or required) return on a security, r_f =the risk-free rate (such as a T-bill), r_m=the expected return on the market portfolio (such as Standard & Poor's 500 Stock Composite Index or Dow Jones 30 Industrials), and b = beta, an index of systematic (nondiversifiable, uncontrollable) risk. For example, assume that the risk-free rate (r_f) is 8 percent, and the expected market return (r_m) is 12 percent. Then if b=0, r=8% + 0 (12% - 8%) = 8% and if b=2.0, r=8% + 2.0(12% - 8%)=16%. It shows that the higher the degree of systematic risk (b), the higher the return on a given security demanded by investors.

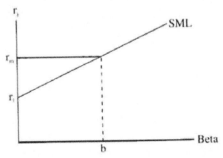

Capital Budgeting the process of making long-term planning decisions for capital investments. There are typically two types of investment decisions: selection and replacement decisions.

Capital Expenditure Budget a budget plan prepared for individual capital expenditure projects. The time span of this budget depends upon the project. Capital expenditures to be budgeted include replacement, acquisition, or construction of facilities and major equipment. *See also* Capital Budgeting.

Capital Expenses the amount of money used to pay off the interest and amortization of a loan.

Capital Formation additions to the stock of real capital. It involves the creation of capital goods made possible through savings; also called *gross investment*. Savings may be spent directly for labor, materials, and other expenses involved in the creation of capital goods. Additions to the stock of real capital after depreciation or capital allowance are called net capital formations or net investments.

Capital Gain or Capital Loss profit or loss from the sale of a capital asset. A capital gain may be either short-term (one year or less) or long-term (more than one year). The maximum tax rate on long-term capital gains is 18% for a stock or mutual fund. This would be calculated by the sales proceeds minus the cost basis of the shares. To calculate gains and losses, you need to determine which shares were sold and the cost basis of those shares.

Capital Gains Distribution income for investors arising from net long-term profits of a mutual fund realized when the portfolio is sold at a gain. Profits from sales of securities are passed on by fund managers to shareholders at least annually.

Capital Gearing the proportion of fixed interest debt to equity capital employed in a firm's capital structure; also called *leverage* or *trading on equity*. It is of major interest to the firm's shareholders since fixed financial charges on debt capital have the effect of gearing up or down the ultimate residual return to them from trading profits. *See* Leverage; Trading on Equity.

Capital Improvements
1. Improvements made to a company's main long-term assets, such as plants and buildings.
2. Costs incurred in connection with real property that increase its worth. Examples are a new roof, an addition, or paneling a room. These improvements increase the cost basis of the property.

Capital Intensive a situation in which a higher proportion of capital is used in the mix of inputs compared with other factor inputs, such as labor in the production process.

Capital Loss Carryover a limit of capital losses that can be allowed on income taxes each year, usually $3,000.

Capital Markets the markets for long-term debt and corporate stocks. The New York Stock Exchange (NYSE), which trades the stocks of many of the larger corporations, is a prime example of a capital market. The American Stock Exchange and the regional stock exchanges are also examples. In addition, securities are issued and traded through the thousands of brokers and dealers on the over-the-counter market.

Capital Rationing a problem of selecting the mix of acceptable projects that provides the highest overall net present value, (NPV), where an entity has a limit on the budget for capital spending. The profitability index is widely used in ranking projects competing for limited funds.

Capital Stock equity shares in a corporation authorized by its Articles of Incorporation and issued to stockholders. Such stock may have a par value or not. The company presents in its annual report the number of shares authorized and issued, par value or stated value per share, and total par value or stated value. Capital stock may be of two types: common and preferred. If only one class of securities exists, it must be voting common stock. If more than one class of stock exists, the additional classes constitute stock that have some preference or restriction of basic rights.

Capital Structure the mix of long-term sources of funds used by the firm, for example, equity capital and debt capital; also called *capitalization*. The relative total percentage (or weight) of each source of long-term financing is emphasized.

Capitalism a system in which capital is privately owned. It is a social and economic system in which individuals are free to own the means of production (land, buildings, equipment and other materials, etc.) of goods and services for consumption by society.

Capitalization

1. total amount of the various securities issued by a corporation. Capitalization may include bonds, debentures, preferred and common stock.
2. a technique used by real estate appraisers to convert the income of a property into a value estimate for that property.

Capitalization Rate (Cap Rate)

1. a tool used by real estate agents to determine a value of an investment; also called cap rate or income yield. It is calculated by dividing a property's net operating income (NOI) by its purchase price. That interest rate, which when applied to the earnings of an investment, determines its appraisal or market value. The higher the cap rate, the lower the perceived risk to the investor and the lower the asking price paid. Whether a piece of property is over-priced or not depends on the rate of the similar type property derived from the market place. The method has two limitations: (1) it is based on only the first year's NOI, and (2) it ignores return through appreciation in property value.
2. a concept that relates the proportion of each class of share or debt capital in a firm to its total market capitalization. Many companies of large size issue several classes of shares.

Capitalize recording an expenditure as a long-term asset rather than as an immediate expense.

Capitalized Cost the "value" established as the "beginning" value for determining lease payments. Sometimes considered to be the "purchase price" associated with the asset for purposes of the lease. This might not be true because of trade-in implications, lease origination fees, how the down payment might be handled, and more.

Capitalized Cost Reduction in a lease, a payment or other item that reduces the "capitalized cost" otherwise used for establishing lease payments. A capitalized cost reduction might be synonymous with a down payment, or any item that reduces the "beginning value" used to compute lease payments. *See also* Capitalized Cost.

CAPM *see* Capital Asset Pricing Model.

Capping a financial institution's putting a ceiling on the interest rate that may be charged on a variable interest rate loan. For example, if a homeowner takes out a variable rate mortgage, the interest rate may be capped not to exceed 15%.

Captive Agent one having the sole privilege to sell in a territory. He or she may be paid a straight salary plus commission.

Captive Finance Company a sales finance company that is owned and operated by a maker of a "big-ticket" item, such as an automobile. It is usually a wholly subsidiary whose objective is to finance consumer purchases from the parent company. An example of a captive finance company is General Motors Acceptance Corporation (GMAC).

Carat
1. a unit of weight for precious stones, such as diamonds. It is equal to 200 milligrams and divided into 100 "points." Thus, a 150-point diamond weighs 1.50 carats. Investment grade diamonds should be at least one-half carat and preferably more than one carat in weight.
2. karat. A unit of fineness for gold equal to 1/24 part of pure gold in an alloy.

Career Planning any systematic attempt to arrange and determine one's work career. Career planning includes an assessment of the opportunities in the chosen vocation or profession as well as the educational requirements and other prerequisites, including any investments.

Carrying Charge
Securities: the fee charged by a broker for carrying a customer's securities on margin.
Commodities: or, holding costs. Expenses incurred because a business keeps inventories. They include interest on money invested in inventory, storage cost, insurance, and taxes.
Real Estate: carrying cost, primarily taxes and debt service costs, of owning land before its development.
Business: the seller's for an installment loan.

Carte Blanche
1. a term connoting full authority to do something. An example is to give someone the full right and authority to fill in any amount he or she wishes on your check. Another example could occur when your employer instructs you to buy whatever is needed for the office.
2. a retail credit card (Carte Blanche) having an annual membership fee. It allows the holder to charge a wide range of retail services wherever it is accepted throughout the world. Carte Blanche does not provide for installment payments, requiring all balances to be paid in full each month. In addition to providing for retail credit purchases it also provides each card holder with airline, rental car, and lost baggage insurance.

Cartel a contractual association of independent businesses formed for the purpose of coordinating the manufacturing, purchasing, or marketing of its members. Firms may be located in one or more countries. Such relationships in the United States could violate antitrust provisions.

Case Studies a pedagogical method used in many business schools to formulate recommended policy and analyze business decisions based on hypothetical situations or actual occurrences in certain companies.

Cash paper currency and coins, bank accounts, and other "near cash" instruments that are very liquid and can readily be converted into cash.

Cash Accounting a basic method of recognizing revenue and expenses when cash is received or paid. This is in contrast to accrual accounting in which revenue and expenses are recorded when earned or incurred.

Cash Basis, Cash Method *see* Cash Accounting.

Cash Budget a budget for cash planning and control presenting expected cash inflow and outflow for a designated time period. The cash budget helps management keep cash balances in reasonable relationship to its needs. It aids in avoiding idle cash and possible cash shortages.

Cash Cow a business or the segment of the business that generates tons of money. "ABC Corporation is a real cash cow—they cannot pay out dividends fast enough!"

Cash Equivalent
1. immediately realizable money that can be obtained in exchange for goods or services.
2. financial instruments of high liquidity and safety (e.g.. Treasury bill, money-market fund).

Cash Flow
1. cash receipts minus cash disbursements from a given operation or asset for a given period. Cash flow and cash inflow are often used interchangeably.
2. in capital budgeting, the monetary value of the expected benefits and costs of a project. It may be in the form of cash savings in operating costs or the difference between additional dollars received and additional dollars paid out for a given period.
3. cash basis net income.
4. the difference between what a business takes in for sales and services and what it lays out in expenses, taxes, and other costs that must be met. It is not the same thing as book income.
5. the stream of cash passing through one's hands before taxes. When one spends more than one takes in, the individual has a negative cash flow. The reverse is a positive cash flow. Examples of cash inflow are salary income, dividend income, and sales of investments. Examples of cash outflow are payments made for rent, utilities, clothing, entertainment, and purchases of assets (e.g., automobile).
6. in real estate, the amount of money available after subtracting all operating expenses and mortgage payments from rental income. For example, Harry acquires an apartment building with the first year of its operation shown on the next page:

Gross rental income	$75,000
Less: Vacancy loss	5,000
Effective gross income	70,000
Less: Operating expenses	50,000
Net operating income (NOI)	20,000
Less: Debt service	15,000
Cash flow before taxes	$ 5,000

Cash-on-Cash Return a percentage return that measures the return on cash invested in an income-producing property. It is cash flow divided by the amount of cash invested. For example, the cash-on-cash return for a $200,000 down payment on an apartment that generates $30,000 a year is 15%. This measure is used to evaluate the profitability of income-producing properties and can be used when comparing investments.

Cash Surrender Value money the insured is entitled to receive from the insurer upon surrendering a cash value life insurance policy. The amount received is the cash value specified in the policy minus a surrender charge and any outstanding loan and interest thereon.

Cash Value the accumulated portion of life insurance premiums as a savings feature that can be borrowed against or obtained as cash upon surrendering the insurance policy. It can be used as a source of loan collateral.

Casualty Insurance insurance that protects a business or homeowner against property loss, damage, and/or bodily injury to a third party.

Casualty Loss loss caused by damage, destruction, or loss of property as the result of an identifiable event that is sudden, unexpected, or unusual. It is covered by most casualty insurance policies, and is tax deductible, with limitations and exclusions, to the extent that it is not reimbursed from insurance.

CAT *see* Catastrophe Bonds.

Catalog directory of file locations.

Catastrophe Bonds a capital market form of reinsurance It is a high-yield, insurance-backed bond meant to raise money in case of a catastrophe such as a hurricane or earthquake. It has a special condition that states that if the issuer (insurance or reinsurance company) suffers a loss from a particular pre-defined catastrophe, then the issuer's obligation to pay interest and/or repay the principal is either deferred or completely forgiven. Owners of these bonds lose money if insured losses exceed an agreed level; "cat" bonds, for short.
Securities: a disparaging description of low-priced, highly speculative stocks with little hope of a strong future.
Business: items accumulating in inventory that have a very low sales turnover.

Catastrophic Medical Coverage a major medical expense insurance policy ($500,000-$1,000,000) designed to pay all medical expenses, above a certain deductible amount, up to the limit of the policy.

Cathode Ray Tube (CRT) a display (for a computer or television set) that uses an electronic gun to draw and paint on the screen.

Causality a cause-effect relationship in which changes in variable x are assumed to cause changes in variable y.

Cause-and-Effect Diagram *see* Fishbone Diagrams.

Cause of Action the circumstances giving an individual cause to seek judicial relief. A cause of action is some intrusion into a person's legal rights, including a breach of contract. A failure to discharge a legal obligation to do, or refrain from performance of, some act. Matter for which a lawsuit may be instituted. Unlawful violation or invasion of right.

Caveat Emptor a Latin term meaning "let the buyer beware" before she buys. According to this principle, the buyers purchase at their own risk, in the absence of misrepresentations. This does not obligate the seller to volunteer information. In recent years, however, the law requires full disclosure by the seller of known defects in the product or service.

Caveat Subscriptor (Venditor) a Latin term meaning "let the vendor beware." Without specific exemptions, the seller is liable for action on the part of the buyer for any alterations in the contract or warranty, whether explicit or implied. This is the basis for the consumer rights movement.

Caveat Venditor *see* Caveat Subscriptor (Venditor).

CBOE *see* Chicago Board of Options Exchange.

CBOT *see* Chicago Board Of Trade.

CC sending a copy of a letter or memo to someone.

CD *see* Certificate Of Deposit; Compact Disc.

CD-ROM *see* Compact Disc-Read Only Memory.

Cell the little rectangle where a row and column intersect in an electronic spreadsheet.

Center of Gravity Location Method mathematical analysis for determining where a warehouse should be located to service a number of retail stores in disparate locations. The method considers three factors: (1) market location, (2) the volume of goods handled in these markets, and (3) shipping expenses to each location.

Central Banks government agencies with authority over the size and growth of the nation's money supply. They commonly regulate commercial banks, act as the government's fiscal agent, and are architects of the nation's monetary policy. Central banks frequently intervene in the foreign exchange markets to smooth fluctuations. For example, the Federal Reserve System is the central bank in the U.S , while the Bundesbank is the central bank of Germany. For the monetary policies and economic performance of central banks, visit the Bank for International Settlements site (*www.bis.org/cbanks.htm*).

Central Limit Theorem one of the most important theorems in statistics. It says: If a large number of random samples are chosen from virtually any population (with mean and standard deviation), the means of these samples will themselves follow a normal distribution .Two important implications of this theorem are as follows: (1) The random samples can be drawn from any population, normally distributed or not. Thus, even if we know that the dollar value of a certain inventory item is not normally distributed, we can invoke the theorem and assume that the sample mean inventory dollar value will be normally distributed. (2) The theorem lets us then make statements about the value of the population mean without looking at the entire population. Thus, we can make interval estimates about the true value of an inventory item. Such interval estimates are called *confidence intervals*.

Central Processing Unit (CPU) a component of a computer hardware system that combines control unit, storage unit, and arithmetic unit. The control unit interprets the instructions given to the computer. Internal storage is where the program of instructions is kept and where data from the input devices are sent. External storage can consist of disks and tapes. The arithmetic unit actually does the calculation required by the program. As technology advances, chip makers are finding ways to make the CPU smaller, faster, and more powerful.

Central Tendency a statistical measure that refers to the average score of a frequency distribution.

Centralization the situation where the power of decision making is at the top of an organization and there is little delegation of authority to make decisions. It is the opposite of decentralization. Centralization and decentralization are really a matter of degree. Full centralization means minimum autonomy and maximum restrictions on operations of subunits of the organization. As an organization grows in size and complexity, decentralization is generally considered to be effective and efficient. *See also* Decentralization.

Certainty a situation in which there is absolutely no doubt about which event will occur, and there is only one state of nature with 100 percent probability attached. Certainty equivalents the amount of cash (or rate of return) that a decision maker would require with certainty to make the recipient indifferent between this certain sum and a particular uncertain, risky sum.

Certificate
1. a document attesting to the performance, or nonperformance, of an act. It can be official when issued by a formally constituted institution, including courts, educational organizations, governmental bodies, or religious organizations. Examples would include marriage certificates, diplomas, licenses, and property deeds. A certificate can also be issued between individuals, as in a simple bill of sale. In the case of formal institutions, a certificate can have a formal seal either affixed to it or impressed on it, further adding to its authenticity.
2. In securities, the stock or bond certificate. The stock certificate is the actual piece of paper with all the special information about the stock, such as the issuer and the number of shares the certificate represents. A bond certificate is the record of your investment.

Certificate in Data Processing (CDP) a certificate granted by the Institute of Computer Professionals (ICCP) to a candidate who demonstrates satisfactory academic accomplishment and work experience in computer-based information systems and passes a written examination.

Certification

1. a written assurance by a responsible party of the correctness and reliability of a statement. As an example, an officer of a corporation might state in writing that specified criteria have been satisfied.
2. written permission to do something, such as receiving a license or franchise to do business.
3. a statement by a governmental agency that a union may bargain for its employees.
4. expression of an unqualified audit opinion on a company's financial statements by a certified public accountant (CPA).
5. a certificate granted by a certification agency to a candidate who demonstrates satisfactory academic accomplishment and work experience in a specialized area such as a CPA.

Certificate of Deposit (CD) special type of time deposit. A CD is an investment instrument, available at financial institutions, that generally offers a fixed rate of return for a specified period. The depositor agrees not to withdraw funds until the CD matures. If the funds are withdrawn, a significant penalty is charged. The fixed rate of return normally increases with the amount or the term of the investment.

Certificate of Incorporation state approval of the articles of incorporation of a corporation.

Certificate of Insurance a document describing the benefits and provisions for people or businesses covered by group insurance.

Certificate of Occupancy (CO) certificate usually granted by a jurisdiction's building department certifying a specified premise has satisfactorily complied with all zoning and building ordinances. This certification is a prerequisite for occupancy for its designated use and often the transfer of title at a sale.

Certificate of Reasonable Value (CRV) a certificate showing the appraised value of the property and maximum VA guaranteed loan a veteran under GI guaranteed mortgage loan may obtain from a private lender.

Certificate of Sale a certificate issued to the buyer at a judicial sale, such as an execution sale. After the time for redemption has expired, the holder of the certificate is entitled to a deed.

Certificate of Title an attorney's opinion of the status of a title, which is attached to the abstract of title.

Certified Check depositor's check that a bank guarantees to pay. The funds are precommitted.

Certified Employee Benefits Specialist (CEBS) a professional designation for employee benefit specialists.

Certified Financial Planner (CFP) a professional designation conferred upon those candidates who demonstrate a high level of skill and competence in the analysis of client financial conditions and the development of client-oriented personal financial plans by passing a series of national examinations administered by the College for Financial Planning, Denver, Colorado. The CFP program consists of six separate parts, each of which is a three-hour written examination. The program includes the following parts: (1) introduction to financial planning, (2) risk management, (3) investments, (4) tax planning and management, (5) retirement planning and employee benefits, and (6) estate planning. The candidates must also meet other educational and work experience requirements of the College in order to obtain the right to use the College's designation of Certified Financial Planner (CFP). *See also* Financial Planner.

Certified Property and Casualty Underwriter (CPCU) a knowledgeable person authorized to aid in the underwriting of property and casualty insurance.

Certified Property Manager (CPM) a professional certification granted by the Institute of Real Estate Management, an affiliate of the National Association of Realtors.

Certified Public Accountant (CPA) title awarded to accountants satisfying rigorous professional education (college degree majoring in accounting), examination (theory, practice, auditing, and law), and experience requirements (e.g., New York State requires two years). The CPA is licensed by the respective state to give an audit opinion on the fairness of a company's financial statements. Because of the CPA's accounting and financial knowledge, she may serve as a good financial adviser in personal financial planning decisions.

Certified Residential Broker (CRB) certification granted by the Realtors National Marketing Institute, which is affiliated with the National Association of Realtors.

Certified Residential Specialist (CRS) certification granted by the Realtors National Marketing Institute upon successful completion of an education program and the required residential sales experience. Candidates must already have achieved the Graduate of the Real Estate Institute designation.

Certiorari a writ issued by a superior court to an inferior court requiring the latter to produce a record of the proceedings of a particular case. The purpose of a writ of certiorari is to review the proceedings of the lower court actions to determine if there is a legal basis for an appeal hearing at the higher court.

Ceteris Paribus A Latin expression meaning "other things being equal". Economic analysis proceeds by considering the effect of varying one or a few variables while other factors remain unchanged. For example, in demand analysis, the demand curve shows the effect of a change in the price of a product on the quantity demanded, assuming that all of the other factors (such as income and the prices of substitute goods) affecting the demand for that product remain unchanged.

CGI *see* Common Gateway Interface.

Chairman of the Board Highest-ranking director in a corporation's board of directors.

Chain of Command an unbroken line of authority that extends from the upper levels of the company down to the lowest levels and clarifies who reports to whom. It helps employees determine whom to go to if they have a problem and also to whom they are responsible.

Chamber of Commerce a group of local business people with similar business interests.

Change in Demand increase or decrease in the quantity demanded due to a change in its price. It is represented by a movement along a demand curve.

Change in Supply increase or decrease in the quantity supplied due to a change in its price. It is represented by a movement along a supply curve.

Channel Length the number of intermediaries that a product has to go through before it reaches the final consumer.

Channels of Distribution all the marketing units through which goods flow from origin to final purchase and use. Channel functions provide transfer of title or ownership as goods move from producer to consumer.

Chapter 7 a statute of the 1978 Bankruptcy Reform Act that covers liquidation proceedings. As a general rule, any debtor subject to Chapter 7 is also subject to Chapter 11. Liquidation proceedings are used to eliminate most of the debts of the debtor. Chapter 7 provides for a court-appointed trustee to make management changes, secure additional financing, and operate the debtor business so as to prevent further loss. The fundamental assumption of proceedings is that honest debtors may sometimes not be able to discharge fully their debts and that fairness and public policy both dictate that the debtor be granted a "fresh start" in both the personal and business lives. *See also* Bankruptcy (Personal); Chapter 11.

Chapter 11 a statute of the 1978 Bankruptcy Reform Act that covers the specific proceedings and provisions covering reorganization and the execution of such a plan of an individual, partnership, corporation, or municipality. This statute provides possible solutions to insolvency and the difficulty of satisfying creditor claims. Under Chapter 11, unless the court rules otherwise, the debtor remains in control of the business and its operations. Debtor and creditors are allowed to work together, thus making possible the restructuring of debt, the rescheduling of payments, and even the granting of loans by the creditors to the debtor. *See also* Bankruptcy (Business); Chapter 7.

Chapter 13 court approved and coordinated plan that pays off an individual's debts over a period of three years; also called *wage-earner plan*. It is a plan for the repayment of debts that allows a credit user in serious financial difficulty to pay off credit obligations without declaring bankruptcy. *See also* Bankruptcy (Personal).

Character

1. In computers, a letter, number, or symbol that occupies one byte of information.
2. credit standard judging the borrower's past record in repaying loans, among other factors regarding the credit worthiness of the borrower. *See also* Five C's of Credit.

Charge

Installment Purchase: term used to describe a credit account purchase. The cost will be billed at a future date.

Finance: the price for a product or service rendered.

Accounting: a cost or expense allocated to a specific account.

Criminal Law: a formal charge filed by a complaint or indictment against a defendant.

Jury: a judge's final statement to a jury in which the case is summarized and the relevant points of law the jury must observe are specified.

Public Charge: a person without means or who is not responsible. A public charge depends on public services for care and survival.

Chart of Accounts a listing of the titles and numbers of all accounts in the ledger. Listed first are the balance sheet accounts—assets, liabilities, and stockholders' equity, in that order. The income statement accounts—revenue and expenses—follow.

Charter an official document of incorporation. It also mean the general purpose of the business.

Chartered Financial Consultant (CFC) a professional designation given by the American College, Bryn Mawr, Pennsylvania, conferred upon those candidates who will provide financial planning services for clients. To earn the CFC designation, the candidate must complete ten courses ; six required and four electives. The six required courses are (1) financial services, (2) income taxation, (3) financial statement analysis/individual insurance benefits, (4) investments, (5) estate and gift tax planning, and (6) financial and estate planning applications. *See also* Certified Financial Planner (CFP); Financial Planner.

Chartered Financial Analyst (CFA) an individual who has passed tests (in economics, accounting, security analysis, and money management) administered by the Institute of Chartered Financial Analysts of the Association for Investment Management and Research (AIMR). Such an individual is also expected to have at least three years of investments-related experience and meet certain standards of professional conduct. These individuals have an extensive economic and investing background and are competent at a high level of analysis. Individuals or corporations utilize their services as security analysts, portfolio managers, or investment advisors.

Chartered Life Underwriter (CLU) a designation granted–by the American College of the American Society of Chartered Life Underwriters in Bryn Mawr, Pennsylvania–only to life insurance agents who meet certain experience or requirements and pass college-level examinations.

Certified Property and Casualty Underwriter (CPCU) an individual who is knowledgeable and authorized to assist in the underwriting of property and casualty insurance.

Chartist an analyst who attempts to evaluate market trends and price behavior of individual securities and predicts movements from a study of charts on prices, price indexes, and trading volumes; also called a *technical analyst* or *technician*. This technique is referred to as technical analysis, which is in contrast to fundamental analysis that focuses on an evaluation of a security's financial statements to determine the value of the security.

Chat Room a facility that allows interactive conversations among persons who are online at the same place at the same time.

Chattel personal (rather than real) property. Examples are furniture, jewelry, automobiles, and computers.

Chattel Mortgage a pledge of personal property, such as an automobile or furniture, to secure a note. If the indebtedness is not paid according to the terms of the agreement, the holder of the mortgage has the right to obtain possession of the mortgaged property. *See also* Mortgage.

Cheap Dollar *see* Appreciation of the Dollar.

Cheap Money *see* Easy or Loose Money.

Check
1. a draft drawn upon a bank, to be drawn upon a deposit of funds, payable upon demand to ("to the order of") the person so named upon the draft.
2. to determine an item's accuracy such as by retotaling changes on an invoice or auditing source documents.

Check Clearing for the 21ˢᵗ Century Act a federal law that went into effect in October, 2004, allowing banks to process checks faster by making electronic copies of checks. People who write checks can no longer count on several days of "float" time and getting back cancelled checks.

Check Truncation the procedure whereby a depository institution keeps the canceled checks and sends only a listing of the month's transactions to the account holder, hence saving on processing and mailing of checks.

Checkable Deposits deposits in depository institutions that are subject to withdrawals by checks; also called *transaction deposits*. Examples include demand deposits, now accounts, super-now.

Chi Square Test a statistical test, based on the Chi-square (X^2) distribution, for the significance of a difference between classification or subclassification. The chi-square test has many applications. It is a statistical test of independence (or association), to determine if membership in categories of one variable is different as a function of membership in the categories of a second variable. It is important to note, however, that there are limitations of this test: (1) The sample must be big enough for the expected frequencies for each cell (rule of thumb is at least 5), and (2) the test does not tell us anything about the direction of an association.

Chicago Board of Options Exchange (CBOE) organized, national exchange where foreign currency, index, and interest rate options are traded by members for their own accounts and for the accounts of customers.

Chicago Board of Trade (CBOT) the world's largest exchange for futures contracts, in terms of the number of contracts traded (243 millions in 1997). Founded in 1848, CBOT trades both financial and commodity futures and futures options. U.S. Treasury bond futures are the most frequently traded instruments. Its big rival is the Chicago Mercantile Exchange, which is particularly strong in agricultural futures contracts.

Chicago Mercantile Exchange (CME) market that trades commodity futures and futures options. Overall, the Chicago Board of Trade is probably bigger in number of contracts traded per year, but the CME is bigger when it comes to agricultural futures and "open interest" contracts.

Chicago School a group of economists at the University of Chicago (among them Milton Friedman and George Stigler) who believed that the money supply should be stabilized and that free markets and competition will lead to the most efficient operation of the economy.

Chief Economist a corporate or business economist who is charged with the main responsibility for business economics as it applies to the entity. The responsibility includes corporate planning, business forecasting, optimal resource allocation, cost reduction, and efficiency.

Chief Executive Officer (CEO) The highest ranking officer of the company, and is often Chairman of the Board as well. The CEO reports only to the board of directors.

Chief Investment Officer (CIO) an executive who is responsible for managing and monitoring the company's investment portfolio. His/her responsibilities include investment portfolio management, investing surplus funds, pension monies management, maintaining liaison with the investment community, and counseling with financial analysts.

Chief Operating Officer (COO) corporate officer in charge of the daily operations of the business. He or she may be the president or executive vice president. The COO reports directly to the chief executive officer.

Chartered Mutual Fund Counselor (CMFC) a new designation offered by the National Endowment for Financial Education, showing a financial advisor's enhanced ability to advise clients on their mutual fund questions and concerns.

Chief Financial Officer (CFO) the top company officer in charge of all accounting and financial affairs, usually reporting directly to the CEO of the company.

Chronic Unemployment long-term unemployment, typically lasting six or more months. *See also* Unemployment.

Churn; Churning trading done in a customer's account that is excessive. Typically, the customer is in a worse situation because of all the commissions he or she has to pay. Such an illegal practice is prompted by the broker's desire to maximize his or her commissions.

Circuit Breakers actions used by stock exchanges during large sell-offs. After market indexes have fallen a certain percentage, the exchanges halt trading for a certain amount of time with an objective of averting panic selling. Circuit breakers exist also for large advances in market price. The rule is to stop the trading if the market drops 250 points and then again if it drops 400 points for the day.

Civil Court a state court where civil disagreements are decided by the judge or jury. A written record is kept of the deliberations. In some states, civil and criminal courts are combined.

Claims Adjuster insurance specialist designated by an insurance company to investigate the insurance claims, including an assessment of whether a loss is covered and the dollar amount the company will pay.

Class A Stock the name given to the basic class of stock when there is another class. There are some differences between the rights of the stock holders of each class—class A and class B stock.

Class Action a legal suit initiated by one or more individuals for the benefit of all members of that group. As an example, a few investors may sue a company for losses incurred on the stock because of alleged false and misleading financial statements. Those investors, on behalf of all investors in the company, file a class action lawsuit to recover the losses.

Class-Action Lawsuit a lawsuit brought by one or more persons of a large group for the benefit of all members of that group. For example, an investor may sue a company for losses because of fraudulent financial statements.

Classical Decomposition approach to forecasting that seeks to decompose the underlying pattern of a time series into cyclical, seasonal, trend, and random sub-patterns.

Classical Economics the economic school of thought that emphasized free markets and competition, including such thinkers as Adam Smith, David Ricardo, and Alfred Marshall. In this school, the product and resource markets will automatically adjust to full-employment levels, as if guided by an "invisible hand." This is because aggregate expenditure equals aggregate income or output.

Classified Stock a stock issue that is divided into two or more classes, carrying different rights and privileges. Shares of stock allow four general rights voting at stockholders' meetings, a share of earnings, a share in the distribution rights: if the company is liquidated, and to subscribe to any additional issues of the stock held. The last right is known as a preemptive right. There can be one class of stock or more. If more, then each class may have more or less of the four general rights. There can be class A and class B stock, each having prescribed rights.

Clayton Antitrust Act one of three major antitrust laws, passed as an amendment to the Sherman Antitrust Act in 1914. The act listed four illegal practices in restraint of competition. It outlawed price discrimination, tying contracts and exclusive dealerships, and horizontal mergers. It also outlawed interlocking directorates (the practice of having the same people serve as directors of two or more competing firms). *See also* Robinson-Patman Act; Sherman Antitrust Act.

Clearing Market applying primarily to many commodity and financial markets; a market where prices are flexible enough to equate supply with demand very rapidly. In this market, no shortage or surplus, unemployment, or rationing exists.

Clearinghouse an organization that settles and guarantees trades in some financial markets.

Click-and-Mortar Companies traditional brick-and-mortar companies that have added e-marketing to their operations.

Click-Only Companies the so-called dot coms, which operate only online without any brick-and-mortar market presence.

Client Middleware a type of operating system that runs business applications on clients such as desktop PCs, hand-held devices, and advance mobile phones.

Client-Server System computers connected by an advanced network in which some computers (clients) process applications while other computers (servers) provide services (e.g., file storage, Internet hosting) to the clients.

Clock Speed, Clock Rate the rate of repetitive machine cycles that a computer can perform; also called *frequency*. It is measured in megahertz (MHz) or gigahertz (GHz).

Close
1. the end of a trading session. The closing price is what's quoted in the newspaper.
2. the command to exit a software program.

Closed Economy an economic system that is completely self-sufficient. It has no international trade (no imports or exports), as opposed to an open economy.

Closed Shop a work place where employees must be members of a specific union as a condition for being hired.

Closed-End Investment Company *See* Closed-End Mutual Fund

Closed-End Mutual Fund a mutual fund whose shares are limited and are traded like the common stock of a corporation. Once shares are issued, the only way an investor can purchase or sell the fund shares is in the open market. An example of a closed-end mutual fund is Prudential-Bache Securities' Global Yield Fund. *See also* Open-End Mutual Fund.

Closely Held Corporation a corporation that has only a few stockholders. It contrasts with a privately held corporation in that a closely held corporation is public although most of the shares are not traded. The so-called corporate pocket-books may become subject to the additional personal holding company tax on income not distributed. For example, deductions and losses in transactions between a major stockholder and the corporation may be disallowed under certain circumstances.

Closing
1. the accounting activities at the end of a period to finalize the accounts and prepare financial statements.
2. the process of financially and legally transferring a house to a buyer, which usually takes place in the office of the lender, an attorney, or an escrow company.

Closing Costs the fees and expenses incurred by a home buyer in negotiating and financing the purchase of a home and paid at the closing. Closing costs consist of loan application fees, loan origination fees, points, title search and insurance, appraisal fees, and other miscellaneous fees such as mortgage taxes and credit reports.

Closing Escrow all of the conditions of the purchase and sale agreement have been fulfilled. Once all the conditions have been met, the escrow agent prepares a summary of the monies received in escrow and the monies paid out of escrow, records the new deed with the county recorder, and finally delivers a new deed to the buyer and the remaining funds from the purchase price to the seller. Escrow is finally closed and official title is given to the buyer.

Closing Statement detailed financial accounting of all the credits and debits for the buyer and seller upon consummation of a real estate sale.

Closing the Books *see* Closing.

Cloud on Title any claim, lien or encumbrance which, if valid, may impair the owner's title to the property; also called a *title defect*. A cloud of title does not hinder transfer of ownership on the property but may diminish its market value. *See also* Quitclaim Deed.

Cluster Zoning a planned subdivision where detached housing is located in close proximity to each other. Additionally, the subdivision shares common open space including parking and recreation areas.

Clue Reports *see* Comprehensive Loss Underwriting Exchange Reports.

CME *see* Chicago Mercantile Exchange.

COBOL (Common Business Oriented Language) a programming language for business data processing. As compared with FORTRAN and BASIC, COBOL statements resemble English sentences and thus are long and wordy, but easy to read.

Cobranding the linking of a credit card with a business trade name offering "points" or premiums toward the purchase of a product or service. Examples are Nordstrom's cobranded Visa and Ford Motor Company's Citibank Visa and MasterCard. Bankers are realizing that cobranded credit cards help build customer loyalty.

Code an organized set of rules and regulations on a particular subject. Often times codes are an accumulation of laws in a particular area of interest. For example, a zoning code or a building code.

Code (Internal Revenue Code) all federal tax laws.

Code of Ethics an organized group of ethical behavior guidelines governing the day-to-day activities of a profession or organization.

Codicil a written supplement or amendment to an existing will.

Coefficient the numerical part of an algebraic expression such as 4x.

Coefficient of Determination a statistical measure of how good the estimated regression equation is, designated as r^2 (read as r-squared). Simply put, it is a measure of "goodness of fit" in the regression. Therefore, the higher the r-squared, the more confidence we can have in our equation. Statistically, the coefficient of determination represents the proportion of the total variation in the y variable that is explained by the regression equation. It has the range of values between 0 and 1.

Coefficient of Variation a measure of the relative dispersion of a probability distribution–that is, the risk per unit of return. Mathematically it is defined as the standard deviation divided by the expected value.

Cognitive Dissonance the tendency for consumers to have doubts following a purchase. It may be alleviated by warranties, prompt service of problems, or money-back guarantees.

Cognovit Clause a provision in a loan agreement where a debtor authorizes a judgment against him in the event of a default. These agreements are widely restricted, but when they are lawful, the creditor is empowered to appear in court and enter a judgment against the debtor.

Coincident Indicators the types of economic indicator series that tend to move up and down in line with the aggregate economy and therefore are measures of current economic activity. Examples are Gross Domestic Product (GDP), retail sales, and industrial production.

Coinsurance a provision in an insurance policy that limits the liability of the insurer by specifying that the owner of property that has experienced damage (e.g., fire or water damage) must have another policy that covers usually at least 80% of the cash value of the property at the time of damage, in order to collect the full amount insured. This serves as an inducement for an individual to carry full coverage.

COLA *see* Cost-Of-Living Adjustments.

Cold Call; Cold Calling a broker (usually one recently hired) telephoning, on an unsolicited basis, individuals to get business, such as pushing particular stocks, bonds, mutual funds, or other investment products. Unfortunately, some cold callers are dishonest and may recommend low quality investments and/or those securities not suitable for the particular investor.

Cold Canvass *see* Cold Call

Collateral assets pledged to secure a debt. The asset will be given up if the borrower defaults on the terms and conditions specified in the debt agreement. An example is pledging inventory to collateralize a bank loan.

Collateralize to pledge assets to secure a debt. These assets will be given up if the borrower defaults on the terms and conditions specified in the debt agreement. An example is pledging inventory to collateralize a bank loan.

Collaterized Mortgage Obligation (CMO) mortgage-backed, pass-through securities that separate mortgage pools into short-, medium-, and long-term time frames. CMOs is an outgrowth of the fact that simple (GNMA) or Federal Home Loan Mortgage Corporation (FHLMC) mortgage-backed securities have uncertain durations (payback of principal and interest factor) because of the possibility of prepayment of the principal amounts remaining on the mortgages. By splitting mortgage pools into different time frames, investors now can buy shares in short term (such as 5-year) or long-term (such as 20-year) pools. CMOs enjoy liquidity and a high degree of safety since they are either government-sponsored or otherwise insured. Most of them are sold, however, in minimum amounts of $25,000, which is out of reach for most small investors. *See also* Mortgage-Backed Securities.

Collection Period number of days it takes to collect accounts receivable. The collection period can be compared with the terms of sale.

Collective Bargaining formal labor negotiations between management and unions.

Collision Insurance a form of automobile insurance that pays for damage resulting from collision or object to an insured automobile regardless of fault.

Color of Title some plausible, but not completely clear-cut indication of ownership rights. It supplements a claim to title of property, but does not actually establish it.

Command Economy an economic system where the allocation of resources, including determination of what goods and services should be produced and in what quantity, is planned by the government.

Commercial Mortgage-Backed Securities (CMBS) securities backed by loans secured with commercial property, such as retail businesses, office buildings, and multifamily homes.

Commercial Paper a financial instrument issued to the public, typically by large financially sound corporations. It usually comes in minimum denominations of $25,000. It represents an unsecured promissory note. It usually carries a higher yield than small certificates of deposit (CDs). The maturity is usually 30, 60, or 90 days. The degree of risk depends on the issuing company's credit rating. Commercial paper is rated by Standard & Poor's as well as Moody's.

Commercial Property business property such as an office building, retail store, medical center, or hotel, that has a profit. A risk/return relationship exists in commercial property. The return is comprised of the net rental income and capital appreciation in price.

Commission
1. a salesperson's fee for sale of goods or services.
2. the broker's fee for buying or selling securities
3. governmental regulatory agency, such as the Federal Trade Commission (FTC).
4. a percentage of the price received for the sale of real estate or of the yearly rental of a property, paid to the real estate agent for selling or renting your property.

Commission Broker a broker who executes the investor's order for the purchase or sale of securities, commodities, and real estate.

Commitment
1. a promise by a bank or lending institution that you will get a loan at a specified amount and interest rate
2. an agreement to buy an asset at a specified price and conditions. The failure to honor the commitment may result in damages.

Committed Costs fixed costs incurred to provide facilities that increase a firm's ability to produce, such as those relating to space, equipment, and factory buildings; also called *capacity costs*. They include rents, depreciation, property taxes, and insurance.

Commodities wheat, eggs, soybeans, silver, pork bellies, and other economic goods.

Commodity Bundling the practice of bundling two or more different products together and selling them at a single "bundle price." For example, travel agencies often sell "package deals" that include airfare, hotel, and meals at a bundled price instead of pricing each component of a vacation separately. PC makers bundle computers, monitors, and software and sell them at a bundled price. Many car dealers bundle options such as air conditioning, power steering, and automatic transmission and sell them at a "special package price."

Commodity Currency Currency made of either silver or gold, or that can be exchanged for silver or gold

Commodity Futures Trading Commission (CFTC) an agency (*www. cftc.gov*) that regulates all commodities traded in organized contract markets, established in 1974 by the U.S. Congress. It is to commodity futures as the SEC is to securities markets.

Commodity Research Bureau (CRB) Indexes the most widely followed commodity index, produced by Knight-Ridder Financial Publishing. It is like the Dow Jones Industrial Averages (DJIA) for stocks. The index measures price changes in commodities, including soybeans, cocoa, coffee, sugar, cotton, and precious metals such as gold, platinum and silver. The Commodity Research Bureau (CRB) has two indexes: one is the CRB Spot Price Index and the other is the CRB Futures Price Index.

Common Costs costs shared by different departments, products, or jobs; also called *joint costs* or *indirect costs*. *See also* Indirect Costs.

Common Gateway Interface special software used in Internet servers that allows the capture of data from a form displayed on a page and the storage of the data in a database. It allows web sites to be interactive for chat rooms and bulletin boards.

Common Law the legal system that uses court precedents where there is no legislation. It was originated in England and was adopted in the United States. It relies on judicial decisions rather than litigation.

Common Market a high degree of regional economic integration. It involves (1) eliminating internal trade barriers and establishing a common external tariff, (2) removing national restrictions on the movement of labor and capital among participating nations and the right of establishment for business firms, and (3) the pursuit of a common external trade policy. The best known is the European Common Market.

Common Stock share (or part-ownership) in a public or privately-held company. It is a security that represents an ownership interest in a corporation. While you may retain part-ownership for a while, you expect to eventually sell to other investors–hopefully at a profit. In the event of liquidation, common stockholders are paid after bondholders and preferred stockholders. The terms common stock and capital stock are often used interchangeably when the company has no preferred stock. A bond, which is a debt issue, does not represent ownership.

Communications Protocol the set of rules that govern data communications. When more than two parties participate in the communication, it is also called *network protocol*.

Communism a socialist economic system based on the ownership of production by the government and requires that government plan and control the economy.

Community Property property owned and held jointly and equally shared by husband and wife. It is acquired by both spouses during their marriage, irrespective of the wage-earning status of either spouse.

Community Property Laws statutes stipulating that the property of deceased individuals is distributed in a way that assumes that property during marriage is jointly owned and equally shared by the spouses, irrespective of how much each paid. Sixteen western states have the community property doctrine.

Compact Disc a small plastic disc read by optical lasers that contains digitized data, animation, or music.

Compact Disc-Read Only Memory (CD-ROM) a device whose data was recorded by the manufacturer and cannot be changed.

Comparable Properties (COMPS) properties similar to the subject property that are used to estimate the value of the subject property.

Comparative Advantage the principle stating that trade is beneficial even if a country does not have an absolute advantage in the production of a good, but does have more of a relative advantage in the cost of producing the good than its trading partner; also called *comparative cost principle*. This principle explains why countries specialize in producing and exporting products based on their endowment of resources. The concept is especially important in international trade, suggesting that countries should specialize in areas in which they have a comparative advantage.

Compensating Balance a balance of a given amount that the firm maintains in its demand deposit account. It may be required by either a formal or informal agreement with the firm's commercial bank. Such balances are usually required by the bank (1) on the unused portion of a loan commitment, (2) on the unpaid portion of an outstanding loan, or (3) in exchange for certain services provided by the bank, such as check-clearing or credit information. These balances raise the effective rate of interest paid on borrowed funds. The compensating balance is usually 10%. No interest is earned on this balance, which increases the effective interest rate on the loan. Assume an individual borrows $10,000 from the bank at a 12% interest with a 10% compensating balance. The compensating balance is $1,000 ($10,000 x 10%). The effective interest rate is: $1,200/($10,000 - $1,000) = $1,200/$9,000 = 13.33%.

Competitive Advantage the process of creating better customer value for the same or lower cost than that of competitors, or creating equivalent value for lower cost than that of competitors.

Competitive Markets a market structure in which a very large number of small buyers and sellers trade independently, and as such, no one trader can significantly influence price.

Complementary Goods goods and services that are complementary to each other. When the demand for one increases (decreases) so does the demand for the other. An example is coffee and sugar.

Compound Interest an interest rate that is applicable when interest in subsequent periods is earned not only on the original principal but also on the accumulated interest of prior periods. For example, assume that the initial principal is $1,000 and annual interest rate is 10%. At the end of the first year, the amount is the principal and interest, which is $1,000 + .1 ($1,000) = $1,000 + $100=$1,100. At the end of the second year, the amount is accumulated: $1,100 + .01($1,100) = $1,100 + $110 = $1, 210. *See also* Future Value.

Compound Rate of Return an accurate measure of the return on an investment over multiple time periods; also called *geometric rate of return*. It is one thing to measure the return over a single holding period and quite another to describe a series of returns over time. When an investor holds an investment for more than one period, it is important to understand how to compute the average of the successive rates of return.

Compounding the process of earning interest on interest. The interest that accrues when earnings for a specified period are added to the principal so that interest for the following period is computed on the principal plus accumulated interest. Interest is calculated on reinvested interest as well as on the original amount invested. *See also* Future Value; Time Value of Money.

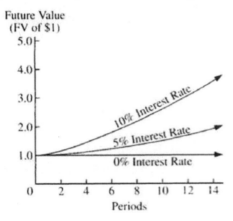

Comprehensive Insurance a provision that covers a variety of perils, such as glass breakage and losses caused by fire, theft, hail, water, flood, vandalism, riot, and accidents with birds and animals. Coverage limits are the same as for collision insurance.

Comprehensive Loss Underwriting Exchange (CLUE) Reports a detailed report covering five years of claims on both home and insurance policies. The reports are used by most insurance companies to set rates and even determine whether they want to extend coverage at all. The CLUE database is maintained by ChoicePointof Alpharetta Ga.,(www.choicepoint.com), which allows consumers to order the two types of CLUE reports online within seconds; review them immediately; and, if needed, request that incorrect information be fixed. Under the Fair and Accurate Credit Transactions Act of 2003, consumers now can order, for free, the two detailed reports.

Complementary Product a product, the demand for which increases with demand for a second product. Motorcycles and helmets, peanuts and beer, and skateboards and medical services are a few examples.

Compressed Files; Compression/Decompression new files that take up significantly less space on the storage medium or take less time to communicate over a channel.

Compressed Workweek a workweek of less than the standard five days. For example, the workweek may be four ten-hour days.

Compression/Decompression *see* Compressed Files

Comptroller
1. a misspelled word for controller.
2. the chief auditor that is found in the government sector. For example, the Comptroller General heads the General Accounting Office, a legislative branch of the government that conducts audits of all government agencies..

Compuserve one of the major commercial online services.

Computer-Aided Design (CAD) use of a computer to interact with a designer in developing and testing product ideas without actually building prototypes.

Computer-Aided Design and Manufacturing (CAD/CAM) computerized system to both integrate part design and to generate processing or manufacturing instructions.

Computer-Aided Manufacturing (CAM) manufacturing system utilizing computer software that controls the actual machine on the shop floor.

Computer-Integrated Manufacturing (CIM) computer information systems utilizing a shared manufacturing database for engineering design, factory production, and information management.

Computer Security the method of protecting information, computer programs, and other computer system assets. It primarily involves hardware and software security. Hardware security, which is the security of computer assets and capital equipment, refers to computer location, access control, fire protection, and storage procedures. Such measures as badges, electronic identification keys, alarm systems, and physical barriers at doors are used for this purpose. Software security entails the protection of software assets such as application programs, operating systems, and database management software. Special user numbers and passwords are typically used to prevent unauthorized access to them. In addition to security for hardware and software, good internal control also requires that measures be taken to prevent loss or accidental destruction of data.

Computer Virus a program that replicates and spreads by attaching itself to other programs. When the infected program is run, the virus executes an event.

Computer Fraud and Abuse Act a federal law making it a crime for any unauthorized use (copying, damaging, obtaining database information, etc.) of computer hardware or software across state lines.

Computer Simulation the use of a computer model that represents the dynamic relationships in a system to predict the behavior of the system. It attempts to answer a variety of "what-if" scenario questions in all business functional areas. Spreadsheet software such as Excel is widely used for this purpose.

Concave and Convex Curves A function that is concave to the origin and whose second derivative is negative. It is at the same time convex, away from the origin. Intuitively, a convex function will have only one highest point. The convex curve is shaped like a big U.

Concentration Measures the measures of the size distribution of firms engaged in economic activities. There are many ratios calculated, based on sales, value added, value of shipments, assets employed, or employment. For example, the ratio of the total assets employed of the top four or eight firms as a percentage of the industry's total assets employed.

Concentration Ratio a measure of the extent to which a few firms dominate an industry, which may be used as a proxy for one dimension of market structure. Using Standard Industrial Classification (SIC) groupings, the U.S. Bureau of the Census publishes industrial concentration ratios for manufacturing census years. It measures the percentage market share held by an industry's top four or eight firms.

Concession
1. a right to undertake and profit by a specific activity in return for services or for a particular use.
2. reduced price used as an incentive.
3. permission or right, usually granted by a governmental unit, to use property for a particular type of business in a specific area or place, such as a service station on a highway.
4. per-share compensation for the investment banker's underwriting service in a new security issue.

Condemnation a legal action involved in eminent domain where the government or other units take ownership of privately held real estate for public use (such as for schools, parks, streets, public parking, or public housing) regardless of the owner's wishes. The property owner must be paid the fair market value of the property taken from him or her.

Condition Precedent a condition that must be met or action performed before something can take effect. For example, in most real estate sales contracts all payments must be made before the buyer may ask for transfer of title.

Conditions
Law: provisions specified in a contractual agreement.
Real estate:
    1. qualifications attached to an estate upon the happening of which the estate is defeated or enlarged.
    2. limitations imposed in a deed.
Insurance: statements in an insurance policy that impose obligation on both the insured and the insurer by establishing the ground rules of the agreement. For example, the insured must pay the premium on time, notify the insurer immediately in the case of an accident, and cooperate with the insurer in defense of the insured in a liability suit.

Conditions Subsequent a condition that comes into being based on an action or event. For example, a contract between buyer and seller will only take effect if the seller is shown to have legal title to the property.

Conference Board a not-for-profit group of business people that examines and studies economic and managerial issues to enhance business activities. The organization puts out such useful statistics as the help-wanted index. Recommendations are given to the business community regarding important business issues. It also compiles the Confidence Index based on a five-question survey of 5,000 households. Each month the survey asks:
- How would you rate present general business conditions in your area (good, normal, bad)?
- Six months from now, do you think business conditions in your area will be (better, same, worse)?
- What would you say about available jobs in your area right now (plentiful, not so many, hard to get)?
- Six months from now, do you think availability of jobs in your area will be (better, same, worse)?
- What would you guess your total family income will be six months from now (higher, same, lower)?

Survey answers are converted into numbers—higher for more confidence, lower for less confidence. The base value of 100 derives from consumers' answers in 1985.

Conference Call A valuable opportunity to hear senior management's take on the company's prospects future earnings and new products in the pipeline. Institutional investors and financial analysts of brokerage firms call in to a special number to listen and ask questions. Yahoo Finance (*http://finance.yahoo.com*) maintains a calendar of upcoming conference calls. Enter a company's ticker to listen in on a current meeting or access an archive of a recent call.

Confidence Interval an estimated range of values with a given probability, including the population parameter of interest. The range of values is usually based on the results of a sample that estimated the mean, and the sampling error or the standard error.

Conforming Loans loans that adhere to national guidelines by Fannie Mae, who buys the loans on the secondary market. Conforming loans typically come with a lower interest rate than larger mortgage, or jumbo loans, which are purchased on the secondary market by another federally-chartered company, the Federal Home Loan Mortgage Corporation (Freddie Mac).

Consideration

Law: anything of value given to induce entering into a contract. It may be money, personal services, or the trading of products. A valid contract must have sufficient consideration.

Securities: the amount actually received from the sale of securities after deducting all the expenses including taxes on the sale and commission to the broker from the gross receipts.

Consignee the receiver of the goods who acts as a trustee but does not have title to the goods.

Consignment when a company places goods in a store but retains the title to the goods. If the products are not sold, the store is not responsible for them.

Consignor the shipper of the goods who maintains the title but not the possession of the goods.

Console Device the devices that communicate with the central processing unit of the computer, such as the keyboard, mouse, and computer monitor.

Consolidated Financial Statements financial statements that bring together all assets, liabilities, and operating accounts of a parent company and its subsidiaries. It presents the financial position and results of operations of the parent company and its subsidiaries as if the group were a single company with one or more branches. The technique for preparing consolidated financial statements is to take the individual statements to be consolidated and to combine them on a worksheet after eliminating all intercompany transactions and intercompany relationships. Most firms prepare consolidated statements when they hold more than 50 percent of the subsidiary's stock.

Consolidation presentation as one economic entity of the earnings of a parent and subsidiary (or subsidiaries) subsequent to the data of acquisition. The parent company owns more than 50% of the voting common stock of the subsidiary, which is therefore controlled by the parent. In consolidation, the reporting mechanism is the entire group and not the separate companies. Note that the entities that make up the consolidated group retain their separate legal entity; adjustments and eliminations are for consolidated financial statements only.

Consortium an alliance of companies formed in order to get more business clout than any individual company could.

Constant Returns to Scale a situation where, if the firm increases the amount of all inputs by the same proportion, output increases by the same proportion. For example, if all inputs double, output is also exactly doubled.

Constant-Cost Industry an industry in which the expansion or contraction of output has no effect on input prices. Therefore, marginal cost of production remains constant regardless of the level of output. A constant-cost industry operating under perfect competition has a horizontal long-run supply curve.

Constraints explicit limitations that will be encountered in achieving an objective. Examples of constraints are limited machine capacity or a limited quantity of necessary materials or skilled labor.

Construction Spending spending on office buildings and other construction projects in addition to housing. Construction spending figures are issued monthly by the Department of Commerce. *See also* Housing Starts.

Constructive Receipt tax concept whereby income not actually received is considered to be constructively received by a taxpayer and thus must be reported. An example is a bond interest coupon. The interest is taxable in the year the coupon matures, even though the holder delays cashing it until a later year.

Consumer Confidence Index a measure of consumer optimism and pessimism about general business conditions, jobs, and total family income. There are two popular indexes that track the level of consumer confidence: one is the Conference Board of New York, an industry-sponsored, non-profit economic research institute and the other is the University of Michigan's index. The Conference Board's index is considered a useful economic barometer because it provides insight into consumer spending, which is critical to any sustainable economic upswing. Many economists pay close attention to the index, which provides insight into consumer attitudes toward spending and borrowing. Consumers account for two-thirds of the nation's economic activity (i.e., national gross domestic product) and thus drive recovery and expansion. The University of Michigan Survey Research Center is another research organization that compiles its own index called the Index of Consumer Sentiment. It measures consumers' personal financial circumstances and their outlook for the future. The index is used by the Commerce Department in its monthly Index of Leading Economic Indicators

Consumer Credit a report of four credit categories of consumer borrowing–cars, revolving credit (credit cards), mobile homes, and other credit, released monthly by the Federal Reserve. The increased use of credit generally is viewed as a signal of improved consumer confidence and overall economy while reductions indicate declining expectations. The data on consumer credit is carefully watched by economists along with retail sales to assess the strength of consumer spending in the economy. It is noted that these two sets of numbers do not always move in tandem, since sometimes consumers are borrowing and not spending, just paying off the bills.

Consumer Credit Protection Act or Truth In Lending Act requires disclosures by lenders to borrowers, such as unusual loan terms, effective interest rate, total interest, and total payments.

Consumer Gap Analysis attempts to determine the difference between what consumers want (or need) and what is currently available to them. Marketers work hard to identify gaps and provide good products to successfully fill the gaps before the competition does and better than the competition can.

Consumer Price Index (CPI) a price index published by the U.S. Bureau of Labor Statistics on a monthly basis; also called *cost-of-living index*. This index attempts to track the change in prices of the typical group of goods and services consumed by an average family of four with a median income. Each monthly survey taken determines the weighting of the chosen representative prices for successive refinements in the computation of the price index. The so-called market basket, covered by the index, includes items such as food, clothing, automobiles, homes, and fees to doctors. *See also* Inflation; Price Indexes.

Consumer Product Safety Commission (CPSC) the federal agency that deals specifically with the risks of injury resulting from a wide range of consumer products.

Consumer Profiling the collection of information about individual shoppers in order to know and serve consumers better.

Consumer Research concerned chiefly with the discovery and analysis of consumer attitudes, reactions, and preferences. It uses tools such as focus groups, interviews, and surveys to get information about how consumers use products, why they buy them, how they respond to sales campaigns, etc.

Consumer Surplus the difference between the amount consumers actually pay for a commodity and the amount they are willing to pay.

Consumer Surveys method that involves interviewing potential customers to estimate demand relations.

Consumption the use of economic resources to satisfy current needs and wants. It means purchase of consumer goods and services and the act of using these goods and services to satisfy human needs and wants.

Consumption Function the assumed direct relationship between the national income level (Y) and the planned consumption expenditures of households (C). There are various hypotheses as to which level of income is most important in determining the level of consumption, including the absolute level of current disposable income, relative income, or permanent income (wealth).

Consumption Taxes indirect taxes imposed on the consumption of products and services. These indirect taxes include excise duties, wholesale or retail sales taxes, value-added taxes or other taxes on intermediate transactions.

Contingency Planning a strategy to minimize the effect of disturbances and to allow for timely resumption of activities. The aim of contingency planning is to minimize the effects of a disruption on your organizations. A disruption is any security violation, man-made or natural, intentional or accidental, that affects normal operations.

Contingent Beneficiary an individual that will become the beneficiary if the original beneficiary dies before the insured. It is the policyholder's second choice as beneficiary, dependent on the standing of the primary beneficiary.

Continuous Improvement (CI) never-ending effort for improvement in every part of the firm relative to all of its deliverables to its customers; also called *Kaizen* in Japanese. It covers improvement of machinery, materials, labor utilization, and production methods through application of suggestions and ideas of team members.

Contract a legally enforceable agreement between two or more competent parties, requiring one party to perform some service in exchange for some form of consideration; the written evidence of such an agreement.

Contracting Out the use of outside sources for the supplying of partially manufactured units or services that were formally made or performed in-house; also called *Outsourcing*.

Contrarianism an investment philosophy based on crowd psychology, which urges investors to do the opposite of what the crowd is doing. When most investors are buying, contrarians may be selling and vice versa.

Contribution Margin (CM) the difference between sales and the variable costs of the product or service. It is the amount of money available to cover fixed costs and generate profits. Example: If sales are $12,000 and variable costs are $5,000, contribution margin is $7,000 ($12,000 less $5,000).

Contribution Margin Analysis a technique based on the concept of contribution margin used for short-term decision making; also called *cost-volume-profit* (CVP) *analysis*. For example, a company can sell an item below the normal selling price when idle capacity exists as long as there is a contribution margin since it will help to cover the fixed costs or add to profits. Further, contribution analysis is effective in evaluating the performance of the department as a whole and its manager.

Contribution Margin Income Statement an alternative format of income statement that organizes the costs by behavior rather than by function in contrast to the traditional income statement. It shows the relationship of variable costs and fixed costs a given cost item is associated with, regardless of the functions. This approach to income determination provides data that is useful for managerial planning and decision making. For example, the contribution approach is useful:

1. for break-even and cost-volume-profit analysis
2. in evaluating the performance of the division and its manager
3. for short-term and non-routine decisions

A comparison is made between the traditional format and the contribution format below.

Traditional Format		
Sales		$15,000
Less: Cost of Goods Sold		7,000
Gross Margin		8,000
Selling	$2,100	
Administrative	1,500	3,600
Net Income		$4,400

Contribution Format		
Sales		$15,000
Less: Variable Expenses		
Manufacturing	$4,000	
Selling	1,600	
Administrative	500	6,100
Contribution Margin		8,900
Less: Fixed Expenses		
Manufacturing	$3,000	
Selling	500	
Administrative	1,000	4,500
Net Income		$4,400

Controllable Costs Costs that are considered to be controlled by managers or at a given level of authority. Categorizing costs as controllable and uncontrollable is important in responsibility accounting. For example, certain advertising spent specifically for a given department would be an expense controllable by the manager of that department. Advertising expenses that benefit many departments or products are, however, uncontrollable costs.

Controller the chief accounting executive of an organization. The controller is in charge of the accounting department. The principal functions of the controller are:

1. planning for control
2. financial reporting and interpreting
3. tax administration
4. management audits, and development of accounting systems
5. internal audits

In contrast with the controller, the treasurer is concerned mainly with the financial problems, including planning the finances, managing working capital, formulating credit policy and managing the investment portfolio. In a large firm, both the controller and treasurer report to Vice-President of Finance, better known as chief financial officer (CFO). In many small or medium-sized firms, the controller is typically a CFO.

Conventional Mortgage a mortgage that requires a large down payment, is typically only available to good credit risks, and has fixed monthly payments for the life of the loan. It typically has a fifteen or thirty-year period of fixed interest rates discharged on an amortized basis with equal monthly payments. It is neither insured by the FHA nor guaranteed by the VA.

Conversion

1. the act of exchanging one class of corporate security for another. An example is the conversion of convertible bonds into stock.
2. a valuation substitution for another. An example is the restatement of historical cost for that of current cost.
3. transfer of mutual fund shares from one fund to another in the same family.
4. switch from one currency to another using an exchange ratio.

Convertible Bond subordinated debentures that may be converted, at the holder's option, to either common or preferred shares of the company issuing the bond at a fixed price. Convertible bonds (CVs) are hybrid securities having characteristics of both bonds and common stock in that they provide fixed interest income and potential appreciation through participation in future price increases of the underlying common stock. The pitfall is that the interest of the CV is slightly lower due to the potential capital gain if the stock price goes up.

Convertible Preferred Stock Preferred stock that can be converted into common stock at the option of the holder.

Convertible Term a term life insurance policy that allows the insured to convert into a whole life insurance policy, or another form of cash value life insurance.

Convertibles, Convertible Security a preferred stock or bond that is convertible into common stock of the issuing corporation at some stated ratio at a later date.

Conveyance the transfer of the title of land, real estate, or personal property from one party to another. This transfer is made typically via a mortgage, trust deed, sales contract, or similar instrument.

Cook the Books to falsify financial records and statements so as to misrepresent the financial position and operating results of the entity. The financial records statements are improperly stated.

Cookie Jar Accounting accounting practice that inflates provisions for expected expenses and later reverses them to boost earnings—in many cases at very convenient times. This is traditionally abused when companies want to push reserves into future earnings. Reserves are set to cover the estimated costs of taxes, litigation, bad debts, job cuts, and acquisitions. Company managers estimate reserves and the outside auditor judges whether the reserves are reasonable. Auditors rarely challenge company estimates because there are unclear guidelines for calculating reserves.

Cookies information stored in the client on behalf of a server for a specified time period. Servers usually use cookies to store user identifications, user habits, and buying tastes. The cookie is sent back to the server in later requests from the client. Cookies are, by default, communicated only to the server that created them.

Cooling-Off Ruling a federal rule that provides a buyer with three business days in which to cancel a door-to-door sales contract. It is the right of rescission.

Cooperative Apartment (Co-Op) apartment building in which each the resident owns a percentage share of the corporation that owns the building.

Co-Payment a stipulation in a health insurance contract requiring that the insured pay a specific dollar portion of specifically covered expense items.

Copyright the exclusive right an individual or company gets to publish specific material. It specifies how and when their works should be used and the compensation for them.

Core Rate of Inflation *see* Consumer Price Index.

Corporate Bond a debt security of a corporation. It represents an agreement that the face value (usually $1,000) of the loan will be repaid at maturity and that interest will be paid at regular intervals (usually semiannually). It is a corporate IOU, which is traded on major exchanges. *See also* Bond; Zero-Coupon Bond.

Corporate Culture the set of basic values, perceptions, and wants that guide daily behavior in the corporate world in general.

Corporate Development Officers (CDOs) the heads of in-house merger and acquisition (M&A) teams.

Corporate Governance the system of checks and balances designed to ensure that corporate managers are just as vigilant on behalf of long-term shareholder value as they would be if it was their own money at risk. It is also the process whereby shareholders—the actual owners of any publicly traded firm—assert their ownership rights, through an elected board of directors and the CEO and other officers and managers they appoint and oversee. On the heels of corporate scandals, including the Enron debacle in 2002, a series of sweeping changes are being sought, such as forcing boards to have a majority of independent directors, granting audit committees power to hire and fire accountants, banning sweetheart loans to officers and directors, and requiring shareholder approval for stock option plans. More specifically, the following principles constitute good governance:
1. To avoid conflicts of interest, a company's board of directors should include a substantial majority of independent directors–"independent" meaning that directors don't have financial or close personal ties to the company or its executives.
2. A company's audit, nominating, and compensation committees should consist entirely of independent directors.
3. A board should obtain shareholder approval for any actions that could significantly affect the relationship between the board and shareholders, including the adoption of anti-takeover measures such as "poison pills."
4. Companies should base executive compensation plans on pay for performance and should provide full disclosure of these plans.
5. To avoid abuse in the use of stock options (and executive perquisites), all employee stock option plans should be submitted to shareholders for approval.

Institutional Shareholder Services, Inc., *(http://www.issproxy.com/)* an influential proxy advisor, started scoring companies on governance issues.

Corporate Raider *see* Raider. an organization or individual investor who attempts to take over particular companies, usually resisted by the management of those firms. The raider, if successful, will reshape the company and then sell it, hoping to gain a quick investment return.

Corporate Stocks all shares, common and preferred, representing ownership of a publicly traded corporation. Stock is traded in a stock exchange.

Corporation a legal entity existing apart from its owners (stockholders). Ownership is evidenced by possession of shares of stock. The corporate form is not the most numerous type of business, but it is the most important in terms of total sales, assets, profits, and contribution to national income. The corporate form is implicitly assumed throughout this course. Corporations are governed by a distinct set of state or federal laws and come in two forms: a state C Corporation or federal Subchapter S.

The general structure of a corporation is depicted below.

Corporate Structure

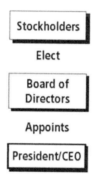

Corpus
  1. the actual, physical and tangible fact in a given situation. Corpus is a substantive body of positive evidence.
  2. the principal or main body of money, as in a trust.

Correction a price reaction, usually downward, leading to an adjustment of typically more than 10%, after experiencing a general period of advancing prices. A true correction is then followed by a continued period of advancing prices, which distinguishes it from a major bearish turn in the overall direction of the stock or the market.

Correlation the degree of relationship between business and economic variables, such as cost and volume, returns on two different stocks, and price and quantity demanded. Correlation analysis evaluates cause/effect relationships. It looks consistently at how the value of one variable changes when the value of the other is changed. A prediction can be made based on the relationship uncovered. An example is the effect of advertising on sales. Positive correlation would mean that the variables typically move in the same direction. Negative correlation would mean that they move in opposite directions.

Correlation Coefficient (r) a statistical measurement of the degree of correlation between the two variables. The range of values it takes is between -1 and +1. A negative value of r indicates an inverse relationship; a positive value of r indicates a direct relationship; a zero value of r indicates that the two variables are independent of each other; the closer r is to + and - 1, the stronger the relationship between the two variables. For example, we may expect a negative relationship between the demand for a product and its selling price, because the higher the selling price charged, the lower the demand.

Cosign to sign a note on behalf of another person and, therefore, to guarantee payment. The cosigner becomes equally responsible for the loan if the borrower does not repay.

Cost
1. the sacrifice, measured by the price paid, to acquire, produce or maintain goods or services. The prices paid for materials, labor, and factory overhead in the manufacture of goods are costs.
2. an asset. The term cost is often used when referring to the valuation of a good or service acquired. When it is used in this sense, a cost is an asset.
3. the concepts of cost and expense are often used interchangeably. When the benefits of the acquisition of the goods or services expire, the cost becomes an expense or loss. An expense is a cost with expired benefits. A loss is an expense (expired cost) with no related benefit.

Cost Accounting a system for recording and reporting measurements of the cost of manufacturing goods and performing services in the aggregate and in detail. It includes methods for reorganizing, classifying, allocating, aggregating and reporting actual costs and comparing them with standard costs. Determination of unit cost to make a product or render a service is needed to establish a selling price or fee to be charged. Also, we have to know the costs for manufacturing a product for inventory valuation needed to prepare the balance sheet and income statement.

Cost Accumulation the collection of costs in an organized fashion by means of a cost accounting system. There are two primary approaches to cost accumulation: a job order system and process cost system. Under a job order system, the three basic elements of manufacturing costs–direct materials, direct labor and factory overhead–are accumulated according to assigned job numbers. Under a process cost system, manufacturing costs are accumulated according to processing department or cost center.

Cost Center the unit within the organization in which the manager is responsible only for costs. A cost center has no control over sales or over the generating of revenue. An example is the production department of a manufacturing company. The performance of a cost center is measured by comparing actual costs with budgeted costs for a specified period of time.

Cost Control the steps taken by management to assure that the cost objectives set down in the planning stage are attained and to assure that all segments of the organization function in a manner consistent with its policies. For effective cost control, most organizations use standard cost systems, in which the actual costs are compared against standard costs for performance evaluation and the deviations are investigated for remedial actions. Cost control is also concerned with feedback that might change any or all of the future plans, the method of delivery services, or both.

Cost Curves a graphical representation of a firm's costs (such as total costs, average costs, marginal costs, fixed costs, or variable costs) in relation to the quantity of output. For example, fixed costs are constant regardless of output and average costs tend to be U-shaped.

Cost Driver a factor that causes a cost item to be incurred (e.g., labor hours, number of patient days, or number of inspections).

Cost Effective among decision alternatives, the one whose cost is lower than its benefit. The most cost effective program would be the one whose cost-benefit ratio is the lowest among various programs competing for a given amount of funds. *See also* Cost-Benefit Analysis.

Cost Effectiveness Analysis an analysis designed to assist public decision makers in their resource allocation and public expenditure decisions when benefits cannot easily be quantified in dollar terms.

Cost Function a mathematical relationship between costs of factor inputs and activity. A cost function may be either linear or nonlinear.

Cost Leadership a low-cost competitive strategy that aims at the broad mass market and requires aggressive construction of efficient-scale facilities, vigorous pursuit of cost reductions from experience, tight cost and overhead control, avoidance of marginal customer accounts, and cost minimization in areas like R&D, service, sales force, advertising, and so on. Because of its lower costs, the cost leader is able to charge a lower price for its products than its competitors and still make a satisfactory profit.

Cost Management management and control of activities to help set enterprise strategies and to determine an accurate product and service cost, improve business processes, eliminate waste, identify cost drivers, and plan operations.

Cost Management System (CMS) cost and management accounting, control, and reporting system that identifies, monitors, and maintains continuous, detailed analyses of a company's activities and provides managers with timely measures of operating results.

Cost of Capital the rate of return that is necessary to maintain market value (or stock price) of a firm, also called a *hurdle rate, cutoff rate* or *minimum required rate of return*. The firm's cost of capital is calculated as a weighted average of the costs of debt and equity funds. Equity funds include both capital stock (common stock and preferred stock) and retained earnings. These costs are expressed as annual percentage rates.

Cost of Funds Index an average of what savings institutions in the 11th District of the Federal Home Loan Bank System (California, Arizona, and Nevada) are paying in interest to depositors and other sources of borrowed money. The index was developed in 1981 to provide a benchmark for adjustable rate mortgages. Currently, about 10 percent of the nation's mortgages are tied to the index. When the index rises, so do interest rates on millions of home mortgages.

Cost of Living Adjustment (COLA) an upward adjustment to an employee's compensation or to Social Security benefits to account for inflation. The adjustment is typically based on a price index such as the Consumer Price Index (CPI).

Cost Per Thousand (CPM) an advertising term referring to the advertising costs of reaching 1,000 customers.

Cost Per Thousand Impressions (CPM) advertising bought on the basis of impression. This is in contrast to the various types of pay-for-performance advertising, whereby payment is only triggered by a mutually agreed upon activity (i.e. click-through, registration, sale). The total price paid in a CPM deal is calculated by multiplying the CPM rate by the number of CPM units. For example, one million impressions at $10 CPM equals a $10,000 total price (1,000,000 / 1,000 = 1,000 units; 1,000 units X $10 CPM = $10,000 total price). The amount paid per impression is calculated by dividing the CPM by 1000. For example, a $10 CPM equals $.01 per impression. $10 CPM / 1000 impressions = $.01 per impression.

Cost Pool a group of related costs that are assigned together to a set of cost objectives (such as services, programs, or activities).

Cost Push Inflation a general rise in prices that occurs when restrictions are placed on the supply of factor inputs (such as labor), or when the prices of those inputs are increased. An example is a wage and price spiral. Wages increase and then producers try to pass on increased wages by charging higher prices to maintain profit margins. As workers realize that prices have increased, and thus their real earnings are no higher, they bargain for even higher wages, and so on. Whether producers are able to pass on costs depends on price elasticity of demand for the products in question. This chain and continuous process will lead to inflation. *See also* Demand Pull Inflation.

Cost-Based Price widely used pricing technique that involves an appropriate cost base plus the markup–usually calculated as some percentage of the cost base.

Cost-Benefit Analysis an analysis to determine whether the favorable results of an alternative are sufficient to justify the cost of taking that alternative. This analysis is widely used in connection with capital expenditure projects in the government sector. A social benefit is any gain in utility and a social cost is any loss of utility as measured by the opportunity cost of the project in question. An example of cost-benefit analysis is where the cost incurred to uncover the reasons for a variance outweighs the benefit to be derived. The cost-benefit ratio or profitability index is widely used for capital expenditure decisions.

Cost-of-Living Index *see* Consumer Price Index (CPI).

Cost-Plus Contract form of contract that requires the customer to pay for all costs incurred plus a predetermined amount of profit.

Cost-Plus Pricing adding a standard markup to the cost of the product.

Costs of Goods Sold the costs of materials used, labor, and overhead in the products and goods that a company makes.

Cost-Volume-Profit (CVP) Analysis analysis that deals with how profits and costs change with a change in volume. More specifically, it looks at the effects on profits of changes in such factors as variables costs, fixed costs, selling prices, volume, and mix of products sold. By studying the relationships of costs, sales and net income, management is better able to cope with many planning decisions. For example, CVP analysis attempts to answer the following questions:
1. What sales volume is required to break even?
2. What sales volume is necessary in order to earn a desired (target) profit?
3. What profit can be expected on a given sales volume?
4. How would changes in selling price, variable costs, fixed costs, and output affect profits?
5. How would a change in the mix of products sold affect the break-even and target volume and profit potential?
See also Break-Even Analysis.

Council of Economic Advisors (CEA) a group established by the Employment Act of 1946, whose function is to help the president formulate and assess the economic policies of the government.

Counter-Advertising advertising that refutes or corrects false claims or misrepresentations. It may be voluntary or required by some regulatory agency. Counter-advertising also includes media messages that present information opposing use of commercially advertised products. Nonsmoking or anti-alcohol usage are two examples.

Counterclaim a legal action by defendant against the plaintiff. It is a counter demand in litigation by the defendant. For example, if a plaintiff sues a defendant for $1,000,000, the defendant may in turn decide to sue the plaintiff for a similar amount. A counterclaim does not constitute an answer to the plaintiff's charges.

Countercyclical (Defensive) Stock a stock of a company that maintains substantial earnings during a general decline in economic activity because its products are needed. Examples are food and entertainment stocks.

Counteroffer an original offer to buy or sell answered with a simultaneous revised offer. For example, a buyer offers $100,000 for a house put on the market. The owner turns down the offer but submits a counteroffer for $125,000. Offers and counteroffers are not restricted to price but include such matters as financing arrangements and apportionment of closing costs.

Countertrade the trade of goods and services for other goods and services.

Country Risk *see* Political Risk.

Coupon; Coupon Rate the interest rate on the face amount of a debt security. For instance, the annual interest to be paid on a $1,000 bond with a nominal interest rate of 8% is $80. Typically, interest payments are made semiannually. The term derives from bearer bonds, once more common than now, which actually bore coupons to be detached and presented for payment as interest becomes due. Even with registered bonds the term survives and is distinguished from yield, which relates the coupon rate to the market price of the bond.

Cournot's Doupoly Model a duopoly model that assumes each of the two firms will maximize profits assuming that its competitor's output remains constant. Covariance a statistical measure of how two variables move together in a linear fashion.

Covenant legal term for a promise, commonly found in the form of restrictions in a loan agreement imposed on the borrower to protect the lender's interest. Examples of typical restrictive provisions are a ceiling on dividends and the required maintenance of a minimum working capital. *See also* Indenture.

Covered Interest Arbitrage a process whereby an investor earns a risk-free profit by (1) borrowing currency, (2) converting it into another currency where it is invested, (3) selling this other currency for future delivery against the initial original currency, and (4) using the proceeds of forward sale to repay the original loan. The profits in this transaction are derived from discrepancies between interest differentials and the percentage discounts or premiums among the currencies involved in the forward transaction.

CPM *see* Critical Path Method (CPM); Cost Per Thousand (CPM).

CPU *see* Central Processing Unit.

Crashing process of reducing an activity time by adding resources and hence usually cost. Crashing involves shifting more resources (money) to those activities or perhaps outsourcing some of the work.

Critical Path longest sequence of activities in a project management network.

Creative Accounting manipulating accounting and financial numbers to suit the results a company desires. *See also* Cook the Books.

Creative Financing any financing arrangement other than a conventional mortgage from a third-party lending institution. This form of financing is popular when the price of real estate is out of reach for many buyers. Creative financing devices include the seller financing; owner carrying (OWC); balloon payment loans; wraparound mortgages; assumption of mortgages; sale-leasebacks; land contracts; alternative mortgage instruments, such as adjustable rate mortgages (ARM) and shared equity mortgages (SEM).

Credit
1. as a noun, an entry on the right side of an account. As a verb, to make an entry on

the right side of an account. Under the double entry bookkeeping system, credits increase liabilities, equity, and revenues and decrease assets and expenses.

2. as a verb, to enter or post a credit.

3. the ability to buy an item or to borrow money in return for a promise to pay later.

4. in taxation, a dollar for dollar offset against a tax liability.

Credit Analysis the process of determining whether a credit applicant meets the firm's credit standards or those of a lender and what amount of credit it should receive, before a line of credit is extended. It typically involves two steps: (1) obtaining credit information (such as financial statements, Dun & Bradstreet reports, etc.) and (2) analyzing the information in order to make the credit decision.

Credit Bureau an agency, typically established and owned by merchants and banks at the local level, which gathers credit information from its members and makes this information available for a specified fee to member creditors, under the requirements of the Fair Credit Reporting Act. Experian is such an example.

Credit History a history of an individual's credit financial transactions including a detailed payment analysis. The credit history is critical for performing a credit analysis to develop a credit rating. A credit history record of prompt and timely payments is important for a strong credit rating. A credit history is kept by major credit rating organizations and is accessible for a fee by commercial organizations as well as by individuals under terms of the Consumer Credit Protection Act. Banks and other major lenders give an individual's credit history serious consideration before extending credit or granting loans.

Credit Rating a rating to help the lender determine if a credit applicant should be granted credit. It is based on the applicant's job history, income, assets owned, credit history, etc. Many firms investigate and maintain credit records of individuals and businesses. Examples are TRW (for individuals) and Dun and Bradstreet (for businesses).

Credit Report, Credit Record a report from an independent agency of the borrower's credit history.

Credit Risk possibility that a loss may occur from the failure of another party to perform according to the terms of a contract. For example, credit risk in bond terminology refers to the risk of default.

Credit Scoring an objective method of evaluating a credit applicant's credit worthiness by assigning values to factors such as income, existing debts, job security and credit history. *See* FICO Credit Score.

Credit Terms

1. the stipulations specified by the bank for the money borrowed by a company, such as the amount of available credit, the percentage rate of interest, and when the funds are due to be paid.

2. The conditions specified by a creditor on accounts receivable. For example, a 2/10, net 30 term means that if you pay within 10 days from the purchase, you

get a 10% discount; otherwise, you must pay within thirty days.

Credit Union a depository institution formed as a cooperative having some common bond, such as the same employer, religion, union, or fraternal association. It is a mutual association owned by depositors. It draws together the deposits of its members and lends these funds out to other members or invests money.

Credit Worthiness financial standing of a debtor as a basis to pay obligations.

Creeping Inflation a gradual and continuous rise in the general price level that is bearable in the short term but may lead to sizable long-term price increases and gradually erodes the purchasing power of money. *See also* Galloping Inflation.

Crisis Management to the practice of management what emergency medicine is to the practice of medicine. It is public relations activities in which an organization attempts to contain and minimize damages and disruptions resulting from an adverse event affecting its products or services. *See also* Business Continuity Plan.

Critical Path the longest path for a project. This is the minimum amount of time needed for the completion of the project. Thus, it is the activities along this path that must be accelerated in order to speed up the project. On the other hand, delays in these activities would cause delays in the project. It is thus important to identify the critical path. The critical path is also the path leading to the final event such that all events on the path have zero slack.

Critical Path Method (CPM) a Program Evaluation and Review (PERT) technique that uses a single time estimate for each activity, rather than three-time estimates–optimistic, most likely, and pessimistic. The primary objective of CPM is to identify the critical path for a project.

Cross Rate the exchange rate between two currencies derived by dividing each currency's exchange rate with a third currency. For example, if yen/$ is 100 and Euro/$ is 1.25, the cross rate between yen and Euro is 100 yens/$ divided by 1.25 Euro = 80 yens/Euro. Because most currencies are quoted against the dollar, it may be necessary to work out the cross rates for currencies other than the dollar. The cross rate is needed to consummate financial transactions between two countries.

Cross Sectional Data observations of a particular variable at the same point in time across economic units (e.g., households, firms, states, or countries). For example, year-end earnings or sales for a group of firms in an industry is cross sectional data.

Cross Subsidization pricing method in which the firm may enhance profits by selling one product at or below cost and the other product above cost.

Cross Training training of employees to be able to do various jobs so that if someone is absent they can fill in.

Crowding Out a situation in which large increases in government spending and the resultant deficit financing are likely to reduce personal consumption and business investment spending. The reasons for this are: (1) financial resources that may otherwise be used by the consumer and business sectors are diverted to public use and, (2) interest rates may be pushed up due to competition between the private and public sectors, which increases the costs of borrowing by the private sector and drives it out of the financial markets. For these reasons, private incentives to work and invest may be diminished, thereby dampening the economy.

CRT *see* Cathode Ray Tube (CRT).

Culture the whole set of social norms, behavior patterns, beliefs, rules, customs, values, techniques, artifacts, institutions, and the like that are distinctive to a population and that condition its behavior. A multinational company (MNC) must consider the culture of all the foreign countries it operates in.

Cultural Risk the risk built-in in operating cross culturally. It is the chance of loss because of an MNC's inaccurate perception of a foreign culture or the manner in which the corporate culture and the foreign culture interface.

Culture Shock the clash of two different cultures.

Cumulative Dividends dividends on designated preferred stock that have not been paid, but will be paid when available, to the preferred stock holders before distributing any future dividends to the common stockholders; also called *accumulated dividends* and *dividends in arrears*.

Cumulative Voting a method of voting for corporate directors that enables a minority group of shareholders to obtain some voice in the control of a corporation. Normally, shareholders must allocate their votes equally among the candidates for the board of directors. Cumulative voting allows them to vote all their shares for a single candidate. For example, a 10-share holder normally casts 10 votes for each or, say, 12 nominees to the board of directors. He/she thus has 120 votes. Under the cumulative voting principle he/she may do that or he/she may cast 120 (10 x 12) votes for only one nominee, 60 for two, 40 for three, or any other distribution he/she chooses.

Currency another word for money, paper, or coin.

Currency Depreciation a fall in the exchange rate of one currency in terms of other currencies under a system of floating exchange rates. This is in contrast with devaluation, which denotes a lowering of fixed rates of exchange.

Currency Revaluation a strengthening of the spot value of a currency that has previously been devalued. The value can be increased by raising the supply of foreign currencies via restriction of imports and promotion of exports.

Currency Risk the risk that the return on an international security to U.S. investors would be negatively affected by a change in the value of the dollar relative to the foreign currency; also called *foreign exchange risk*, *exchange rate risk*, or *exchange risk*. A weaker dollar would boost the security's return, since the stronger foreign currency would be exchanged for more U.S. dollars. A stronger dollar would lower the security's return.

Current Account an account in the balance of payments, analogous to the revenues and expenses of a business, the sum of the merchandise, services, investment income, and unilateral transfer accounts. When combined, they provide important insights into a country's international economic performance, just as a firm's profit and loss statement conveys vital information about its performance. *See also* Balance of Payments (BOP).

Current Assets assets that will be converted into cash within one year. Examples of current assets are cash, accounts receivable, inventory, and prepaid expenses.

Current Liabilities liabilities payable within one year. Examples are accounts payable, notes payable, and taxes payable.

Current Ratio the current assets divided by the current liabilities. It measures how well a company can meet its short-term obligations.

Current Value a present market value of an asset; also called *replacement value*, *market value*, *fair market value*, or *present value*. This is in contrast to historical cost, which is the original cost of the asset.

Current Yield the measurement of investment return that relates income to the market price. For a bond, it is annual interest divided by its current market price. For a common or preferred stock, it is the ratio of the annual cash dividend income received to the price paid by the investor. For example, a 12 percent coupon rate $1,000 par value bond is selling for $960. *See* Bond Yields; Yield To Maturity (YTM).

Cursor the blinking line on the screen that demonstrates position.

Cusip Number a nine-digit identification number used to identify all stocks and registered bonds that trade in the U.S. CUSIP stands for Committee on Uniform Securities Identification Procedures, which is a committee set up by the American Banker's Association.

Custodian
1. anyone having the responsibility of caring for and managing the property of another. An example is an individual's having the responsibility of managing a custodial account for a minor.
2. an agent, bank, trust company, or other organization which holds and safekeeps an individual's or an investment company's assests for them.

Custody
1. the situation in which one person has another's assets and is charged with the legal management of those assets.
2. the care and management of children or money as set by law.

Customer Relationship Management Systems (CRM) a set of applications designed to gather and analyze information about customers. CRM systems automate customer service and support. They also provide for customer data analysis and support e-commerce storefronts. While CRM is constantly evolving, it's already led to some remarkable changes in the way companies interact with customers. The ultimate development of CRM remains to be seen but undoubtedly mobile communication will play a significant role. Many companies are already experimenting with systems to send messages to cell phone users offering them special discounts and buying "opportunities." Example: Federal Express allows customers to track their packages on the Web. Amazon.com uses CRM technology to make suggestions to customers based on their personal purchase histories.

Customer Relationship Management (CRM) Software software that automate customer service and support. They also provide for customer data analysis and support e-commerce storefronts. While CRM is constantly evolving, it's already led to some remarkable changes in the way companies interact with customers. For example, Federal Express allows customers to track their packages on the Web. This service is becoming commonplace, but it didn't exist 10 years ago. Amazon.com uses CRM technology to make suggestions to customers based on their personal purchase histories.

Customer Value the difference between what a customer receives (customer realization) and what the customer gives up (customer sacrifice).

Cyber Investing investing such as on-line trading on the Internet.

Cybermall a virtual shopping mall on the Web.

Cyberspace originally used in *Neuromancer*, William Gibson's novel of direct brain-computer networking; refers to the collective realms of computer-aided communication.

Cycle Time time required to produce and deliver a product or service. Thus, total cycle time is the sum of value-added processing time and total non-value-added time.

Cyclical Stock a stock whose prices is directly and significantly tied to economic conditions. If the economy is improving, stock prices rise but if the economy is deteriorating, stock prices decline. Cyclical stocks are somewhat risky. Examples of cyclical stocks are General Motors, International Paper, American Airlines, and Kaufman & Braud. Noncyclical stocks are not as directly affected by economic changes.

Cyclical Unemployment unemployment caused by cyclical movements (i.e., downswings) of the business cycle–that is, a broad-based decline in the overall level of aggregate demand in the economy. This situation can be managed through economic policies. *See also* Unemployment.

Dd

Damages

Injury or Loss: a monetary restitution, which may be recovered either through insurance indemnification or by judicial settlement, for losses or injuries incurred either through an accident or illegal action.

Compensatory: financial settlement to compensate a victim of a personal injury or property loss. The intent is not to benefit from the injury or loss but merely to compensate for the damages incurred.

Exemplary or Punitive: punishment for unacceptable or illegal conduct. Exemplary or punitive damages are primarily intended to deter future unacceptable acts. Such damages are awarded to the plaintiff in a legal action on an increased scale and are over and above the actual pecuniary value of the loss or injury.

Data Mart a data file consisting of logical records. It is an element of a data warehouse furnishing summarized information that can be used in decision making by a department or division manager.

Data Mining software that searches a database to find trends, patterns, associations, or relationships in order to make informed decisions. Patterns indicate the occurrence of something that infers the presence of something else. Sequential patterns uncover chronological events. In clustering, we look for groupings and high-level classifications.

Data Privacy security measures and devices employed by the company to assure that confidential information (e.g. customer files) are not improperly accessed. For example, a password may be required to obtain access to electronic data files of customers.

Data Processing (DP) a process that involves transformation of data into information through classifying, sorting, merging, recording, retrieving, transmitting, or reporting. Data processing can be manual or computer based.

Data Warehouse a database structured to tactical information that can be used to answer specific questions about transactional company history.

Data Warehousing subject-oriented, timely integrated database providing important information to management in making business decisions.

Database a collection of related data records independently managed apart from any specific program or information system application. It is then made available to a wide variety of individuals and systems within the organization. In essence, it is an electronic filing cabinet providing a common core of information accessible by a program. An example is a database of inventory items.

Database Administrator (DBA) the person who manages all activities related to the database. A qualified DBA should be able to understand the hardware configuration (such as the client server environment) and take advantage of existing hardware capability to improve the performance of the database management system. He/she should have expertise in terms of database engine (such as SQL) and front-end tools (such as Visual Basic and Power Builder) to create a good user interface. A DBA should be able to do limited trouble shooting in both the application area and system level since a database crash may involve both application and system software.

Database Management System (DBMS) the software (computer programs) used to manage data in the database. It is a set of programs that provides for defining, controlling, and accessing the database. The database program allows managers to enter, manipulate, retrieve, display, select, sort, edit, and index data. Advantages of a database management system include (1) elimination of data redundancy, (2) improved efficiency in updating, (3) data sharing, (4) easy data access, and (5) reduced program maintenance cost. An example of database management systems is Microsoft Access.

Databasification assembling consumer information on Internet-connected computer servers that store billions of pieces of data, covering almost every American. Victims of identity theft learn that their credit histories and other information are stored by data brokers, who gather and sell the information to institutions such as lenders and companies vetting job candidates.

Dataquick a national company that maintains a huge database that tracks 83 million properties. The firm provides information and analysis to clients such as newspapers, appraisers, mortgages and lending, and title insurance.

Date of Record the date on which stockholders of record in a company's stock ledger are entitled to receive dividends or stock rights. Stock usually trades ex-dividends or ex-rights beginning the fourth business day before the date of record.

Day Order order placed by an investor to purchase or sell securities or commodities that will end if not transacted or cancelled on the trading day. An order is always deemed to be a day order unless noted otherwise. The primary exception is a good-till-cancelled order. However, even this type of order may be fulfilled on the trading day depending on whether certain conditions are met. *See also* Buy Order.

Day Trading the purchase and sale of a security on the same day so that the profit or loss is settled by the end of the trading day. Day trading aims at taking advantage of price swings during that day. Due to the popularity of online trading, day trading has a significant impact on the stock market in terms of price and volume. Day trading has the disadvantage of high commissions.

DBA (Doing Business As) certification by a state that a principal is doing business under an assumed name. The certificate also states the address where the business is being conducted. The primary purposes of the DBA certificate are:
1. registration of a business and its assumed name giving the principal's name and address.
2. protect the business name from being used by others.
3. provide a public source of redress.

De Facto (*Latin*) in deed, in fact, in reality, actually. An act or fact that occurs as a matter of practice and reality as distinguished from de jure, meaning a lawfully and rightfully occurring act. A de facto action or occurrence is accepted as a matter of fact, but is illegal or illegitimate. For example, a homeowner has been notoriously using the premise as a de facto two family house although the single family residence zoning makes this an illegal practice.

De Jure *see* De Facto.

Dead-End Job a job or career having no further growth, salary increase, or promotions. The present job holder can advance no further than his or her present position. In such a circumstance, the job holder will have to determine whether he or she is satisfied with this eventuality or should seek a new position or career. Most people become very discouraged when discovering they are in a dead-end position. Management should try to restructure dead-end positions to allow for career advancement recognition in order to prevent low morale and turnover and encourage higher productivity growth.

Dealer
1. an individual or a company that owns and offers securities. The dealer acts as a principal rather than as an agent. Typically, a dealer buys for his/her own account and sells to a customer from his/her own inventory, as distinguished from the broker who acts as the buyer's or seller's agent for a fee.
2. an individual dealing in auto sales.

Death Benefit
1. in taxation, a payment or receipt of proceeds to a specified beneficiary or beneficiaries by an employer, by virtue of the death of the employee. This can be a survivor annuity from a pension plan, a life insurance payment, or a lump sum.
2. the portion (tax exempt) of the proceeds of a life insurance policy representing protection as distinguished from investment value. Policy loans reduce the death benefit by the amount of the outstanding loan balance.

Debenture a long-term debt instrument that is not secured by a mortgage or other lien on specific property. Because it is an unsecured debt, it is issued usually by large, financially strong companies with excellent bond ratings. There are two kinds of debentures: a senior issue and a subordinated (junior) issue, which has a subordinate lien. The order of a prior claim is set forth in the bond indenture. Typically, in the event of liquidation, subordinated debentures come after senior debt.

Debit

1. as a noun, an entry on the left side of an account. As a verb, to make an entry on the left side of an account. Under the double entry bookkeeping system, debits increase assets and expenses and decrease liabilities, equity and revenues.
2. as a verb, to enter or post a debit.
3. an accounting lingo, an entry made on the asset or expense side of a ledger or account.
4. legal obligation to pay, the principal and interest on, which must be repaid. It may be either short term (e.g., accounts payable, taxes payable, notes), intermediate term (e.g., bank loans), or long term (e.g., bonds, mortgages).
5. the amount of money owed by a country to the public or another country.
6. future services due from an advance payment such as a retainer for management consulting services.
7. term designating the left side of a balance of payment account.

Debit Card a card issued for making electronic transfers of funds in stores, depository institutions, and other businesses to make transactions. These cards replace the need for cash or checks by initiating automatic transfers of funds via computer systems. No cash or check is needed.

Debt

1. money or services owed to another in accordance with an agreement. The debtor may have to give collateral for a loan, such as a mortgage on his or her house. Principal and interest on the loan will have to be paid. Debt may either be short term or long term.
2. one of the two basic methods of raising capital for a company. *See* Debt Financing.

Debt Consolidation Loan a type of loan that combine all of an individual's debts into one large loan with small monthly payments. The idea is to pay off several smaller debts with varying due dates and interest rates and instead have one monthly payment that is usually lower in amount than the payments on the other debts combined. The high rate of interest for the new loan greatly increases the total cost of the credit, although the monthly payment may be lower than the sum of all the former payments.

Debt Coverage Ratio (DCR); debt service coverage ratio

1. ratio of monthly consumer debt payments to monthly take-home pay. This ratio helps a consumer determine how much debt to handle. The absolute maximum is 20 percent. This maximum limit includes payments due on credit cards, and personal, school and car loans--but not mortgages, home-equity loans or rent.
2. operating income divided by annual debt service; the ratio of a company's operating income to its loan payments or debt service.

Debt/Equity Ratio total liabilities divided by stockholders' equity. It indicates whether or not a company has a great amount of debt in its capital structure. Large debts mean that the borrower has to pay significant periodic interest and principal. Also, a heavily indebted firm takes a greater risk of running out of cash in difficult times. The interpretation of this ratio depends on several variables, including the ratios of other firms in the industry, the degree of access to additional debt financing, and stability of operations.

Debt Financing raising money by selling bonds, notes, or mortgages and borrowing the money directly from financial institutions. The presence of debt financing in a firm's capital structure provides financial leverage, which tends to magnify the effects of increased operating profits on the stockholder's returns. Since debt is normally the cheapest form of long-term financing, due to the tax deductibility of interest, it is a desirable component of the firm's capital structure as long as the borrowed funds produce a return in excess of their cost. Also, during inflation, the company will be paying back the debt in cheaper dollars. However, too much debt can result in higher levels of financial risk in meeting the principal and satisfying interest payments. Excessive debt will make it more difficult to raise funds and will increase the cost of capital.

Debt Limit

1. the legal and maximum amount of indebtedness that a governmental entity can undertake. This maximum debt amount minus the outstanding debt is the legal debt margin.

2. a provision often found in a covenant in a corporate loan agreement.

Debt Restructuring

1. an adjustment or realignment of debt structure reflecting concessions granted by creditors, to give the debtor a more practical arrangement for meeting financial obligations. Restructuring is needed when the debtor has severe financial problems. The agreement to restructure may be the result from legal action or simply an agreement to which parties consent. *See also* Chapter 11; Chapter 7.

2. a realignment of debt structure based on a voluntary financial management decision–for example, to replace short-term debt with long-term debt.

Debt Securities securities that serve as evidence to the existence of a debt, such as bonds, notes, etc., as opposed to equity securities, such as stocks, which manifest evidence of ownership. *See also* Fixed Income Securities.

Debt Service the interest and principal paid on a loan. Debt service is normally paid bi-weekly, monthly, quarterly, or annually depending on the terms of the loan. Note that the initial interest payments are substantially higher than the principal payments but begin declining as the principal payments steadily increase. *See also* Amortization.

Debug process of tracing and correcting flaws in a software program or hardware device. Computerized routines may be used to find bugs.

Decentralization the delegation of decision making to the subunits of an organization. It is a matter of degree. The lower the level where decisions are made, the greater is the decentralization. Decentralization is most effective in organizations where subunits are autonomous and costs and profits can be independently measured. The benefits of decentralization include (1) decisions are made by those who have the most knowledge about local conditions, (2) greater managerial input of decision making has a desirable motivational effect, and (3) managers have more control over results. The costs of decentralization include (1) managers have a tendency to look at their division and lose sight of overall company goals, (2) there can be costly duplication of services, and (3) costs of obtaining sufficient information increase.

Decision Making the purposeful selection from among a set of alternatives in light of a given objective. Decision making is not a separate function of management. In fact, decision making is intertwined with the other functions, such as planning, coordinating, and controlling. These functions all require that decisions be made. For example, at the outset, management must make a critical decision as to which of the several strategies would be followed. Such a decision is often called a *strategic decision* because of its long-term impact on the organization. Also, managers must make scores of lesser decisions, tactical and operational, all of which are important to the organization's well-being.

Decision Making Under Certainty a decision situation where for each decision alternative there is only one event and therefore only one outcome for each action. For example, there is only one possible event for the two possible actions: "Do nothing" at a future cost of $3.00 per unit for 10,000 units or "rearrange" a facility at a future cost of $2.80 for the same number of units. A decision matrix (or payoff table) would look as follows:

State Of Nature		
Actions	Cost	(with probability of 1.0)
Do nothing	$30,000	(10,000 units x $3.00)
Rearrange	28,000	(10,000 units x $2.80)

Note that there is only one state of nature in the matrix because there is only one possible outcome for each action (with certainty). The decision is obviously to choose the action that will result in the most desirable outcome (least cost), that is to "rearrange."

Decision Making Under Uncertainty a decision situation that involves several events for each action with its probability of occurrence. The decision problem can best be approached using a payoff table (or decision matrix).

Decision Rule a designation of a specific condition or combination of conditions that may arise in the decision-making process and the appropriate action to take if the conditions exist. For example, in a capital budgeting decision, under the NPV method, a project should be accepted if its net present value (NPV) is positive. Also, under the internal rate of return (IRR) approach, a project should be accepted if the IRR of the project exceeds the cost of capital.

Decision Support System (DSS) a branch of the broadly defined Management Information System (MIS). It is an information system that provides answers to problems and that integrates the decision maker into the system as a component. The system utilizes such quantitative techniques as regression, linear programming, and financial planning modeling. DSS software furnishes support to the accountant in the decision-making process. It analyzes a specific situation and can be modified as the practitioner wishes. Models are constructed and decisions analyzed. Planning and forecasting are facilitated. *See also* Management Information System (MIS).

Decision Tree a pictorial representation of a decision situation, normally found in discussions of decision making under uncertainty or risk. It shows decision alternatives, states of nature, probabilities attached to the state of nature, and conditional benefits and losses.

The tree approach is most useful in a sequential decision situation. For example, assume XYZ Corporation wishes to introduce one of two products to the market this year. The probabilities and present values (PV) of projected cash inflows are given below:

Product	Initial investment	PV of cash inflows	Probabilities
A	$225,000		1.00
		$450,000	0.40
		200,000	0.50
		-100,000	0.10
B	80,000		1.00
		320,000	0.20
		100,000	0.60
		-150,000	0.20

• A decision tree analyzing the two products is shown on the next page.

Decision Tree

	Initial Investment (1)	Probability (2)	PV of Cash Inflows (3)	PV of Cash Inflows (2) X (3) = (4)
		0.40	$450,000	$180,000
	$225,000	0.50	$200,000	100,000
Product A		0.10	-$100,000	-10,000
			Expected PV of Cash Inflows	$270,000
Choice A or B				
Product B		0.20	$320,000	$64,000
	$80,000	0.60	$100,000	60,000
		0.20	-$150,000	-30,000
			Expected PV of Cash Inflows	$ 94,000

Based on the expected NPV, choose product A over product B.

Note: this analysis fails to recognize the risk factor in project analysis.

Declaration Date the date on which the dividend is voted and announced (declared) by the board of directors. At the declaration date, the dividend is a legal liability of the company.

Declaration of Homestead statement filed with a governmental authority declaring property a homestead for the purposes of securing a homestead exemption. The declaration of homestead has no effect on the property title and is not a conveyance. For example, Bill Jones makes a declaration of homestead to the municipality for his home in order to qualify for a homestead exemption of a 25% property tax deduction.

Declaration Page the first page of an insurance policy summarizing the policy benefits.

Declarations

1. an announcement to pay dividends as a result of the board of directors' decision. The front page of an insurance policy that provides basic descriptive information about the insured person and/or property, the premium to be paid, the time period of the coverage, and the policy limits.
2. a legal record used to create a condominium.

Declining-Balance Depreciation a method of accelerated depreciation in which a constant percentage of an asset's value is written off each year. A depreciation rate is determined by doubling the straight-line rate. For example, the double-declining rate for a 10-year asset is 20% (10%x 2). *See also* Depreciation.

Declining Market a market in which there are more sellers than buyers, thereby causing prices to fall. Declining markets for securities may be caused by unfavorable business conditions and high interest rates.

Decreasing Cost Industry an industry where the long-run supply curve is negatively sloping, meaning that the equilibrium price of the industry tends to fall as industry output increases. One example is the case of a young industry that springs up in a relatively underdeveloped area where resource markets are poorly organized, marketing facilities are primitive, and transportation is inadequate. An increase in the number of firms and in the output of the industry may stimulate the development of marketing and transportation facilities that reduce the costs of individual firms.

Decreasing Returns to Scale a situation where inputs increase by a certain percentage and the resulting output increases by a smaller percentage. For example, when all inputs increase 200 percent (i.e., doubled), output grows by only 90 percent.

Decreasing Term term insurance in which the protection decreases over the life of the policy.

Decree the judicial decision in a litigated case, rendered by a court of law. For example, the court decision may require one party to a contract to carry out a specific condition under it.

Decryption process of converting encrypted data back into its original form, so it can be understood. *See also* Encryption.

Deductible the amount that an insured must pay on any insured loss before payment by the insurance company begins, usually on a per illness or per accident basis. The deductible is paid by the insured or by another insurance policy in the event that multiple coverage exists.

Deductions
1. itemized deductions, which are deductions from adjusted gross income (AGI). Certain personal expenditures are allowed by the Tax Code as deductions from adjusted gross income if they exceed the zero bracket amount. Examples include, interest on home mortgages, real estate taxes, and charitable contributions. Itemized deductions are reported on Schedule A of Form 1040.
2. deductions for adjusted gross income, such as employee business expenses and contributions to an IRA pension plan.
3. adjustment to an invoice.

Deed a written document used to convey title to real estate, when properly executed and delivered.

Deed Description a property description contained in a title deed. A deed description is intended to inform a reasonable person where property is located. It can be described by metes and bounds, by reference to a lot on a filed map by monuments, or by a government survey. A street address may be used, but it is not the best method. The deed description should also include any street rights or rights of neighbor's property.

Deed in Lieu of Foreclosure a legal instrument that conveys real estate to the lender after the borrower defaults on his or her mortgage payments. The borrower should demand cancellation of the unpaid debt and a letter to that effect from the lender. This method relieves the lender of the inconvenience of foreclosure proceedings and waiting out any required redemption periods. It is a voluntary act by both borrower and lender.

Deed Restriction a written statement in a deed limiting the number, type, size, and use of property. An example would be a deed restriction stating the described property can only be used for educational purposes. It is illegal for deed restrictions to be imposed against individuals because of color, creed, nationality, race, or sex.

Deep in the Money term used to describe the value of stock or index options that differ significantly from the market price of the underlying security or index. A call option is deep-in-the-money if its striking price is much lower than the market price. Such a call could be written or sold if a stockholder of the underlying securities is bearish on the stock and wants to protect the original investment if the stock does indeed fall in price. A put option is deep-in-the-money if its striking price is significantly above the market price of the related security. This put would be desirable to sell by an individual who shorted the underlying stock and is anticipating that it may rise in price. The price increase of the shorted stock would be covered by the proceeds of the put option up to the striking price of the put. Options that are deep-in-the-money have very little premium since their striking price is significantly different from the market price of the underlying security.

Deep Pockets individuals or companies with lots of money.

Default failure of a debtor to pay principal or interest on a debt when due. In the event of default, debtors may make claims against the assets of the issuer in order to recover their principal.

Defeasance
Contract: a specific act that causes a contract to become null and void.
Corporate finance: a way to remove low interest-cost loans from a balance sheet by securing higher interest-bearing securities to satisfy the loan payments. Such an action involves depositing the higher yielding securities in an irrevocable trust dedicated to redeeming the lower cost loan. In a variation of them, a client could instruct a broker to perform a market purchase of an older outstanding bond issue of a company and then exchange it for a security issue that is later sold at a profit.
Real estate: a mortgage clause permitting the mortgagee to redeem the property after a default. Thus, if the borrower defaults on the mortgage and agrees to pay the entire debt within the defeasance period, the property can be purchased by the borrower.

Deferred Annuity an annuity whose first payment or receipt does not begin until sometime after the first period. An annuity of, say, $1,000 that will be paid at the end of each year from the fourth through the end of that annuity is an example of a deferred annuity.

Deferred Compensation salary or bonuses that are not paid during the year in which they are earned, but later, usually after retirement.

Deferred Maintenance in real estate, a type of physical depreciation owing to lack of normal upkeep, such as broken windows and discolored paint that adversely affect the value of a piece of property. It should be fixed right away.

Deficiency an amount of money below what is expected.

Finance: when a person's liabilities exceed his or her assets.

Income tax: an additional amount of money the IRS determines a taxpayer owes. Deficiency rulings can be appealed to the Tax Court.

Deficit an excess of expenditure over income, resulting in insufficient funds that must be made up by either reducing savings or investments or through borrowing.

Deficit Spending any spending by the government that exceeds what it takes in as revenues.

Defined Benefit Plan, Defined Benefit Pension Plan a pension plan where the benefit is defined by a formula and frequently founded on the last final years of employment. It typically has a predefined retirement income benefit formula with a variable contribution formula. The pension benefit formula usually is based on the worker's salary level as the retirement date is approached. Defined benefit pension plans are dependent on an adequate funding pattern to assure that sufficient funds are available to satisfy the promised benefits. There are two types of defined benefit pension plans:

1. **Fixed dollars:** under this concept are the (a) unit benefit approach having discrete units of benefits being credited for years of service, (b) the level percentage of compensation in which all employees after a minimum age (usually 50) receive the same percentage of earnings after a minimum period of service (usually 20 years), and (c) the flat amount in which all employees receive the same total dollar amount of retirement benefits after they meet minimum requirements for age (over 50) and years of service (usually over 20).

2. **Variable dollars:** there are two concepts in the variable dollar approach: (a) in the cost-of-living plan, the dollar amounts of the pension are varied according to increases in the cost of living as normally measured by the consumer price index (CPI) and (b) the equity annuity plan in which employee premiums purchase units in a variable annuity plan; on the employee's retirement, these are converted to fluctuating retirement units consistent with the value of the underlying common stock portfolio.

Defined Contribution Plan, Defined Contribution Pension Plan a method for an employer to add an unused profit sharing plan deduction (credit carryover) to a future contribution on a tax deductible basis, such as 401(k) plans. It is a pension plan in which employee contributions are fixed and benefits vary according to a formula. The formula may consider such factors as years of service, salary levels, and age. The organization benefits from a defined contribution plan because it knows what its employee benefit costs will be. The employee benefits since there is no fixed retirement benefit, allowing for the possibility of future growth. A defined contribution plan forces the organization to budget for continuous benefit payments, but it faces no future pension liability since most defined contribution plans are also funded pension plans. Thus, employees are assured of receiving their benefits irrespective of whether the organization is in existence when they retire.

Deflation a general decrease in prices. It is the opposite of inflation and distinguished from disinflation, which is a reduction in the rate of price increases. Deflation is caused by a reduction in the money stock of the economy. Deflation can also be brought about by direct contractions in spending, either in the form of a reduction in government spending, personal spending, or investment spending. Deflation has often had the side effect of increasing unemployment in an economy since the process often leads to a lower level of demand in the economy. Other downside effects include possible pay cuts and more expensive repayment of consumer debts. The upside of falling prices: mild deflation would assure working people (at least those who fend off pay cuts) of steadily rising real wages.

Default Risk the likelihood that a bondholder will not receive the promised interest and bond redemption when due. Investment advisory services rate firms according to their ability to repay debt. *See also* Bond Ratings.

Deficit Financing borrowing by a government to cover a revenue shortfall. This can stimulate the economy for a time but dampen the economy in the long run by putting upward pressure on interest rates. Government borrowing can create the "crowding out" of consumers and businesses from the credit markets. *See also* Crowding Out.

Deflator a price index used to convert an economic time series in current dollars into a series expressed in constant dollars of a prior period.

Degree of Freedom (DF) number of data items that are independent of one another. Given a sample of data and the computation of some statistics (e.g., the mean), the degrees of freedom are defined as the number of observations included in the formula minus the number of parameters estimated using the data. For example, the mean statistic for N sample data points has n DF, but the variance formula has (n-1) DF because one parameter (the mean X) has to be estimated before the variance formula can be used.

Degree of Financial Leverage (DFL) percentage change in earnings available to common shareholders that is associated with a given percentage change in net operating income. The greater the DFL, the riskier the firm; however, if the return on assets exceeds the cost of debt, additional leverage is favorable.

Degree of Operating Leverage (DOL) change in operating income (earnings before interest and taxes) resulting from a percentage change in revenues. It measures the extent to which a firm incurs fixed rather than variable costs in operations. Thus, the greater the DOL, the greater the risk of loss when sales decline, and the greater the reward when sales increase.

Degree of Total Leverage (DTL) percentage change in net income that is associated with a given percentage change in sales. It is the product of the degree of financial leverage (DFL) and the degree of operating leverage (DOL).

Delaware-Based Corporation the state of Delaware is known to have favorable laws towards businesses, thus many companies are incorporated in Delaware to be governed by those state laws.

Delinquency being in arrears in a payment on a tax or debt obligation when due (on the due date of payment or before the grace period).

Delisting Withdrawal of a particular security from trading on a securities exchange. Stocks can be delisted when the company violates minimum standards of the exchange including failure to maintain a minimum net worth, not having the required number of shareholders, or conviction of certain illegalities. Of course, when a company is merged into another company or is no longer publicly traded, it will be removed from the exchange. This activity should not be confused with delisting in which the company's stock is not permitted to be traded because of nonconformance with basic exchange policies.

Delivery Cycle Time *see* Cycle Time

Delivery Time time period between product completion and customer receipt of the item.

Delphi Method a qualitative forecasting method that seeks to use the judgment of experts systematically in arriving at a forecast of what future events will be or when they may occur. It brings together a group of experts who have access to each other's opinions in an environment where no majority opinion is disclosed.

Delta
1. the mathematical symbol for an incremental difference.
2. a mathematical term meaning change.
3. ratio of change of the option price to a small change in the price of the underlying asset.

Demand the quantity of a good or service that consumers are willing and able to purchase at various prices during a period of time. Thus, demand is a schedule of amounts that will be purchased at various prices.

Demand Curve a graph of a demand schedule, showing the negative relationship between price and quantity demanded during a period of time, all other things remaining the same. Price is on the vertical axis and quantity demanded is on the horizontal axis.

Demand Function mathematical relationship showing how the quantity demanded of a good or service responds to changes in a number of economic factors, such as its own price, the prices of substitutes and complementary goods, income, and advertising.

Demand-Pull Inflation one explanation for inflation. It is inflation that occurs when total planned spending increases faster than total output, that is, when too much money is chasing two few goods. *See also* Cost-Push Inflation.

Demand-Side Economics the economic policy that stresses the demand for goods and services, often by government spending or tax cuts, to stimulate the economy.

Demarketing a shift from urging to discouraging consumption. The campaign to get people to use less gasoline during fuel shortages is a prime example.

Deming Prize a major award given annually to Japanese companies that demonstrated outstandingly high levels of quality. *See also* Canada Awards for Business Excellence; Malcolm Baldrige National Quality Award.

Demise
1. the giving or transference of an estate by bequest, charger, or contract for a period of time or life.
2. the making of a charter or lease for period of years.

Demographics
1. population data by age, sex, education, location, and income level that is helpful in market research for business.
2. an analysis of housing needs, household size, ages, occupations, marital status, and other factors.

Denomination the amount stated on the face of currency, stock, bonds. For example, a bond is usually issued in $1,000 denominations and the value of $1,000 will be inscribed on its face. This term corresponds to face value or par value.

Density
1. the distribution of population over a given area of land. For example, the population density per square mile for the United States is 69 inhabitants.
2. the number of bits that can be recorded on one disk. The greater the density, the more information the disk will hold.
3. the number of anything per whatever unit of size.

Dental Coverage a type of health insurance to pay for dental care, typically including preventive expenses, such as oral examinations, cleanings, and fillings, as well as dental injuries sustained through accidents.

Department of Housing and Urban Development (HUD) the department of the U.S. government (*www.hud.gov*) that handles programs like low-income housing, urban renewal, and urban planning.

Dependent Variable a variable whose value depends upon the values of other variables and constants in some relationship. For example, in the relationship $Y=f(X)$, Y is the dependent variable. For example, market price of stock is a dependent variable influenced by various independent variables, such as earnings per share, debt-equity ratio, and beta. *See also* Independent Variable.

Depletion the physical exhaustion or using up of a natural resource, for example, a depleted coal mine or oil well. Depletion is an expense of the company.

Deposit
1. earnest money, money that the purchaser puts down to indicate her willingness to follow through with the purchase agreement. Deposit or earnest money can be forfeited if the depositor defaults on the terms of the contract.
2. funds placed in an account and credited to the depositor.

Deposition a witness's testimony to a series of written questions or interrogatories, not in open court but in pursuance of a court order. A written word-for-word account is taken in all depositions. They are witnessed and intended to be used in civil or criminal actions. Depositions are given under oath outside the courtroom, often in an attorney's office.

Depreciation
1. the spreading out of the original cost over the estimated life of the fixed assets, such as plant and equipment. Depreciation reduces taxable income. Among the most commonly used depreciation methods are the straight-line depreciation and accelerated depreciation, such as the sum-of-the-years'-digits and double-declining balance methods.
2. the decline in economic potential of limited life assets originating from wear and tear, natural deterioration through interaction of the elements, and technical obsolescence. To some extent, maintenance (lubrication, adjustments, parts replacement, and cleaning) may partially arrest or offset wear and deterioration.
3. decline in value of a currency; also called *cheap* (*weak*) *dollar*. The depreciation of the dollar is its reduction in value pegged to other currencies or gold.

Depreciation of the Dollar a drop in the value of the dollar that is pegged to other currencies or gold; also called *cheap dollar*, *weak dollar*, or *devaluation*. *See also* Appreciation of the Dollar.

Depression a bottom phase of a business cycle in which the economy is operating with substantial unemployment of its resources (such as labor), a depressed rate of business investment and consumer spending, and the loss of the over-all confidence in the economy. An example is the Great Depression of the 1930s. Depression is a much more serious state of economic decline than recession. The economy is at a virtual standstill. *See also* Business Cycle; Recession.

Deregulation removing government regulation on a certain industry or sector of the economy.

Derivative
1. transaction, or contract, whose value depends on, or, as the name implies, derives from the value of underlying assets such as stocks, bonds, mortgages, market indexes, or foreign currencies. One party with exposure to unwanted risk can pass some or all of that risk to a second party. The first party can assume a different risk from the second party, pay the second party to assume

the risk, or, as is often the case, create a combination. The objectives of users of derivatives may vary. A common reason to use derivatives is so that the risk of financial operations can be controlled. Derivatives can be used to manage foreign exchange exposure, especially unfavorable exchange rate movements. Speculators and arbitrageurs can seek profits from general price changes or simultaneous price differences in different markets, respectively. Others use derivatives to hedge their position; that is, to set up two financial assets so that any unfavorable price movement in one asset is offset by favorable price movement in the other asset.

2. a major calculation in calculus representing the slope of the curve.

Derived Demand the demand for a factor of production or product that is derived from the demand for other goods. For example, the demand for lumber is derived from the demand for a house and an industrial product using lumber. The demand for gasoline is derived from the demand for automobile transportation. When the demand for a good is derived, as in the case of intermediate goods and capital goods, considerable information may be obtained from examining the markets for the final goods to which the good in question is ultimately related.

Descriptive Economics economic analysis of facts and data: "the way things are"; also called *positive economics*. It only seeks to explain and describe exiting economic phenomena without involving value judgments. *See also* Normative Economics.

Deseasonalized Data removal of the seasonal pattern in a data series. Deseasonalizing facilitates the comparison of month-to-month changes.

Devaluation a deliberate downward adjustment of a country's currency relative to gold and/or currencies of other nations. The opposite is revaluation.

Deviation the difference between the value of a variable and its mean. *See also* Standard Deviation.

Device any hardware component connected to the computer, such as a mouse, disk drive, or keyboard.

Device Drivers programs allowing input and output devices to communicate with other parts of the computer system.

Devise a gift of real estate by will or last testament. The individual obtaining the property is the devisee while the person giving the property is the devisor.

DDB *see* Double-Declining-Balance Depreciation.

Dialog Box the screen (or box) that pops up to allow a variety of options such as the next step in the use of the software.

Differential a difference in revenues and/or costs caused by an extraordinary event or circumstance.
Securities: amount paid to a dealer or odd-lot trader, for the completion of an odd-lot transaction. An odd-lot transaction is any purchase of shares that numbers fewer than a round lot, 100 shares. Normally the charge is one-eighth of a point

or .125 cents per share, which is either added to the purchase price or subtracted from the sale price.

Personal: an extra amount added to a wage for working either in unusual conditions or nonstandard work hours. Anyone who works under these conditions is entitled to the wage differential. Wage differentials often are the subject of collective bargaining agreements.

Commodities: the premium or discount paid for quality differences in selected commodities.

Differential Cost The additional costs of one alternative over another; also called *incremental cost.*

Differentiation the mathematical process of calculating derivatives of a function.

Diffusion Index index showing the percentage of economic series that experience increases over the time interval being measured. Often, the 50 percent mark is used as a guide. For example, if more than 50 percent of the leading indicators are rising, it might be plausible to predict an upturn in aggregate economic activity. In a more general sense, however, diffusion indexes can be employed to help measure and interpret the breadth and intensity of recessions and recoveries, the state of economic conditions, and the degree of optimism or pessimism on the part of businessmen. *See also* Economic Indicators.

Diffusion Process the manner in which innovations or new products are adopted by consumers and spread through a segment or social unit. Typical progression would include stages of (1) innovation, (2) minor acceptance, (3) early majority, (4) late majority, and (5) laggards.

Digital transmission of data by varying digits, versus analog, which varies the frequency or voltage. Digital transmission has the definition of using either digital signals or analog signals to transmit information in digital format. That means all data or information must be converted into digital representation prior to transmission. For example, an image can be converted into digital file and this digital file will be transmitted by analog signals, which carry this digital representation to the destination. Digital transmission uses repeaters instead of amplifiers for long distance transmission. It is considered the best way for information transmission. *See also* Analog.

Digital Cash cash in electronic form.

Digital Certificate electronic file acting as a container for a public key. Its like your electronic identification.

Digital Identifications digital certificates from certificate authorities (e.g., VeriSign) having an entity's encrypted public key and limited information about the entity (e.g., company name and address, division, department, e-mail address).

Digital Signature signatures attached to messages or documents transmitted electronically for security purposes so as to assure the sender's authenticity and the written communication's integrity. The signature provides verification that the document has not been improperly altered.

Digital Subscriber Lines (DSL) lines that provide the capability of carrying data at speeds of up to 1.5 megabits per second (Mbps) over standard copper telephone wires. DSL also permits users to receive voice and data simultaneously.

Diminishing Returns *see* Law of Diminishing Returns.

Direct Cost costs that can be directly identified and traced to specific objects such as departments, products, or other segments of a business.

Direct Deposit of Payroll an agreement to utilize an automated clearing house to deposit worker paychecks automatically into employee accounts.

Direct Investments
1. investment in a foreign corporation in which the investor has a controlling interest.
2. the purchase of an active ownership interest in a company, whether it is of a controlling or a substantial minority interest. This is contrasted with purchasing shares in a company and taking a nonactive posture.

Direct Labor labor directly involved in making the product (e.g., the wages of assembly workers on an assembly line).

Direct Marketing selling directly to customers, rather than via a mass medium. It includes methods such as direct mail and telemarketing.

Direct Material an integral part of the finished product (e.g., steel used to make an automobile).

Direct Quote the price of a unit of foreign exchange expressed in the home country's currency. For example, the direct quote is $.95 per Euro if the home country is U.S.

Director
1. the head of a governmental agency.
2. a member on the board of directors of a corporation. The board of directors, which is selected by the shareholders, is the chief governing body of the corporation. It has the sole responsibility for the declaration of dividends. It also decides on major areas, including expansion, retraction, change of product, and the selection of corporate officers.

Disability the inability, either in part or in whole, of the insured to perform duties related to her present occupation.

Disability Insurance insurance to provide regular cash income when an insured person is unable to work as a result of a covered illness, injury, or disease. Most disability payments are tax-exempt as long as the individual policyholder pays the premium. The rule is that an adequate disability plan should provide at least

60 percent of the individual's current gross income. This figure is based on the assumption that some of her disability benefits will be tax free. If one owns a business or practice, she may need higher coverage to provide cash flow to cover business overhead.

Discharge

General: remove a financial obligation by making the appropriate payment in full.

Mortgage: a document formally stating that a mortgage debt has been fully satisfied and is usually recorded in a local property deeds registry.

Bankruptcy: an order whereby the bankrupt debtor is relieved of responsibility to pay his or her obligations. Although the debtor is no longer liable for discharge obligations, the bankruptcy will remain in his or her credit report for ten years.

Lien: an order withdrawing a property lien subsequent to satisfaction of the claim through payment or other means.

Disclaimer

Accounting: statement by an auditor not having sufficient evidence to form an audit opinion. For example, some uncertainty, such as a pending lawsuit, exists, which could seriously jeopardize the firm's profitability.

Ownership: giving up an ownership claim to property to which ownership has formerly asserted.

Real Estate: renunciation of a claim to real property. For example, a piece of property becomes dilapidated and the absentee owner disclaims any ownership rights to the property.

Warranty: wording that specifically renounces any responsibility if certain circumstances occur. For example, the warranty on a camera is voided if the camera is submersed in water.

Disclosure

Accounting: all material and relevant information concerning a company's financial position and the results of operations, shown in the footnotes accompanying the statements. Disclosure usually contains information regarding the terms of major borrowing arrangements and the existence of large contingent liabilities, contractual leasing arrangements, employee pension and bonus plans, major proposed asset acquisitions, accounting methods and changes in those methods used in preparing the financial statements, and other significant events including labor strikes, raw material shortages, and pending legislation or lawsuits. The SEC also requires special disclosures detailing any specific and unique developments affecting a company's financial position in Form 8-K. For example, a publicly traded company suffering an extreme disaster directly affecting its financial position should file this form.

New securities: revelation by a company of all the pertinent financial and legal information concerning the company. Such information which is included in the prospectus, is required by the SEC when a firm seeks to make s security or bond public.

Loans: Statement by the lending agency of the full amount of all the associated costs when making a loan. The Truth-In-Lending Act (TILA), as amended in 1970, requires that credit costs be expressed both in dollar amounts and in annual percentage terms based on the unpaid account balance. This act extends to the issuance, liability, and use of consumer credit cards.

Discount

1. the difference between future (or face) value and present value of a payment.
2. a reduction in price given for prompt payment. *See also* Cash Discount; Quantity Discount; Trade Discount.
3. a purchase price for a bond bought below its face value. *See also* Bond Discount.
4. manner in which Treasury bills are sold at less than face value and are redeemed at face value.
5. taking into account all available good or bad news about the company's prospects in evaluating its current security price. It is called discounting the news.
6. reduction in the unit selling price of merchandise due to a large quantity order.
7. *see* Discount Loan.

Discount Broker a stock broker who charges a reduced commission and does not provide investment advice.

Discount Loan a loan in which the whole interest charge is deducted in advance from the face value of a loan. The borrower receives the face value of the loan minus this deduction, which increases the effective interest rate on the loan. Assume an individual borrows $10,000 from the bank at a 10% interest on a discount basis. The effective interest rate is: $1,000/($10,000 - $1,000) = $1,000/$9,000 = 11.11%

Discount Rate

1. the interest rate used to convert future receipts or payments to their present value. The cost of capital (cutoff, hurdle, or minimum required rate) is used as the discount rate under the net present value (NPV) method. *See also* Capitalization Rate. The interest rate charged by the Federal Reserve Bank to its member banks for loans; also called the *rediscount rate*. The federal discount rate is less than the prime rate.

2. A change in the discount rate will have a significant impact on the economy. For example, the following is a summary of the possible effect of cutting the discount rate on the economy. *See also* Prime Rate.

The Effects Of Lowering The Discount Rate
• **The players:** The Federal Reserve is the nation's central bank. It regulates the flow of money through the economy.
• **The action:** The discount rate is what the Federal Reserve charges on short-term loans to member banks. When the Fed cuts the discount rate, it means banks can get cash cheaper and thus charge less on loans.
• **The first effect:** Within a few days, banks are likely to start passing on the discounts by cutting their prime rate, which is what banks charge on loans to their best corporate customers.
• **Impact:** Businesses are more likely to borrow. Second, adjustable consumer loans are tied to the prime, such as credit card rates. These become cheaper, stimulating spending.
• **The second effect:** Within a few weeks, rates on mortgages and consumer loans, such as auto loans decline.
• **The third effect:** The lower interest rates go, the more investors move their cash to stocks, creating new wealth.
• **The goal:** To kick start the economy. Lower interest rates cause businesses to start growing again, laid-off workers get jobs, retailers start selling, and the economy starts to roll again.

Discounted Cash Flow (DCF) Techniques methods that involve discounting the future cash flows generated by a project, product, business, or security. These techniques are used primarily for valuation. Under this method, the asking price (or value of an investment) is the present worth of the future after-tax cash flows from the investment, discounted at the rate of return required by the investor.

Discounting

1. the process of finding the present worth of a future sum of money. *See also* Discounted Cash Flow; Present Value; Time Value of Money.
2. interest deducted in advance from a loan. *See also* Discount Loan.
3. reduction in selling price of a product or service to stimulate buyer interest.

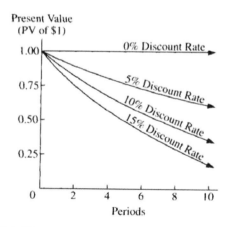

Discretionary Account an account in which the investor gives full or partial written permission to an investment adviser or broker to buy or sell securities at the adviser's discretion. Discretion can be limited to a specific security or group of securities. Investment advisers or brokers having discretionary accounts have complete latitude, unless specifically restricted, to choose the securities as well as their price and timing.

Discretionary (Fixed) Costs those fixed costs that change because of managerial decisions, also called *management (fixed) costs* or *programmed (fixed) costs*. Examples of this type of fixed costs are advertising outlays, training costs, and research and development costs. Management sometimes unjustly reduces these costs below normal levels in order to pad current net income, which may place the future net income of the company at risk.

Discretionary Income any portion of income that is not committed to such essentials as food and rent payments and therefore can be spent at the discretion of an earner.

Diseconomies of Scale the decreases in a firm's long-run average costs as the size of its plant is increased. This may be due to (1) competition among firms in bidding up prices of scarce resources and (2) difficulties of maintaining efficient supervision and coordination. *See also* Economies of Scale.

Disequilibrium a state of imbalance or not being in equilibrium. For example, in a situation where the quantities demanded and supplied of a good at a given price are not equal, there is a tendency for market prices and/or prices to change. Shortages or surpluses so created tend to bring the market to an equilibrium.

Disgorgement returning any ill-gotten gains obtained by a company and/or individuals from violating security rules to investors. In the past, disgorgement funds went back to investors, but civil penalties went to the U.S. Treasury. Under a 2002 change in law, all civil penalties will be return to investors.

Disinflation slowing down of the rate of inflation. This condition usually occurs during a recession, when a lack of consumer demand prohibits retailers from passing on higher prices to consumers.

Disintermediation investing directly in securities as opposed to placing your money with banks that will in turn decide where to invest that money.

Disinvestment
1. withdrawal of the capital invested in a company or a foreign country.
2. selling-off or closing down all or part of a foreign investment (e.g., foreign subsidiaries) for some financial or other reason; also called *divestiture*.
3. the selling of a part of the business that has not been profitable or is no longer serving the best interest of the firm.
4. sale of fixed assets without replacing them.
5. failure to properly maintain property, plant and equipment.**Disk** hard disks or floppies that are used to store information.

Diskette a floppy to be distinguished from hard disks.

Dispersion a statistical measurement of variability of data values. This is measured in terms of standard deviation.

Disposable Income personal income minus personal income tax payments and other government deductions. It is the amount of personal income available for people to spend or save; also called *take-home pay*.

Distressed Property
1. foreclosed real estate or subject property in a bankrupt estate.
2. income property which is making an inadequate return and has a negative capitalization rate.

Dissaving an excess of spending over income. It occurs when one lives beyond one's means. This may be accomplished by drawing on past saving, borrowing, or credit card charges.

Dissident; Dissenting Shareholder a shareholder who objects to a proposed corporate action or position.

Distribution
Marketing: the movement of goods from the manufacturer to the consumer through wholesalers and retailers.
Economics: the allocation of national income throughout the population.
Estate: the distribution of property to the legal heirs by the executor of a properly drawn and executed will.
Securities: selling, over a period of time, of a large block of stock without unduly depressing the market price; also called *professional selling*. A stock is under distribution when volume expands on days when price moves down.
Mutual funds: the payout by mutual funds and closed-end investment companies of realized capital gains on securities contained in the underlying portfolio.
Investments: a return of capital invested, such as dividends, to distribute part of the net income.
Retirement: a redemption from a retirement account.

Distribution Cost any cost incurred to fill an order for a product or service. It includes all money spent on warehousing, delivering, and/or shipping products and services to customers.

Diversifiable Risk that part of the risk of a security associated with such random events such as lawsuits, strikes, winning or losing a major contract, and other events that are unique to a particular firm. This type of risk can be eliminated by proper diversification.

Diversification
1. a corporate strategy in which a firm attempts to build its business in areas outside of its core activities.
2. the spreading of investment money among many investment vehicles so as to reduce risk. Diversification is also offered by the securities of many individual

companies because of the wide range of their activities. Investing in a mutual fund will also accomplish diversification.

3. having different jobs or sources of income to protect against the loss of one.

Diversity conditions in which cost objects place different demands on activities, activities place different demands on resources, or processes place different demands on resources. This situation arises, for example, when there is a difference in mix or volume of products that causes an uneven assignment of costs. Different types of diversity include batch size, customer, market, product mix, distribution channel, and volume.

Diversity Management efforts concerned with developing organizational initiatives that value all people equally, regardless of their differences. One approach to diversity management requires that diverse individuals be assimilated into the workforce by the use of affirmative action programs, so that an employee "melting pot" is achieved.

Divestiture the selling-off of a company's assets or segments (such as divisions and subsidiaries) for economic or other reasons. *See also* Disinvestment.

Dividend

Securities: distribution of earnings paid to stockholders based on the number of shares owned; also called *payout*. The most typical type of dividend is a cash dividend. Dividends may be issued in other forms such as stock, property, and strip (note). Dividends are customarily paid quarterly. The Board of Directors of the company decides on how much dividends should be declared and in what form. The investor must include cash dividends received as taxable income. For example, Company X has 4,000,000 common shares outstanding and declares a $.10 cash dividend per share. Total dividends will be $400,000.

Insurance: cash returned to an insurance policyholder by the insurance company. Insurance dividends are not deemed to be taxable by the IRS as they are considered to be a refund of the premium paid.

Dividend Growth (Discount) Model model that allows an investor a way of determining if the stock is priced correctly for the investor's projected estimate of earnings; also called *Gordon's growth model*. It involves the next expected dividend per share, the expected growth rate in dividends or earnings, and the investor's required return.

Dividend Payout Ratio the dividend payment as a percentage of net earning of a company. It equals dividends per share divided by earnings per share. Generally speaking, newer and smaller companies pay a much lower percentage of earnings in dividends than larger, more mature companies. A company having a relatively large dividend payout ratio may have that much less capital for reinvestment purposes. Utilities commonly have high dividend payout ratios.

Dividend Reinvestment Plan (DRIP)

1. corporate plan that allows their shareholders to invest cash, dividends, or both directly through the company (or its agents) to buy more shares of the compa-

ny's stock. In some cases, the company will not charge or will have a minimal charge for this service. In some cases, the company may even discount the stock price. Most people have not heard abut them for one simple reason— companies can't advertise their DRIPs.

2. a plan offered by a mutual fund to reinvest dividends without a service charge.

Dividend Restrictive Provision a clause in a loan agreement or bond indenture placing a restriction on the amount of dividends a company can pay.

Dividend Yield ratio providing an estimate of the return per share on a common or preferred stock investment based on the market price at the end of the reporting period. The ratio equals dividends per share divided by market price per share. For example, cash dividends are $80,000, market price per share is $10, and 80,000 shares are outstanding. The dividend yield is .10 ($1/$10). Dividend yields of stocks are presented in stock tables in financial newspapers such as the *Wall Street Journal* or *Investor's Business Daily*.

Dividend Yield Ratios	
Boeing	1.48%
General Motors	3.78%
Wells Fargo	2.22%
General Electric	1.87%
Coca-Cola	1.69%
Procter & Gamble	1.79%

Diversionary Pricing a technique intended to deceive the consumer into believing all of a firm's prices are low when in actuality it is only those advertised.

Divorce the legal termination of a marriage. The agreement specifies the settlement rights of the parties. Alimony and/or child support may be involved. Alimony payments are tax deductible to the payor and taxable to the receiver. Child support payments are not tax deductible to the payor.

Documentation, Document

1. anything printed, written, or otherwise noted that is relied on to record or prove something. Examples are wills, brokerage statements, and leases.

2. to substantiate an assertion by providing written or oral evidence to support it. An example are documents filed in a case against the spouse in a divorce action.

3. the thick book that accompanies a computer or software program that often is difficult to read.

Dodge Index a monthly market index that assesses the building industry in terms of the value of new construction projects. The index is prepared by the F.W. Dodge Division of McGraw-Hill.

Dollar Indexes various measures of the value of the dollar, provided by the Federal Reserve Board (FRB), Morgan Guaranty Trust Company of New York, and Federal Reserve Bank of Dallas. They show different movements since they include different countries and are based on different concepts and methodologies. The data are provided in nominal values (market exchange rates) and in real values (purchasing power corrected for inflation). The FRB index is published in a press release and in the monthly Federal Reserve Bulletin, the Morgan index is published in the bimonthly World Financial Markets, and the FR Dallas index is published monthly in Trade-Weighted Value of the Dollar. The FRB and Morgan indexes include 10 and 18 industrial nations respectively, and the FR Dallas index includes all of the 131 U.S trading partners.

Dollar Cost Averaging (DCA) a time diversified investment method in which a constant dollar amount of stock is bought at regularly scheduled dates. It is a constant dollar plan. This approach is especially appropriate for "blue chip" stocks. Because the same dollar amount of stock is invested in each period, less shares are purchased at higher prices and more shares are bought at lower prices. This strategy typically results in a lower average cost per share.

Domain, Domain Name
1. in cyberspace, the part of an address following the @ sign.
2. in a database, the name of a field or attribute.

Donee individual receiving a gift or bequest. A donee receives without first giving a consideration. Person receiving a power, right, or interest.

Donor
Trust: an individual who devises a trust for a donee. A person acting as a grantor.
Gift: making a gift to an educational, community, or philanthropic organization.

Dormant Account an account in which there is no activity for a sustained period of time. When depositors move without notifying the bank or die, leaving the estate uninformed about the account, the account becomes dormant. In many states, dormant accounts are publicly advertised, and if there are no verifiable claims made for the account, the money reverts to the state.

Double-Counting a problem in national accounting that arises since the value of inputs to production is included in the value of output. This problem can be eliminated by totaling only the value of final output.

Double-Declining-Balance Depreciation (DDB) an accelerated depreciation method where a constant percentage factor of twice the straight-line rate is multiplied each year by the declining balance of the asset's book value. The straight-line rate is simply the reciprocal of the useful life in years, multiplied by 100. If the useful life is 5 years, the straight-line rate is $1/5 \times 100 = 20\%$. Therefore, the double declining rate is 40%. To determine the annual depreciation expense, we simply multiply the asset's book value at the beginning of the period by the double declining rate. See also Depreciation.

Double-Digit Inflation a yearly rate of inflation of 10% or higher.

Double-Entry Accounting a method of accounting that recognizes the duality of a transaction such that any a change in one account also causes a change in another account.

Double Taxation taxation of dividends in which (1) the Federal government taxes corporate profits once as corporate income and (2) any part of the remaining profits distributed as dividends to stockholders is taxed again as individual income.

Dow-Jones Industrial Average (DJIA) an average developed by Charles Dow in 1885 to study market trends. It is the average of the closing prices of 30 representative blue-chip stocks, which have been selected by Wall Street Journal editors. The Dow is often viewed as a proxy for the overall market. DJIA was originally composed of 14 companies (12 railroads and 2 industrials), the rails by 1897 were separated into their own Average, and 12 industrial companies of the day were selected for the Industrial Average. The number was increased to 20 in 1916 and to 30 in 1928. The stocks included in this Average have been changed from time to time to keep the list up-to-date or to accommodate a merger. The only original issue still in the Average is General Electric.

Components Of The Dow Jones Industrial Average February 27, 2006	
Ticker Symbol	Name
AA	Alcoa, Inc.
MO	Altria Group
AXP	American Express
PFE	Pfizer
BA	Boeing Co.
CAT	Caterpillar Inc.
DD	Du Pont
KO	Coca-Cola Co.
DIS	Disney (Walt) Co.
AIG	American International Group
HON	Honeywell
XOM	Exxonmobilcorp.
GE	General Electric
GM	General Motors
HWQ	Hewlett-Packard
HD	Home Depot
INTC	Intel

IBM	Intl. Bus. Machine
VZ	Verizon
JNJ	Johnson & Johnson
MCD	McDonalds Corp.
MRK	Merck & Co.
MSFT	Microsoft
MMM	Minn. Mining (3m)
JPM	JP (Morgan Chase)
PG	Procter & Gamble
SBC	SBC Communications
UTX	United Tech Corp.
DIS	Walt Disney
WMT	Wal-Mart Stores

Dow Theory a theory of market analysis based upon the performance of the Dow Jones industrial and transportation stock price averages. The theory says that a bull market is supposed to continue as long as one average continues to make new highs that are "confirmed" by the other. A reversal is signaled when one average does not confirm the other. A bear market is supposed to continue as long as one average makes new lows that are confirmed by the other.

Down Payment a partial payment of the purchase price that is required to be made at the time a purchase agreement is entered into. Normally, down payments are made in cash. The down payment represents only a portion of the total cost. *See also* Earnest Money.

Download transmitting a file or program from a communications network to a personal computer. *See also* Upload.

Downside Risk
1. an investment risk evaluation derived by estimating the total loss that could occur in a worst-case scenario. A variety of factors enter into such an evaluation, including book value and net earnings as well as general market conditions.
2. a company's risk of loss in a downturn in business activity. For example, an auto manufacturer has downside risk in an economic downturn because it cannot slash its fixed costs, which results from the capital-intensive nature of the industry.

Downswings a widespread downward movement in employment and total output.

Downsizing an organizational action that reduces the size of the workforce through extensive layoffs. Often called *rightsizing*, *RIFs* (reductions in force), and *restructuring*, downsizing has both the positive and negative impacts:

- **Positive**–increase in productivity, company earnings, and stock market performance
- **Negative**–high human cost, low morale, and mistrust of management

Downturn a shift in the stock market cycle from increasing to decreasing. The stock market is in a downturn when it goes from a bull to a bear market.

Draft

In general: a written order in which the first party (drawer) instructs a second party (drawee) to pay a third party (payee).

International trade: the instrument normally used in international commerce to effect payment, also called a *bill of exchange*. It is simply an order written by an exporter (seller) requesting an importer (buyer) or its agent to pay a specified amount of money at a specified time. The person or business initiating the draft is known as the maker, drawer, or originator. The party to whom the draft is addressed is the drawee.

Bank draft: drawn by one bank on another.

Clean draft: a draft having no shipping documents attached.

Documentary draft: one to which various shipping documents are attached.

Sight draft: a draft payable upon presentation.

Bill of exchange: draft used in foreign transactions.

Time draft: payable on a specific date or time after presentation or demand.

Drawee individual to whom a bill of exchange or check is directed. For example, in a checking account the bank is the drawee, the person writing the check is the drawer or maker, and the person to whom the check is written is the payee.

DRIP *see* Dividend Reinvestment Plan (DRIP).

DSL *see* Digital Subscriber Lines (DSL).

Du Pont Formula the breakdown of return on investment (ROI) into margin and turnover.

$$ROI = \text{Net Profit Margin} \times \text{Total Asset Turnover}$$

For example, consider the following financial data:

Total assets=$100,000
Net income=18,000
Sales=$200,000

Then,	ROI	= \$18,000/\$100,000=18%
	Margin	= \$18,000/\$200,000 =9%
	Turnover	= \$200,000/\$100,000=2 times
Therefore,	ROI	= 9% x 2 times = 18%

The breakdown provides a lot of insights to financial managers on how to improve profitability of the business and investment strategy. Specifically, it has several advantages over the original formula (i.e., net profit after taxes/total assets) for profit planning. They are:

1. The importance of turnover as a key to overall return on investment is

emphasized in the breakdown. In fact, turnover is just as important as profit margin in enhancing overall return.

2. The importance of sales is explicitly recognized, which is not in the original formula. The breakdown stresses the possibility of trading margin and turnover since they complement each other. Weak margin can be complemented by a strong turnover, and vice versa.

3. It shows how important turnover is as a key to profit making. In effect, these two factors are equally important in overall profit performance.

4. The formula indicates where your weaknesses are: margin or turnover, or both. Owners or managers can take various actions to improve ROI including:
   • Reduce expenses, (for example, improve productivity, automate, or cut down on discretionary expenses) thereby increasing net profit.
   • Reduce assets, (for example, improve inventory control, speed up receivable collections, etc.) without decreasing sales.
   • Increase sales while maintaining profit margin.

Dual Listing

Securities: a listing of a security on more than one stock exchange. An example is a listing of a multinational stock on both a domestic stock exchange and a foreign stock exchange.

Real Estate: a piece of property listed for sale with two real estate brokers.

Dual Pricing Scheme an arrangement or agreement that allows a selling division to record the transfer of goods or services at a market or negotiated price and a buying division to record the transfer at a lower cost-based amount. *See also* Transfer Pricing.

Dual Problem a linear programming (LP) problem, which is one part of associated LP problems called *the primal* and *the dual*. In other words, each maximizing problem in LP has its corresponding problem, called *the dual*, which is a minimizing problem; similarly, each minimizing problem has its corresponding dual, a maximization problem. For example, if the primal is concerned with maximizing the contribution from the three products A, B, and C from the three departments X, Y, and Z, then the dual will be concerned with minimizing the costs associated with the time used in the three departments to produce those three products. An optimal solution to the dual problem provides a shadow price of the time spent in each of the three departments.

Due Diligence a qualitative assessment of management's character and capability. Due diligence evaluation is like "kicking the tires" of the company by conducting plant tours, trade checks, and interviews with competitors, suppliers, customers, and employees. Comprehensive due diligence may also include an examination of the books and records, asset appraisals, reviews of the company's other debt obligations, legal and accounting affairs, internal controls, planned capital expenditures, and other matters that bear on the company's future success and profitability. Due diligence is a legal requirement before public offerings.

Dummy Variable often referred to as a binary variable whose value is either 0 or (.) It is a variable frequently used to quantify qualitative or categorical events. For example, a peace or war situation could be represented by a dummy variable.

Dumping the practice of selling goods or services in foreign markets for less than their worth, meaning prices below the cost of production or market price of the same product in domestic or other markets; also known as *differential pricing* in GATT. Since it is generally viewed as an unfair trading practice, this may subject the company to antidumping tariffs or penalties. It is illegal in the U.S. if the practice harms (or threatens to harm) an industry in the U.S. Article VI of the GATT permits levy of antidumping duties equal to the difference between the price sought in the importing country and the normal value of the product in the exporting country.

Dun & Bradstreet Reports a published source of credit information about companies. The report includes a credit history, any legal proceedings, current debts, and any other useful financial information.

Dunning Letter creditor notices that insistently demand repayment of debts from customers or borrowers.

Durable Goods costly manufactured products expected to last at least three years, including appliances and automobiles. The Census Bureau of the U.S. Commerce Department keeps track of them. The bureau tracks the dollar value of new orders. Separately, it also tracks shipments, unfilled orders, and inventories. Orders for durable goods can help forecast future manufacturing activity, although the overall number needs to be used with care, because it can be strongly influenced by large orders in a particular sector, such as defense spending. For more information, two web sites are helpful: *www.census.gov/ftp/pub/ indicator/www/m3/index.htm* and *biz.yahoo.com/c/terms/durord.html*.

Durable Power Of Attorney A legal device allowing individuals to grant others general or specific powers for managing their finances. It remains in effect even if the person is incapacitated.

Duration an attempt to measure risk in a bond by considering the maturity and the time pattern of cash inflows (i.e., interest payments and principal). It measures a bond's sensitivity to changes in interest rates.

Ee

EAFE *see* Europe, Australia, Far East (EAFE) Index.

Early Withdraw Penalty
1. a charge assessed against a holder of a fixed-term investment, such as certificates of deposit (CDs), if she withdraws the money before maturity. This penalty would be assessed, for instance, if someone who has a six-month certificate of deposit withdraws funds after four months.
2. a penalty for taking a benefit plan or IRA distribution prematurely, such as before age fifty-nine.

Earned Income income from personal services. Earned income generally includes wages, salaries, tips and other employee compensation. Compensation includes items that can be excluded from gross income, such as lodging, or meals furnished for the employer's convenience. Earned income also includes any net earnings from self-employment. Pension and annuity payments are not included.

Earnest Money a deposit in advance of the down payment on a real estate purchase as evidence of good faith.

Earnings money earned as opposed to income received from investments, such as interest income.

Earnings Announcements the company's preliminary results of operations. This includes the most recent quarterly date announced as well as revenue, earnings, and earnings per share (EPS) information for that quarter.

Earnings Forecast projection of earnings or earnings per share (EPS) frequently made by management and independent security analysts. Examples of forecast sources include (1) Lynch, Jones and Ryan's Institutional Brokers Estimate System (IBES), (2) Standard & Poor's Earnings Forecaster, (3) Zacks Investment Research's Icarus Service, and (4) First Call.

Earnings Growth a weighted average of the one-year earnings growth rates of the stocks in the fund. This calculation excludes stocks whose earnings changed from a loss to a gain and stocks whose earnings gains exceeded 999.99%.

Earnings Management both legitimate and less than legitimate efforts to smooth earnings over accounting periods or to achieve a forecasted result. It is the responsibility of a company's audit committee members to identify, by appropriate questioning and their good faith judgment, whether particular earnings management techniques, accounting estimates and other discretionary judgments are legitimate or operate to obscure the true financial position of the company. *See* Managed Earnings.

Earnings Multiple *see* Price-Earnings Ratio.

Earnings Multiplier *see* Price-Earnings Ratio.

Earnings Per Share profit accruing to stockholders for each share held in a simple capital structure, basic earnings per share equals:

$$\frac{\text{Net Income - Preferred Dividends}}{\text{Weighted-Average Common Stock Outstanding}}$$

In a complex capital structure, basic earnings per share and diluted earnings per share are presented. Diluted earnings per share considers the dilutive effect of stock options, warrants, and convertible securities. As such, diluted earnings per share will be less than basic earnings per share. It is generally an indication of the amount of retained earnings that are available for dividends or reinvestment projects.

Earnings Surprises a company's announced net income for the reporting period that is above or below that expected by analysts (i.e., the consensus forecast). Stock price will typically increase if the earnings report is better than anticipated with the opposite effect if the earnings report is less than that expected. In fact, if earnings reported are much lower than that being forecasted by securities' analysts, a drastic falloff in stock price may occur because of the disappointment. An example of a company that closely monitors earnings surprises is First Call (*www.firstcall.com*).

Earn-Out a deferred payment plan, under which an acquiring firm agrees to make a specified initial payment of cash or stock and additional compensation if the acquired company can maintain or increase earnings.

Easy or Loose Money an increase in the amount of money available for business and individual spending as a result of reduction in the interest rate in the economy. Easy money tends to encourage investment spending and promote economic growth, which can be inflationary. *See also* Tight Money.

E-Business the use of electronic platforms—intranets, extranets, and the Internet—to conduct a company's business.

EC *see* European Community. An abbreviation for European Community.

Ecoefficiency a concept that maintains that organizations can produce more useful goods and services while simultaneously reducing negative environmental impacts, resource consumption, and costs.

E-Commerce buying and selling processes supported by electronic means, primarily the Internet.

Econometric Models statistically based models where relationships among economic variables are expressed in mathematical equations, single or simultaneous in nature and then estimated using such techniques as regression methods. The simplest kind of econometric models would be a single equation, expressing some dependent variable as a function of some other set of variables. For example, gross domestic product (GDP) might be expressed as a function of past GDP, construction activity, changes in the unemployment rate, and the level of interest rates. Some models attempt to capture the complexity of the entire economy; they may contain hundreds of equations that must all be estimated simultaneously. The Wharton model is a good example.

Econometrics branch of economics concerned with empirical testing of economic theory using various statistical methods such as regression analysis.

Economic Feasibility Study an evaluation of whether the benefits outweigh the costs of a project over the life of the proposal.

Economic Forecasting forecasting future values of key economic variables such as gross domestic product, inflation, interest rates, and unemployment.

Economic Indicators data, statistics, ratios, or other figures that attempt to size up where the economy seems to be headed and where its been. Each month government agencies, including the Federal Reserve, and several economic institutions publish economic indicators.

Economic Life the length of time an asset is expected to yield economic benefits, such as information systems, computers, equipment, or machinery.

Economic Losses the amount by which the accounting expenses, the opportunity cost of capital, and the risk cost of doing business exceed a firm's sales revenues. This is the opposite of economic profit.

Economic Model statistically based models where relationships among economic variables are expressed in mathematical equations, single or simultaneous in nature, and then estimated using such techniques as regression methods.

Economic Order Quantity (EOQ) The most economic quantity of materials or inventory for a company to purchase at one time. It is the order size that minimizes the sum of carrying and ordering costs. At the EOQ amount, total ordering cost equals total carrying cost. Usually calculated by a mathematical model. See the chart on the next page.

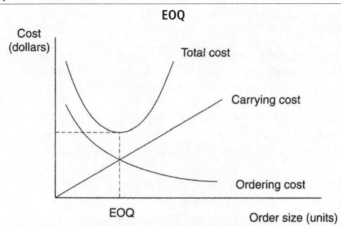

EOQ

Economic Order Quantity (EOQ) Model a mathematical model that determines EOQ. In the original version of the model, demand is assumed to be known and constant throughout the year. Ordering cost is assumed to be a fixed amount per order, and carrying costs are assumed to be constant per unit. EOQ is computed as:

$$EOQ = \sqrt{\frac{2\,(\text{annual demand})\,(\text{ordering cost})}{\text{carrying cost per unit}}}$$

If the carrying cost is expressed as a percentage of average inventory value (say, 12 percent per year to hold inventory), then the denominator value in the EOQ formula would be 12 percent times the price of an item.

Economic Policy strategy concerned with finding solutions to economic problems. While policy makers use economic theory to help them, they must go beyond it as well. They must consider the cultural, social, legal, and political aspects of an issue if they are to formulate a successful policy.

Economic Profits difference between the total revenue and the total opportunity costs.

Economic Resources the factors used in the production of goods. These resources are broken down broadly into two categories: human resources such as labor and management and nonhuman resources such as land, capital, and technology.

Economic Risk the chance of loss due to economic conditions. Economic risks include inflation risk, purchasing power risk, foreign exchange risk, and interest rate risk.

Economic System a particular system of organization for the production, distribution, and consumption of products and services people use to achieve a certain standard of living. All societies and nations do not agree on the optimal way to address these economic issues. For example, the U.S. economy uses a capitalist or free-market system while the former Soviet economy was a socialist or planned economy. Every economic system must answer the following questions: What goods and services should be purchased? How much of these goods and services should be produced? How should these goods be produced? For whom should these goods be produced?

Economic Union a group of countries committed to (1) removing all barriers to the free flow of goods, services, and factors of production between each other, (2) the adoption of a common currency, (3) the harmonization of tax rates, and (4) the pursuit of a common external trade policy.

Economic Value Added (EVA) variation of residual income (RI) that defines the variable in specific ways. EVA = After-tax Income – (Cost of Capital x Capital Invested). The major difference between RI and EVA is that RI uses the market value or book value of assets for the capital invested in the division or firm while EVA uses the market value of total equity and interest-bearing debt.

Economics the science focusing on the study of how scarce resources should be allocated in an efficient manner for the production and distribution of products and services to satisfy demand. Economics is generally classified into microeconomics and macroeconomics. Microeconomics is the study of the individual markets (for oil, agriculture, corn, and so on) that operate within the broad national economy, while macroeconomics is the study of the national economy as a whole, dealing with the "big picture," and not details.

Economies of Scale a situation in which the average cost of production declines as plant size and output is expanded. Some of the reasons are (1) increased specialization and division of labor, (2) better use and specialization of labor, and (3) use of more efficient or high-tech machinery and equipment.

Economist, The a monthly international business magazine that covers and comments on international business and economics.

Economy

1. efficiency, thrift, and the avoidance of waste by prudent planning and use of resources.
2. a particular system of organization for the production, distribution, and consumption of all things human beings use to achieve a certain standard of living, such as the U.S. or the Soviet economy.

Effective Interest Rate (Effective Annual Yield)

1. the yield on debt as calculated from the purchase price. A more accurate measure of the return on a bond investment than the simple coupon payment. Computed using both the capital gain from price appreciation and the bond's yield. *See also* Yield to Maturity.
2. the effective annual yield, better known as the annual percentage rate (APR). Different types of investments use different compounding periods. For example, most bonds pay interest semiannually; banks generally pay interest quarterly. If a financial manager wishes to compare investments with different compounding periods, he or she needs to put them on a common basis.

3. annual percentage rate (APR), which is a measure of the cost of credit, is expressed as a yearly rate. It includes interest as well as other financial charges such as loan origination and certain closing fees. The lender is required to tell you the APR. It provides you with a good basis for comparing the cost of loans, including mortgage plans.

Effective Rate of Return *see* Effective Interest Rate (Effective Annual Yield).

Effective Tax Rate the average tax rate equal to the tax divided by taxable income. If the tax is $20,000 on taxable income of $60,00, the average tax rate is 33.33% ($20,000/$60,000).

Effectiveness the extent to which actual performance compares with targeted performance. For example, if a company has established a target sales plan of 10,000 units at the beginning of the year and the company's salespeople only sold 8,000 units during the year, the sales people are appropriately considered "ineffective," as opposed to "inefficient." *See also* Efficiency.

Efficiency the cost of inputs for each unit of output produced. For example, the assembly department spent 2,320 hours of direct labor in order to produce 2,000 actual units of output, while the budget allows only 2,000 direct labor hours for that level of output. Then the department was clearly inefficient (or wasteful) in the use of labor since it spent 320 hours more than allowed.

Efficient Market
1. a market that is analyzed systematically and everyone has lots of information available about it.
2. a controversial theory that a stock's price is the same as its investment value. In an efficient market, all data are fully and immediately reflected in the stock price. Price changes are as likely to be positive as negative. Thus, holders of this theory argue that it is useless to try to find undervalued stocks or to predict market movements. You cannot beat the market.

Efficient Portfolio the central theme of Markowitz's portfolio theory. Efficient portfolio theory states that rational investors behave in a way reflecting their aversion to taking increased risk without being compensated by an adequate increase in expected return. Also, for any given expected return, most investors will prefer a lower risk and, for any given level of risk, prefer a higher return to a lower return.

Elastic Demand exists when a relatively small change in a product's price results in a more than proportional change in quantity demanded.

Elastic Coefficient the ratio of percentage changes in demand due to percentage changes in factors such as price, advertising, and income.

Elasticity of Demand a measure of how sensitive quantity demanded is to the change in a factor in the demand function. The principal factors involved with demand elasticity are:
1. The price of the good (in the case of price elasticity).

2. The price of a substitute-product (in the case of cross elasticity).

3. Income (in the case of income elasticity).

4. Advertising (in the case of advertising elasticity).

Example: Firms need to be aware of the elasticity of their own demand curves when they set product prices. For example, a profit maximizing firm would never choose to lower its price in the inelastic range of its demand curve--such a price decrease would only decrease total revenue (see the above chart) and at the same time increase costs, since output would be rising. The result would be a drastic decrease in profits. In fact, when costs are rising and the product is inelastic, the firm would have no difficulty passing on the increases by raising the price to the customer. On the other hand, when there are many substitutes and demand is quite elastic, increasing prices may lead to a reduction in total revenue rather than an increase. The result may be lower profits rather than higher profits. Similarly, managers are sometimes surprised by a lack of success of price reductions, this merely being a reflection of the fact that demand is relatively inelastic. In such a case, they may have to rely on other marketing efforts such as advertising and sales promotion in an effort to increase their market share. Various elasticity measures will allow marketing managers to see how effective each of the demand determinants (i.e., advertising, price change, and external factors) is going to be. In this way, marketing resources may be utilized more profitably and efficiently.

Electronic Commerce (EC) the buying and selling of goods and services on the Internet, especially the World Wide Web. In practice, this term and a new term, *e-business*, are often used interchangeably. For online retail selling, the term *e-tailing* is sometimes used. It is also called *e-commerce* for short, *on-line commerce, Internet commerce, e-business,* or *cyberspace commerce.* E-commerce can be divided into (1) E-tailing or "virtual storefronts" on web sites with online catalogs, sometimes gathered into a "virtual mall." It is the gathering and use of demographic data through web contacts. (2) Electronic Data Interchange (EDI), the business-to-business exchange of data. (3) E-mail and fax and their use as media for reaching prospects and established customers (for example, with newsletters). (4) Business-to-business buying and selling. (5) The security of business transactions.

Electronic Data Gathering, Analysis, and Retrieval (EDGAR) service that the Securities & Exchange Commission uses to transmit company documents to investors. Those documents, which are available via Smart Edgar service, include 10-Qs (quarterly reports), 8-Ks (significant developments such as the sale of a company unit) and 13-Ds (disclosures by parties who own 5% or more of a company's shares).

Electronic Data Interchange (EDI) standardized electronic exchange of documents among computers of different business entities. Business documents exchanged include sales invoices, purchase orders, quotes, credit memos for damaged or returned goods, and shipping reports. EDI transactions are usually between a buying company and its supplier.

Electronic Filing the ability to file your taxes electronically online.

Electronic Fund Transfer (EFT) mechanism facilitating the making of electronic payments between parties such as remittance advices among banks and direct deposits of salaries into the bank accounts of workers.

Electronic Fund Transfer, Electronic Banking a cashless transaction technique where the price of a purchase is automatically deducted from the buyer's account and credited to the seller's.

Electronic Transfer Funds (ETFs) equity indexes that were introduced in 1993 as a way for investors to buy into a liquid, transparent, and diverse basket of stocks while paying less than for a mutual fund. The shares are priced in real time, tracking the value of their underlying index, and can be held as long-term investments, flipped for a quick profit, or sold short to hedge equity risk.

11th District Index a cost of funds index that most adjustable rate mortgages (ARMs) written in California in recent years are tied to. Computed by the Federal Home Loan Bank of San Francisco, it reflects the cost of deposits at savings and loans in California, Arizona and Nevada.

Eligibility Requirements
Insurance: essential requirements needed to qualify for certain types of insurance. For example, only nonsmokers can qualify for reduced life insurance premiums.
Pensions: essential requirements needed to receive pension benefits. For example, 20 years of employment service may be necessary for one to begin receiving pension benefits.

Elimination Period or grace period. A period that must elapse before an insured becomes eligible for coverage under an insurance policy.

E-Marketing the marketing side of ecommerce — company efforts to communicate about, promote, and sell products and services over the Internet.

Emerging Markets the stock markets of countries whose markets or economies tend to grow at considerably faster rates over the coming years than the economies of industrial nations. Emerging markets attract foreign investors because their potential for rapid economic growth is better than in more mature markets. However, the risks, both economic and political, are high. Note: One way to get exposure to emerging markets is through unit investment trusts or regional funds that specialize in this type of investment.

Eminent Domain governmental right to take private property for public use, as long as fair compensation is paid to the owner. Land for schools, parks, roads, public parking, highways, and other social and public purposes is obtained in this manner. A condemnation proceeding is required when government exercises this right.

Employee Assistance and Wellness Programs (EAPS) programs designed to offer employees a variety of services that will help them to become mentally and physically healthy, which in turn reduces absenteeism and productivity losses due to accidents.

Employee Benefits the cost of all benefits paid to employees, which can include medical and life insurance, pensions, and 401(k) savings plans.

Employee Contract a legal agreement between the employer and employee specifying the particulars of the arrangement, such as employment terms and compensation. The contract affords the employee protection in the relationship.

Employee Empowerment placing the authority to make critical decisions with those closest to the problem, for example, those in the work area directly affected. *See also* Decentralization.

Employee Retirement Income Security Act (ERISA) Federal legislation ensuring that private retirement plans are fair and secure. This law was passed in part to improve the chances that employees who are eligible for a pension actually receive those benefits. It also permits uncovered employees to establish their own individual tax-sheltered retirement plans.

Employee Stock Ownership Plan (ESOP) a stock bonus plan that encourages employees to invest in the company's stock, usually at a discount from the current market price through payroll deductions. Many plans defer delivering the stock to the employee until he or she leaves the plan or retires. This allows for the deferral of tax on the stock accumulation until a later year when the employee may be in a lower tax bracket. Because most of the funds are concentrated in the stock of one company, the plan does not provide any safety through diversification.

Employee Turnover the percentage of employees that leave a company, usually measured on an annual basis. A turnover of 20 percent means that 20 percent of a company's employees left during the year. The U.S. Department of Labor suggests the following formula:

$$\frac{\text{Number of employee separations during the month}}{\text{(Total number of employees at midmonth)}} \times 100$$

where separations are people who left the company.

Employment Cost Index (ECI) the most comprehensive and refined measure of underlying trends in employee compensation as a cost of production. Measures the cost of labor and includes changes in wages and salaries and employer costs for employee benefits. ECI tracks wages and bonuses, sick and vacation pay plus benefits such as insurance, pension and Social Security and unemployment taxes from a survey of 18,300 occupations at 4,500 sample establishments in private industry and 4,200 occupations within about 800 state and local governments. This index can be obtained free from the Bureau of Labor Statistics' Internet site (*www.stats.bls.gov*). *See also* Inflation.

Encryption conversion of data into a form, called a *cipher*, that cannot be easily intercepted by unauthorized people. *See also* Decryption.

Encumbrance
1. any claim, right, lien, estate, or liability that limits a clear title to property. Encumbrances include easements, mortgages, and judgment liens.
2. debt secured by a lien on assets.

Endorsement

1. a statement attached to an insurance policy (such as property and casualty insurance) changing the terms of the policy.
2. a written signature appearing on the back of a check or other financial instrument assigning and transferring property to another. To be effective, an endorsement must be for the entire instrument rather than just a portion.

Conditional endorsement: an endorsement subject to the fulfillment of a special condition to be effective. For example, only upon the completion of contractually stated terms will the endorsement be effective.

Financial instrument: a signature making checks and other financial documents negotiable and transferable to a third party. The endorser's signature guarantees ownership of the instrument and has the rights to assign it to another party.

Full endorsement: order by the endorser for money to be paid to some named individual only.

Endorsement in Blank; Blank Endorsement.

The simple affixing of an endorser's signature on the back of note or bill without mentioning the name of any person for whom the endorsement is made. An endorsement in blank specifies no individual endorsee and may consist of a simple signature.

Endowment

1. generally the permanent gift of money or property to a specified institution for a particular purpose, for example, a gift of money to a university for the specific purpose of constructing a library facility. Often an endowment may be a gift of money to be used as an investment vehicle to derive income for funding a particular activity. For example, a research foundation may be funded in whole or in part from the income of an endowment.
2. an insurance policy that either pays a specified sum if the policy holder dies within a certain period or pays a specified sum to the holder if the policy holder survives the endowment period.

Energy Efficiency Ratio (EER)

the ratio of energy output of an appliance to its energy input.

Engel's Law

the law, advanced by Ernst Engel, stating that (1) the higher the family money income, the less the percentage of that income spent on food and more on education, automobiles, and on saving, and (2) the proportion of a nation's income spent on food is a good index of its welfare–that is, the lower the proportion, the higher the welfare of the nation.

Enrolled Agent (EA)

an individual who has completed a course of study and passed a rigorous exam by the IRS.

Enterprise Resource Planning (ERP)

latest phase in the development of computerized systems for managing organizational resources. ERP is intended to integrate enterprise-wide information systems. ERP connects all organizational operations (personnel, the financial accounting system, production, marketing, distribution, etc.) and also connects the organization with its suppliers and customers. ERP systems grew out of material requirements planning (MRP) systems which have been used for more than 20 years. ERP systems update MRP systems with better integration, relational databases, and graphical user interfaces (GUI). Features now encompass supporting accounting and finance, human resources, and various e-commerce applications including supply chain management (SCM) and customer relationship management (CRM).

Enterprise Resource Planning (ERP) Software system that grew out of material requirements planning (MRP) systems, which have been used for more than 20 years. MRP systems computerized inventory control and production planning. Key features included an ability to prepare a master production schedule, a bill of materials, and generate purchase orders. ERP systems update MRP systems with better integration, relational databases, and graphical user interfaces. Features now encompass supporting accounting and finance, human resources, and various e-commerce applications including supply chain management (SCM) and customer relationship management (CRM).

Enterprise Risk Management (ERM) a broad term for risk management system that:
1. Makes each area manager responsible for documenting and evaluating financial controls in his or her own area. People closest to each business unit manage the data, which improves accuracy and completeness.
2. Identifies areas with inadequate control measures so action plans can be initiated to resolve problems.
3. Tracks the progress of outstanding action plans, describes who is responsible for those actions, and sets the expected time for resolution.
4. Protects against fraud with systematic data management that ensures multiple reviews and verification.
5. Raises the level and precision of reporting to management.
6. Puts "localized knowledge" to work. Area managers become empowered to understand the impact of their roles on corporate results.
See also Risk Management.

Enterprise Zone a zone designated by a municipality to give benefits to businesses. The benefits may include tax credit, low financing, and the like to encourage business in depressed areas.

Entitlement Spending portion of the budget that is fixed and hence difficult to cut as a result of prior program commitments such as unemployment insurance, student loans, and Social Security, as contrasted with discretionary spending.

Entrepreneur a visionary self-starter who loves the adventure of a new enterprise. Entrepreneurship creates the new jobs. These jobs are created by an absolutely unique partnership—the marriage of money and work. The money comes from a unique system of venture-capital financing. The work comes from the driving force of the entrepreneur.

Entrepreneur Magazine a business magazine targeting small business owners.

Environmental Analysis part of strategic management, concerned with examining those forces that are not under the direct control of the firm or its industry but that can strongly influence the industry and firms within the industry.

Environmental Costs costs that are incurred because poor environmental quality exists or may exist. Environmental costs can be classified in four categories: prevention costs, detection costs, internal failure costs, and external failure costs.

Environmental Impact Statement a report that contains information regarding the effect of a proposed project on the environment.

Environmental Protection Agency (EPA) the agency that assures that a company prepares, if necessary, an environmental impact statement and decides whether it is acceptable for the activity to proceed.

Equal Credit Opportunity Act (ECOA) a federal law making it illegal to discriminate when giving credit based on such factors as race, religion, marital status, and age. A lender must respond to credit applications within 30 days. If the application is denied, reasons must be given. The Federal Trade Commission is responsible for enforcing the provisions of the act.

Equilibrium a state within an economy where no pressures are forcing changes in supply or demand. Equilibrium in a competitive market is determined by the intersection of the market demand and supply curves. Equilibrium price is the price of a commodity (good and service) toward which a competitive market will move and, once there, at which it will remain. It is the price at which the market "clears"; that is, the price determined by the intersection of the market forces of demand and supply. Equilibrium quantity is the quantity that corresponds to the equilibrium price. It is the output level at which the market "clears."

Equilibrium Price

1. the price of a commodity (good and service) toward which a competitive market will move and, once there, at which it will remain. It is the price at which the market "clears"; that is, the price determined by the intersection of the market forces of demand and supply.

2. the price that maximizes a firm's profit.

Equilibrium Quantity the quantity that corresponds to the equilibrium price. It is the output level at which the market "clears."

Equipment Trust Certificate a type of debt security used to pay for new equipment. Title to the equipment is held by a trustee until the notes are paid off. An equipment trust certificate is usually secured by a first lien of the equipment.

Equity

1. assets minus liabilities; also called *net worth*. In a sole proprietorship, it the owner's equity. In a corporation, it is stockholders' equity.

2. any right to assets; property rights; a liability. An equity holder may be a creditor, stockholder, or proprietor.

3. in real estate, the portion of an asset owned by an individual, that is, the market value of the property less any amount owed on the property.

Equity Buildup the increase of one's equity in real estate resulting from a reduction in the mortgage loan balance and appreciation in the property's price.

Equity Funds A mutual fund that invests in the equity (stock) market *See also* Mutual Funds.

Equity Spread calculation of equity value creation by multiplying beginning equity capital by the difference between the return on equity (net income/equity) and the percentage cost of equity.

Equity Transfer Funds (ETFs) equity indexes that were introduced in 1993 as a way for investors to buy into a liquid, transparent, and diverse basket of stocks while paying less than for a mutual fund. The shares are priced in real time, tracking the value of their underlying index, and can be held as long-term investments, flipped for a quick profit, or sold short to hedge equity risk.

Equivalent Before-Tax Yield *see* Equivalent Taxable Yield.

Equivalent Bond Yield comparison of yields on bonds with coupons and discount yields. For example, if a 10%, 180-day T-bill with a face value of $10,000 cost $9,500, the equivalent bond yield is 10.67%, calculated as follows:

$$\frac{\$500}{\$9,500} \times \frac{365}{180} = 10.67\%$$

Equivalent Taxable Yield what the return on a nontaxable security would be if it were taxable at an individual's tax rate. To compute the equivalent taxable yield divide the interest rate by the net of tax rate (1 – the tax rate). For example, assume a municipal bond that pays an interest rate of 7%. If one's tax rate is 28%, the equivalent rate on a taxable instrument is

$$\frac{7\%}{1-.28} = 9.7\%$$

Ergonomics the science of designing and modifying machines to better suit people's health and comfort.

Escheat the right of the state to take property when no one is legally qualified to inherit or make claim to the property of a deceased person.

Escrow the arrangement in which a buyer puts a deed and/or money into the care of a neutral third party (an escrow agent) to hold until certain conditions are fulfilled. After those conditions are met, the escrow agent releases the deed and/or money to the seller. The escrow is designed to benefit both parties involved. Escrow periods can be for any amount of time agreed to by the parties who are buying and selling property. For example, a buyer of a home may insist that the seller place funds into an escrow account for unexpected repairs when the buyer actually moves into the home.

E-Selling utilizing e-mail to generate leads.

ESOP *see* Employee Stock Ownership Plan.

Estate the real and personal assets of an individual at the time of death. The distribution of the assets to the heirs is based on the will. If there is no will, the distribution is in accordance with a court order. It is a liquidation process. Court-supervised probate achieves the following purposes: determines ownership of property, ascertains who is to received the benefits, assures the property transfer of property, and provides for the payment of debts and taxes. The executor of a will is the individual selected by the decedent during his or her lifetime to fulfill the terms of the will. Some functions of the executer are to manage the property, collect estate assets, pay creditors, and distribute the remaining property. In general, expenses applicable to settle a decedent's estate reduce the principal. Expenses to operate, preserve, and manage income-producing property are charged against income.

Estate Planning deriving the most favorable tax effect for wealth that has been accumulated. This is the financial strategy through which you provide for others in case something happens to you and then the eventual distribution of your assets to these beneficiaries.

Estate Taxes taxes charged by the federal government or state on a deceased person's net worth that will be passed on to his or her heirs. The estate is a separate taxable entity and is reported on IRS Form 1041. For example, if someone dies leaving an estate of greater than $600,000 to a non-spouse, under current law there is a federal estate tax.

Estimated Tax quarterly payments for the estimated liability on taxable income that is not being withheld.

Estoppel bar preventing one from making an allegation or a denial that contradicts what one has previously stated as the truth.

ETFs *see* Equity Transfer Funds (ETFs).

Ethernet
1. the design, introduced and named by Xerox, for the contention data communications protocol.
2. a popular local area network (LAN).

Ethics standards of professional conduct and business practices adhered to by professionals in order to enhance their profession and maximize idealism, justice, and fairness when dealing with the public, clients, and other members of their profession. Ethics in business is a big current issue.

Ethnocentric Behavior behavior that is based on the belief in the superiority of one's own ethnic group or culture; often shows disregard or contempt for the culture of other countries.

Ethnocentric Staffing a staffing approach within the multinational company in which all key management positions are filled by parent-country nationals.

eToken a car key-sized authentication token that plugs into a computer's Universal Serial Bus (USB) port, a standard feature on virtually all PCs and laptops manufactured since 1997.

Euro new currency that is intended to unite 17 European economies. The symbol is €.

Eurobond a bond underwritten by a multinational syndicate of banks and placed outside of the countries of the issuer and of the currency denomination. The issue thus escapes national restrictions.

Eurocurrency a dollar or other freely convertible currency outside the country of the currency in which funds are denominated. A U.S. dollar-denominated loan, deposit, and bond in Europe is called a Eurodollar. There are Eurosterling (British pounds deposited in banks outside the U.K.), Euromarks (Deutschemarks deposited outside Germany), and Euroyen (Japanese yen deposited outside Japan).

Eurodollar a dollar-denominated bank deposit held in a bank outside the U.S. In general, these are time deposits ranging from a few days up to one year. Eurodollars are basically an international currency.

Europe, Australia, and Far East (EAFE) Index compiled by Morgan Stanley Capital International (MSCI), the Morgan Stanley Europe, Asia, and Far East Index is a value-weighted index of the equity performance of major foreign markets. The EAFE index (it is pronounced EE-feh.) is, in effect, a non-American world index of over 1,000 stocks. It is considered the key "rest-of-the-world" index for U.S. investors, much as the Dow Jones Industrial Average is for the American market. The index is used as a guide to see how U.S. shares fare against other markets around the globe. It also serves as a performance benchmark for international mutual funds that hold non-U.S. assets. Morgan Stanley also compiles indexes for most of the world's major stock markets as well as for many smaller, so-called emerging markets. In addition, there are Morgan Stanley indexes for each continent and the entire globe. The index is quoted two ways: one in local currencies and a second in the U.S. dollar.

European Terms foreign exchange quotations for the U.S. dollars, expressed as the number of non-U.S. currency units per U.S. dollar. For example, 0.95 Euro/$.

European Union (EU) a formal arrangement linking some, but not all, of the currencies of the EU. The common currency is called the Euro.

Eviction the act of removing, dispossessing or expulsion of an individual from a premises by force or law.

Excise Tax tax levied on specific products or services (such as alcohol, tobacco, gas, guns, and airline tickets) for specific purposes. For example, an excise tax on gasoline might be used to fund road construction and repair. Excise taxes are levied at all levels of government, primarily federal and state. They are normally a percentage of the purchase price. A tax on certain consumer items.

Exclusion

Income tax: portions of income that are excluded from taxation because of specific exemptions. For example, an IRA contribution would be excluded from total taxable income.

Insurance: a provision in a policy that denies or restricts coverage; those specified items that are not included in the insurance policy.

Gift tax: the amount a donor may transfer to another without tax consequences from the IRS.

Exclusive Agency an exclusive grant of authority given to an agent or broker to sell within a specified market or area. If a sale is made by any other broker during the contract period, the broker holding the exclusive agency is entitled to all commissions in addition to the commissions payable to the broker effecting the transaction.

Exclusive Right to Sell an agreement with a real estate agent that pays a commission to the agent even if the property is sold to a buyer found by the owner.

Executive Compensation a variety of pay packages to provide incentives for performance of the executives of a company, including bonuses, deferred compensation, and stock options.

Executive Information System (EIS) provides information on how the company is currently performing in its operating and financial activities. The EIS provides detailed information as needed to bring management up-to-date in executive decision making.

Executive Opinions the subjective views of executives or experts from sales, production, finance, purchasing, and administration that are averaged to generate a forecast about future sales. Usually this method is used in conjunction with some quantitative method such as trend extrapolation. The management team modifies the resulting forecast based on their expectations.

Excel Software popular spreadsheet software by Microsoft.

Excess Capacity the overproduction by a firm or industry of a good or service, causing some of the facilities to remain idle (unused). The possible causes for excess (over) capacity include too many suppliers, overinvestment in plant and equipment, less than expected demand, and inability to sell overseas. *See also* Idle Time.

Executor/Executrix a male (or female) person given the job of settling the estate.

Exempt Employee an employee who is exempt from receiving overtime pay if he or she works more than the standard workweek.

Exemption Organization an organization that is exempt from Federal income taxes. An example is a not-for-profit corporation organized for religious, charitable, scientific, literary, educational, or certain other purposes.

Exemption a deduction allowed in computing taxable income. There are basically two types: personal exemptions and dependency exemptions. There are five categories of exemptions, including personal and dependency types: (1) exemption for the taxpayer, (2) exemption for the taxpayer who is age 65 or older, (3) exemption for the taxpayer who is blind, (4) exemption for the taxpayer's spouse, and (5) exemption for dependent children and other dependents where more than one-half of the dependent's support is provided.

Exception Reports periodic or ad hoc reports that red flag facts or numbers that deviate from preset standards or budgets. *See also* Redflag.

Exchange Fee a fee charged if an investment is shifted from one mutual fund to another within the same company.

Exchange, 1031 transfers of assets or property from one taxpayer to another that are specifically exempted from federal income tax consequences; also called a *like-kind exchange*. Real Estate held for these purposes are called *like-kind/1031 properties*. Examples are exchanges of property or assets to certain corporate entities in which ownership of transferred assets are still maintained; a controlled corporation (Section 351) or like-kind exchanges under Section 1031. In the year of exchange, there is no recognized gain or loss. However, there is an adjustment to basis of the assets received in the transfer, in effect deferring the gain upon future disposition.

Exchange
1. a reciprocal transfer of goods or services from one entity to another.
2. a market for securities or commodities, such as the New York Stock Exchange (NYSE) or the Chicago Mercantile Exchange.
3. exchange rate.

Ex-Dividend a term used to indicate that a stock is selling without a recently declared dividend. The ex-dividend date is four business days prior to the date of record, according to rules applicable to NYSE-listed companies, and are observed generally by other exchanges. *See also* Date Of Record.

Ex-Rights a term used to indicate that a stock is selling without a recently declared stock right. As with dividends, the ex-right date is generally four business days prior to the date of record.

Exchange-Traded Funds (ETFs) index portfolios that you buy or sell just like stocks. The best of them are super-cheap—iShares S&P 500 Index (IVV) costs 0.09% a year, half the price of the Vanguard 500—and they can be traded instantly, sold short, or bought on margin. And ETFs track an astonishing variety of indexes, from biotech to Brazilian stocks.

Index fund	Expense ratio	Typical commission
Vanguard 500 index	0.18%	None
iShares S&P 500 index	0.09%	$4 to $30 per trade*

*The commission on an automatic investment plan is $4; the top base rate for one national discount brokerage is $30.

Existing-Home Sales sales of single-family homes that were owned by someone other than their builders, an economic statistic gathered by the National Association of Realtors. Existing homes account for about 80% of all U.S. home sales. Existing-home sales provide a quick check on how healthy the U.S. residential real-estate market is. If sales are high, then the market is considered healthy, with many people able to purchase their first homes or trade up to larger ones. That is good news for homeowners wishing to sell. Falling home sales may indicate a saturated or overpriced housing market, sometimes due to higher interest rates or to generally bleak economic conditions that make people wary of taking on a new mortgage. Falling sales can be bad news for home sellers but good news for would-be buyers with both money and fortitude.

Expected Value weighted average using the probabilities as weights. For decisions involving uncertainty, the concept of expected value provides a rational means for selecting the best course of action.

Expenditure an actual expense or amount paid to satisfy an obligation.

Expense
1. the cost of an item or service. In business, an expense is the cost of goods sold or services rendered.
2. the result of using up a resource, depreciating a resource, or incurring a liability. For example, a contractual obligation for the purpose of deriving revenue in the current period.

Expense Account an allowance given to executives and salespeople for travel and entertainment.

Expert Systems computer software involving stored reasoning schemes and containing the knowledge of experts in an area. This is the area of Artificial Intelligence (AI) that has received great attention from business decision makers. There are recent advances in this area of software systems that are designed to mimic the way human experts make decisions. They represent an attempt to capture in computer program software the reasoning and decision making processes of human experts, providing computerized consultants. In effect, the expert system evaluates and solves problems requiring human imagination and intelligence that involve known and unknown information. The components of the systems include a knowledge base, inference engine, user interface, and knowledge acquisition facility.

Expertise the skill and knowledge, primarily gained from experience, whose input into a process results in performance that is far above the norm.

Exponential Distribution probability distribution used to describe the pattern or service times for some waiting lines.

Exponential Smoothing a mathematical, statistical methodology of forecasting that assumes future price action is a weighted average of past periods; a mathematical series in which greater weight is given to more recent price action. It uses a weighted average of past data as the basis for a forecast. The procedure gives heaviest weight to more recent information and smaller weights to observations in the more distant past. The reason for this is that the future is more dependent upon the recent past than on the distant past.

Export-Import Bank (EXIMBANK) the U.S. agency charged with providing the backbone support for American exports through credit risk protection and funding programs; also called as *EX-IM bank* for short throughout the world. The programs provided through the Export-import Bank of the United States make international factoring more feasible because they offer credit assurance alternatives that promise funding and sources the security they need to agree to a deal.

Extensible Business Reporting Language (XBRL) formerly code named XFRML, a freely available electronic language for financial reporting. It is an XML-based framework that provides the financial community a standards-based method to prepare, publish in a variety of formats, reliably extract, and automatically exchange financial statements of publicly held companies and the information they contain.

Extension
1. suffixes for computer files that indicate the type of file it is. Examples are bat, com, exe, and doc.
2. an allowed delay to file your IRS tax return.

Extensive Advertising a shotgun advertising technique with the goal of reaching a large number of consumers but with a low frequency of repetition; wide but not deep.

External Failure Costs category of quality costs incurred because products fail to conform to requirements after being sold to customers. They include warranty costs, returns, and lost sales. *See also* Failure Costs.

Extortion The illegal collection of money by a public official usually by coercion or threats.

Extranet private network that uses the Internet protocols and the public telecommunication system to securely share part of a business's information or operations with suppliers, vendors, partners, customers, or other businesses. An extranet can be viewed as part of a company's intranet that is extended to users outside the company.

Extrapolation a projection of an unknown variable outside or beyond the range of a series of known values. Techniques for extrapolation include procedures ranging from simple coin tossing to complicated mathematical techniques. They are generally mechanical and are not closely integrated with relevant economic and statistical data.

Ff

5W2H Approach (5 Whys, 2 Hows) asking various questions about the current process and how it can be improved. 5W2H refers to "why? when? who? where? what? how to do? and how not to do?"

F Distribution or Ratio a statistical test between the variances or standard deviations of two distributions to see how similar they are or not. F-TEST ratio of two mean squares (variances) often can be used to test the significance of some item of interest. For example, in regression, the ratio of the mean square due to the regression to the mean square due to error can be used to test the overall significance of the regression model. By looking up F-tables, the degree of significance of the computed F-value can be determined.

F Key (Function Key) a key on a computer keyboard that triggers commands.

F-Test *see* F Distribution or Ratio.

Face Amount *see* Face Value.

Face Value
1. nominal (par) amount of a debt obligation (e.g., bond, mortgage, note) or equity security as stated on the instrument or certificate. It excludes interest and dividends. Bonds are typically in denominations of $1,000. State and city municipal bonds are usually stated in $5,000 face values.
2. in insurance, the amount that is paid to a beneficiary when an insured person dies; the amount the person was insured for.

Factoring the outright sale of a firm's accounts receivable to another party (the factor) without recourse, which means the factor must bear the risk of collection. Some banks and commercial finance companies factor (buy) accounts receivable. The purchase is made at a discount from the account's value. Customers either remit directly to the factor (notification basis) or indirectly through the seller (non-notification basis).

Factoring Procedure

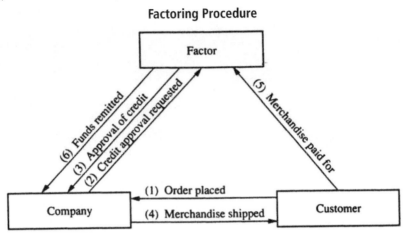

Factors of Production those essential elements necessary for the production of goods and services. These factors include natural resources, labor, capital, and entrepreneurship or management.

Factory Orders new orders received by manufacturers of durable goods other than military equipment. Durable goods are defined as those having a useful life of more than three years. Non-defense equipment represents about one-fifth to one-third of all durable goods production. Factory orders include engines, construction, mining, and materials handling equipment; office and store machinery; electrical transmission and distribution equipment and other electrical machinery (excluding household appliances and electronic equipment); and railroad, ship, and aircraft transportation equipment. Military equipment is excluded because new orders for such items do not respond directly to the business cycle. The factory order series is released by the Department of Commerce. Each month approximately 2,300 companies are asked to file a report covering orders, inventories and shipments. Economists typically count on factory production, particularly of "big ticket" durable goods ranging from airplanes to home appliances, to help lift the economy from a downturn. A decline in this series suggests that factories are unlikely to hire new workers. A drop in the backlog of unfilled orders is also an indication of possible production cutbacks and layoffs. The wider dispersal of gains in many types of goods is looked upon as a favorable sign for the economic recovery. The broader the dispersal of orders increases, the broader the rehiring.

Factory Overhead all costs of manufacturing except direct materials and direct labor; also called *manufacturing overhead, indirect manufacturing expenses, factory* *expense*, and *factory burden*. Some of the many examples include depreciation, rent, property taxes, insurance, fringe benefits, payroll taxes, setup costs, waste control costs, quality costs, engineering, workmen's compensation, and cost of idle time.

Failure Costs the costs resulting from products or services not conforming to requirements or customer/user needs. Failure costs are divided into internal and external failure cost categories.

Internal Failure Costs: Failure costs occurring prior to (a) delivery or shipment of the product or (b) the furnishing of a service to the customer. Examples are the costs of scrap, rework, reinspection, retesting, material review, and down grading.

External Failure Costs: Failure costs occurring after (a) delivery or shipment of the product or (b) during or after furnishing a service to the customer. Examples are the costs of processing customer complaints, customer returns, warranty claims, and product recalls.

Fair and Accurate Credit Transactions (FACT) Act of 2003 a law that mandates the public's access to free copies of their reports, which track the amount of debt consumers have and whether they pay their bills on time. The law is better known as the FACT Act.

Fair Credit Billing Act (FCBA) a law designed to correct errors and abuses in credit billing and the handling of credit complaints. This act established time limits within which bills must be sent and complaints answered.

Fair Credit Reporting Act (FCRA) a law that regulates the use of credit information and allows consumers access to their own credit files. It is designed to force credit bureaus to keep only correct information about borrowers on file. It also requires a lender to explain how loan interest is calculated.

Fair Debt Collection Practices Act of 1978 a federal act that protects consumers against unreasonable collection practices.

Fair Housing Laws Federal, state, and local laws that guarantee people of all races and genders freedom from discrimination when buying, renting, selling, or making any real estate transaction.

Fair Labor Standards Act (FLSA) act enacted in 1938 that applies to workers involved in interstate commerce. It sets standards with respect to working condition, including such aspects as minimum wage and working hours. It has been periodically amended and adjusted to keep the standards relevant to the current working environment.

Fair Market Value (FMV)
1. amount that could be received on the sale of a security in the market. There exist willing and financially capable buyers and sellers who have informed knowledge; also called *market value*. No unusual circumstances exist such as emergencies.
2. appraisal amount derived by an independent appraiser.
3. in real estate, tax, and other applications, the market value, or the value someone is willing to pay. Current value of a property.

Fair Plan; Fair Program An insurance program sponsored by the federal government for individuals unable to get insurance through private carriers. It is also a governmental insurance plan that covers property that would otherwise have difficulty being covered.

Fall Out of Bed vernacular term used in the stock market to describe a precipitous decline in the market price of a particular security.

Falling Out of Escrow situation where one of the parties is unable to comply with the conditions of the purchase and sale agreement. For example, if the buyer is unable to obtain a loan by the time escrow was to close, the sale may become null and void.

False Advertising deceptive or misleading advertising. For example, a rental advertisement claims the rental price of an apartment includes air conditioning even though the air conditioning unit has never been installed.

Family and Medical Leave Act (FMLA) the law that requires governmental employers and the private employers of 50 or more workers to provide their employees up to 12 weeks of unpaid leave for their own serious illness, the birth or adoption of a child, or the care of a seriously ill child, spouse, or parent.

Family of Funds a group of mutual funds, all with different investment objectives, that are under the same management company. A shareholder can switch between the funds, sometimes at no charge as his/her investment objectives and perceptions change.

Fannie Mae *see* Federal National Mortgage Association.

FAQ *see* Frequently Asked Questions (FAQ).

FASB pronounced as FAS-bee, a board created by the accounting profession to set rules and standards for all accountants to follow. The primary accounting association, AICPA, requires all members to comply with FASB rules or justify any variations. *See also* Financial Accounting Standards Board (FASB).

FDI *see* Foreign Direct Investment (FDI).

Feasibility Study an evaluation of a contemplated project or course of action, according to preestablished criteria (such as net present value, internal rate of return, and payback) to determine if the proposal meets management requirements. An analysis is also made of alternative means of accomplishing the task. *See also* Capital Budgeting.

Federal Deposit Insurance Corporation (FDIC) the federal agency that insures bank accounts. Most commercial and all national bank accounts carry FDIC insurance up to $100,000. It is important to note that insurance is for each depositor and not for each account. If the amount held by one depositor exceeds $100,000, another account should be opened with a different bank or additional deposits with the same bank could be made in another person's name.

Federal Fair Housing Law originally passed as Title VIII of the Civil Rights Act of 1968, the law prohibits discrimination in the sale or rental of residential dwelling units or vacant land on the basis or color, national origin, race, religion, or sex.

Federal Funds Rate the rate that bankers charge one another for very short-term loans, although the Fed heavily manages this rate as well. The Fed Funds rate is the major tool that the nation's central bank, the Federal Reserve, has to manage interest rates. Changing the target for the Fed Funds rate is done when the Fed wants to use monetary policy to alter economic patterns.

Federal Home Loan Bank Board (FHLBB) the agency of the federal government that supervises all federal savings and loan associations and federally insured state-charted S&Ls. It is a central bank in this industry. It also operated the Federal Savings and Loan Insurance Corporation (FSLIC).

Federal Home Loan Mortgage Corporation (FHLMC) known as "Freddie Mac," a stockholder-owned corporation, chartered by Congress in 1970. Its purpose is to provide ongoing assistance to the secondary market for residential mortgages by increasing liquidity of mortgage investments and improving the distribution of investment capital available for residential mortgage financing.

Federal Housing Administration (FHA) a federal agency within the Department of Housing and Urban Development that provides financing opportunities for home buyers, especially those with little down payment funds or with a need for smaller monthly payments. It insures mortgage loans that meet its standard.

Federal Insurance Contribution Act (FICA) law dealing with social security taxes and benefits. The taxes withheld from the employee's wages for Social Security are called FICA taxes. The FICA taxes depend upon the tax rate and the base amount of the wages subject to the tax.

Federal National Mortgage Association (FNMA) a government-sponsored corporation engaged in the buying and selling of FHA, FHDA, or VA mortgages; also known as *Fannie Mae.*

Federal Open Market Committee (FOMC) a body of the Federal Reserve System that determines the amounts of government securities and other obligations that Federal Reserve banks buy or sell and controls Federal Reserve purchases of foreign currencies in the international money markets.

Federal Reserve Bank a district bank of the Federal Reserve System. *See also* Federal Reserve Board (System).

Federal Reserve Board (System) the system, created by an act of Congress in 1913, that is made up of twelve Federal Reserve District Banks, their 24 branches, and all national and state banks that are part of the system scattered throughout the nation. It is headed by a seven-member Board of Governors. The primary function of the Board is to establish and conduct the nation's monetary policy. The System manages the nation's monetary policy by exercising control over the money stock. It controls the money supply primarily in three ways: (1) by raising or lowering the reserve requirement; (2) by setting the discount rate through loans to commercial banks; and (3) through its open market operations by purchasing and selling the government securities, mainly three-month bills and notes issued by the U.S. Treasury. The System also serves as the central bank of the United States, a banker's bank that offers many of the same services that banks provide their customers. It performs many other functions. It sets margin requirements, regulates member banks, and acts as a Fiscal Agent in the issuance of U.S. Treasury and U.S. Government agency securities.

Source: Federal Reserve System

Source: Adapted from the Board of Governors of the Federal Reserve System

Federal Reserve Requirements The Federal Reserve can change the ratio of reserves a bank is required to hold against deposits.

Federal Savings and Loan Insurance Corporation (FSLIC) a defunct federal agency that insured deposits in savings and loan associations and similar institutions. It was an entity created to insure deposits and depositors against loss by insolvency of these federally chartered savings and loan institutions. Its duties have been largely assumed by the Federal Deposit Insurance Corporation (FDIC).

Federal Trade Commission (FTC) the organization, created by the Federal Trade Commission Act passed in 1914, that is responsible for thwarting "unfair methods of competition" among firms. It exists to ensure free and fair competition, and to prevent monopolies and activities in restraining trade. It also investigates cases of industrial espionage, bribery for the purpose of obtaining trade secrets or gaining business, and boycotts.

Federal Unemployment Tax Act (FUTA) a social security legislation affecting labor costs and payroll records. Unlike FICA, which is strictly a federal program, FUTA provides for cooperation between state and federal governments in the establishment and administration of unemployment insurance. Under FUTA, an employer must pay an unemployment insurance tax to the federal government. While the federal act requires no employee contribution, some states levy an unemployment tax on the employee.

Fee Simple a property owned without encumbrances. The fee simple represents all the rights in real estate.

Feedback a term used to refer to information concerning actual performance, particularly in comparison with the plan. The feedback process is a critical part of a management control system in order to see if a given system or model is performing as planned. Timely feedback enables quick corrective action to be taken when things get out of hand.

Fee-For-Service
1. a term used for health insurance where you are free to select whichever doctor you wish.
2. one method of pricing nonprofit services. It is the price agreed in advance, such as college tuition and Medicaid.

Fiber Optics the technology of using laser light to send information through glass fibers as opposed to the older technology of using metal wires.

FICA The Social Security taxes you and your company pay each year. Payments into the governmental program of Social Security including disability and Medicare. *See* Federal Insurance Contribution Act (FICA).

FICO Credit Score an acronym for Fair, Isaac & Company. A computer-generated credit score that predicts a lender's risk in doing business with a borrower. Any company or individual that issues mortgage loans, home-equity loans, car loans, insurance policies, or healthcare services (even the IRS) bases much of its lending decisions and terms on the applicant's FICO score. FICO scores are determined by computers and released through the three credit bureaus to their subscribing members. At Experian the scores are called Experian/Fair, Isaac; at Equifax, they are called Beacon scores; and at Trans Union, they are called Empirica scores. FICO scores five main kinds of credit information. Listed from most important to least important showing the percentage of the score based on the category, the categories are: payment history (approximately 35% of the score), amount owed (approximately 30% of the score), length of credit history (approximately 15%), new credit (approximately 10%), and types of credit in use (approximately 10%). Credit scores range from 300 to 850. Scores provide an extremely valuable guide to future risk based solely on credit report data. The higher the consumer's score, the lower the risk to lenders when extending new credit to a consumer.

Fiduciary an individual or institution responsible for holding or administering property owned by another. An executor, guardian, trustee, or an administrator would be examples of a fiduciary. The prudent man rule is one way states ensure that fiduciaries invest responsibly.

Field

1. a group of adjacent characters. For example, in a company's payroll system, separate fields can exist for an employee's name, employee's Social Security number, and hourly rate.
2. in cyberspace, a place to input information.

FIFO *see* First In, First Out (FIFO).

15-Year Mortgage a mortgage loan where for a slight increase in the monthly payment, the loan can be paid off in only 15 years. The overall savings in interest paid to the lender over the life of the 15-year mortgage can be quite substantial, yet the monthly payment is not significantly higher.

File

1. a collection of information stored as records; the contents of a disk file are just like those in a file cabinet. For example, the records for all charge customers at the local department store collectively form the accounts receivable file. Thus, Mr. Smith's account is an accounts receivable record. A record that describes a single business activity is called a transaction record. Thus, when Mr. Smith buys a new suit on credit, the sales clerk writes up a credit sales ticket as a transaction record. The total set of credit sales tickets for that day would collectively comprise a daily credit sales transaction file.
2. act of making formal submission of a document to an entity, such as the submission of a tax return to the IRS.

File Transfer Protocol (FTP) protocol associated with the transfer of information on the Internet between client computers and file servers. Files may be transferred, downloaded, and uploaded individually or in batch form.

File Transfer Protocol TCP/IP protocol allowing users to download data to their client PC.

Filing Status one of four basic categories for taxpayer filing: (1) married, filing a joint return; (2) married, filing separately; (3) head of household; and (4) single. The filing status determines the tax rate schedules to be used to compute tax liability. The tax rates generally increase in each category with the respective order listed above.

Finance Charge fee for the cost of a loan including interest and points. Points (1 point = 1% of the total loan) are advance charges for a mortgage, whereas interest is charged over the life of the mortgage. Interest and points add to the total cost of the loan. The Truth-in-Lending Act requires any costs to be disclosed to the prospective homebuyer before final acceptance. *See also* Consumer Credit Protection Act; Regulation Z.

Financial Accounting accounting methods used to provide financial information to outside parties such as investors, creditors, and governments. To protect those outside parties from being misled, financial accounting is governed by what are called *generally accepted accounting principles* (GAAP). This is in contrast to management accounting, which provides internal cost information for managerial analysis and decision making.

Financial Accounting Disclosure *see* Disclosure.

Financial Accounting Standards Board (FASB) (*www.fasb.org*)set up to establish best practice for accounting and reporting. It provides guidance on the implementation of transparent and accurate accounting procedures, and promotes the convergence of international accounting standards. *See also* FASB.

Financial Adviser a professional who gives professional financial advice and may sell a particular financial and investment product. The financial adviser should be knowledgeable in investments, tax planning, insurance, estate planning, or similar fields. *See also* Financial Planner.

Financial Analysis the use and transformation of financial data into a form that can be used to monitor and evaluate the firm's financial position, to plan future financing, and to designate the size of the firm and its rate of growth. Financial analysis includes the use of financial statement analysis and cash flow analysis. *See also* Financial Statement Analysis.

Financial Analyst *see* Analyst.

Financial Derivative *see* Derivative.

Financial Engineering application of economic principles to the dynamics of securities markets, especially for the purpose of structuring, pricing, and managing the risk of financial contracts.

Financial Highlight a section of corporate annual reports that summarizes key financial data on a comparative basis. Sales, earnings per share (primary and after dilution), and dividends are always highlighted along with other information the company considers noteworthy.

Financial Institutions institutions, such as banks, that serve as intermediaries between suppliers and users of funds. In general, they are wholesalers and retailers of funds. It is in the financial market that entities demanding funds are brought together with those having surplus funds. *See also* Financial Markets.

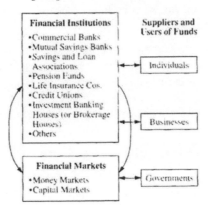

Financial Intermediary an institution that receives funds from savers and lends them to borrows; also called *financial institutions*. These include depository institutions, such as commercial or savings banks, and non-depository institutions, such as mutual funds and insurance companies.

Financial Leverage a portion of a firm's assets financed with debt instead of equity and therefore involving contractual interest and principal obligations. Financial leverage benefits common stockholders as long as the borrowed funds generate a return in excess of the cost of borrowing, although the increased risk can offset the general cost of capital. For this reason, financial leverage is popularly called *trading on equity*. Financial leverage is measured by the debt-to-equity ratio.

Financial Markets markets in which companies demanding funds are brought together with those having surplus funds. Financial markets provide a mechanism through which the financial manager obtains funds from a wide range of sources, including financial institutions. The financial markets are composed of money markets and capital markets. Money markets are the markets for short-term (less than one year) debt securities. Examples of money market securities include U.S. Treasury bills, commercial paper, and negotiable certificates of deposit issued by government, business, and financial institutions. Capital markets are the markets for long-term debt and corporate stocks. The New York Stock Exchange, which handles the stocks of many of the larger corporations, is an example of a major capital market. The American Stock Exchange and the regional stock exchanges are still other examples. In addition, securities are traded through the thousands of brokers and dealers on the over-the-counter (OTC) market, a term used to denote all buying and selling activities in securities that do not occur on an organized stock exchange.

Financial Planner a planner engaged in providing personal financial planning service. A financial planner assists a client in the following ways: (1) assesses a client's financial history, such as tax returns, investments, retirement plan, wills, and insurance policies; (2) helps decide on a financial plan, based on personal and financial goals, history, and preferences; (3) identifies financial areas where a client may need help, such as building up retirement income or improving investment return; (4) prepares a financial plan based on the individual situation and discusses it thoroughly; (5) helps implement the financial plan, including referring the client to specialists, such as lawyers or accountants, if necessary; and (6) reviews the situation and financial plan periodically and suggests changes in the program when needed. Financial planners come from a variety of backgrounds and, therefore, may hold a variety of degrees and licenses. They include such credentials as Certified Financial planner (CFP), Chartered Financial Consultant (CFC), lawyers (JD), and Certified Public Accountant (CPA).

Financial Planning the process of developing and implementing plans to achieve financial goals.

Financial Planning Software personal finance computer programs that keep track of income and expenses by budget categories, reconcile accounts, store tax records, figure net worth, track stocks and bonds, and print checks and financial reports. Some programs are sophisticated enough to generate a detailed, long-term personal financial plan covering planning for college education, investment planning, and retirement planning. Examples of financial planning software are Quicken and Managing Your Money.

Financial Responsibility Law a state law mandating that the driver of an automobile must be properly insured so as to have sufficient funds to pay for losses arising from an accident. A minimum amount of automobile liability insurance is typically required.

Financial Risk
Personal: the risk a person has of running into financial problems and/or incurring financial losses. An example is an individual who has most of his or her funds invested in junk bonds.
Corporate: portion of total risk resulting from using debt. The greater the proportion of debt to equity the firm has, the greater is its financial risk.

Financial Statement Analysis the analysis of financial statements used by interested parties such as investors, creditors, and management in order to evaluate the past, current, and projected conditions and performance of the business firm. Ratio analysis is the most common form of financial analysis. It provides relative measures of the firm's conditions and performance. Horizontal and vertical analyses are also popular forms. Horizontal analysis is used to evaluate the trend in the accounts over the years, while vertical analysis, also called a *common size statement approach*, discloses the internal structure of the firm. It indicates the existing relationship between sales and each income statement account. It shows the mix of assets that produce income and the mix of the sources of capital, whether by current or long-term debt or by equity funding. When using the financial ratios, a financial analyst makes two types of comparisons:

Industry comparison: The ratios of a firm are compared with those of similar firms or with industry averages or norms to determine how the company is faring relative to its competitors. Industry average ratios are available from a number of sources, including (a) Dun & Bradstreet. Dun & Bradstreet computes 14 ratios for each of 125 lines of business. They are published in *Dun's Review and Key Business Ratios*. (b) Risk Management Associates. This association of bank loan officers publishes *Annual Statement Studies* in which 16 ratios are computed for more than 300 lines of business, as well as a percentage distribution of items on the balance sheet and income statement (common size financial statements).

Trend analysis: A firm's present ratio is compared with its past and expected future ratios to determine whether the company's financial condition is improving or deteriorating over time. After completing the financial statement analysis, the firm's financial analyst will consult with management to discuss their plans and prospects, any problem areas identified in the analysis, and possible solutions.

Financial Statements a written report that quantitatively summarizes the financial status of an organization for a stated period of time. Financial statements consist of a balance sheet, an income statement, and a cash flow statement. These statements must be developed in accordance with generally accepted accounting principles, GAAP for short.

Finder's Fee a fee paid to an individual or company for bringing the parties together in a business deal. The finder may also serve as a consultant until the deal is finalized. The fee may be a flat rate, a percentage of the sale, or a percentage of gross margin. For example, finder's fees are paid in bringing a lender and borrower together or finding a customer for a particular service or good.

Firewalls security controls for information transferred over a network between two parties. It provides protection against the misuse of data. It guards against protocols or databases being compromised. However, firewalls do not safeguard a network against viruses nor assure authentication or privacy.

First In, First Out (FIFO) a system of inventory valuation that firms use to compute ending inventory cost from most recent purchases and cost of goods sold from older purchases including beginning inventory. This is in contrast to LIFO (last in, first out) that uses the last inventory first.

First Mortgage the original or senior mortgage on a piece of property. Because of its precedence, it has priority over all subsequent mortgages, and the mortgagee has precedence in payment in the event of default.

First World in contrast with the third world, the industrialized countries. They are primarily members of the Organization for Economic Cooperation and Development (OECD).

Fiscal Policy a government policy to stimulate the economy by increasing or decreasing government spending or increasing or decreasing taxes.

Fiscal Year twelve consecutive months used by a business entity to account for and report on its business operations. Typically, businesses use a fiscal year ending December 31. (The year-end December 31 is referred to as a calendar year). However, many entities use the natural business year, referring to a year ending at the annual low point in activity or at the end of the season. An example is a fiscal year-ending June 30. A company prepares its financial statements and includes them in the annual report at the end of the fiscal year. It is a company's accounting year, which may or may not coincide with a calendar year, either by chance or some peculiarity of the company's business.

Fishbone Diagrams way of determining likely root causes of a problem, often called *cause-and-effect diagrams*; also called an *Ishikawa diagram.*

Fisher Effect named for Irving Fisher, the tendency for the level of interest rates to be affected by the magnitude of expected inflation. It is a relation in which the nominal interest rate equals the real interest rate plus the expected inflation rate.

Five C's of Credit five elements used by lenders in evaluating a borrower's credit application. They are:
1. Character (willingness to pay)
2. Capacity (cash flow)
3. Capital (wealth)
4. Collateral (security)
5. Conditions (economic conditions)

Character reflects a customer's integrity and reliability in meeting financial obligations. The borrower's credit history indicates how reliable the borrower is in paying bills on time. Capacity looks at a borrower's earning power and/or cash flow. Capital analyzes a borrower's balance sheet (assets and liabilities revealing whether net worth is positive or negative). Collateral refers to assets that can be secured and liquidated by the lender if a loan is not repaid. Finally, conditions mean economic conditions at the time of the loan and a borrower's vulnerability to business downturn or credit crunch. When much money is available, especially at low interest rates, it is much easier to obtain credit, whereas in a credit crunch, many applicants would be rejected who would normally have been approved for credit. Once the five C's are analyzed, a borrower is assigned to a credit rating category, which will determine the default risk premium for the borrower. Generally, the higher a customer's credit risk, the higher the loan rate.

Fixed Asset any tangible assets of a permanent nature such as a building, equipment, or furniture required for the usual activities of a business that will not be consumed or sold in the immediate future. Fixed assets are necessary to conduct operations and therefore are not the object of sale. Fixed assets are usually referred to as property, plant, and equipment.

Fixed Costs costs that remain constant in total regardless of changes in activity within a relevant range. Examples are rent, insurance and taxes. Fixed cost per unit changes as volume changes. *See also* Variable Cost.

Fixed Disk an older name for hard disk or drive.

Fixed Exchange Rates a system under which the values of currencies in terms of other currencies are fixed by intergovernmental agreement and by governmental intervention in the currency exchange markets.

Fixed Income Securities investment vehicles that provide a fixed periodic return. Examples are debt securities such as bonds.

Fixed-rate Mortgage a mortgage loan that is at a set specified interest rate for the lifetime or maturity of the mortgage.

Flagship
1. the main, downtown, central, or oldest unit of a multiunit department store group.
2. a store, office, or product that is the most significant, largest, best-selling, or most identified with its company.

Flash Report a report that provides the highlights of key information promptly to the responsible managers. An example is an exception report such as performance reports that highlight favorable or unfavorable variances. A flash report allows managers to take corrective action for an unfavorable variance.

Flat Tax one in which the income tax rate is the same for all income levels. It is a proportional tax. A pure flat tax would eliminate all deductions, exemptions, and loopholes, and tax all income at the same low tax rate. The tax would also make the tax system less complex and more equitable.

Flexible (Variable) Budget a budget based on different levels of activity; also called a *variable budget*. It allows for the variation in costs associated with changes in output volume. The costs, for example, at 75% of capacity, are different from costs incurred at 90% capacity. It is an extremely useful tool in cost control in that the actual cost incurred is compared to the cost allowable for the activity level achieved. It is dynamic in nature rather than static.

Flexible Factory the objective of a flexible factory is to provide a wide range of services across many product lines in a timely manner. An example is a fabrication plant with several integrated manufacturing cells that can perform many functions for unrelated product lines with relatively short lead times.

Flexible Manufacturing System (FMS) computer-controlled process technology suitable for producing a moderate variety of products in moderate, flexible volumes. This system reduces setup or changeover times and facilitates the production of differentiated products in small numbers. The shift in emphasis is from mass production of a few products to a job-shop environment in which customized orders are manufactured. Automation allows for better quality and scheduling, rapid changes in product lines, and lower inventories and costs. *See also* Computer Integrated Manufacturing (CIM).

Flexible Spending Accounts (FSAs) in contrast to health savings accounts (HSAs) FSAs are not attached to health plans, but are separate benefits offered each year by many employers at open-enrollment time. When you sign up for an FSA, you must declare in advance the amount you want deducted from your paycheck over the course of following year. You are committed to that amount, with a few exceptions. Like a HSAs, you can use the money for medical expenses not covered by your insurance. Unlike HSAs, however, you may not roll the money over. It's a strictly use-it-or-lose-it proposition.

Flextime a work scheduling concept which allows for non-traditional work hours to be employed on a systematic basis. Hours can be arranged for different times or periods of time to accommodate such aspects as efficiency, traffic, parenthood, disabilities, continuous operations, etc.

Flipping buying an investment—such as real estate or stock in an initial public offering (IPO)—in anticipation of reselling it quickly at a profit. Analysts argue that a period of growing popularity of flipping in a rising housing or stock market can signal that a downturn is near.

Float
1. amount of funds represented by checks that have been issued but not yet collected.
2. time between the deposit of checks in a bank and payment. Due to the time difference, many firms are able to "play the float," that is, to write checks against money not presently in the firm's bank account.
3. to issue new securities, usually through an underwriter.
4. shares in public hands, as opposed to shares outstanding, which are shares held by company's insiders as well as shares owned by the public, including institutional and individuals investors. *See also* Outstanding Shares.

The figure below illustrates the float resulting from a check issued and mailed by the payer company to the payee company

Total Float Time

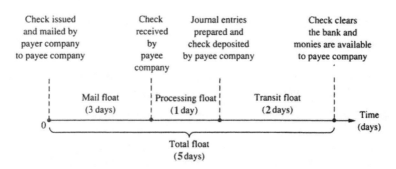

Floater Endorsement an addition to a policy that itemizes specific item(s) for insurance protection under the endorsement. An example is a policy covering personal property within a home or personal property like jewelry.

Floating (Flexible) Exchange Rate the system of foreign exchange rate where the exchange rate is determined in the foreign exchange market and can change from moment to moment. After 1973, exchange rates between the dollar and other foreign currencies were allowed to float and to be determined by the supply and demand for foreign exchange.

Floor
1. the actual trading floor area of the stock exchange where securities' trading occurs among brokers and traders. Exchange rules allow only members to trade on the floor.
2. the price below which a stock must be sold, as in a sell stop order. If the price penetrates the floor price, it will be "stopped out."
3. a contract on an interest rate, whereby the writer of the floor periodically pays the difference between a specified floor rate and the market interest rate if, and only if, this difference is positive. This is equivalent to a stream of put options on the interest rate.

Flowchart the traditional method of representing in a schematic form the flow of data in a system. The flowchart shows the points of input and output, the logic or sequence of the various processing steps in the system, and the relationship of one element of the system to the other parts of the system or to other information systems.

F.O.B. Price "free on board" a railroad car, a ship, a plane, or a motor truck. Under this price, the seller assumes the transportation charges to a given shipping point, and the buyer incurs the costs beyond that point. *See also* Free On Board (FOB).

Focus Group a small group of people put together for a marketing research purpose. A facilitator engages the group in a discussion that explores the merits of a new consumer product being tested.

Forbes a biweekly business magazine.

Forecast
1. a projection or an estimate of future sales, revenues, earnings, or costs.
2. a projection of future financial positions and operating results of an organization.

Foreclosure a legal means whereby the owner of property loses his legal rights and interests therein. It arises from a default on the part of the mortgagor in paying a mortgage lien or taxes against the property.

Foreign Bond a bond underwritten by a syndicate composed of members from a single country, sold principally within that country, and denominated in the currency of that country. The issuer, however, is from another country. A bond issued by a Swedish corporation, denominated in dollars, and sold in the U.S. to U.S. investors by U.S. investment bankers, would be a foreign bond. Foreign bonds have nicknames: foreign bonds sold in the U.S. are "Yankee bonds"; foreign bonds sold in Japan are "Samurai bonds"; and foreign bonds sold in the United Kingdom are "Bulldogs."

Foreign Bonds To U.S. Investors		
Sales		
	In the U.S.	**In Foreign Countries**
Domestic issuer	Domestic bonds	Eurodollar bonds
Foreign	Yankee bonds	Foreign currency bonds
		Eurodollar bonds

Foreign Corporation

1. a corporation that is chartered under the state law and resides in a particular state of the union or other country, which is considered a foreign corporation to the remaining states.
2. a corporation formed under the laws of a foreign country.

Foreign Corrupt Practices Act (FCPA) a law designed to prevent U.S. companies from offering or giving bribes (directly or indirectly) to foreign officials for the purpose of influencing those officials (or causing them to use their influence) to help the companies obtain or retain business.

Foreign Direct Investment (FDI) investment that involves ownership of a company in a foreign country. In exchange for the ownership, the investing company usually transfers some of its financial, managerial, technical, trademark, and other resources to the foreign country. It is distinguished from foreign portfolio investment.

Foreign Exchange the exchanges of the currency of one country for that of another country. Foreign exchange (FOREX) is not simply currency printed by a foreign country's central bank. Rather, it includes such items as cash, checks (or drafts), wire transfers, telephone transfers, and even contracts to sell or buy currency in the future. Foreign exchange is really any financial that fulfills payment from one currency to another. The most common form of foreign exchange in transactions between companies is the draft (denominated in a foreign currency). The most common form of foreign exchange in transactions between banks is the telephone transfer. Foreign Exchange is the backbone of all international capital transactions. The FOREX market has vital implications for the economic prospects of the countries concerned and the general prosperity of the free world economy. The reason is that some $1.5 trillion worth of international currencies are bought and sold every single trading day (*www.knewmoney.com*). This volume of trade is equivalent to over two months of trading in the New York Stock Exchange. Note: A foreign exchange market is now available to individual investors for trading foreign exchanges.

Foreign Exchange Rate an exchange rate for short, specifies the number of units of a given currency that can be purchased with one unit of another currency. Exchange rates appear in the business sections of newspapers each day and financial dailies such as *Investor's Business Daily* and *The Wall Street Journal*. Exchange rates are also available at many finance web sites such as the Bloomberg World Currency Values website.

Foreign exchange rates are determined in various ways:

Fixed exchange rates: it is an international financial arrangement in which governments directly intervene in the foreign exchange market to prevent exchange rates from deviating more than a very small margin from some central or parity value.

Flexible (floating exchange) rates: it is an arrangement by which exchange rate levels are allowed to change daily in response to market demand and supply. Arrangements may vary from free float, i.e., absolutely no government intervention, to managed float, i.e., limited but sometimes aggressive government intervention in the foreign exchange market.

Forward exchange rate: it is the exchange rate in contract for receipt of and payment for foreign currency at a specified date, usually 30, 90, or 180 days in the future, at a stipulated current or "spot" price. By buying and selling forward exchange, importers and exporters can protect themselves against the risks of fluctuations in the current exchange market.

Foreign Trade Zones areas near a customs port of entry that are physically on U.S. soil but considered to be outside U.S. commerce.

Forfeiting a means of export financing similar to factoring, which is the sale of receivables by an exporter for cash. Forfeiting is the discounting—at a fixed rate without recourse—of medium-term export receivables denominated in fully convertible currencies (e.g. U.S. dollar, Swiss franc).

Forfeiture loss of rights, assets, or property as a result of the nonfulfillment of some obligation or condition. In some instances, forfeiture mandates a formal judicial action whereas in others, the nonfulfillment of a contractual obligation is sufficient to cause a forfeiture. For instance, the space loss of a lease can result from the failure to pay the current rent due. *See also* Default; Foreclosure.

Format

1. used as a verb, the process of initializing or preparing a disk or form of computer data storage medium, by recording a special pattern of data over the medium's reactive surface, thereby allowing a computer operating system the ability to store and retrieve data.
2. used as a noun, the type or version of format used on the storage medium.

FORTRAN (Formula Translation) the first high-level programming language, developed by IBM in the late 1950s, that allows programmers to describe calculations by means of mathematical formulas. FORTRAN includes arrays and may consist of subroutines of functions that are compiled separately from the main program. The program allows for easy use of arrays, matrices, and loops.

Fortune a biweekly news magazine in business.

Fortune 500 a listing of the largest 500 companies in the country by the business publication *Fortune* magazine.

Forward Contracts contracts similar to futures. However, forward contracts are not uniform or standardized. They are not traded on exchanges. In such a contract, goods are actually delivered at a future date or settlement may be in cash. Forward contracts may be on commodities or instruments. The contract fixes the quantity, price, and date of purchase or sale.

Forward Exchange Rate the contracted exchange rate for receipt of and payment for foreign currency at a specified date, usually 30, 90, or 180 days in the future, at a stipulated current or "spot" price. By buying and selling forward exchange contracts, importers and exporters can protect themselves against the risks of fluctuations in the current exchange market.

Forward Earnings estimated earnings by analysts of what companies will earn in the coming 12 months. In a period of earnings growth, trailing earnings produce a higher P/E ratio. In a period of earnings declines, the opposite is true. *See also* Trailing Earnings.

4/5th Rule the rule stating that discrimination generally is considered to occur if the selection rate for a protected group is less than 80% of the group's representation in the relevant labor market or less than 80% of the selection rate for the majority group.

Four I's (of Services) four basic characteristics that distinguish services from goods: intangibility, inseparability of production and consumption, inventory, and inconsistency. These characteristics are important because they pose several unique marketing problems.

Four P's four basic elements in the marketing mix–product, place, price, and promotion.

Franchise; Franchisee/Franchisor a license granted to an owner-operator of a business to use a company's name and product. It is also a legal agreement that grants the franchisee the rights to market and distribute a trademarketed product or service in exchange for royalties. This could be a way for some small business owners with little experience to tap into a built-in market and proven product. Franchise agreements usually run 15 to 20 years. For more, visit: *www.franchise. org*.

Franchising An arrangement between a franchisor (grantor) and the franchisee (i.e., a retailer) under which the franchisor's product(s) or services, including productive (usually) and marketing knowledge (names and practices) are provided to the franchisee for a specific consideration.

Freddie Mac *see* Federal Home Loan Mortgage Corporation (FHLMC).

Free Cash Flow amount of cash that remains after deducting the funds a company must commit to continue operating at its planned level; net cash flows from operating activities, minus dividends, minus net capital expenditures.

Free On Board (FOB) free on board some location (e.g., shipping point or destination). It indicates that the invoice price includes delivery at seller's expense and seller's risk to the specified location. For example, "FOB our warehouse in Deluth, Minnesota," means, to a buyer requesting New York City delivery, that the seller who might have its headquarters and billing office in Chicago, will pay shipping costs from Deluth to New York. Title usually passes from seller to buyer at the FOB point.

Free Trade a governmental policy by which no intervention or restrictive devices are exercised in trading between nations–by tariffs, quotas, or other measures. North American Free Trade Agreement (NAFTA) is an example of such an attempt.

Free Trade Area association of trading countries whose members agree to promote free trade (impose no restrictive measures), such as the North American Free Trade Association (NAFTA).

Freeware truly free computer software available from the Internet or user groups. *See also* Shareware.

Frequency Distributions a table in which possible values for a variable of interest (e.g., weekly wage, cash collection days) are grouped into classes, and the number of observed values that fall into each class is recorded (i.e., frequency). The data organized in a frequency distribution are called grouped data. From here, percentages and averages can be calculated. In many cases, statistical data in the raw can appear little more than a confusing mass of numbers. An efficient way to reorganize the data in such a way to bring some order out of chaos is to construct a frequency distribution.

Frequently Asked Questions (FAQ) in the Internet and in many newsgroups, questions commonly asked by the users.

Fringe Benefit compensation or other benefits provided by the employer to the employee at no charge that is above and beyond salary or wages. Examples include health plans, cafeteria plans, and life insurance.

Front Money the seed money needed to get a project going.

Front-End Ratio the percentage of monthly income that can be applied toward monthly house payments. It is calculated by dividing a person's total monthly mortgage payment by his or her monthly gross income. In more traditional markets, mortgage lenders don't allow housing expenses to be more than 28 percent to 33 percent of a borrower's household monthly gross income.

FTC *see* Federal Trade Commission (FTC).

Full Disclosure
General: a requirement to present all material facts relevant to a certain matter.
Securities: the Securities Act of 1933 calls for full disclosure of new securities. To receive approval from the Securities and Exchange Commission (SEC), the applicant must provide the SEC with economic and financial data relevant to the company and the new offering. It does so in the form of a prospectus.
Insurance: the insured is required to provide all pertinent information on any matter to the insurer to issue a policy.
Real Estate: a broker is required to present all known facts about the financial and physical condition of the subject property.

Banking: a lender is required to disclose to borrowers the true cost and terms of loans.

Full Employment The availability of work at prevailing wage rates for all persons who desire it. Full employment does not mean 100 percent employment. There always is some unemployment, owing to job changes, seasonal factors, and so on. Most economists define full employment, as meaning that a given percentage of the work force is employed. Until the mid-1970s, this figure was 96 percent; meaning that with full employment, unemployment was no higher than 4 percent. By the early 1980s, many economists agreed that in view of increased structural unemployment, this was an unrealistic goal and needed to be revised to 6 to 7 percent unemployment.

Full Faith and Credit the backing of a debt of a government entity representing all the resources of the entity, including its taxing and borrowing power. Bonds backed up by the full faith and credit of the issuer are called general obligation bonds.

Full Product Cost cost that includes not only the costs of direct materials and direct labor, but also the costs of all production and nonproduction activities required to satisfy the customer.

Full-Cost-Plus Pricing a pricing method in which the cost base is the full manufacturing cost per unit. Selling and administrative costs are provided for through the markup that is added to this base.

Full-Service Broker a broker providing a wide range of services to clients. Unlike discount brokers, full-service brokers provide buy and sell advice on stocks, bonds, options, commodities, and mutual funds. A full-service broker may offer research services, asset management accounts, tax shelters, and limited partnerships as well as allowing participation in new security issues.

Function Keys (F-Keys) *see* F-Keys (Function Key).

Functional Currency as defined in FASB No. 52, in the context of translating financial statements, the currency of the primary economic environment in which a foreign affiliate operates and in which it generates and expends cash.

Fund Accounting a system used by nonprofit organizations. Since there is no profit motive, accountability is measured instead of profitability.

Fund Managers professionals who manage a mutual fund.

Fundamental Analysis
1. appraisal based on economic theory and models to forecast exchange rate movements. The factors to consider are money supply, inflation rate, interest rate, and balance of payments.
2. predicting economic direction by examining such conditions as gross domestic product, inventory levels, and unemployment.
3. evaluation of a company's stock based on an examination of the firm's financial statements; also called *fundamental investment analysis*. It considers overall

financial health (e.g., solvency, earning potential, revenue generation, rate of return on assets, earnings quality), economic and political conditions, industry factors, marketing aspects, management quality, and future outlook of the company.

Funding

1. providing the necessary financial resources to carry out a particular activity.

2. refinancing a debt prior to its maturity; also termed *refunding*.

3. putting money into investments or another type of reserve fund to provide for future pension plans.

Future Dollars *see* Future Value (FV).

Future Value (FV)

1. the future sums of money resulting from an investment. *See also* Compounding.

2. the valuation of an asset projected to the end of a particular time period in the future. An example is projecting what an individual's house will be worth in ten years.

Futures a contract to purchase or sell a given amount of an item for a given price by a certain date (in the future–thus the name "futures market"). Note: It is like deals made now to take place in the future. The seller of a futures contract agrees to deliver the item to the buyer of the contract, who agrees to purchase the item. The contract specifies the amount, valuation, method, quality, month and means of delivery, and exchange to be traded in. The month of delivery is the expiration date; in other words, the date on which the commodity or financial instrument must be delivered. Commodity contracts are guarantees by a seller to deliver a commodity (e.g., cocoa or cotton). Financial contracts are a commitment by the seller to deliver a financial instrument (e.g., a Treasury bill) or a specific amount of foreign currency. Futures can by risky; to invest in them, you will need specialized knowledge and great caution.

Futures Contracts *see* Futures.

Fuzzy Logic a rule-based method used in artificial intelligence to solve problems with imprecise conditions.

FY *see* Fiscal Year.

Gg

GAAP *see* Generally Accepted Accounting Principles.

Galloping Inflation extremely high rate of inflation; also called *hyperinflation.*

Game Theory a theory that deals with competitive situations where two or more participants pursue conflicting objectives. The theory attempts to offer a solution that resolves the conflict among the participants. In games, the participants are competitors; the success of one is usually at the expense of the other. Each person selects and executes those strategies that he believes will result in "winning the game." Game theory attempts to provide a guideline for a variety of game situations.

Gantt Chart graphical representation of a project schedule used to plan or monitor progress. Table 1 provides the symbols frequently used in a Gantt chart. An open bracket indicates the scheduled start of the activity, and a closing bracket indicates the scheduled completion. The symbol [−] indicates the currently completed portion of the activity. A caret at the top of the chart indicates current time. Figure 1 shows a Gantt chart of a business student preparing for final exams. Project activities are listed down the page and time is listed across the page. The project activities are studying for exams in Marketing, Human Resource Management (HRM), Operations Management (OM), and Information Systems (IS). OM is broken into two subactivities — studying new concepts since the last exam and studying concepts covered on previous exams, for review. By examining the horizontal time axis, we see that all activities must be completed in three and one-half weeks. Studying Human Resource Management, for example, is scheduled to start at the beginning of week 1 and end after one and one-half weeks. The caret at the top indicates that one and one-half weeks have already passed. The heavy lines show how much of each activity has already been done. Students can use this chart to visualize their progress and to adjust their study activities. As you can see, one of the strengths of project scheduling with Gantt charts is the simplicity of the schematic model.

Table 1
Gantt Chart Symbols

Symbol	Meaning
[	Start of an activity
]	End of an activity
[—]	Actual progress of the activity
V	Point in time where the project is now

Figure 1
Gantt Chart For Project Scheduling

Project activity	Week 1	Week 2	Week 3	Week 4
Study HRM	[___	]		
Study Marketing		[___	]	
Study OM				
Study new concepts since last exam		[___	]	
Study concepts covered on previous exams			[ ]	
Study IS				[ ]

Garbage In-Garbage Out (GIGO) Inputting incorrect data in computers, which leads to inaccurate results.

Garnishment an official proceeding whereby an individual's property, salary, or other assets are attached and used to pay a debt or other legal obligation. Normally, the practice of garnishment orders an employer to withhold part of the disposable salary payments of an employee for payment to the court until the legal obligation has been satisfied.

Gateway software or device enabling two networks to communicate together and have data transfers between them even though there exist different protocols.

GATT *see* General Agreement on Tariffs and Trade (GATT).

GDP *see* Gross Domestic Product (GDP).

GDP Deflator another index of inflation that includes a wider array of goods and services than either the Consumer Price Index (CPI) or Producer Price Index (PPI); also called *implicit price index*. The GDP Deflator is a weighted average of the price indexes used to deflate the components of GNP. Thus, it reflects price changes for goods and services bought by consumers, businesses, and governments. The GDP deflator is found by dividing current GDP in a given year by constant (real) GDP. Because it covers a broader group of goods and services than the CPI and PPI, the GDP Deflator is a very widely used price index that is frequently used to measure inflation. The GDP deflator, unlike the CPI and PPI, is available only quarterly–not monthly. It is published also by the U.S. Department of Commerce.

Gear Up Mobilizing resources to get a job done.

Gen X *see* Generation X

General Accounting Office (GAO) a legislative branch, headed by the Comptroller General, that was established to assist the Congress in its oversight of the executive branch and to serve as the independent legislative auditor of the Federal Government. Among others, roles of the GAO are (1) prescribing principles and standards for Federal agency accounting systems, (2) assisting agencies in accounting system design, and (3) reporting to Congress on the status of agency accounting systems.

General Agreement on Tariffs and Trade (GATT) an agreement signed at the Geneva Conference in 1947 that became effective on January 1, 1948. It set a framework of rules and guidelines for international trade, including a negotiation of lower international trade barriers and settling trade disputes. Over the years, the agreement has been modified as needed, through various rounds of negotiations. GATT also acts as an international arbitrator with respect to trade agreement abrogation. More specifically, GATT has four basic long-run objectives: (1) reduction of tariffs by negotiation, (2) elimination of import quotas (with some exceptions), (3) nondiscrimination in trade through adherence to unconditional most-favored-nation treatment, and (4) resolution of differences through arbitration and consultation.

General and Administrative (G&A) Expenses G&A for short, the costs incurred for administrative activities (e.g., executive salaries and legal expenses). It is simply called *administrative expenses.*

General Fund a primary operating fund of a governmental unit.

General Ledger the book of all accounting transactions and events of a company.

General Obligation Bonds bonds whose payment is unconditionally promised by a governmental unit that has the power to levy taxes. Many of state, county, city, town, and school district obligation bonds are of this type. General obligation bonds are backed by the full faith and credit (and taxing power) of the issuing government whether it be the U.S. or a municipality.

General Partner
1. a member of a partnership who is jointly and severally liable for all debts incurred by the partnership; that is, does not have limited liability.
2. a managing partner of a limited partnership who is in charge of its operations. A general partner has unlimited liability. *See also* Limited Partner.

Generally Accepted Accounting Principles (GAAP more often known as *U.S. GAAP*) standards, conventions, guidelines, rules and procedures accountants follow in recording and summarizing transactions, and in the preparation of financial statements. GAAP is based on authoritative accounting pronouncements, such as American Institute of CPAs' Opinions, Financial Accounting Standards Board Statements, industry practice, and accounting literature in the form of books and articles. In the audit report, the CPA must indicate that the client has followed GAAP on a consistent basis.

Generation X the 45 million people born between 1965 and 1976 in the "birth dearth" following the baby boom; also known as *Gen X*, or *GenXers*. The next generation of Generation X has been called the *Millennium generation* because their births will span two centuries.

Generation Y the more than 70 million children of the baby boomers, born between 1977 and 1997; also called *Echo Boomers*.

Generic Brand a plain, unadvertised brand. Also, aspirin and nylon are examples of former brand names now used as general terms for a class of products.

Geocentric Staffing a staffing policy where the best people are sought for key jobs throughout a multinational company, regardless of nationality.

Geometric (Average) Rate of Return the compounded rate of return. It is a measure of return over a single holding period or over multi-periods. When an investor holds an investment for more than one period, it is important to understand how to compute the average of the successive rates of return. There are two types of multi-period average (mean) returns: arithmetic average return and the geometric average return. The arithmetic return is simply the arithmetic average of successive one-period rates of return. The arithmetic average return, however, can be quite misleading in multi-period return calculations. A more accurate measure of the actual return generated by an investment over multiple periods is the geometric average return. The geometric return over n periods is computed as follows:

$$\text{Geometric return} = \sqrt[n]{(1 + r_1)(1 + r_2)...(1 + r_n)} - 1$$

Geometric Mean an average computed by first finding the product of "N" numbers and then taking the Nth root of the product. For example, to determine the geometric mean of 10 and 40, multiply the two numbers to get 400, and then take the second (square) root of this product to get 20 as the appropriate mean. For more than just a few numbers, logarithms should be used to make the calculations. The geometric mean is the appropriate measure to use when dealing with ratios or index numbers and the primary interest is in proportional change from one period to another. *See also* Geometric (Average) Rate of Return.

Giffen Good any good or service whose demand tends to rise as its price rises and vice versa, thus contradicting the law of demand. A good must be an inferior good to belong in this category. So named after Sir Robert Giffen who observed during the potato famine in Ireland in the mid-1840s that the poor buy more potatoes as its price rises. This situation occurred when the price increase drained the income of the peasants so that they became even more reliant on potatoes for food.

Gift Tax a tax levied on the transfer of money or property made without consideration. The donor pays the tax based on the fair market value of the property at the transfer date. A parent may give a child up to $10,000 per year tax free. Gifts between spouses are unlimited.

Gigabyte (G, GB) a billion or so bytes.

Ginnie Maes the "pet name" given for Government National Mortgage Association (GNMA)'s securities.

Global Bond Funds funds seeking a high level of income by investing in the debt securities of companies and countries worldwide, including issuers in the United States. The funds' money managers deal with varied currencies, laws, and regulations. Because of these factors, although global funds provide added diversification, they are also subject to more risk than domestic bond funds.

Global Business, Global Marketing the selling or buying of products and services overseas. It involves currency risk and more complex planning and financing.

Global Economy an economy characterized by the international trade of goods and services, the international movement of labor, and international flows of capital and information.

Global Fund a mutual fund that invests in both U.S. and foreign securities. Unlike an international fund, it invests anywhere in the world, including the United States. However, most global funds keep the majority of their assets in foreign markets.

Global Marketing the use of a standardized marketing approach in all the countries in which it markets on the principle that the world is really just one market.

Global Village a term used to refer to our world in the age of information and telecommunications, because people are highly accessible to each other.

Globalization a changeover in local markets from competition among nations or local suppliers to competition among international suppliers.

Glocalization the planning and design of global web sites so that they also can cater to local needs and preferences.

Glut a very significant oversupply of a product or service. This situation may be due to overproduction or favorable weather conditions in the case of agricultural products. Glut may lead to a drop in the price of the item since supply exceeds demand.

Goal Congruence sharing the same goals by top managers with their subordinates. This is one of the many criteria that is used to judge the performance of an accounting system. The system can achieve its goal more effectively and perform better when organizational goals can be well aligned with the personal and group goals of subordinates and superiors. The goals of the company should be the same as the goals of the individual business segments. Corporate goals can be communicated by budgets, organization charts, and job descriptions.

Goal Programming a form of linear programming (LP) allowing for consideration of multiple goals that are often in conflict with each other. With multiple goals, all goals usually cannot be realized exactly. Goal programming does not attempt to maximize or minimize a single objective function as does the linear programming model. Rather, it seeks to minimize the deviations among the desired goals and the actual results according to the priorities assigned. The objective function of a goal programming model is expressed in terms of the deviations from the target goals. Example: Consider an investor who desires investments that will have a maximum return and minimum risk. These goals are generally incompatible and therefore unachievable. Other examples of multiple conflicting objectives can be found in organizations that want to (1) maximize profits and increase wages, (2) upgrade product quality and reduce product cost, (3) pay larger dividends to stockholders and retain earnings for growth, and (4) reduce credit losses and increase sales.

Goal Seeking the situation where a manager wishes to determine what change would have to take place in the value of a specified variable in a specified time period to achieve a specified value for another variable. For example, a manager can ask the following "goal seeking" question: What would the unit sales price have to be for the project to achieve a target return on investment of 20%? Spreadsheet software such as Excel can help answer this type of question.

Going Dark process of deregistering. It involves a company with no more than 300 holders of record (not the same as shareholders) or 500 holders of record and less that $10 million in assets that files Form 15 with the SEC to indicate that it will stop meeting previous reporting requirements. Company control and ownership do not change. Technically, the shares can still be bought and sold. They are listed on the "pink sheets," the National Quotation Bureau's list of daily quotes for companies not listed on any stock exchange. See also Going Public.

Going Private involves a group or individual buying all outstanding shares of a company, which alters control, capitalization, and ownership of the company. Typically the buyers believe the stock is undervalued. The process is more costly and time consuming that going dark. When it is complete, the company's shares are no longer publicly traded. *See also* Going Dark; Going Public.

Going Public the process by which shares of common stock are first offered for sale in the public markets (through the organized exchanges or over-the-counter); also called *initial public offering*. The advantages of going public must be weighted against the disadvantages. Going public may give the company and major stockholders greater access to funds as well as additional prestige and wealth. It also means that shares assume a market value (a value placed on expected future earnings). On the other hand, the company must open its books to the public through the SEC and state filings and put up with the pressure for short-term performance placed on the company by security analysts and large institutional investors.

Gold Standard a country's currency expressed on its equivalent value to gold such as one U.S. dollar equating to 23.22 grains of fine gold. It displays how much of the units of a currency are exchangeable into a certain amount of gold. If a significant outflow of gold occurs, a deficit in the balance of payments may arise. A gold standard may aid stability in exchange rates. The gold standard worked acceptably for a period of more than 40 years up to World War I. The U.S. dropped this standard in the early 1930s.

Golden Handcuffs a contractual agreement, almost virtually assuring that the stockbroker will stay with the brokerage firm for a specified time period. The incentive may be in the form of high commission rates, bonuses, participation in a forthcoming initial public offering (IPO) of the brokerage firm itself, or other attractive fringe benefits. The contract may specify a penalty the broker will incur such as forfeiting past commissions if he or she leaves the brokerage firm before a specified date.

Golden Handshake a clause in an executive employment contract that provides the executive with a lucrative severance package in the event of his/her termination. It may include a continuation of salary, bonus and/or certain benefits and perquisites, as well as accelerated vesting of stock options.

Golden Parachute a highly lucrative contract, giving a senior corporate executive monetary or other benefits if his or her job is lost in a merger or acquisition. Examples of benefits are generous severance pay, bonus, and stock options.

Good Till Cancelled (GTC) Order an investor's order to his or her broker to buy or sell a security or option at a given price. The order continues in effect until it is executed or cancelled by the investor. In the event the GTC order has not been executed for an extended time period, the broker will typically contact you to ascertain whether you still want to keep the order open. *See also* Buy Order.

Good-Faith Bargaining; Good Faith (Goodwill) in the carrying out of a transaction, an indication that each party will be ethical and fair and will act without malice or deception. Good faith implies honest intentions and observance of the concept of reasonableness. If deception did occur without prior knowledge, the transaction, conducted in good faith, is still valid. For example, if a property deed is transferred to another in the course of a good faith sales, and it later becomes evident that a prior owner had not properly signed the certificate, the sales is still valid. Contrary to good faith is bad faith, where one of the participants knowingly commits fraud or deception. Should this be proved, the transaction is rendered invalid.

Goodness-Of-Fit a degree to which a model fits the observed data. In a regression analysis, the goodness-of-fit is measured by the coefficient of determination (R-squared).

Goodwill
Personal: the good name and reputation an individual enjoys.
Corporate: the additional value accruing to a company because of its favorable public reputation, customer relations, and other intangible factors that give the company a measurable competitive edge.
Accounting: the intangible asset that has tangible value at the time of the sale of a company. The purchase price of a company is equal to net assets values plus goodwill. For example, if the net assets of company XYZ are $5,400,000 and its goodwill is $600,000, then the purchase price would equal $6,000,000. Goodwill is an intangible asset amortizable over 40 years.

Google a popular search engine. Reportedly named by an infant. Google is a 1 with 100 zeroes behind it.

Gopher menu-based client/server structure having search engines obtaining requested data from information servers. Gopher client software is usually on a client PC interacting with software on a specified Gopher server. This Gopher server searches many FTP sites to find the needed data to send to the Gopher client.

Government Accounting Standard Board (GASB) an organization that formulates accounting and budgeting standards for governmental units.

Government National Mortgage Association (GNMA, Ginnie Mae) government-owned corporation, nicknamed *Ginnie Mae*. GNMA primarily issues pass-through securities. These pass through all payments of interest and principal received on a pool of federally insured mortgage loans. GNMA guarantees that all payments of principal and interest will be made on the mortgages on a timely basis and its guarantee is backed by the full faith and credit of the U.S. Treasury.

Grace Period
Insurance: the 30-day period after the due date allowed on life and health insurance policies, which maintains the policy coverage although the premium has not yet been paid.
Banking: the time period in days in which savings deposits or withdrawals can be made and still earn interest from a given day of the interest period.
Credit: the number of days between the billing date on a credit card or charge account statement and when finance charges begin.

Graduated Payment Mortgage (GPM) a special type of fixed rate mortgage; conventional mortgage in which the monthly payments are lower in the early years of the loan than they are in the later years.

Grandfather Clause a stipulation in a new law or regulation exempting those already a part of the existing system from its effects. A grandfather clause permits those already participating in an activity about to be restricted to continue in their present activities and associations. For example, if an individual is currently piloting a boat without a newly required license, a grandfather clause may permit the individual to continue as before. In certain cases, a modified grandfather clause may allow a certain period of time to elapse before compliance with the newly imposed condition is required.

Grapevine

1. the communication system that results from an informal organization. Superimposed upon the formal organization, the informal organization nurtures and carries much important information.
2. the current gossip within an office.

Graphic Rating Scales Performance Evaluation Method a number of employee performance rating factors on which a supervisor indicates an evaluation. Rating factors include quantity and quality of work, attendance, timeliness, behavior attitudes, willingness to learn new techniques, and other factors that management feels are important.

Graphical User Interface (GUI) a program interface that takes advantage of the computer's graphics capabilities to make the program easier to use. It uses the easy-to-use icons and pull-down windows that give a program its commands.

Green Fund a mutual fund that only invests in companies that meet certain ethical and moral standards. An example is a fund that only invests in environmentally conscious companies.

Green Marketing the term to describe the activities of marketers who offer products that are environmentally friendly rather than environmentally harmful. Green marketers develop products that are less toxic, can be recycled and reused, and are of better quality.

Greenback slang for dollar.

Greenmail payoff given to a potential acquirer by a company targeted for a takeover. For example, this premium payment may be made to the raider due to a proxy contest. In most cases, the targeted company buys back its shares at a significantly higher price. In reciprocation for selling the stock back, the suitor agrees to end the attempted takeover. Sometimes management pays this exorbitant price to protect their positions. The premium may be made to thwart the takeover if the raider concurs not to purchase additional shares or to otherwise pursue the takeover for a stipulated number of years.

Gretham's Law a law that is popularly phrased as "bad money drives good money out of circulation." More accurately, the law asserts that when an item has a use as both a commodity and money, it will be used where its value is greater. The rapid disappearance of silver certificates is an example of Gretham's law. If a one dollar silver certificate entitles the holder to more than a dollar's worth of silver, the certificate will be hoarded, exported or exchanged for silver bullion, thereby disappearing from circulation. The law is named after Sir Thomas Gresham, Master of the Mint under Queen Elizabeth I during the sixteenth century.

Gross Domestic Product (GDP) an economic indicator that measures the value of all goods and services produced by the economy within its boundaries and is the nation's broadest gauge of economic health. GDP is divided among personal consumption, investment, net exports, and government spending. Consumption makes up roughly two-thirds of the total. GDP is normally stated in annual terms, though data are compiled and released quarterly. The U.S. Bureau of Economic Analysis releases an advance estimate of quarterly GDP, followed by a "preliminary" estimate and a "final" figure. It is reported as a "real" figure, that is, economic growth minus the impact of inflation. The figure is tabulated on a quarterly basis, coming out in the month after a quarter has ended. It is then revised at least twice, with those revisions being reported once in each of the months following the original release. Changes in the GDP of the U.S. are calculated quarterly, and announced in annualized terms (what the annual change would be if the quarter's pace of growth or contraction continued for a year). GDP reports appear in most daily newspapers and online at services like America Online. Also visit the Federal Government Statistics website on the Internet at *www.bea.gov/bea/newsrel/gdpnewsrelease.htm*, *www.fedstats.gov/* or *www. economicindicators.gov*. GDP is often a measure of the state of the economy. For example, many economists speak of recessions when there has been a decline in GDP for two consecutive quarters. The GDP in dollars and real terms is a useful economic indicator.

Gross Income (GI)

1. the amount of money earned (which is collected or will be collected) from the sale of goods minus the cost of the goods sold, also called *gross profit* or *gross margin*. For example, assume sales is $4,000 and the cost of goods sold is $1,200, the gross income is $2,800 ($4,000 - $2,800). Gross profit less operation expenses equals net income.

2. to the IRS, gross income is gross taxable income, salary, any investment earnings, and any other income subject to income tax..

Gross Income Multiplier (GIM) a method of determining the price to pay for an income-producing property by dividing the asking price (or market value) of the property by the current gross rental income. Example: Assume that current gross rental income = $23,600 and the asking price = $219,000, then the gross income multiplier is $219,000/$23,600 = 9.28.

A property in the similar neighborhood may be valued at "8 times annual gross." Thus, if its annual gross rental income amounts to $23,600, the value would be taken as $188,800 (8 x $23,600). This approach should be used with caution. Different properties have different operating expenses that must be taken into account in determining the value of a property.

Gross Margin *see* Gross Income (GI).

Gross Profit *see* Gross Income (GI).

Gross Profit Margin *see* Gross Income (GI).

Gross Rent Multiplier (GRM) the ratio of the selling price of property to its gross rental income. It is a popular income method that is used to appraise an income producing property. For example, if the selling price of property was $350,000 and the gross rental income generated was $50,000, the GRM would be 7 times.

Gross Revenues, Gross Sales the total sales amount without any adjustments for discounts or returns.

Ground Lease a long-term lease (such as 20 years) of only land.

Group of Five a group of five countries, that is, France, Japan, United Kingdom, United States, and West Germany. Finance ministers and central bankers of these countries met in the mid-1980s to discuss coordinating global economic policies.

Group of Seven a group of seven countries—Canada, France, Germany, Italy, Japan, United Kingdom, and the United States. Political leaders from these countries met in 1990 and 1991 to discuss common issues including economic aid to the Soviet Union and whether to intervene in the foreign exchange markets to attempt to stop the rising value of the U.S. dollar.

Group of Ten a group of ten non-Communist countries, meeting in the mid-1980s to establish the Basle Accord as well as deal with other common global economic issues.

Group of Thirteen (G-13) a group of thirteen countries formed in 1984 by the Group of Seven to compete with the OECD. This group includes Algeria, Argentina, Egypt, India, Indonesia, Jamaica, Malaysia, Nigeria, Peru, Senegal, Venezuela, Yugoslavia, and Zimbabwe.

Group Technology concept for identifying and classifying part families to efficient mass-production-type layouts. It can be designed for items usually manufactured by a process layout.

Groupware type of client/server software facilitating collaborative work; also called *workflow software*. It includes electronic mail, electronic messaging, and electronic meeting capabilities, among other features. Groupware enables individuals to communicate and accomplish activities together electronically. As a result, productivity and communication are enhanced irrespective to time or place. Groupware allows people to work together and share information in various ways.

Growth and Income Fund a mutual fund that seeks both current dividend income and capital gains. The goal of the fund is to provide long-term growth without much variation in share value. An example is Fidelity Investors' Growth and Income Fund.

Growth Fund a mutual fund that seeks to maximize its return through capital gains. It typically invests in the stocks of companies that are expected to rise in value faster than inflation. These stocks are best for an individual desiring steady growth over a long term period but feeling little need for income in the meantime. An example is T. Rowe Price Capital Appreciation Fund.

Growth Rate

In General: the percentage change in earnings per share, dividends per share, sales, market price of stock, or total assets, compared with a base year amount.

Securities: the compounded annual rate at which a security appreciates (depreciates). *See also* Time Value of Money.

Economics: the periodic growth rate in the gross domestic product (GDP) of the economy, expressed as a percentage over the preceding year or quarter. The growth rate generally signifies the state of the economy–prosperity or recession.

Growth Stock stock usually paying a small or no dividend that puts a priority on earnings per share growth, often the stock of a young company with little or no earnings history. The company is valued on the basis of anticipated future significant earnings and thus has a high price-earnings ratio. The growth company generally grows faster than the economy as a whole and also faster than the industry of which it is a part, but may also vacillate more in price. Such a company is risky because capital gains are speculative, especially in the case of young companies in new industries. An example of a growth company is a high-tech company. Growth stocks usually pay no or minimal dividends. Note: Growth stocks are more popular with investors who desire capital appreciation instead of dividend income. *See also* Common Stock.

Grubb & Ellis Office Space Study a measure of office vacancy rates, building and new leasing (locally, regionally, and nationally) compiled by Grubb & Ellis Commercial Real Estate Services. Economists use it to judge the health of a region's construction industry and determine whether businesses are expanding or shrinking. Developers and lenders use it to assess whether an area needs commercial or industrial construction. Firms can use it to negotiate leases; for example, they can demand concessions during high vacancy periods.

G.T.C. Order *see* Good Till Canceled (GTC) Order.

Guaranteed Invest Contracts (GIC)

1. an arrangement whereby an insurance company guarantees a rate of return for a limited time period, typically five to ten years, to be applied to the amount invested.
2. a frequent investment option in a 401(k) that pays a relatively attractive rate of interest, because a high number of employees were expected to select the option.

Guaranteed Renewable Policy a policy that is always renewable as long as the premiums are paid, although the company can raise the policy's rates.

Guardian one having the legal authority to take care of another as a parent; one acting as an asset administrator for an individual who is judged to be incompetent because of mental of physical impairment.
Testamentary: individual appointed as a child's guardian in the parent's will.
General guardian: one having the general care responsibility for an individual and his or her estate.

Special guardian*:* individual having limited authority of a guardian. For example, a special guardian may have no authority over the assets of an estate but must nurture and care for a child.

Guerrilla Marketing a low-cost marketing strategy targeting urban and street consumers, which employs the tactics and techniques and the weapons and the savvy of the guerrilla; also called *guerrilla street marketing*. Guerrilla marketing is needed because it gives small businesses a delightfully unfair advantage: certainty in an uncertain world, economy in a high-priced world, simplicity in a complicated world, and marketing awareness in a clueless world

GUI *see* Graphical User Interface (GUI).

Hacker a person who accesses a computer system without permission.

Hard Copy output printed directly onto paper. They are physical copies of letters, memos, or reports rather than electronic files. It is the fancy name for a printed out copy.

Hard Currency *see* Hard Money.

Hard Disk the long-term, main storage device for the computer.

Hard Dollars actual payment made by a client firm for certain services.

Hard Money
  1. convertible currency that has wide acceptance. For example, the United States dollar and the Japanese Yen are considered hard money.
  2. gold or silver coins, as compared with paper currency; also called *hard currency*.

Hardware the "computer name" given to all the electronic and mechanical devices that make up a computer, as opposed to software that refers to programs.

Harmonic Mean an average of a series of numbers computed as follows: (1) compute the reciprocal of each, (2) add these, (3) divide by the number of items, and (4) then determine the reciprocal of that result. For example, a firm buys $1,000 worth of a given supply at $1.00 per unit and a month later buys another $1,000 worth at $2.00 per unit. The average cost per unit is not the arithmetic average of $1.50, which is clearly incorrect. The proper answer is the harmonic mean of $1.33, which is obtained from:

$$\frac{1}{[(1/1) + (1/2)]/2}$$

Harvard Business Review a business journal containing in-depth articles on different facets of business.

Hay Points a job evaluation system, designed by a compensation firm called Hay, in which points are determined for specific activities.

Hazard a condition that affects the probability of losses or perils occurring. An example is possible earthquake or flood damage to a house.

Hazard Insurance insurance that lenders require borrowers to have so as to protect the lender's financial interest in a house. It guards against risks like storms or fires.

Head and Shoulders a chart pattern for a stock or stock market in which the highest point of the stock, or stock market, is preceded and followed by intermediate highs. When the pattern is graphed, it has the characteristic look of a head atop a pair of shoulders, hence the name. It is considered bearish when a head and shoulder formation is completed and moves to the right shoulder. According to classic chartist interpretations, the next move would then be down. However, an inverted head and shoulder formation is considered to be bullish since the completion of the chart's right shoulder normally precedes an upward movement.

Head Hunters a slang term for personnel or personnel firms that specialize in recruiting executives from other firms, usually for higher-income positions.

Head of Household a category of the filing status of a taxpaying entity. The head of household is an unmarried individual who maintains a household for another and satisfies the following conditions: (1) the taxpayer maintains a home in which a dependent relative lives for the whole year, (2) the taxpayer pays more than 50% of the cost of maintaining the home, and (3) the taxpayer is either a U.S. citizen or a resident alien. *See also* Filing Status.

Health Insurance insurance that provides protection against financial losses resulting from illness, injury, and disability. It is any insurance program covering medical expenses and/or income lost owing to illness or accidental injury, such as comprehensive or major medical, and through such means as fee-for-service, managed care, HMO, and PPO.

Health Maintenance Organization (HMO) a medical organization consisting of a group of hospitals, physicians, and other health care personnel who have joined together to provide necessary health services to its members. Major emphasis is on preventive medicine. Members pay an annual fee for the service.

Health Savings Accounts (HSAs) accounts that were created in the Medicare reform package passed by Congress in late 2003; work very much like individual retirement accounts; often called *health-care IRAs*. Each year you or your employer can put pre-tax dollars into an account. You can then use the money to pay for medical expenses not covered by insurance—such as deductibles, prescription-drug co-payments, and elective treatments—or roll the money over into subsequent years, thus building up a health-care nest egg.

Hedge
1. the process of protecting oneself against unfavorable changes in prices. Thus one may enter into a offsetting purchase or sale agreement for the express purpose of balancing out any unfavorable changes in an already consummated

agreement due to price fluctuations. Hedge transactions are commonly used to protect positions in (1) foreign currency, (2) commodities, and (3) securities.

2. financing an asset with a liability of similar maturity.

Hedge Fund

1. a limited partnership of investors that invests in speculative stocks.
2. a mutual fund that seeks to make money betting on a particular bond market, currency movements, or directional movements based on certain events such as mergers and acquisitions. It attempts to hedge in order to minimize an exposure to currency risk. In general, international short-term bond funds usually hedge most of the currency risk while longer-term funds have substantial exposure. Funds use currency options, futures, convertible bond arbitrage, merger arbitrage, and elaborate cross currency hedges, but the most effective hedges are expensive. Among the most successful hedge fund strategies in recent years has been convertible bond arbitrage. Hedge funds buy convertible bonds, which carry a low coupon but can be exchanged for equity at a certain price. They then take short position against the company's stock, trading on the relationship between the company's stock and bond prices.
3. a mutual fund that hedges the risk by buying or selling options to protect its positions against market risk. For example, a fund specializing in government debt securities may hedge its position by selling call options against its position to protect it against downside risk. Contrary to popular opinion, a hedge fund constructively uses options to protect investment positions and is pursuing an extremely conservative investment philosophy. Investors buy hedge funds as a way of diversifying portfolios and bolstering performance when other asset classes, such as equities or bonds, are having a rough ride. This is because hedge funds are classified as an alternative asset class in which returns are not correlated closely with other investments.

Help-Wanted Advertising Index an economic indicator that tracks employers' advertisements for job openings in the classified section of newspapers in 50 or so labor market areas. The index represents job vacancies resulting from turnover in exiting positions such as workers changing jobs or retiring and from the creation of new jobs. The help-wanted figures are seasonally adjusted. The help-wanted advertising figures are obtained from classified advertisements in newspapers in major labor markets. Herfindahl-Hirshman Index sum of the squared market shares multiplied by 10,000 to eliminate the need for decimals. By squaring the market shares before adding them up, the index weight firms with high market shares more heavily. The value of the Herfindahl Hirshman Index lies between 0 and 10,000. A value of 10,000 exists when a monopolist exists in the industry. A value of zero results when there are numerous infinitesimally small firms. This index is often used by the Department of Justice to determine an antitrust policy.

Herzberg' Theory For Motivation Fredrick Herzberg's theory on job satisfaction as a key component of motivation. He divided work into motivators and hygiene factors as shown on the next page.

Hygiene Factors	Motivators
• Pay, status, security	• Meaningful and challenging work
• Working conditions	• Recognition for and feeling of achievements
• Fringe benefits	• Increased responsibility
• Policies and practices	• Opportunity for growth and advancement

Hertz (Hz) the frequency of electrical cycles per second. One Hz is equal to one cycle per second.

HH Bonds *see* Series HH Savings Bond.

Hidden Clauses purposely vague contractual language that may lead an unsuspecting purchaser to incur obligations or risks that are not readily apparent.

Hidden Reserve the understatement of owners' equity or net worth. This understatement can arise either from the undervaluation of assets or a complimentary overaccrual of liabilities. For purposes of published financial statements, full disclosure must be made with respect to this departure from standard reporting practices. The ultimate effect of putting up a hidden reserve is that in a future period, net income will be inflated by the amount of hidden asset values converted to cash.

High-Yield Bonds bonds, or mutual funds that invest in bonds and that pay a higher rate of return than normal because they are rated lower than investment grade; also called *junk bonds*.

Histogram (Frequency Diagram) a graphical representation of a frequency distribution. It is a series of rectangles, each proportional in width to the range of values within a class and proportional in height to the number of items falling in that class.

HMDA *see* Home Mortgage Disclosure Act (HMDA).

HMO *see* Health Maintenance Organization (HMO).

Hog-Corn Price Ratio number of bushels of corn necessary to purchase 100 pounds of hog (live pork). It is simply the ratio of the prices of these two products. When the ratio is relatively high, hog production increases since farmers find it more profitable to use corn to feed more hogs than to sell their corn; vice versa.

Hold
1. the practice of a long-term investor buying and retaining a security over an extended period of time; this allows the earnings of the company to grow, resulting in a concomitant increase in the stock's market value.
2. an analyst's recommendation on a stock between accumulate and sell.
3. the practice of retaining an asset in an account until an item is collected or a liability is satisfied. For example, a passbook loan requires the amount of the loan to be held in a savings account until the loan has been satisfied.

Holders of Record owners of a firm's shares on the date of record indicated on the firm's stock ledger. Holders of record receive stock rights or dividends when they are announced. Because of the time needed to make bookkeeping entries when a stock is traded, the stock will sell ex-dividend for four business days prior to the date of record.

Holding Company corporations that own enough voting stock in one or more companies to assume control over their policies and management. The other corporations are generally referred to as subsidiaries. Holding companies control many subsidiaries in widely different business areas. Advantages of holding companies are (1) ability to control sizable operations of fractional ownership, (2) isolation and diversification of risks through subsidiaries, and (3) approval of stockholders of the acquired company not required. Disadvantages of holding companies are (1) partial multiple taxation when less than 80% of a subsidiary is owned, (2) ease of enforced dissolution by the U.S. Department of Justice, and (3) risks of negative leverage effects in excessive pyramiding.

Holding Period the time interval for which an investor holds an investment. The return on a given investment depends primarily on this period of time. The period is used for income tax purposes to determine whether a profit earned or loss incurred is treated as short- or long-term capital gains or losses.

Holding Period Return (HPR) the total return earned from holding an investment for the holding period of time.

Holographic Will a will not meeting all the requirements of a valid will.

Home Affordability Index a measure of the typical U.S. family's ability to buy a home, published by the National Association of Realtors. When the Index measures 100, a family earning the median income has exactly the amount needed to purchase a median-priced, previously owned home, using conventional financing and a 20 percent down payment. For example, the index of 140.9 means that half the families in the nation have at least 140.9 percent of the income needed to qualify for the purchase of a home with a median price of, say, $250,000.

Home Banking a telecommunications method of doing ordinary consumer banking using a home computer, modem and a telephone line or a television with an interface device and telephone connection. Home banking allows the depositor to get up-to-the-minute information on account balances as well as to pay bills. While home banking is still in its infancy, its future seems assured as telecommunications and computers gain consumer acceptance.

Home Mortgage Disclosure Act (HMDA) the act that created public loan data that can help determine whether financial institutions are serving the housing needs of their communities and identify possible discriminatory lending patterns. The law applies to financial institutions including banks, savings associations, credit unions and other mortgage lending institutions. Using this loan data, the Federal Financial Institutions Examination Council (FFIEC) creates reports for the nation, states, and each major metropolitan area. The data can be found online at the FFIEC's website at *www.ffiec.gov.*

Home Office Deduction a deduction allowed for income tax purposes if certain requirements are met for maintaining an office in the home. Requirements are that the portion of a home is exclusively used on a regular basis (a) as a principal place of business or (b) as a place for meeting with clients or customers in the normal course of the taxpayer's business. An additional requirement for employees holds that the office must be maintained only for the convenience of the employer.

Home Owners Warranty (HOW) Program builder's ten-year guarantee that their workmanship, materials, and construction are up to established standards. The HOW provides reimbursement for the cost of remedying specified defects.

Home Page the opening page of a website.

Home-Equity Loans the loan secured by a house. It is one of the few loans whose interest payments can still be tax deductible. They come in two varieties: the traditional second trust deed (mortgage) and the home-equity line of credit.
Second trust deed: a second trust deed is similar to a first trust deed (mortgage), except that in the event of foreclosure, the holder of the first mortgage has priority in payment over the holder of the second mortgage.
Line of credit: under the line of credit provision, a check may be written whenever funds are needed. Interest is charged only on the amount borrowed. Under the Tax Reform Act of 1986, interest incurred on the first and second homes is deductible for tax purposes.

Homestead legal status conferred by certain states on a homeowner's principal residence. In certain states, homestead status may provide protection against creditor claims or forced land sales providing the homeowner continues to maintain his or her residence there. Homestead status may also qualify the homeowner for a homestead exemption.

Horizontal Analysis a financial statement analysis that covers more than one period for the purpose of calculating percentage change in an account. *See also* Vertical Analysis.

Horizontal Integration the combining of businesses manufacturing and/or distributing similar products. The main goals of horizontal integration are to expand market share and hurt competition. It may be in violation of antitrust laws in certain cases. *See also* Vertical Integration.

Horizontal Mergers mergers between companies whose operations compete or that perform roughly the same function in the economy.

Host Country the target or recipient country of direct foreign investment and in which a multinational company is based and operates externally to its domestic jurisdiction.

Hot Link a link between two applications such that changes in one affect the other. For example, some desktop publishing systems allow one to establish hot links between documents and databases or spreadsheets. When data in the spreadsheet change, the corresponding charts and graphs in the document change accordingly.

Hot Money money that moves internationally from one currency to another either for speculation or because of interest rate differentials, and swings away immediately when the interest difference evaporates. A multinational company is likely to withdraw funds from a foreign country having currency problems.

Hotel-Occupancy Report a local, regional, and national report of the average monthly occupancy percentage of hotels in a given area, compiled by Pannell Kerr Forster, a national accounting firm that specializes in the hospitality industry. It is an indicator of business travel as well as of the health of the tourism industry.

Hotspot provides high-speed wireless internet access in convenient public locations or at home. Using either a laptop or PDA that is 802.11 wirelessly-enabled, people can download their email attachments, watch a live webcast, or listen to streaming audio.

House Poor buying more house than a buyer can afford. This is the situation of having very little cash because virtually all of one's net worth is tied up in her house.

House Price Index (HPI) a quarterly report, compiled by the Office of Federal Housing Enterprise Oversight (based on the nation's largest database of U.S. mortgage records) tracking transactions involving the same single-family homes over time.

Housing And Urban Development Department (HUD) created by Congress in 1965, the agency is principally responsible for federal programs relating to housing and urban improvement. HUD's programs include mortgage insurance for home-buyers, low-income rental assistance, and programs for urban revitalization that are developed in conjunction with state and municipal authorities.

Housing Starts a measure of actual starts of houses, condominiums, and apartment construction. When an economy is going to take a downturn, the housing sector is the first to decline. The strength in housing starts means not only the housing industry is healthy but suggests strength in the overall economy. At the same time, it is closely related to interest rates and other basic economic factors. Housing starts figures are issued monthly by the Department of Commerce. Housing is a key interest-sensitive sector that usually leads the rest of the economy out of the recession. Also, housing is vital to a broader economic revival, not only because of its benefits for other industries but also because it signals consumer's confidence about making long-term financial commitments. For the housing sector to be sustained, housing start figures need to be backed by building permits. Permits are considered a leading indicator of housing starts.

Housing Stock the total number of housing units.

HPI *see* House Price Index (HPI).

HR 10 Plan *see* Keogh Pension Plan.

HRM *see* Human Resource Management (HRM).

HTML The formatting language of the World Wide Web. It determines the appearance of the pages and it defines the links in the website. *See* Hypertext Markup Language.

HTTP *see* Hypertext Transport Protocol (HTP).

Hudson Employment Index a monthly nationwide survey, done by Hudson Highland Group (*www.hudson-index.com*) of more than 9,000 employed Americans on U.S. workers' attitudes regarding employment conditions. The Hudson Employment Index is the first monthly measure of employee attitudes on critical work issues, including career opportunities, job satisfaction, and workplace performance. The Index reflects the opinions of a diverse cross-section of U.S. employees, at all career levels within all industries.

Human Development Index an attempt by the United Nations to assess the impact of a number of factors on the quality of human life in a country.

Human Resource Accounting recognizing a variety of human resources and showing them on a company's balance sheet. For example, the idea of human resource accounting was well received, especially by human resource oriented firms such as those engaged in accounting, law, and consulting. However, practical application is limited, primarily because of the difficulty and the lack of uniform, consistent methods of quantifying the values of human resources. Under human resource accounting, a value is placed on people based on such factors as experience, education, and psychological traits and, most importantly, future earning power (benefit) to the company.

Human Resource Management (HRM) the part of the organization that is concerned with the "people" dimension. It involves staffing, training, management development, motivation, performance evaluation, compensation activities, and maintenance of employees so as to achieve organizational goals. HRM is complicated in an international business by the profound differences between countries in labor markets, culture, legal systems, economic systems, and so on.

Human Resource Planning the process of analyzing and identifying the need for and availability of human resources so that the firm can meet its objectives.

Human Resources (HR) the company function that oversees hiring, training, compensation, benefits, and other related activities.

Hybrid Loans mortgages that have a fixed rate for the first few years, then adjust annually—usually turn into constant-maturity Treasury (CMT)-indexed mortgages when they enter their adjustment periods.

Hyperlink *see* Hypertext.

Hypertext database approach linking related data, programs, and pictures. A hypertext document has highlighted 'words, called hyperlinks, which when clicked on, will direct one to more information about the word.

Hypertext Markup Language (HTML) uniform coding for defining web documents. The browser used by the user examines the HTML to ascertain the manner in which to display the graphics, text, and other multimedia components. The use of HTML is recommended in developing intranets/extranets because it is easier to program than window environments such as Motif or Microsoft Windows. HTML is a good integrating tool for database applications and information systems. It facilitates the use of hyperlinks and search engines enabling the easy sharing of identical information among different responsibility segments of the company. Intranet data usually goes from back-end sources (e.g., mainframe host) to the web server to users (e.g. customers) in HTML format.

Hypertext Transport Protocol (HTTP) the basic protocol for the World Wide Web (www).

Hypotheses Testing in statistics, the use of a statistical test to discriminate between two hypotheses–called the null (H_0) and the alternative (H_1) hypothesis—at two specific risk (or probability) levels. These two hypotheses are usually stated in terms of (anticipated) population parameters, e.g.,

$$H_0: = \$100$$
$$H_1: \neq \$100$$

Statistics (e.g., x) from the random sample may serve as estimators of the population parameters (e.g., μ). The risk levels, symbolized as "α" and "β" are specified for two types of errors—Type I and Type II, respectively—which can occur in the decision process. A Type I error occurs when the null hypotheses (H_0) is rejected when it is in fact true, but the sample results lead you to believe otherwise. A Type II error occurs when the null hypothesis is accepted when, in fact, it is false (i.e., H_1 is true). The decision to accept or reject the null hypothesis is based on (1) statistics computed from the random sample and (2) the probability of obtaining such values (determined from the underlying sampling distribution).

Ii

IBRD *see* International Bank for Reconstruction and Development.

Icon a small picture that represents an object or program. Icons are very useful in applications because an icon is used in place of words or commands. You click on the icons to open different programs.

Ideal Capacity
1. the volume of activity that could be attained under ideal operating conditions, with minimum allowance for inefficiency, also called *theoretical capacity, engineered capacity* or *maximum capacity*. *See also* Capacity.
2. the presence of unused capacity together with insufficient raw materials or skilled labor a firm needs. When idle capacity exists, a firm can take on an incremental order without increasing the fixed costs.
3. economic situation wherein the market will not absorb all of the maximum possible output at a price exceeding the variable cost of production.

Idle Time the cost of direct labor for employees unable to perform their assigned tasks due to machine breakdowns, shortage of materials, power failure, sloppy production scheduling, and the like; also called *down time*.

Illiquid
1. the inability to convert an investment to cash in a short period of time with a minimum capital loss.
2. lacking cash (or working capital) or having a low current ratio. *See also* Liquid.
3. the lack of sufficient liquid assets, like cash or marketable securities, to pay short-term debt.

ILO *see* International Labor Office (ILO).

IMF *see* International Monetary Fund (IMF).

Immediate Annuity
1. an annuity that is purchased with one premium and whose payments begin immediately.

2. an annuity to be started immediately, in opposition to a deferred annuity, which will be paid sometime in the future.

Impact Statement a document that analyzes the projected effects of a contemplated project. A primary reference point within this statement concerns probable externalities (e.g., negative implications to the outside). An example would be the proposal of a large industrial corporation located on an upriver site that would dump some level of pollutants into the air and streams (e.g., an environmental impact report). The effects upon health would be considered.

Impaired Credit a reduction in credit given by a business to a customer who has experienced deterioration in creditworthiness.

Impairment of Capital
1. the amount by which stated capital has been decreased by distributions such as dividends or losses.
2. a legal restriction enacted to protect creditors by limiting payments of dividends to current or retained earnings.
3. the excess of liabilities over assets due to losses.

Impairment of Value a permanent decline in the value of an asset. The entry is to debit the loss account and credit the asset for the reduction in utility. Recovery of its cost or book value is not a realistic expectation.

Imperfect Competition a situation in which each marketer's product is differentiated enough and produced in large enough quantities to affect the market price. Retailers are usually imperfect competition examples, as buyers cannot compare all price quality offerings at all retail outlets.

Imperfect Markets markets where imperfect competition exists. Imperfect competition includes monopoly and oligopoly where one or more sellers can control the market price. *See also* Perfect Market.

Implicit Costs or opportunity cost. The return foregone from an alternative use of time or facilities. For example, if an individual goes to the health spa on Tuesday night instead of working overtime and earning $260, the monetary return foregone is $260.

Implied Warranty a warranty in effect whether expressed individually or not. It is mandated by state law. It provides that products sold are warranted to be suitable for sale and will work effectively whether there is an express warranty or not.

Impound
1. to take custody and seize property or money by some legal action (e.g., court mandate).
2. in governmental accounting, to reduce authority to incur financial obligations by withholding some portion or all of an appropriation.

Improvement a capitalized expenditure usually extending the useful life of an asset or improving it in some manner over and above the original asset. Thus if an expenditure adds years to an asset or improves its rate of output, it would be considered an improvement that is capitalized. In contrast, a maintenance or repair expense is not capitalized.

Impulse Buying unplanned retail consumer buying motivated by a whim or a spur-of-the-moment impulse. Impulse buying is a strategy exploited by many retailers. For example, newspapers are strategically placed at the checkout counter of a store.

Imputed Costs implicit costs that are not reflected in the financial reports of the firm; also called *implicit costs*. They consist of the opportunity costs of time and capital that the manager has invested in producing the given quantity of production and the opportunity costs of making a particular choice among the alternatives being considered.

In Escrow the period in which the escrow agent informs both the buyer and the seller as to what documents or funds need to be deposited with the escrow agent in order to fulfill the conditions of the purchase and sales, and in which the parties collect the items requested. These items include such things as funds to cover mortgage insurance premiums, taxes, hazard insurance, and title insurance. Title insurance indicates that no one else has an ownership right to the property, confirmation that the seller has obtained an adequate loan to cover the purchase price, there has been an inspection of the property for termites, and the seller's original deed to the property has been obtained.

In the Money a term describing the exercise price of a call option that is less than the current market price of the related stock. For example, a 50 calls option on a stock selling at 53 is in the money. A 50 put option on a stock selling at 48 would also be in the money. Such an option has intrinsic value.

In the Tank
1. a slang term meaning that market prices of securities are down significantly.
2. a slang term referring to the rapid decline in stock market prices at the conclusion of a trading day.
3. a street slang used to describe a situation in which your investment is in a deep hole. In other words, it is doing poorly.

Inadequacy a loss or expense incurred by virtue of lost or reduced capacity, technological obsolescence, abnormal wear and tear, and that requires premature replacement or abandonment.

Inc. "Incorporated." American English word for a business formed as a corporation. *See also* Limited.

Inc. Magazine a business magazine for small business owners and entrepreneurs.

Incentive Bonus
1. salary paid in consideration of other factors than hours worked. For example, wages may be tied to units produced as an indicator of productivity.
2. a bonus paid to employees who meet a production quota within a prescribed period of time.

Incentive Compensation *see* Incentive Bonus.

Incentive Stock Options (ISOs) stock received under an option plan that provides a more favorable tax effect than the qualified stock option for employees receiving such stock. With incentive stock options, employees receive the right to purchase a specified number of shares of company stock at a specified price during a specified period. ISOs are not taxable at the time of grant or at the time of exercise. Only when they are sold, the gains are subject to federal taxation. Under Tax Reform Act of 1986, gains from incentive stock options will be taxed at an ordinary income tax rate. However, for 1987 the law capped capital-gain taxes at 28 percent. Options are exercised in any order. Also, an employer may not grant an employee more than $100,000 in stock options that first become exercisable in any one year.

Income
1. money earned or accrued during an accounting period that results in the increase in total assets.
2. items such as rents, interest, gifts, and commissions.
3. revenues arising from sales of goods and services.
4. The excess of revenues over expenses and losses for an accounting period (i.e., net income). *See also* Gross Income.

Income Bonds bonds on which the payment of interest is required only when earnings are available from which to make the payment. Typically, interest that is bypassed does not accumulate. It is commonly used during the reorganization of a failing or failed business firm.

Income Distributions one of the ways a mutual fund pays its shareholders. Dividends earned by stocks are accumulated and paid to investors during the year according to a schedule.

Income Dividends *see* Income Distributions.

Income Shifting a strategy of moving a person's income from a high income bracket or tax rate to a lower one. One popular form of income shifting is applying some of a person's income to their child.

Income Statement an accounting schedule that itemizes a firm's revenues, costs and profits (or losses) for a given period of time; also called the *profit and loss statement* and is used as a comparative measure of performance. While a balance sheet shows the condition of a company at a particular point in time, the income statement shows the results of a company's operations during a specific time frame such as from January 1st through December 31st.

The Putnam Company
Income Statement
For the Year Ended December 31, 20B

Sales	$900,000
Less: Cost of goods sold	$492,000
Gross margin	$408,000
Less: Selling and administrative expense	278,000
Operating income	130,000
Less: Interest expense	5,625
Net income before taxes	124,375
Less: Income taxes	60,000
Net income after taxes	$64,375

Income Stocks a stock that pays a high current yield and has a good record of earnings and dividend payments over a period of years.

Income Tax A government levy on the taxable income of an individual or corporation. The taxable income equals the gross income less deductions and exemptions. The tax rate is graduated, increasing as taxable income goes from one tax bracket to another. Tax rates also depend on the status of the taxpayer (e.g., married, single). Income tax may be paid to federal, state, and local governments.

Incorporated a legal state of existence signifying that a corporate entity has been recognized. That is, a legal entity has been authorized by a state or other political authority to operate according to the entities' approved articles of incorporation or charter. An incorporated entity shares basic attributes: an exclusive name, continued and independent existence from shareholders or members, paid-in capital, and limited liability.

Increasing Return to Scale a phenomenon where if all inputs increase by a certain percentage, output grows more than that percentage. For example, when all inputs are doubled, output more than doubles. *See also* Economies of Scale, Returns to Scale.

Incremental Analysis the real-world counterpart to marginal analysis. Also called *differential analysis*, it is a decision-making method requiring that an estimate be made of the changes in total cost and/or revenue that result from a decision as to pricing, whether to add or drop a product, accept or reject a special order, or undertake a new investment.

Incremental Cost the real-world counterpart to marginal cost. Also called *differential cost*, it is the additional costs incurred by the firm if it undertakes a new program or manufactures an additional batch of output.

Indemnify

1. to agree to compensate for a loss or damage experienced by a person. The indemnifier may be an insurance company or employer.
2. a legal principle that determines the amount of the economic loss reimbursed for destroyed or damaged property.

Indenture a legal document that specifically states the conditions under which a bond has been issued, the rights of the bondholders, and the duties of the issuing corporation; also called a *deed of trust*. An indenture normally contains a number of standard and restrictive provisions (covenants), including a sinking fund requirement, a minimum debt-equity ratio to be maintained, and an identification of the collateral if the bond is secured. It also covers redemption rights and call provisions. The indenture provides for the opportunity of a trustee to act on behalf of bondholders.

Independent Agent in insurance, one representing several insurance companies who scrutinizes the market for the best place for a client's insurance business. The independent agent has his or her own records and is not directed by any one company, paying all agency expenses from the commissions derived from securing insurance clients.

Independent Contractor a person or business that provides goods or services to another entity under terms specified in a contract. Unlike an employee, an independent contractor does not work regularly for a company.

Independent (Outside) Director member of the Board of Directors of an entity who is an outsider, meaning he or she is not an employee of that entity. An example is a broker sitting on the Board of a client company. Such directors are important because they bring unbiased opinions regarding the company's decisions and diverse experience to the company's decision making process. In order not to have a conflict of interest, independent directors should not participate on the boards of directly competing businesses. Directors are typically compensated based on a standard fee for each board meeting.

Independent Variable An explanatory variable that may take on any value in a relationship. For example, in a relationship $y=f(x)$, x is the independent variable. For example, independent variables that influence sales are advertising and price. *See also* Dependent Variable.

Index

1. a statistical yardstick expressed in terms of percentages of a base year or years. For instance, the Department of Commerce's Consumer Price Index (CPI) is based on 1982-84 as 100. In April 1990, the index stood at 128.9, which meant that CPI that month was almost 29 percent higher that in the base period. An index is not an average. The index differs from an average in that it weighs changes in prices by the size for the companies affected. The Standard & Poor's Index of 500 stocks calculates changes in prices as if all the shares of each company were sold each day, thus giving a giant like General Motors its due influence.

2. in real estate, the basis for setting an adjustable rate such as the one-year Treasury bill average, three-month certificate of deposit (CD) rate, 11ᵗʰ District of cost of funds, London Inter-Bank Offering Rate (LIBOR), or prime rate.

Index Fund a mutual fund that has as its primary objective the matching of the performance of a particular stock index such as the S&P 500 index. The beauty of index funds is twofold: (1) They minimize costs. All the fund company has to do is construct a portfolio out of the stocks in a chosen index. The fund is passively managed, with changes being made only to fine-tune the fund's performance to match more closely the index's results. The alternative is an actively managed fund, which even sounds more expensive. (2) The index funds eliminate your need to work so hard and worry too much. You can be fairly assured that your performance will be as good—or as bad—as the overall performance of the market or markets you select a drawback to index funds is that since the index is made of the stocks of large, well-known, and highly regarded companies, they can miss out on the opportunity of superior stock-price appreciation that some small companies often provide.

Index Lease a lease agreement in which the tenant's rent is based on a change in the price of some measure, such as the consumer price index.

Index of Consumer Confidence the index that tracks the level of consumer confidence based on a survey by the Conference Board of New York, an industry-sponsored, non-profit economic research institute. It measures consumer optimism and pessimism about general business conditions, jobs, and total family income. The Conference Board's index is calculated on a 1985 basis of 100 and derived from a survey of 5,000 households nationwide, covering questions that range from home-buying plans to the outlook for jobs, both presently and during the next six months. Economic forecasters say that the index must exceed 80 over several months to conclude that the economy is solidly growing. *See also* University Of Michigan's Index Of Consumer Sentiment.

Index of Leading Economic Indicators (LEI) the economic series of indicators that tend to predict future changes in economic activity; officially called *Composite Index of 11 Leading Indicators*. This index was designed to reveal the direction of the economy in the next six to nine months. This series is the government's main barometer for forecasting business trends. Each of the series has shown a tendency to change before the economy makes a major turn--hence, the term "leading indicators." The index is designed to forecast economic activity six to nine months ahead (1982=100). The Index consists of 11 indicators, and are subject to revision. For example, petroleum and natural gas prices were found to distort the data from crude material prices and were subsequently dropped from that category. It is found in *Business Conditions Digest* published by the Bureau of Economic Analysis of the U.S. Department of Commerce. If the index is consistently rising, even only slightly, the economy is chugging along and a setback is unlikely. If the indicator drops for three or more consecutive months, look for an economic slowdown and possibly a recession in the next year or so. A rising (consecutive percentage increases in) indicator is bullish for the economy and the stock market, and vice versa. These 11 components of the index are adjusted for inflation. Rarely do these components of the index all go in the same direction at once. Each factor is weighted. The composite figure is designed to tell only in which direction business will go. It is not intended to forecast the magnitude of future ups and downs. This series consists of:

1. **Average workweek of production workers in manufacturing:** Employers find it a lot easier to increase the number of hours worked in a week than to hire more employees.
2. **Initial claims for unemployment insurance:** The number of people who sign up for unemployment benefits signals changes in present and future economic activity.
3. **Change in consumer confidence:** It is based on the University of Michigan's survey of consumer expectations. The index measures consumers' optimism regarding the present and future state of the economy and is based on an index of 100 in 1966. Note: Consumer spending buys two-thirds of GNP (all goods and services produced in the economy), so any sharp change could be an important factor in an overall turnaround.
4. **Percent change in prices of sensitive crude materials:** Rises in prices of such critical materials as steel and iron usually mean factory demands are going up, which means factories plan to step up production.
5. **Contracts and orders for plant and equipment:** Heavier contracting and ordering usually lead economic upswings.
6. **Vendor performance:** Vendor performance represents the percentage of companies reporting slower deliveries. As the economy grows, firms have more trouble filling orders.
7. **Stock prices:** A rise in the common stock index indicates expected profits and lower interest rates. Stock market advances usually precede business upturns by three to eight months.
8. **Money supply:** A rising money supply means easy money that sparks brisk economic activity. This usually leads recoveries by as much as fourteen months.
9. **New orders for manufacturers of consumer goods and materials:** New orders mean more workers hired, more materials and supplies purchased, and increased output. Gains in this series usually lead recoveries by as much as four months.
10. **Residential building permits for private housing:** Gains in building permits signal business upturns.
11. **Factory backlogs of unfilled durable goods orders:** Backlogs signify business upswings.

Index of Saturation a formula: Ci x REi where Ci = the number of RFi of customers; REi = the dollar expenditure per customer; and RFi = total square feet of unit area allotted to a product or service. The objective is to have the optimum per capita sales per square foot of space.

Index Options call or put option contracts purchased and sold on the Standard & Poor's (S&P) 100 index, Standard & Poor's (S&P) 500 index, major market index, international market index, computer technology index, oil index, and institutional index. Essentially, the investor is risking a specified amount of money, the price of the option contract, on the possibility that the selected index will move up, in the case of the call option, or down, in the care of the put option, sufficiently for the investor to make a profit by selling the option prior to the expiration date of the contract. All options are short term in nature and the time value of their premiums depreciates over their life. Thus, index options are an extremely speculative investment, but do not have as much leverage or risk as a futures contract.

Indexation feature of a contract or agreement designed to adjust its value for general price level changes. An example is cost of living adjustments (COLA) in a labor contract.

Indexed Bond a bond whose interest payments are tied to an inflation index. Thus if the price levels rise, the rate of bond interest is adjusted accordingly. *See also* Indexation.

Indexed Loan a noncurrent loan in which the principal, interest, or maturity is related to a particular index. Therefore, periodic adjustments are necessary to conform to the change in the applicable index. A case in point is an adjustable rate mortgage.

Indexing a method of changing the rate on an adjustable rate loan according to some selected index.

Indirect Costs costs that are difficult to directly trace to a specific costing object; also called *common costs*. National advertising that benefits more than one product and sales territory is an example of an indirect cost. Fixed factory overhead is another example of an indirect cost. *See also* Direct Cost.

Indirect Labor the labor not directly involved in production but essential to the manufacturing process, such as supervisory personnel and janitors. It is classified as part of factory overhead. *See also* Factory Overhead.

Indirect Liability
1. an obligation that has not yet occurred but for which responsibility for payment or satisfaction of such an obligation may arise in the future. An example is cosigning a loan for another party.
2. a potential obligation, the eventual occurrence of which usually depends on some future event beyond the control of the company, called *contingent liability*. Contingent liabilities may originate with such events as lawsuits, credit guarantees, and contested income tax assessments.

Indirect Manufacturing Expenses *see* Factory Overhead.

Indirect Materials primarily supplies including glues, nails, and other minor items and are classified as part of factory overhead. *See also* Factory Overhead.

Indirect Quote the price of a unit of a home country's currency, expressed in terms of a foreign country's currency. For example, in the case of U.S., 100 yens per dollar. *See also* Direct Quote.

Individual Investor an individual, as opposed to an institutional investor such as a mutual fund or pension fund.

Individual Retirement Account (IRA) a personal retirement account in which an employee can set up, with a deposit that is tax deductible, up to $3,000 a year ($6,000 for both spouses working). If you are 50 or over, that max is $3,500. IRA funds are available to their depositors, penalty-free, at the age of 59½ or sooner in cases of death or disability. Early withdrawal of deductible contributions for any reason will cost the taxpayer a 10 percent penalty.

Industrial Espionage the attempt by an outsider to steal or illegally obtain protected trade, process, or technology secrets from a business. The attempt is made by, for instance, eavesdropping, hacking into the target firm's computer database, or bribing a key company employee or scientist.

Industrial Park a separate zone set aside in a city where traffic and utilities are designed specifically for industrial use.

Industrial Production Index more precisely, the Federal Reserve Board Index of Industrial Production: A measure of changes in the output of the mining, manufacturing, and gas and electric utilities sectors of the economy. Detailed breakdowns of the index provide a reading on how individual industries are faring. Data for the index are drawn from 250 data series obtained from private trade associations and internal estimates. *See also* Capacity Utilization Rate; Factory Orders; Purchasing Manager's Index.

Industry Demand the total sales in any given product and service category and is, in part, determined by the price level.

Industry Standard the norm or benchmark set and accepted by the industry in technical specifications, production procedures, labor time required, materials used, etc.

Inefficient Markets markets in which at least some relevant information is known to some but not all parties involved. *See also* Information Asymmetry.

Inelastic Demand demand for certain items tends to remain constant even when price increases. Gasoline, cigarettes, and medicines are examples.

Inflation
1. a general rise in the price level. When inflation is present, a dollar today can buy more than a dollar in the future. Higher inflation could mean less attractive bond prices and less attractive stock prices. In the presence of hyperinflation, with prices rising at 100% or more, there is a tendency for people to prefer hard assets (such as real estate and precious metals) to financial assets (stocks and bonds) in their investment choice.
2. the general rise in prices of consumer goods and services. The federal government measures inflation with five key indexes: Consumer Price Index (CPI), Producer Price Index (PPI), Gross Domestic Product (GDP) Deflator, personal consumption expenditure price index, and Employment Cost Index

(ECI). Price indexes are designed to measure the rate of inflation of the economy.

Inflation-Indexed (-Linked, -Protected) Security an anti-inflation security that promises a higher return than the rate of inflation if the security is held to maturity. An example is inflation-linked 10-year U.S. Treasury notes. *See also* Treasury Inflation-Protected Security.

Infomercial one form of direct-response, nonstore retailing media. It is a program-length TV commercial that presents products in an entertainment-like atmosphere.

Information Asymmetry condition in which at least some relevant information is known to some but not all parties involved. Information asymmetry causes markets to become inefficient, since all the market participants do not have access to the information they need for their decision making processes.

Information Overload a situation in which people have too much information from which to choose for their problem solving and decision making.

Information Superhighway the Internet; also known as the *electronic highway* or *cyberspace*. It is a buzz word that refers to the Clinton/Gore administration plan to deregulate communication services allowing for the integration of all aspects of the Internet, cable TV, telephone, business, entertainment, information providers, education, etc.

Information Technology (IT) the technological side of an information system. It includes hardware, software, networks, databases, and all technologies that collectively facilitate construction and maintenance of information systems. In its broad sense, *IT* is used interchangeably with *information system*.

Information Transfer the transference of information from one nation to another within a multinational company. This sometimes develops into a political issue in relations among the governments because some types of information being transmitted are viewed as sensitive by the governments.

Infrastructure roads, airports, sewage and water systems, housing, schools, railways, the telephone, and other public utilities through expenditures made usually by governments; also called *social overhead*. It is regarded as a prerequisite for economic development and improvements in the standards of living.

Ingress entrance or path to a land parcel.

Inheritance Tax a state tax levied on the value of assets received as the result of an inheritance. Unlike the Federal Estate Tax, the inheritance tax is charged on the value of the property actually received by the heir rather than the value of the entire estate left by the decedent.

In-House any job done within a house as opposed to outsourcing.

Initial Margin partial payment required by an investor to a broker when he or she buys securities with the remainder on credit. The broker retains the securities as collateral and charges the investor interest on the money owed. The Federal Reserve Board determines margin requirements. The initial margin requirement for stocks is higher than that for bonds because of greater risk. Assume that with an initial margin requirement of 50% (present requirement for stocks and convertible bonds), 100 shares of Company XYZ stock are bought at $100 per share. The actual amount invested is $5,000, with a margin of $5,000 on credit. The current initial margin requirement on a short sale is 50% of the proceeds.

Initial Margin Requirement amount of cash or eligible securities required by the Federal Reserve Board and one's brokerage to be deposited with one's brokerage before buying on margin.

Initial Public Offering (IPO) a corporation's first offering of stock to the public. It is typically an opportunity for the present investors, participating venture capitalists, and entrepreneurs to make big profits, since for the first time their shares will be given a market value reflecting expectations for the company's future growth.

Injunction a court order issued to a defendant in an action either prohibiting or commanding the performance of a defined act. A violation of an injunction could lead to a contempt of court citation. There are many different types of court ordered injunctions; however, the most frequently used are the permanent, preliminary, and temporary injunctions.

Input-Output Analysis analysis of linear production processes with fixed input coefficients; also called *interindustry analysis*. It attempts to develop a matrix relationship between the flow of goods and services between industries or branches of an economic system. It employs historical tabular data on intersectional output and material flows to predict demand and supply changes for individual industries.

Inside Director an individual on the board of directors of a company who is an employee of that company. *See also* Outside Directors.

Inside Information privileged information obtained regarding material business results and pending security transactions that will not be made public until a certain date. Taking advantage of inside information for the purpose of making a profit is illegal.

Insider as defined by the Securities and Exchange Act of 1934, a corporate director, officer or shareholder with more than 10% of a registered security, who obtains knowledge through the influence of position, that may be used primarily for unfair personal gain to the detriment of others. The definition has been extended to include relatives and others in a position to capitalize on inside information.

Insider Trading
1. the buying and selling of the company's securities based on material information relating to the company that has not been made public. Insider trading according to this definition is against the law in most countries.
2. the buying and selling of shares of a public company by its officers, directors and stockholders who own more than 10% of the company's stock. In the USA,

such transactions must be reported monthly to the SEC under Section 16 of the Securities Exchange Act of 1934: reporting rules for similar trading may also exist in different countries or markets.

Insolvency the inability to meet financial obligations.

Insolvent

1. any person incapable of meeting current liabilities because of insufficient assets. Insolvency usually precedes bankruptcy; in the latter case, a court-appointed administrator develops a financial plan to help the debtor meet creditor payment demands. Insolvency is distinguished from illiquidity in that in illiquidity, there are sufficient assets to meet creditor demands, but they are not in a cash form.
2. the inability of a business to pay debt when due. An evaluation of insolvency is directed at the financing mix, cost structure, and the debt/equity ratio.

Insourcing the opposite of outsourcing.

Installment Loan a loan that is repaid in a series of periodic, fixed scheduled payments rather than in a lump sum. It is usually associated with the purchase of durable goods and services, such as autos and appliances.

Installment Sales

1. sales made on installment basis. Many business firms, such as TV dealers, furniture stores, and appliance dealers, make installment sales. Typically, a customer purchases merchandise by signing an installment contract in which the customer agrees to a down payment plus installment payments of a fixed amount over a specified period. The installment receivable so created by the contract is usually classified as a current asset.
2. transaction with a predetermined contract price in which payments are made on an installment basis over a period of time.
3. in real estate, a method of selling and financing property by which the seller retains title but the buyer takes possession while he or she makes the installment payments. The tax on the gain is paid as the mortgage principal is collected.

Installment (Sales) Method a revenue recognition method by which revenue is recognized when cash is collected. That is, when each payment is received from the customer, a portion of gross profit on the sale (and the gain) is recognized (based on the gross profit percentage in the year of the sale), so that by the final payment the entire gross profit is recorded.

Institute for Supply Management's Index the index, based on a survey of 375 companies in 17 industries, that measures new orders, inventories, exports, and employment in the service sector. Services account for five-sixths of the $10-trillion U.S. economy and includes industries such as entertainment, utilities, health-care, farming, insurance, retail, restaurants, and zoos.

Institute of Chartered Financial Analysts (ICFA) an educational branch of the Financial Analysts Federation, which was founded in 1947. The ICFA grants the Chartered Financial Analyst (CFA) designation to persons who have met certain professional qualifications. Essentially, candidates must serve a 2-year apprenticeship and also pass a series of three annual examinations about such topics as accounting, economics, ethical standards and laws, and security analysis to obtain the CFA designation. The ICFA is headquartered at the University of Virginia, Charlottesville, Virginia.

Institute of Internal Auditors (IIA) a professional organization that was established to develop the professional status of internal auditing. It administers and confers the CIA (Certified Internal Auditor).

Institute of Real Estate Management (IREM) a professional organization for real estate managers.

Institutional Advertising a form of advertising designed to develop or reinforce an image, concept or idea about a firm, a product, or a product line. The American Dairy Association used commercials with the message: "Drink milk and eat cheese" to develop an image that dairy products are healthy.

Institutional Investor an institution (such as a mutual fund, bank, insurance company, or pension fund) operating on behalf of a broad client base that trades large blocks of securities.

Instrument a written document, such as a contract, deed, will, lease, mortgage agreement, or bond, that provides rights and obligations for the parties concerned. An instrument gives formal notice of an agreement, creating rights and duties for the affected parties, such as a contractual commitment. An instrument serves as evidence of the terms agreed to.

Insurance an agreement through an insurance contract, termed a *policy*, that one party, for an agreed premium, will provide insurance or pay the insured a specified sum of money, contingent upon the specified conditions within the insurance contract, such as loss of life or property of the insured. Employers provide many types of insurance for employees, including health, disability, and life insurance.

Insured the individual indemnified against specific perils in an insurance policy. The insured may also contain others not specifically named within an insurance policy, such as family members or others in a fire insurance policy. Group insurance policies may include many individuals as the insured.

Insurer an insurance company or insurance underwriter that issues an account to indemnify the insured. An insurance policy is a legally enforceable contract issued for a stated premium by an insurer to an insured, assuming the risk of loss for stated perils.

Intangible Asset an asset that has no physical substance, such as a trademark, a patent, reputation, or goodwill.

Integrated Circuit (IC) a small electronic device made out of a semiconductor material; also known as a *chip*. Integrated circuits are used for a variety of devices, including microprocessors, audio and video equipment, and automobiles.

Integrated Services Digital Network (ISDN) a network that can transmit voice, data, and video.

Intellectual Property Rights (IPRs) the ownership of the right to possess or otherwise use or dispose of products created by human ingenuity. Examples are trademarks, patents, trade names, trade secrets, and copyrights. There are international organizations that deal solely with intellectual property, such as International And Territorial Operations.

Interest

1. amount charged by a lender to borrower for the use of money. Interest rates are normally expressed on an annual basis. The total interest = principal x interest rate x period of time. For example, the interest on a $20,000 loan at 9% for 10 months = $20,000 x 9% x 10/12 = $1500.

2. equity ownership of an individual or company in a business property, expressed in a percentage of dollars. For example, if an investor owns 100,000 shares of a company having 1,000,000 shares outstanding, the investor has a 10% ownership interest.

Interest Rate the rate, usually expressed annually, charged on money borrowed or lent. The interest rate may be variable or fixed. *See also* Variable Rate Loan. There are various types of interest rates. They are:

1. **Prime (interest) rate.** It is the rate charged on business loans to the most credit worthy customers by the nation's leading banks. The prime rate fluctuates with changing supply and demand relationships for short-term funds.

2. **Nominal or stated interest rate.** It is the interest that was predetermined for a loan. The effective rate of interest often differs from the stated rate. If the interest is paid when a loan matures, the actual rate of interest paid is equal to the stated interest rate. When interest is paid in advance, it is deducted from the loan so that the borrower actually receives less money than requested, which will raise the interest rate above the stated rate. The actual rate paid is called the effective rate of interest; also called the *yield*. It is computed by dividing the dollar interest paid by the amount of loan proceeds available to the borrower. For example, for a $1,000 loan with an annual interest of 10% with a provision of interest paid in advance, the effective rate is 11.11% ($100/($1,000 - $100) = $100/$900). The bond yield usually differs from the nominal (coupon) interest rate. *See also* Bond Yields.

3. **Discount rate.** It is the rate that the Federal Reserve charges member banks for loans. It is also the interest rate used in determining the present value of future cash flows. *See also* Discount Rate.

Interest Rate Parity a condition where the differences between national interest rates for securities of similar risk and maturity should be equal to but opposite in sign to the forward exchange rate differential between two currencies.

Interest Rate Risk the risk that the value of an asset will change adversely as interest rates change. For example, when market interest rates rise, fixed-income bond prices fall.

Interest-Only Loan a special loan in which the borrower pays only the interest for a specified time and then the principal in one lump sum at the end of the loan period.

Interface interaction between two computer devices or systems that handle data (e.g., formats, codes) differently. An interface is a device that converts signals from one device into signals that the other device needs.

Interim Financing a temporary source of financing on a short-term basis until a long-term financing source may be arranged. An example is a bride loan made to a new company until a stock issue can be floated.

Interlocking Directorates members of boards of directors serving on more than one firm's board, or one or more firms having a number of overlapping members.

Internal Audit an employee of a company, usually an independent contractor, who is responsible for auditing various aspects of the accounting procedures and internal systems, checking for fraud and errors and promoting efficient operations.

Internal Auditor *see* Internal Audit.

Internal Controls ways and policies to minimize errors and fraud and promote efficient operations.

Internal Failure Costs *see* Failure Costs.

Internal Financing a source of financing raised internally within the firm, such as retained earnings, as opposed to external financing, such as equity and debt financing.

Internal Rate Of Return (IRR)

1. the rate earned on a proposal. It is the rate of interest that equates the initial investment with the present value of future cash inflows. Under the internal rate of return method, the decision rule is accept the project if IRR exceeds the cost of capital; otherwise, reject the proposal.
2. The annual yield or rate of return on an investment for the term of ownership. For example, bond yield is the IRR on bond.

Internal Revenue Code federal statutes defining the income tax law. The Internal Revenue Code is extremely detailed and covers all aspects of the income tax law.

Internal Revenue Service (IRS) a branch of the U.S. Treasury Department that collects income tax and enforces the tax code.

Internalization extension of ownership by a firm to obtain new sources of materials, new stages of the production process, and new markets, as opposed to externalization. By growing internally, a business attains greater control, efficiency, and productivity. It is usually less costly than growing through acquiring other businesses. It is the business strategy opposite to vertical and horizontal integration.

International Accounting Standards (IAS) a set of international accounting and reporting standards that will help to harmonize company financial information, improve the transparency of accounting, and ensure that investors receive more accurate and consistent reports.

International Accounting Standards Board (IASB) *www.iasb.org.uk;* an independent regulatory body, based in the United Kingdom, which aims to develop a single set of global accounting standards.

International Accounting Standards Committee (IASC) a group that consists of members from influential accounting bodies in the United States, England, West Germany, France, Canada, Japan, etc. The organization proposes internationally accepted accounting standards. Discussion papers, drafts, and formal statements are issued. There is adherence to universally adopted and accepted concepts. It was founded in 1973.

International Bank for Reconstruction and Development (IBRD) the bank that was established to assist less developed countries in developing their economies; also called the *World Bank*. It attempts to promote economic and social progress through the creation of modern economic and social infrastructures. It makes loans to countries or firms for such purposes as roads, irrigation projects, and electric generating plants.

International Banking Facility (IBF) a separate banking operation within a domestic U.S. bank, created to allow that bank to accept Eurocurrency deposits from foreign residents without the need for domestic reserve requirements, interest rate ceilings, or deposit insurance premiums.

International Diversification
1. an ability to reduce the multinational company's risk by operating facilities in more than one country, thus lowering the country risk.
2. the effort to reduce risk by investing in more than one nation. By diversifying across nations whose business cycles do not move in tandem, investors can typically reduce the variability of their returns.

International Economics the branch of economics that deals with such topics as international trade, finance, foreign exchange, balance of payments, and similar subjects.

International Financing
1. Also called *foreign financing*, raising capital in the Eurocurrency or Eurobond markets.
2. A strategy used by multinational companies for financing direct foreign investment, international banking activities, and foreign business operations.

International Fisher Effect a theory that states that the spot exchange rate should change by the same amount as the interest differential between two countries.

International Fund a mutual fund that invests only in foreign stock or bond markets; also called a *foreign fund* or an *overseas fund*. Because these funds focus only on foreign markets, they allow investors to control what portion of their personal portfolio they want to allocate to non-U.S. stocks. International funds may be open-end or closed-end, equity or bond, small cap or large cap.

International Labor Office (ILO) a U.N. affiliate with representation from employers, unions, and governments dealing with trade union rights, employment terms and conditions, and the protection of the right of workers to organize and bargain collectively.

International Monetary Fund (IMF) a fund created at the Bretton Woods agreement in 1944 to supervise the international financial system, to lend official reserves to nations with temporary payments deficits, and to decide when exchange rate adjustments are needed to correct chronic payments deficits. The IMF has an international paper currency called special drawing rights (SDRs) to increase international liquidity. The IMF is affiliated with the United Nations and funded by member contributions.

International Product Cycle a theory of trade advanced by Vernon explaining why a product that begins as a country's export eventually becomes its import. The theory illustrates both trade flows and foreign investments based on product position in the following stages: (1) exports of an industrialized nation, (2) initiating foreign manufacture, (3) overseas competition in export markets, and (4) import competition in the country where the product was produced originally.

International Standard Book Number (ISBN) the number assigned by the Library of Congress to each book or serial publication such as magazines, newspapers, and newsletters.

International Trade Association (ITA) a division of the U.S. Dept. of Commerce who offers to help U.S. exporters and businesses compete in the global marketplace. It has information about export opportunities for specific industries, as well as information about specific nations. The ITA's home page on the Internet is *http://www.ita.doc.gov/*.

International Trade Commission (ITC) an independent, nonpartisan, quasi-judicial federal agency (*www.usitc.gov*) that provides trade expertise to both the legislative and executive branches of government, determines the impact of imports on U.S. industries, and directs actions against certain unfair trade practices, such as patent, trademark, and copyright infringement.

Internet system of linked smaller computer networks, international in scope, that facilitates data communication such as file transfer, electronic mail, and newsgroups between different entities. It all began as a network of computers for the United States Defense Department called the Defense Advanced Research Projects Agency Network (DARPANET). It already provides access to information provided by government (.gov), for-profit business (.com), nonprofits (.org), universities (.edu), and networks (.net).

Internet Address the actual full address for the Internet or World Wide Web location. *See also* URL.

Internet Marketing a form of direct marketing; also called *online marketing*. It requires that both the retailer and the consumer have a computer and a modem.

Internet Protocol (IP) *see* TCP/IP.

Internet Service Provider (ISP) business to service customers so they may access the Internet (such as America Online), and sometimes other related services, to subscribers.

Internet2 super-fast network that connects universities researching the next-generation Internet. It is used by several millions college students, researchers, and professionals around the world, but is generally inaccessible to the public.

Intranet private network used within the company. An intranet serves the internal needs of the business entity. Intranet users are able to access the Internet, but firewalls keep outsiders from accessing confidential data. It makes use of the infrastructure and standards of the Internet and the Web. Intranets use low-cost Internet tools, are easy to install, and offer flexibility. Intranets have already been established by at least two-thirds of the Fortune 500 companies and many other organizations.

Intrinsic Value

1. the natural value of an item. For example, land is worth its resale value.
2. a theoretical "true value" of something after detailed analysis. The value may be determined by incorporating relevant information in a model. An example might be the theoretical "real value" of a company based on financial analysis, which may be different from its book value or market value.
3. theoretical value of a call or put option.

Inventory the current stock of finished goods, goods in process, raw materials, and supplies, such as packing and shipping materials.

Inventory Control methods and procedures designed to minimize the costs of inventory, such as economic order quantity, reorder point, and safety stock.

Inventory Management planning and control of inventory of raw materials, work-in-process, and/or finished products involving a decision as to how much of some item to order (or produce) and when to place an order (or commence production).

Inventory Turnover The number of times inventory is sold during the year. It equals cost of goods sold divided by the average dollar balance. Average inventory equals the beginning and ending balances divided by two.

Inventory-to-Sales Ratio a ratio comparing the amount of current inventory against the sales of specific goods. It's a measure of how long it would take to sell existing inventory.

Investment

1. a capital asset.
2. an expenditure to acquire property, equipment, and other capital assets that produce revenue.

3. securities of other companies held for the long term, called long-term investments shown on the noncurrent asset section of the balance sheet.

4. securities of other companies held for a very short term, which are short-term investments.

Investment Adviser

1. the investment banker who may advise client companies on a continuing basis about the types of securities to be sold, the number of shares for distribution, the timing of the sale, and mergers and takeovers.

2. professionals registered with the SEC who advise their investor clients about the types of securities and the timing of purchases and sales; also called *advisor* or *financial advisor* or *investment advisor* or *investment counsel.*

Investment Banker a financial organization (employee thereof) that specializes in selling primary offerings of securities. Investment bankers buy new securities from issuers and resell them publicly, that is they underwrite the risk of distributing the securities at a satisfactory price. They can also perform other financial functions, such as (1) advising clients about the types of securities to be sold, the number of shares or units of distribution, and the timing of the sale; (2) negotiating mergers and acquisitions; and (3) selling secondary offerings. Most function as broker-dealers and offer a growing variety of financial products and services to their wholesale and retail clients.

Investment Center a responsibility center within an organization that has control over revenue, cost and investment funds. It is a profit center whose performance is evaluated on the basis of the return earned on invested capital. The corporate headquarters or division in a large decentralized organization would be an example of an investment center. Return on investment and residual income are two key performance measures of an investment center.

Investment Club a group of individuals joining together for the purpose of sharing security investment ideas. Normally, an investment club develops a pool of capital contributed by its members, which is subsequently invested in securities. Additional money is also contributed at monthly or quarterly intervals, depending on the wishes of the members. Investment decisions are made through a vote of the membership.

Investment Grade

1. highly rated bonds that are purchased by institutional investors because they are very marketable, and hence carry less risk. Standard & Poor's considers investment grade items to be from AAA through BBB-minus whereas Moody's considers them to be rated from AAA to Baa-3. *See also* Bond Ratings; Junk Bonds.

2. an investment situation in which a company is recognized as a leader in its industry and has a strong balance sheet, considerable capitalization, and continuous dividends.

Investment Income or unearned income. Passive income derived from any of several financial investments. Investment income includes annuities, capital gains, dividends, interest, option premiums, rents, and royalties. Under current law interest paid on a margin account can be used to offset any investment income.

Investor's Business Daily a daily newspaper for investors.

Invoice a bill prepared by a seller of goods or services and submitted to the buyer. The invoice describes such items as date, customer, vendor, quantities, prices, freight, and credit terms of a transaction.

Involuntary Bankruptcy bankruptcy that is legally and formally declared by petition of the debtor's creditors, and not by the debtor. *See also* Chapter 7; Chapter 11.

IOU a letter of debt written to the lender indicating, "I owe you" a specified sum of money to be paid at a certain date. The debtor must sign the letter to make it effective. If it is witnessed, it may be enforceable as a contract.

IP Address identification of a computer in the network by a numeric address.

IRA *see* Individual Retirement Account.

IRA Rollover a tax-free reinvestment of a distribution from a qualified retirement plan into an IRA or other qualified plan within a specific time frame, usually 60 days. These transfers can happen when leaving a job at an employer who offered a retirement plan such as a 401(k).

IRR *see* Internal Rate Of Return (IRR).

Irrevocable Trusts a trust that cannot be broken without the express permission of the beneficiary.

IRS Regulations Treasury Department Regulations representing the government's interpretation of the Internal Revenue Code. The regulations are published in the Federal Register.

IRS Rulings income tax rulings made by the Internal Revenue Service regarding specific applications of the Internal Revenue Service Code. They are administrative rulings, having the force of law, that can be appealed in the federal courts.

ISDN *see* Integrated Services Digital Network (ISDN).

iShares index funds that trade like stocks on stock markets. Each share represents a proportion of ownership in each stock that makes up an index. iShares are a great way for smaller investors to get the diversification of 50 or more companies without having to buy each individual stock.

ISO *see* Incentive Stock Options (ISOs).

ISO 9000 certification standards developed by the International Organization for Standardization (ISO) that serves as a basis for quality standards for global manufacturers. The 9000 is a block of numbers set aside for manufacturing standards, whereas other block numbers are for other standards. It includes:
ISO 8402: Quality — Vocabulary
ISO 9000: Quality management and quality assurance standards — Guidelines for

selection and use

ISO 9001: Quality systems—Model for quality assurance in design/development, production, installation, and servicing

ISO 9002: Quality systems—Model for quality assurance in production and installation

ISO 9003: Quality systems—Model for quality assurance in final inspection and test

ISO 9004: Quality management and quality system elements—Guidelines

Itemized Deduction a deduction from adjusted gross income for individual taxpayers. Examples of such allowable deductions are mortgage interest, certain casualty losses, medical expenses, contributions, and miscellaneous. The actual amount of the deduction allowed is only the excess of the total itemized deductions less the standard deduction (previously called *zero bracket amount*). Only this residual amount is deducted from adjusted gross income to compute taxable income.

Jj

Java Sun Microsystems object-oriented programming language used in the World Wide Web. It is a programming language used to create programs running on the client side of a web client/server application. Java enables web pages to include animation, sound, and interactivity.

Job Analysis the study of a work/task activity to determine the basic requirements. Once identified, the information is used to find personnel, evaluate performance, and set wages.

Job Burnout the emotional exhaustion that results from being overworked, overwhelmed, or stressed over a period of time. Burned-out workers develop negative or impersonal responses to others. Some workers experience decreased professional commitment and plan to leave their job.

Job Description a listing of your job duties. The job description is the basis for a performance evaluation for a merit salary increase.

Job Enlargement the horizontal expansion of a job through increasing job scope — the number of different tasks required in a job and the frequency with which these tasks are repeated.

Job Enrichment the vertical expansion of a job by adding planning and evaluating responsibilities It can improve the quality of work output, employee motivation, and satisfaction.

Job Jumper or job hopper. An individual who changes jobs frequently, usually in the hope of improving career opportunities. Research does not demonstrate that job jumpers are any more successful than others staying with an organization over a sustained period of time. Being termed a job jumper can be detrimental to one's career and job opportunities as employers may be reluctant to employ such an individual for fear he or she may leave soon.

Job Order Costing the accumulation of costs by specific jobs, contracts, or orders. This costing method is appropriate when direct costs can be identified with specific units of production. Job order costing is widely used by custom manufacturers such as printing, aircraft, construction, auto repair, and professional services. Job order costing keeps track of costs as follows: Direct material and direct labor are traced to a particular job. Costs not directly traceable (factory overhead) are applied to individual jobs using a predetermined overhead (application) rate. A compensation departments task is to determine the relative value of various jobs within a company. Often, there are subjective aspects to determining the ranking, such as how important or difficult the tasks of one job are, as compared with another in the company.

Job Rotation a form of job design where employees are systematically moved, or rotated, from one job to another. An objective of job rotation is to diminish the boredom and accidents often associated with job specialization.

Job Satisfaction an attitude that reflects the extent to which an individual is gratified by or fulfilled in his or her work. Extensive research conducted on job satisfaction has indicated that personal factors such as an individual's needs and aspirations determine this attitude, along with group and organizational factors such as working conditions, work policies, compensation and relationships with coworkers and supervisors.

Job Specialization the process of dividing work into smaller processes for the purpose of simplification. Job specialization makes work so simple that workers become interchangeable. The disadvantage is that the lack of challenge in simplified work processes oftentimes leads to boredom and subsequent accidents.

Jobber a middleman in the sales process who buys goods from a wholesaler and sells them to a retailer.

Job-Cost Sheet a record of the costs of a unit or batch of goods, usually including the direct materials costs, direct labor costs, and the allocation of factory overhead.

Jobless Claims a weekly compilation of the number of individuals who filed for unemployment insurance for the first time. This economic indicator, and more importantly, its four-week moving average, foretells trends in the labor market. Jobless claims are an easy way to measure the strength of the job market.

Joint and Several Liability a legal concept in which two or more persons have an obligation that can be enforced against them by joint action, against all members, and against themselves as individuals, hence several liability or responsibility.

Joint Costs all the common manufacturing costs incurred prior to the point, referred to as the split-off point, where the joint products are identified as individual products.

Joint Products the products that have a relatively significant sales value when two or more types of products are produced simultaneously from the same input by a joint process. For example, gasoline, fuel oil, kerosene, and paraffin are the joint products that are produced from crude oil.

Joint Return an income tax return that effectively provides that the income earned by a husband and wife will be treated as though it had been earned by both equally. This is allowed even though one spouse may not have income or deductions. A joint return usually provides a favorable tax effect compared with the filing of a non-joint return.

Joint Tenancy two or more persons to whom real or personal property is deeded or who together own an undivided interest in such property as a whole. Upon the death of one of the joint tenants, the deceased's property goes to the survivor joint tenant(s) without becoming an element of the estate of the deceased; also called *joint tenancy with right of survivorship.*

Joint Tenancy with Rights of Survivorship joint tenancy requiring that upon the death of a joint tenant (one owner), the surviving tenant automatically becomes the sole owner of the property.

Joint Venture a cooperative business activity, formed by two or more separate organizations for strategic purposes, that creates an independent business entity and allocates ownership, operational responsibilities, and financial risks and rewards to each member, while preserving their separate identity/autonomy; also called *strategic alliances.* Joint ventures occur because the companies involved do not want to or cannot legally merge permanently. Joint ventures provide a temporary way to meld the partners' strengths so that an outcome of value to both is achieved.

Journal of Commerce Index an 18-item industrial spot (not futures) price index for commodities, owned by Knight-Ridder Financial Publishing Company and calculated only once a day by the Center for International Business Cycle Research Center at Columbia University. Along with the Commodity Research Bureau (CRB) Index, it is frequently used as an indicator of inflation trends. Unlike the CRB, which is very much dominated by grains, it has no food components. Some economists contend that this index, though confined to spot conditions, is a superior predictor to the CRB futures index since its prices, including those used in manufacturing and construction, are more likely to be passed along the production chain than are prices of, say, soybean, grains, or wheat.

Journal/Journal Entry the method of entering the detail of a transaction into the company's accounting system. Journal entries are then posted to a general ledger.

Judgment

In General: a final opinion on some matter formed after consideration of all known evidence.

Accounting: an accountant's opinion regarding a set of financial facts as well as the implications they could have.

Law: an official judicial decision on a matter brought before the court in which the rights and claims of all the parties have been considered. A judicial judgment includes a conclusion regarding facts found or admitted by the parties followed by a decision or sentence of the law. The law's last word in a judicial matter.

Real Estate: a court decree placing a financial indebtedness on another to satisfy a claim. For example, Jones defaults in his lease obligations to Smith, and the court places a judgment against Jones upon completion of a judicial action initiated by Smith.

Jumbo Loans loans that differ from conforming loans because they are in excess of the conforming amount and reflect each lender's own guidelines. Jumbo loans are purchased on the secondary market by Freddie Mac.

Junior Stock a certain kind of stock issued to employees that is usually subordinate to regular common stock. The subordination may apply to voting rights, dividends, and liquidation rights. Junior stock may be converted to common stock when the employees meet certain performance requirements.

Junk Bonds a high-yield bond with a speculative credit rating of BB or lower, as opposed to an investment-grade bonds.

Juran, Joseph M. a quality theory guru. Juran believes that over 80% of all quality problems are caused by factors controllable by management. In consequence, management continually needs to seek improvements through sound quality management, which Juran defines as a trilogy of quality planning, control, and improvement. He defined quality as "fitness for use," including reliability, productibility, maintainability, and conformance.

Just-In-Yime (JIT) Inventory an inventory approach of ordering inventory from suppliers so that no storage is necessary. It arrives just when the inventory is needed.

Just-In-Time (JIT) Manufacturing; Just-In-Time Production approach to manufacturing in which items are produced only when needed in production.

Just-In-Time (JIT) Production Systems demand pull system. Purchases of materials and output depend on actual customer demand. Inventories are reduced greatly or eliminated, a few suppliers must reliably deliver small amounts on a frequent basis, plant layouts must become more efficient, a zero defects policy is established, and workers must be able to perform multiple tasks, including continuous monitoring of quality.

Kk

Kaizen Japanese term for continuous improvement. Kaizen budgeting incorporates expectations for continuous improvement into budgetary estimates. Kaizen costing determines target cost reductions for a period, such as a month. Thus, variances are the differences between actual and targeted cost reduction. The objective is to reduce actual costs below standard costs. The cost-reduction activities associated with the Kaizen approach minimize costs throughout the entire product life cycle. Therefore, it has the advantage of being closely related to the entity's profit-planning procedures. *See also* Target Costing.

Kanban Japanese word for card or ticket. It is essentially a Japanese information system for coordinating production orders and withdrawals from in-process inventory to realize just-in-time production. Originated from the use of cards to indicate a work station's need for additional parts. A basic kanban system includes a withdrawal kanban that states the quantity that a later process should withdraw from its predecessor, a production kanban that states the output of the preceding process, and a vendor kanban that tells a vendor what, how much, where, and when to deliver.

Kelly Blue Book a source listing the wholesale and retail values of used cars. The book may be purchased or used at a library.

Keogh Pension Plan (HR-10) a tax-deferred retirement plan established by a Self-Employment Individual Tax Retirement Act of 1962 (HR-10) under which self-employed persons have the right to establish for themselves and their employees retirement plans that permit them the same tax advantages available to corporate employees covered by qualified pension plans; also known as *HR-10 plan*. The contributions are tax deductible, and earnings are tax deferred until withdrawn. Keogh plans can take different forms, such as a defined benefit plan, a defined contribution plan, or a hybrid plan.

Keynesian Economics a body of economic thought and principles that originated with the British Economist John Maynard Keynes (1882-1946) in the 1930s. It has since been modified, extended, and empirically tested to the point where many of its basic prescriptions, ideas, and tools are now an integral part of general economic theory and governmental economic policy.

Kickback or, a payoff.

Finance: an illegal payment that sales finance companies reward dealers with cash for discounting installment purchase paper through them.

Government or business: a clandestine payment to an individual in government or business for favorable treatment or a business contract.

Labor relations: the illegal practice of requiring employees to return to the employer a portion of contractually determined wages as the price for obtaining a job.

Kiddie Tax the tax obligation for children under the age of 14 who must pay tax on investment income exceeding a certain amount at their parents' highest marginal tax rate. This requires the filing of IRS Form 8615.

Killing

1. an action resulting in the stopping or prevention of some activity. For example, the budget director killed the project because of a lack of funds.

2. making a significant gain on a stock market investment that resulted from an unusual combination of chance and timing.

Kilobyte (K, KB, or Kbyte) roughly one thousand bytes.

Kinesic Communication messages conveyed through actions. A wink, a frown, a smile, a sigh, a nod–they all convey messages.

Knowledge Management the combination of activities in gathering, sharing, analyzing, and disseminating knowledge to improve an organization's performance.

Knowledgement Managenent a broad strategic approach to identifying and using a company's knowledge to improve its efficiency. One subset of knowledge, structured data, can be managed using business intelligence tools.

Krugerrand a bullion coin from South Africa that contains one ounce of gold.

Kurtosis a descriptive statistic that measures the peakness of a frequency distribution.

Ll

Labor Economics a branch of economics that is concerned with earnings, employment patterns by industry and region, and job mobility of labor.

Labor Force the aggregate of individuals who either hold existing jobs or who are available for work. According to the U.S. Bureau of Labor Statistics, the labor force consists of people over the age of sixteen who are employed.

Labor Laws legislation enacted for the purpose of protecting workers' rights and the working environments. Significant labor laws were enacted with the National Labor Relations Act of 1935 (Wagner Act) and the Taft-Hartley Act of 1948.

Labor Market the market in which wages and the conditions of employment are determined by market forces.

Labor Standard labor efficiency standard that is often set via time and motion studies and laboratory experiments of the various labor operations needed to produce the finished good.

Labor Unions organized groups of employees of trades or sectors of the economy to represent employee interests in bargaining for wages, working conditions, work rules, and employee benefits.

Laffer Curve named after a supply-side economist, Arthur Laffer, a curve showing a hypothetical relationship between the marginal tax rate and tax revenues. The theory states that as tax rates increase too high, the total amount of tax revenues tends to level off. As Figure 1 indicates, eventually tax receipts will fall all the way back to zero if the rates grow too high. There is no empirical evidence to support this relationship and it still remains a hypothesis.

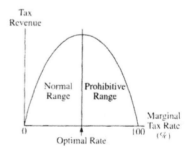

Laggard Industry an industry that lags behind the rest of the economy in output, employment, and contributions to the gross domestic product (GDP). A laggard industry in one nation may not be one in another nation.

Lagging Indicators the economic series of indicators that follow or trail behind aggregate economic activity. There are currently six lagging indicators published by the government. They are unemployment rate, business expenditures, labor cost per unit, loans outstanding, bank interest rates, and book value of manufacturing and trade inventories. *See also* Coincident Indicators; Index Of Leading Economic Indicators (LEI).

Lagrangean Multiplier measure of the marginal change in the value of the objective function resulting from a one-unit change in the value on the right-hand side of the equality sign in the constraint.

Lagrangean Multiplier Technique a method of solving constrained optimization problems in which the constraint (in a form in which it will be equal to zero when it is satisfied) is added to the original objective function. A new, augmented objective function is called Lagrangean, which constitutes an unconstrained optimization problem. Through creation of a new independent variable, (the Lagrangean multiplier), the satisfaction of the constraint becomes a first order condition for the new function.

Laissez-Faire the economic doctrine, as popularized by Adam Smith, that government should not interfere with commerce. It can be characterized by an attitude of non-interference and an absence of government from the markets.

LAN *see* Local Area Network (LAN).

Land Contract or, contract for deed; installment sales contract. A method of creative financing in real estate that enables the seller to finance a buyer by permitting him or her to make a down payment followed by monthly payments. However, title remains in the name of the seller until the mortgage is paid off.

Large Cap Stocks a company with large capitalization.

Laspeyres Price Index a price index that measures the cost, relative to the base period, of purchasing the base-year quantities at the given-year prices. It is a base-year weighted price index.

Last In, First Out (LIFO) a system of inventory valuation under which the cost of goods sold equals the cost of the latest inventory purchases and a firm computes the ending inventory cost from the costs of the older units. In periods of rising prices and increasing inventories, LIFO leads to higher reported expenses and therefore lower reported income and lower balance sheet inventories than does FIFO (first in, first out).

Latte Factor a simple notion that all you need to finish rich is to look at the small things you spend your money on every day and see whether you redirect that spending to yourself. Putting aside as little as a few dollars a day for your future rather than spending it on little purchases such as lattes, fancy coffee,

bottled water, and so on can really make a difference between accumulating wealth and living paycheck to paycheck. Say, you save $ 5 per day:
$5 per day (average cost of latte and fancy coffee) x 7 days = $35 per week, $35 per week =$160 per month, $150 per month invested at a rate of 10% annual return=

$1,885	after 1 year
$3,967	after 2 years
$11,616	after 5 years
$30,727	after 10 years
$62,171	after 15 years
$339,073	after 30 years

Law of Diminishing Returns the law that states that as the amount of a variable input (such as labor) is increased, with the amount of other fixed inputs (such as capital) held constant, the output that is produced by the additional units of the variable factor will continue to increase, but at a decreasing rate—a point is reached beyond which marginal product declines; also called the *law of variable proportions.*

Law of Large Numbers a statistical concept holding that as the number of units in a group increases, predictions about the group become increasingly accurate. This is the mathematical foundation of insurance, which states that the larger the group of objects under one's management, the smaller the variation between actual and probably losses.

Law of One Price *see* Purchasing Power Parity (PPP).

Law of Supply and Demand the law that postulates that market price will converge to the level at which the quantity buyers wish to purchase just equals the quantity that suppliers wish to offer.

Lawn *see* Local Area Wireless Network. A Lan connected by radio rather than actual wires.

Layaway buyers put down a deposit to hold items for final payment and purchase in the future.

Layout the arrangement of equipment and fixtures, merchandise, selling and sales-supporting departments, displays and checkout stands, where needed, in proper relationship to each other and in accordance with a definite plan.

L/C *see* Letter of Credit.

Lead Time
1. in purchasing, the time interval between placing an order and receiving the delivery. For example, if it will take two weeks to receive a new delivery, the lead time is two weeks. *See also* Reorder Point.
2. in manufacturing, it is the time from initial startup to the completed product.
3. in project management, it is the time from the start of a project to its completion.

Leader Merchandising a practice under which retailers sell certain items with a markup less than normal. Markup on lost leaders is less than average cost (total expenses) of doing business.

Leading (Economic) Indicators the economic series of indicators that tend to predict future changes in economic activity; officially called *Composite Index of 11 Leading Indicators*. This series is published monthly by the U.S. Department of Commerce, including average work week, average weekly initial claims, index of net business formation, new orders, and stock prices. The index of leading indicators, the components of which are adjusted for inflation, has an excellent track record of forecasting ups and downs in the business cycle.

Lean and Mean a company that has just the right number of workforce. The workforce is highly motivated to the organizational tasks and highly efficient.

Learning Curve a curve depicting the productivity of a manufacturing process over time. In the initial stages of the learning curve, the productivity of the manufacturing process is lower than in the later stages because the manufacturer is learning how to resolve problems occurring in the process that reduce overall productivity. After the producer learns how to deal with the obstacles, the manufacturing process can be done more quickly and inexpensively and with a higher quality output. Resources are used more productively, and better manufacturing methods are developed. More specifically, it is based on the statistical findings that as the cumulative output doubles, the cumulative average labor input time required per unit will be reduced by some constant percentage, ranging between 10 and 40 percent. The curve is usually designated by its complement. For example, if the rate of reduction is 20 percent, the curve is referred to as an 80 percent learning curve. The learning curve theory has found useful applications in many areas, including:
1. budgeting, purchasing, and inventory planning
2. scheduling labor requirements
3. setting incentive wage rates
4. pricing new products
5. negotiated purchasing

Business people use the learning curve theory in setting wage rates and contract prices and also determining labor requirements for a job or project. Budget analysts must take into account the learning rate in budgeting direct and indirect labor costs.

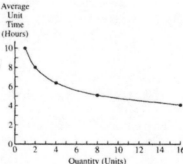

Lease

1. a contract in which the lessee pays rent to the lessor for the use of real property for a designated period of time, instead of owning them outright. Examples are the tenant's lease of an apartment and the rental of a car.
2. the written, legal document for a rental agreement.

Lease Agreement a contractual agreement between a lessor and a tenant for the use and possession of property for a certain period of time at a certain cost.

Gross lease: a total figure for the lease of the property from which the landlord must pay all taxes, utilities, insurance, and other expenses.

Month-to-month lease: a form of tenancy in which there is no formal lease agreement between the landlord and the tenant. Normally, the landlord must give a one-month notice prior to canceling the lease.

Net lease: a lease in which the tenant is required to pay all the related property costs including insurance, taxes, utilities, and others.

Lessee/Lessor a legal term for the tenant and the landlord.

Leased Fee Estate a lease contract to possess a parcel of property for a certain period of time. A leased fee estate is a conditional estate conveyance in real property for a specified period of time. The lease permits the lessee to possess, use, and enjoy the property for the specified lease period. For example, Smith agrees to lease a home at the rate of $1,200 per month for two years as a leased fee estate.

Leasehold Estate possession and use of a property estate by virtue of a lease.

Leasehold Improvements upgrading made by a lessee to leased property. Examples are paneling and wallpapering. These improvements revert to the lessor at the expiration of the lease term. As improvement costs are incurred under an operating lease, the leasehold improvement account is charged. The leasehold improvement is amortized to expense over the shorter of the life of the improvement or the remaining lease term. The improvements are considered long-term assets.

Least-Squares Method a statistical technique for fitting a straight line through a set of points in such a way that the sum of the squared distances from the data points to the line is minimized. *See also* Regression Analysis.

Ledger *see* General Ledger.

Legacy a gift by will of personal and real property.

Absolute legacy: an unconditional and immediate gift.

Conditional legacy: the bequest of a gift depending upon the occurrence or nonoccurrence of a specific event. For example, the beneficiary will receive the gift upon becoming employed or married.

Contingent legacy: a legacy dependent upon the passage of time. For example, a particular gift is given to a minor "at the age of 21." A contingent legacy is dependent upon a predetermined event occurring.

Specific legacy: a specific bequest for a beneficiary. For example, a particular beneficiary is designated to receive a particular piece of furniture.

Legal Capital the amount of stockholders' equity that cannot be reduced by the payment of dividends. It is defined by the par-value of par-value issued stock or the stated value of no-par issued stock.

Legal Description a description of real property including metes and bounds, government rectangular survey, or lot numbers of a recorded plot. All property deeds have a legal description.

Legal Liability

1. a legal obligation with specified terms and conditions by which a defined payment amount in money, goods, or services is to be paid within a defined time period in return for a current benefit.
2. legal responsibility of the accountant to the client and third parties relying on the accountant's work. Accountants can be sued for fraud and negligence in performance of duties.

Lehman Brothers Bond Index a popular bond index that measures the total return of a diversified portfolio of corporate bonds.

LEI *see* Index of Leading Economic Indicators (LEI).

Lemon Law a law passed by several states guaranteeing a full refund of money from a dealership to automobile purchasers who buy a new automobile that subsequently has major unresolved mechanical difficulties; also called *lemon protection*. If the purchaser can demonstrate that he or she has brought the car to the dealership a specific number of times to have a problem resolved with no satisfaction, then, under the lemon law, the consumer would qualify for a full refund from the dealer.

Lerner Index measure of the difference between price and marginal cost as a percentage of the product's price.

Less-Developed Countries (LDC) countries, most of whose trade involves the export of raw materials, fuels, minerals, and some food products to the industrialized, rich, and developed countries in exchange mostly for manufactured goods. More and more less-developed countries, however, are striving to industrialize their nations by concentrating on manufacturing labor-intensive products and exporting them at prices lower than the ones offered by developed nations.

Letter of Credit (L/C) a credit letter normally issued by the buyer's bank in which the bank promises to pay money up to a stated amount for a specified period for merchandise when delivered. It substitutes the bank's credit for the buyer's and eliminates the seller's risk. It is used in international trade. The letter of credit (L/C) can be revocable or irrevocable. A revocable L/C is a means of arranging payment, but it does not carry a guarantee. It can be revoked, without notice, at any time up to the time a draft is presented to the issuing bank. An irrevocable L/C, on the other hand, cannot be revoked without the special permission of all parties concerned, including the exporter. A letter of credit can also be confirmed or unconfirmed. A confirmed L/C is an L/C issued by one bank and confirmed by another, obligating both banks to honor any drafts drawn in compliance. An unconfirmed L/C is the obligation of only the issuing bank. The three main types of letter of credit, in order of safety for the exporter, are (1) the irrevocable, confirmed L/C; (2) the irrevocable, unconfirmed L/C; and (3) the revocable L/C.

A summery of the terms and arrangements concerning theses three types of L/Cs is shown below.

	Irrevocable confirmed L/C	Irrevocable unconfirmed L/C	Revocable L/C
Who applies for	Importer	Importer	Importer
Who is obligated to pay	Issuing bank and confirming bank	Issuing bank	None
Who applies for amendment	Importer	Importer	Importer
Who approves amendment	Issuing bank, exporter, and confirming bank	Issuing bank and exporter	Issuing bank
Who reimburses paying bank	Issuing bank	Issuing bank	Issuing bank
Who reimburses issuing bank	Importer	Importer	Importer

Letter Stock *see* Tracking Stock.

Leverage
1. the use of other people's money (OPM) to create a greater return than normal. OPM is then invested in a higher-risk investment, with hopes of greater-than-normal returns.
2. the ability to only pay a portion for a property with the remaining being mortgaged or secured by financing one way or another.
3. a term commonly used in finance and accounting to describe the ability of fixed costs to magnify returns to a firm's owners. Operating leverage, a measure of operating risk, refers to the fixed operating costs found in the firm's income statement. Financial leverage, a measure of financial risk, refers to financing a portion of the firm's assets, bearing fixed financing charges in hopes of increasing the return to its owners. Total leverage is a measure of total risk. The way to measure total leverage is to determine how earnings per share (EPS) is affected by a change in sales.

Leveraged Buyout (LBO) a takeover of a company using borrowed funds. In the classic leveraged buyout, the assets of the target company are used as collateral to finance the takeover by the raider (potential acquirer). The cash flow of the target company is used to repay the loan. At times, the LBO may be used by management to take the company private, so it is not publicly held, to prevent a raider from using the LBO against them. Of course, it is possible for the raider to use his or her own assets to collateralize a loan in an LBO attempt against another company. In any event, the shareholders of the target company are always offered a premium price to induce them into selling their shares to the raider.

Leveraged Lease
1. a lease arrangement of property financed by someone other than the lessee or lessor. A long-term creditor finances the lease and recourse in the event of default is generally not available to the creditor via the lessor.
2. a special lease arrangement involving a creditor, lessor and lessee. A creditor finances most of the cost to acquire an asset, the lessor may put in a small amount of cash if not totally financed by the creditor, and the lessor acquires the asset, using the asset as security. The asset is then leased to the lessee on a non-cancelable basis and the periodic payments to the lessor service the debt. The lessor, having borrowed most of the funds to acquire the asset, has "leveraged" himself while having both the rewards and risks of the lease.

Leveraging
1. using borrowed money to control an investment. The advantage of leveraging is that a small amount of equity can be used to create a larger rate of return. The risk is that leveraging can substantially increase the risk of loss in the event the investment is unsuccessful.
2. using borrowed money to finance elements of a business. Highly leveraged companies have a lot of debt in relation to their equity.

Level of Significance *see* Statistical Significance.

Levy the imposition or collection, usually by legal or governmental authority, of an assessment of a specified amount. An example is a tax assessment.

Liabilities a very broadly defined term implying legal or financial responsibilities to others.
Corporate: an amount of money owed by one company to another or unearned revenue requiring the performance of future services. Examples of corporate liabilities include accounts payable, accrued expenses payable, and bonds payable.
Legal: an obligation one is legally bound to perform immediately or in the future.
Life Insurance: future benefits obligated to policyholders and their beneficiaries. Insurance companies are required by state law to maintain sufficient reserves to meet any liability claim made against them. The cash surrender value of a life insurance company's policies is also considered part of the liabilities.
Personal: an amount of money owed or services to be provided based on advance

payment received (e.g., a retainer). Examples of liabilities to an individual include taxes payable, loans payable, credit card balances, and a mortgage payable.

Liability Exposure the extent to which one is at a liability risk in any matter. The amount of damages or legal liability for which one could be responsible.

Primary liability: a liability in which one is directly responsible. For example, if one were to fall on a homeowner's front step and sustain injuries, the homeowner would bear primary liability responsibility for any damage claims or other legal liability.

Secondary liability: contingent claims for which one could be liable if the primary obligator fails in his or her responsibilities.

Liability Insurance the insurance to protect against the liability the insured becomes legally obligated to pay due to bodily injury, property damage, or professional liability or libel. The two categories of liability insurance are:
1. personal exposures liability
2. professional liability
Personal exposures liability is for acts of omissions that result in lawsuits against an individual for bodily injury and/or property damage to a third party. Professional liability is the liability created when an individual with professional training claims expertise in a specialized area greater than the layman. In liability insurance, the insurer agrees to indemnify the insured for financial indebtedness that the insured might owe a third party as well as legal expenses incurred for his or her liability.

LIBOR *see* London Interbank Offer Rate (LIBOR). A short-term interest rate in the Eurodollar market.

License a legal document given by a regulatory agency to conduct some activity subject to prescribed terms. Typically, a fee is charged. Examples are a marriage license or driver's license.

Lien the right of a party, typically a creditor, to hold, keep possession of, or control the property of another to satisfy a debt, duty or liability. A mortgage would create such a security interest or lien upon property in the event of default.

Life Cycle
1. the movement of a person through the different stages of life from birth through death.
2. the movement of a product of business through the stages of development, growth, expansion, maturity, saturation, and decline. Most new products seem to have life-cycles. Some examples include high-tech items such as computers, VCRs, and black-and-white TVs. *See also* Product Life Cycle.

Life-Cycle Costing
Personal: The costs for an individual that change over the life cycle. For example, a major cost in young parenthood is buying a home. Later in life, a major cost is the college education of the children.

Corporate: estimates of a product's revenues and expenses over its expected life cycle. The result is to highlight upstream and downstream costs in the cost planning process that often receive insufficient attention. Emphasis is on the need to price products to cover all costs, not just production costs.

Life Estate a freehold interest in an estate, limited to the duration of the life of the grantee or other stipulated individual. Upon the demise of the grantee, or other stipulated individual, the estate reverts to the grantor. For example, the U.S. government granted former President Eisenhower and his wife, Mamie, a life estate at their Gettysburg Farm as a historical site. Upon their deaths, the property reverted to the U.S. government as a historical landmark.

Life Expectancy the average number of years a person is expected to live based on actuarial tables. The life expectancy for females exceeds that of males. Insurance plans or retirement plans are dictated by an individual's average life expectancy.

Life Insurance insurance coverage against the death of a person, with payment going to a named beneficiary, typically another family member. The insured pays a periodic lump sum premium, and on his or her death, the face value of the policy (less any loans against it) is payable to the beneficiary. Some policies provide for living benefits to the insured during his or her lifetime, such as cash surrender value of income payments.

LIFO *see* Last In, First Out.

Like-Kind Exchange a tax deferred exchange of assets, usually real estate, without immediate taxation.

Limit Order order to purchase or sell a stock, bond, or commodity at a particular price or better. The trade will occur only if the investor's price limitations are satisfied. For example, an investor places a limit order to buy AT&T at $20 when the stock is at $21. Even if the stock went down to $20 1/4 the buy will not occur. If an investor places a limit order to sell AT&T at $22 when the price is $21, the trade will not take place until the stock reaches $22. A higher commission is typically charged for a limit order. A limit order may be appropriate when market prices fluctuate or uncertainty exists. *See also* Buy Order.

Limited British English word for a business formed as a corporation. It is the same as "Inc."

Limited Liability
Business: a liability that does not go beyond the owner's investment in a business. A corporation and limited partners enjoy this particular feature. The stockholders of a corporation usually have limited liability; they risk only their investment in the business. Sole proprietors and general partners have unlimited liability. *See also* Partnership; Unlimited Liability.
Law: Any illegal or contractually restricted obligation.

Limited-Liability Company (LLC) business form that provides limited personal liability, as a corporation does. Owners, who are called members, can be other corporations. The members run the company unless they hire an outside management group. The LLC can choose whether to be taxed as a regular corporation or pass through to members. Profits and losses can be split among members any way they choose. The LLC rules vary by state.

Limited Partner a partner whose liability for partnership obligations is limited to the investment in the partnership. A limited partner is not allowed to take active part in the management of the partnership. The important use of limited partnerships have always been tax shelters. However, under the Tax Reform Act of 1986 limited partnerships are ruled passive investments and their tax benefits are severely limited. General partners have unlimited joint and several liability and manage the partnership.

Limited Partnership a type of partnership in which the limited partner is legally liable only for the amount of his or her initial investment. Typically there are two classes of partners: the general partner (usually the organizer), who operates the syndicate and has unlimited financial liability and the limited partners (the investors), who receive part of the profits and the tax-shelter benefits but who have no voice in the management of the business. The sponsor or general partner manages the partnership and uses the cash of the limited partners for ventures such as gas or oil exploration, real estate, or equipment leasing.

Limited Warranty a written warranty that fails to meet the conditions of a full warranty in one or more respects. For example, a limited warranty granted by an appliance manufacturer may be limited to the parts, but not the labor, in repairing an appliance.

Line
1. a bank commitment to lend funds to a borrower up to a specified amount over a specified future period.
2. an insurance term describing the maximum liability the insurer assumes for a particular item.
3. the major activities of a company, such as products. It can refer to the selection of products a company offers or can refer to the production line where products are assembled.

Line and Staff typical categorical classifications in which authority and personnel structure are organized in a company. Line personnel usually are defined as deriving from direct operational activities such as financing, distribution, leadership, and strategic decision making. A manager is a line person. Staff personnel are usually advisory and facilitative in nature for the line personnel. An accountant is a staff person to upper management because accounting advice is given. Thus, line personnel contributes directly to the firm's objectives, while staff indirectly contribute to the accomplishment of these objectives by advising and facilitating the execution of such objectives.

Line Authority the authority to give orders to subordinates. It contrasts with staff authority, which is the authority to advise but not command others. Line managers are responsible for attaining the goals set by the organization as efficiently as possible. Production and sales managers typically exercise line authority. *See also* Staff Authority.

Line Balancing process of distributing the workloads evenly.

Line Item Budget a budget typically used by governmental entities in which budgeted items are grouped by administrative entities and object costs. These budget item groups are usually presented in an incremental fashion, that is in comparison with previous periods. Line item budgets are used also in private industry for the comparison and budgeting of selected object groups and their previous and future estimated expenditure levels within an organization.

Line Responsibility *see* Line and Staff.

Line of Credit the maximum preapproved amount that a person can borrow without completing a special lease arrangement involving a creditor, lessor and lessee. A creditor finances most of the cost to acquire an asset, the lessor may put in a small amount of cash if not totally financed by the creditor, and the lessor acquires the asset, using the asset as security. The asset is then leased to the lessee on a non-cancelable basis and the periodic payments to the lessor service the debt. The lessor, having borrowed most of the funds to acquire the asset, has "leveraged" himself while having both the rewards and risks of the lease.

Linear Function a mathematical relationship in which the slope is constant and it is graphed as a straight line. It is formulated as additive elements, with no multiplicative or power components. *See also* Nonlinear Function; Power Function.

Linear Programming (LP) the problem of allocating limited resources among competing activities in an optimal manner. Specifically, it is a mathematical technique used to maximize revenue, contribution margin (CM), or profit function, or to minimize a cost function, subject to constraints. Linear programming consists of two important ingredients: (1) objective function and (2) constraints, both of which are linear. To formulate the LP problem, the first step is to define what are called the decision variables that one is trying to solve for. The next step is to formulate the objective function and constraints in terms of these decision variables.

Linear Regression a regression that deals with a straight line relationship between variables. It is in the form of y=a + bx whereas nonlinear regressions involve curvilinear relationships such as exponential and quadratic functions. *See also* Linearity; Regression Analysis.

Linear Thinking incremental step-by-step logic.

Linearity

1. in linear programming (LP), the requirement that the measure of effectiveness such as contribution margin or cost and resource usage must be proportional to the level of each activity conducted individually. For example, each unit of a resource must make the same contribution to the objective function that every other unit of that resource makes.
2. in linear regression, the requirement that the relationship between a mixed cost and an activity variable, such as machine hours, is a straight line in the form of

$y = a + bx$. This means that the variable portion changes by a constant amount per hour no matter how many hours are used.

Liquid Descriptive of the condition in which an individual has adequate cash and near-cash assets to meet current debt.

Liquid Asset any asset that can easily be converted to cash.

Liquidated Damages an amount of money specified in a contract as compensation to be paid if the contract is not satisfactorily consummated. An example is an offer to buy real property that includes a statement to the effect that once the seller accepts the offer, if the buyer fails to complete the purchase, the seller may keep the buyer's deposit (the earnest money) as liquidated damages.

Liquidating Value an estimated amount of money an asset would sell for if the company was liquidated or closed down; called *break-up value*.

Liquidation
In general: conversion of assets into money.
Business: the breaking up and selling of a company and its assets for cash distribution to its creditors and then owners. Chapter 7 of the Federal Bankruptcy Code covers a forced liquidation.
Stocks: in the event of an unmet margin call, a brokerage firm would liquidate a sufficient amount of the client's securities to meet the cash margin requirement.

Liquidity
1. the immediate convertibility of various assets into cash without significant loss of value. For example, a person's holding of marketable securities is more liquid than his or her house.
2. a person's ability to meet current liabilities when due. This ability may depend upon a person's current assets and expected future cash flow. It may be important for a person's assets to be sufficiently liquid to meet financial near-term commitments and to take advantage of new investment opportunities.

Liquidity Ratio the ratio of liquid assets divided by current debt. A low ratio indicates that the company (or individual) has a liquidity problem and may be unable to meet its debt obligations at a near-term date. The company may have to take steps to improve the situation, such as consolidating several loans into one with a longer maturity date.

Listed Securities securities traded on an organized security exchange such as the New York Stock Exchange (NYSE) and the American Stock Exchange (AMEX). They are distinguished from unlisted securities, which are traded in the over-the-counter (OTC) market. The organized exchanges have certain requirements that firms must meet before their stock can be listed. Among the requirements are size of the company, number of years in business, earnings record, number of shares outstanding, and market value of shares.

Living Trust a trust that is set up with assets while a person is alive.

Living Will a document that specifies how one is to be treated for medical purposes if he/she becomes incapacitated.

Load sales charge assessed by a mutual fund to buy shares (front-end load) or sell shares (back-end load). A no-load mutual fund is one that does not assess a fee when buying or redeeming shares in the mutual fund. Typically, the front-end load ranges from 1% to 8% of the initial investment. For example, if a mutual fund has a 2% front-end load and you invest $5,000, then $4,900 would go into the fund. The load charge is added to the net asset value per share when determining the offer price. Note: The absence of a sales charge in no way affects the performance of the fund's management, and eventually, the return on investment.

Load Chart a modified Gantt chart. Instead of listing activities on the vertical axis, load charts list either whole departments or specific resources. This arrangement allows managers to schedule capacity by workstations.

Load (Mutual) Fund a mutual fund sold to the public that charges sales commissions, usually called a *front-end load* when purchased.

Loan an agreement by which the owner of property (the lender) and a borrower agree to let the borrower use the property for a specified time period, and in return the borrower will pay the lender a payment (usually interest) and return the property (usually cash) at the end of the time period. A loan is usually evidenced by a promissory note. Examples of a loan are a commercial loan, consumer loan, mortgage loan, or auto loan.

Loan Amortization the systematic repayment of the loan principal and interest. For example, on 1/1/20X1 a $100,000 loan is taken out and 10% interest payable over three years at year end. The annual loan payment is $40,209.

Loan Origination Fee the lender's charge to the borrower for doing all the paperwork and setting up the mortgage loan, such as credit checks, appraisal, and title expenses. For example, the lender approves a $100,000 mortgage loan with a 1% loan origination fee. The loan origination fee is then $1,000.

Loan-To-Value (LTV) Ratio the ratio of the loan principal (amount borrowed) to the property's fair market value or sales price. For example, on a $100,000 home with a mortgage loan principal of $80,000, the ratio is 80%. The LTV ratio on a conventional loan is 80%. Home mortgages at more than an 80% LTV ratio generally require private mortgage insurance (PMI).

Loan Value
In general: the amount of money a lender agrees to lend on pledged collateral.
Securities: the amount of money a broker can lend to an investor on marginable securities. If the margin rate is 50%, then for a portfolio of stocks qualifying as marginable worth $20,000, the broker can lend $10,000.
Insurance: the ceiling an insured can borrow against his or her life insurance contract. For policies having a cash surrender value, the amount that can be borrowed equals the surrender value. The policy serves as collateral.

Local Area Network (LAN) linking of computers and other devices for intersite and intercompany applications in a small geographic area.

Local Area Wireless Network (LAWN) a LAN connected by radio rather than actual wires.

Local Taxes taxes collected through local municipalities.

Locational Break-Even Analysis comparison of potential plant locations based on an economic basis by estimating the variable and fixed costs and then graphing them for a representative sales or production volume at each location. Assuming equal revenues from all locations considered, you would select the location with lowest total cost.

Lockbox a box in a U.S. Postal Service facility, used to facilitate collection of customer remittances. The use of a lockbox reduces processing float. The recipient's local bank collects from these boxes periodically during the day and deposits the funds in the appropriate corporate account.

Lock-In-Clause a clause inserted in a loan agreement, where a lender guarantees a quoted interest rate on a loan for a specified period of time. The lock-in-clause is an incentive for the borrower to close the loan before the expiration date. In relatively stable economic periods characterized by a low rate of inflation, lock-in-clauses can be made for longer periods of time than during inflationary periods where there may be rapid changes in interest rates.

Logarithm the power to which another number, called the base, must be raised in order for the whole term to be equal to the original number in question. Thus, since $3^2 = 9$, we can say $\log_3 9 = 2$, where 3 represents the base. In general, we can say that $\log_a N = x$, which means that $a^x = N$. Two bases are commonly used: the base 10 and the base $\underline{e}$. Logs taken to the base 10 are called common logarithms and are often used in computations. Logs taken to the base $\underline{e}$ are called natural logarithms (where $\underline{e}$ is approximately equal to 2.7181) and often used to describe growth or decay over time.

Logarithmic Curve a nonlinear curve that uses logarithms.

Logistic Curve the typical S-shape often associated with the product life cycle. It is frequently used in connection with long-term curve fitting as a technological method and to describe the sales growth of a new product; an initial learning period when sales are low, rising rapidly as sales spread through the entire market and then leveling off and slowing down as new demand for the product reaches a saturation point.

Logo a symbol, design, picture, or any figure that represents an individual or firm. Trademarks, unique trade names, or associated sounds are all "logotypes."

London Interbank Offer Rate (LIBOR) the most prominent of the interbank offered rates, the rate of interest at which banks in London lend funds to other prime banks in London. LIBOR is frequently used as a basis for determining the rate of interest payable on Eurodollars and other Eurocurrency loans. The effective rate of interest on these Eurocredits is LIBOR plus a markup negotiated between lender and borrower. The rate, however, varies according to circumstances at which funds can be borrowed in particular currencies, amounts, and maturities in the market.

Long Bond

Ownership: term indicating a debt security owned outright by an investor who can transfer the title to others upon a sale.

Maturity: a bond having a maturity of ten years or longer. Such long-term bonds generally have a higher yield than short-term bonds as the longer maturity increases the market risk of the bond.

Long Range Budget projections that cover more than one fiscal year; also called *strategic budgeting*. The five-year budget plan is the most commonly used in practice. *See also* Annual Budget.

Long-Term Capital Gain or Loss a gain or loss on an investment or asset held over a period exceeding one year, under IRS rules.

Long-Term Debt bonds issued by a company that mature longer than one year.

Lorenz Curve a graphical device for illustrating the distribution of income within an economy, that is, the extent of income inequality. It is mostly used to compare a nation's actual income distribution among families with an equal distribution.

Loss Leaders a concept illustrating one type of product-line pricing of complementary goods. This concept refers in retailing to the sale of a commodity at less than invoice cost or at a price sharply below normal price and publicizing of the fact through advertising. The intention is (1) to draw in customers who will buy other products and/or (2) to provoke customer interest that will eventually shift the demand curve to the right.

Lotus 1-2-3 a popular spreadsheet program.

Lowballing setting low standards or goals so they can be met easily.

Low-Grade

1. an item of poor quality.
2. a quality rating meeting minimum qualifications. A low-grade quality rating is a poor one. Securities are rated as to qualify by underwriting houses including Fitch's, Moody's, and Standard & Poor's. A low-grade security would be one rated B or lower. D indicates default. A low-grade debt security will be forced to pay a higher rate of interest because of the high risk associated with it. Low-grade equity issues are normally not kept in the portfolios of institutions investing large sums of money in securities. *See also* Bond Ratings.

LP *see* Linear Programming (LP).

LTD see Limited.

Lump-sum Distribution a single one-time payment for something rather than many payments made over time. For example, upon retirement an employee may receive a single lump-sum distribution of his or her pension benefits.

Luxury Tax tax charged on purchases of "luxury" items. Under current tax law, there is a 10% federal luxury tax on cars selling for more than $30,000, furs and jewelry selling in excess of $10,000, and private boats selling above $100,000.

Mm

M1, M2, and M3 a measure of money supply in an economy. M1 is currency and checking accounts, M2 is savings accounts, and M3 is money market funds. *See also* Money Supply.

Maastricht Treaty treaty agreed to in 1991 and ratified in mid-1993 that committed the 12 member-states of the European Community to a closer economic and political union.

MAC; Macintosh a series of personal computers developed by Apple Computers.

MACRO a short computer program within a regular program designed to carry out a specific command or function.

Macroeconomic Policy fiscal and monetary policies that aim at achieving economic goals, such as control of economic stability, growth, full employment, and balance-of-payments equilibrium.

Macroeconomics study of the workings of the whole national economy or large sectors of it. It deals with national price, output, unemployment, inflation, and international trade. It is the study of the big picture. Typical macroeconomic questions include What determines national income and employment levels? What determines the general price level or rate of inflation? What are the policies that combat typical economic problems such as inflation, unemployment, and recession? *See also* Economics; Microeconomics.

MACRS *see* Modified Accelerated Cost Recovery System (MACRS).

Magnetic Ink Character Recognition (MICR) a magnetic coding imprinted on checks and deposit slips to speed up the check and deposit clearing process.

Magnuson-Moss Warranty Act of 1975 the act that regulates express written warranties. One of the objectives of the act is to prohibit written warranties from limiting the implied warranty to a shorter period than that covered by the written warranty. Before passage of this act, many written warranties contained clauses that relieved the seller of an implied warranty. However, the seller can still avoid an implied warranty by the selling of the product "as is."

Mainframes a large, powerful computer system capable of serving more than one user at a time.

Maintenance periodic expenditures undertaken to preserve or retain an asset's operational status for its originally intended use. These expenditures do not improve or extend the life of the asset. It is an expense, which is distinguished from capital improvements (which are capitalized). An example is the cost of a tune-up for an automobile.

Major Medical health insurance primarily for large surgical, hospital, and other medical expenses.

Make-Or-Buy (Outsource) Decision the decision whether to produce a component part internally or to buy it externally from an outside supplier. This decision involves both quantitative and qualitative factors. The qualitative considerations include ensuring product quality and the necessity for long-run business relationships with the subcontractors. The quantitative factors deal with cost. *See also* Outsourcing.

Malcolm Baldrige National Quality Award established by Congress in 1987, a major recognition to those U.S. companies that demonstrate outstanding quality in their products, services, and customer satisfaction. *See also* Canada Awards for Business Excellence; Deming Prize.

Managed Care prepaid health plans that provide comprehensive health care to members. Managed care is offered by health maintenance organizations (HMOs), preferred provider organizations (PPOs), exclusive provider organizations, point-of-service plans, and traditional indemnity insurance companies. There is some sort of restriction on which doctors one can see.

Managed Earnings manipulating (pumping up or down) earnings to shed a more favorable light on companies. All companies have flexibility in how they account for some revenues and costs. For example, they can depreciate a capital cost (say, a fleet of cars) in one year or over several years. If they take it in one chunk, their earnings look lower that year and larger every year after that. If they report it in many smaller pieces, they avoid the big hit in the first year. Even though earnings are not perfect, investors' love affair with earnings is here to stay. To paraphrase Winston Churchill's famous quote about democracy:

> *"Earnings are the worst way to measure corporate performance*
> *except all those other ways that have been tried from time to time."*

Management the Board of Directors, elected by the stockholders, and the officers of the corporation, appointed by the Board of Directors.

Management by Exception a management concept or policy by which management devotes its time to investigating only those situations in which actual results differ significantly from planned results. The idea is that management should spend its valuable time concentrating on the more important items (such as the shaping of the company's future strategic course). Attention is only given to material deviations requiring investigation. The tools that facilitate this use of this concept include Decision Support Systems (DSS), Expert Systems, and Performance Reporting.

Management by Objective (MBO) a system of performance appraisal having the following characteristics: (1) it is a formal system in that each manager is required to take certain prescribed actions and to complete certain written documents and (2) the manager and subordinates discuss the subordinate's job description, agree to short-term performance targets, discuss the progress made towards meeting these targets, and periodically evaluate the performance and provide the feedback.

Management Consulting Service a broad service area covering aspects of organizational management such as planning, finance, inventory, computers, and personnel. These services may include the design and implementation of management information systems, strategic planning, data processing, hardware and software evaluation, data privacy and security, evaluation of management and suggestions for improvement. Public accounting firms have expanded their services into management consulting and some have expressed concerns that this may weaken auditor independence.

Management Control System a system under which managers assure that resources are obtained and used effectively and efficiently in the accomplishment of the organization's goals. Major characteristics of a management control system are as follows: (1) it focuses on programs and responsibility centers; (2) it is a total system in that it encompasses all aspects of a firm's operation; (3) it is usually built around a financial and accounting structure; and (4) it uses two types of information for managerial control, planned data (such as budgets, standards and projections) and actual data.

Management Fee
1. annual fee (delineated by the fund's expense ratio) assessed to shareholders of a mutual fund for its management, administration, and shareholder relations. The mutual fund may be an open-or closed one. The management fee is a constant percentage (e.g., 1%) of the fund's net asset value. The management fee reduces the shareholders' assets once a year. The SEC requires full disclosure by the mutual fund of its management fee in the prospectus.
2. fee charged by an investor, a stockbroker, or financial advisor for managing an investor's portfolio for a specified time period.
3. fee charged by a real estate management company to manage real estate property.

Management Game a form of simulation. Both simulation and management games are mathematical models, but they differ in purpose and mode of use. Simulation models are designed to simulate a system and to generate a series of financial and operating results regarding system operations. Games do the same thing except that in games, human beings play a significant part. That is, participants make decisions at various stages. Thus, the games are distinguished by the idea of play. The major goals of the game are:

1. To improve decision making and analytical skills.
2. To develop awareness of the need to make decisions lacking complete information.
3. To develop an understanding of the interrelationships of the various functions of business (accounting, finance, marketing, production, etc.) within the firm and how these interactions affect overall performance.
4. To develop ability to function cooperatively and effectively in a small group situation. Management games offer a unique means of training accountants and have been used successfully as an executive training device. Management games generally fall into two categories: executive games and functional games. Executive games are general management games and cover all functional areas of business and their interactions and dynamics. Executive games are designed to train general executives. Functional games, on the other hand, focus on middle management decisions and emphasize particular functional areas of the firm.

Management Information System (MIS) a computer-based or manual system that transforms data into information useful in the support of decision making. MIS can be classified as performing three functions:

1. MIS that generates reports. These reports can be financial statements, inventory status reports or performance reports that are needed for routine and nonroutine purposes.
2. MIS that answer "what-if" kinds of questions asked by management. For example, questions such as What would happen to cash flow if the company changes its credit term for its customers? can be answered by MIS. This type of MIS can be called *Simulation* or *What-If model.*
3. MIS supports decision making. This type of MIS is appropriately called Decision Support System (DSS). DSS attempts to integrate the decision maker, the database, and the quantitative models being used.

Management Science a collection of mathematical and statistical methods used in the solution of managerial and decision-making problems; also called *operations research.* There are numerous tools available under these headings, such as linear programming, economic order quantity, learning curve theory, PERT, and regression analysis.

Management Style the general orientation or attitude of an executive or company toward the business or employees.

Management Technology the know-how used to run a business. It is the managerial skills that enable a multinational company to compete in the global market by using its limited resources optimally and profitably.

Management Training training courses and seminars to enhance the knowledge of people in a company. Topics often include presentation skills, time management, and how to be a better manager.

Manager an executive whose function is to plan, organize, control, and make decisions in order to achieve organizational objectives.

Managerial (Management) Accounting the process of identification, measurement, accumulation, analysis, preparation, interpretation, and communication of financial information, which is used by management to plan, evaluate, and control within an organization. It is the accounting used for the planning, control, and decision making activities of an organization. Managerial accounting is concerned with providing information to internal managers who are charged with directing, planning and controlling operations and making a variety of management decisions. Managerial accounting can be contrasted with financial accounting, which is concerned with providing information, via financial statements, to stockholders, creditors, and others who are outside the organization.

Managerial Economics a branch of economics that applies economic theory and decision science methodology to solve business and managerial decision problems; also called *Business Economics*.

Manufacturer's Agent or Representative a person outside a company who officially sells for the company; also called *rep.*

Manufacturing and Production System a system that either creates goods or provides services (or both). Manufacturing and production systems produce output that ranges from highly standardized to highly customized. Depending on the type of system used, an appropriate cost accounting system can be designed. For example, a job order system is used by custom manufacturers, such as ship builders, aircraft manufactures, and printers, while a process cost system is used by processing industries, such as refineries and chemical manufacturers.

Manufacturing Costs those costs are associated with the manufacturing activities of the company. They consist of three categories: direct materials, direct labor, and factory overhead.

Manufacturing Overhead *see* Factory Overhead.

Manufacturing Resource Planning (MRP-II) integrated information system that steps beyond first-generation MRP to synchronize all aspects (not just manufacturing) of the business, including production, sales, inventories, schedules, and cash flows. MRP-II uses an MPS (master production schedule), which is a statement of the anticipated manufacturing schedule for selected items for selected periods. MRP also uses the MPS. Thus, MRP is a component of an MRP-II system.

Maquiladora a special case of joint venture cooperation. It is a manufacturing plant located in Mexico that processes imported materials and reexports them, tariff-free, to the United States.

Margin

1. The difference between cost and selling price.
2. amount of equity used (down payment given) for buying a security or futures contract with the balance being on credit; also called *Performance Bond*.

Margin Account a line of credit with a broker. With a margin account, you can leverage, or borrow, up to a certain percent of the price of a stock from your broker. If the value of a stock on margin falls to a certain level, your broker will make a margin call. *See also* Margin Call.

Margin Call a demand from your broker asking you to put up additional funds or collateral in the form of stocks or bonds into your margin account. A margin call occurs when the equity in a customer's margin account goes below a specified minimum amount established by an exchange or by the brokerage firm. This takes place when the market value of assets collateralizing the customer's account unexpectedly falls. The margin call occurs when the value of your Investment falls below 75% of its original value. Brokerage firms may set their own margin levels, but not less than 75%.

Margin of Safety the difference between the actual level of sales and the break-even sales. It is the amount by which sales revenue may drop before losses begin, and is often expressed as a percentage of budgeted sales:

$$\text{Margin of safety} = \frac{\text{Budgeted sales - Break-even sales}}{\text{Budgeted sales}}$$

The margin of safety is often used as a measure of operating risk. The larger the ratio, the safer is the situation since there is less risk of reaching the break-even point.

Marginal Analysis an analysis that utilizes such concepts as marginal revenue, marginal cost, and marginal profit for economic decision-making. For example, decisions for allocating scarce resources are typically expressed in terms of the marginal condition(s) that must be satisfied in order to attain an optimal solution. The familiar profit maximizing rule for the firm of setting production or sales volume at the point where "marginal revenue equals marginal cost" is one such example. *See also* Incremental Analysis.

Marginal Cost the change in total cost associated with a unit change in quantity. For example, the marginal cost of the 500th unit of output can be calculated by finding the difference in total cost at 499 units of output and total cost at 500 units of output. MC is thus the additional cost of one more unit of output. It is calculated as:

$$\text{MC} = \text{change in total cost/change in quantity}$$

MC is also the change in total variable cost associated with a unit change in output. This is because total cost changes, whereas total fixed cost remains unchanged. *See also* Marginal Analysis; Marginal Revenue.

Marginal Propensity to Consume the fraction or proportion of any change in income that subsequently is spent for consumption.

Marginal Revenue the rate of change of total revenue with respect to quantity sold. Marginal revenue indicates to a firm how total sale revenue will change if there is a change in the quantity sold of a firm's product. An approximation to marginal revenue is the change in total revenue by the change in quantity sold. In a discrete range of activity, marginal revenue is equivalent to incremental revenue. *See also* Marginal Analysis; Marginal Cost.

Marginal Tax Rate the highest tax rate used in computing a company's total tax obligation, which is the tax rate applicable to the next dollar of income. The federal income tax rate is graduated, meaning that as additional profits are earned, the tax rate on the incremental earnings increases. *See also* Average Tax Rate.

Marginal Utility the additional utility or satisfaction that an individual derives from consuming an additional unit of a good or service. Marginal utility is the slope of a utility function. *See also* Utility Function.

Marital Deduction a deduction allowed upon the transfer of property and the reduction of its tax basis from one spouse to another. This deduction is allowed under the Federal gift tax for lifetime transfers or under the Federal estate tax for testamentary transfers of a decedent.

Markdown

Business:

1. reduction in the original retail-selling price, which was determined by adding a percentage factor, called a *markon*, to the cost of the merchandise. Anything added to the markon is called a *markup*, and the term *markdown* does not apply unless the price is dropped below the original selling price.
2. in retail, reduction in selling price.

Securities:

1. amount subtracted from the selling price when a customer sells securities to a dealer in the over-the-counter market. Had the securities been purchased from the dealer, the customer would have paid a markup, or an amount added to the purchase price.
2. reduction in the price at which the underwriters offer municipal bonds after the market has shown a lack of interest at the original price.
3. downward adjustment of the value of securities by banks and investment firms, based on a decline in market quotations.

Marked-To-Market

1. the daily adjustment of margin accounts to reflect profits and losses. At the end of each day, the futures contracts are settled and the resulting profits or losses are paid.
2. valuing a trading security or available-for-sale security at its market value at the end of the reporting period. The security is presented at its market value whether it is below or above cost.

Market Analysis

Finance: research on the stock market and individual securities as well as debt securities to determine future trends and directions. There are two schools of market analysis. These are technical and fundamental analysis. *See also* Fundamental Analysis; Technical Analysis.

Marketing: the study of various markets and their existing clients to determine their potential and existing needs; also called *market research*. This research includes all aspects of a market, including the psychology of the marketplace, prices, monetary variables, seasonality and timing, the demography of the market's clients, competitiveness, and so on. The objective of this type of market analysis is to forecast and, if possible, control trends and develop goods and services to take advantage of opportunities.

Market Breadth an analysis of the stock market's performance by comparing the number of stocks that rose as opposed to those that fell. The greater the number of stocks that went up as opposed to those that fell, the more bullish the indicator. Conversely, the larger the number of stocks falling as opposed to those rising, the more bearish the indicator.

Market Cap (Market Capitalization) value of a business entity equal to its outstanding shares multiplied by the current market price per share. For example, if 5,000,000 shares are issued and outstanding and the market price per share is $10, the company's market capitalization is $50,000,000. Institutional investors, including insurance companies, pension plans, etc., will not invest in a company unless its market capitalization is a minimum amount, (e.g., $100 million) predetermined by them. Higher market capitalization reflects a larger and higher quality company that is probably more widely held and actively traded. *See also* Book Value.

Market Correction a decline after a period of rising prices of at least 10% for a stock, bond, commodity, or index. A healthy market will correct from time to time. A correction is often considered beneficial for the long term health of the market, in that the prices had risen too quickly and the drop put them back to more realistic levels.

Market Cycles up and down movements in the market as business activities shift. The market moves up in a bull market and back down in a bear market.

Market Demand the horizontal sum of the individual demands of all consumers in the market; also called *industry demand*. At each price, market quantity demanded is the sum of all individual quantities demanded at the same price.

Market Economy the economy that emphasizes private ownership, individual economic freedom, competition, the profit motive, and the price system in the achievement of economic goals; also called *capitalistic, market-based,* or *market economic system*. Each economic unit decides what choices and policies are best for it, the thesis being that in encouraging the drive for individual economic self-interest, the outcome proves also to be in the overall best interests of society because of the strong incentives for efficiency, productivity, and satisfaction of consumers. The "what," "how much," and "for whom" questions are primarily solved by a system of free markets.

Market Equilibrium

1. the point at which the market demand and supply curves intersect.

2. the situation in which expected returns on a security equal required returns.

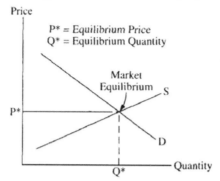

Market Forces the dynamics of supply and demand and of market price movements.

Market Indexes and Averages market gauges used to track performance for stocks and bonds. In theory, an average is the simple arithmetic mean while an index is an average expressed relative to a pre-established market value. In practice, the distinction is not all that clear. There are many stock market indexes and averages available. Each market has several indexes published by Dow Jones, Standard & Poor's, and other financial services. Different investors prefer different indexes. Indexes and averages are also used as the underlying value of index futures and index options.

Market Momentum the rate of change in stock prices in the market by volume. Momentum investors seek to take advantage of upward or downward trends in stock prices or earnings.

Market Order order to purchase or sell a stock or bond at the best available market price when the order reaches the trading floor. Most orders placed by investors are of this type. *See also* Buy Order.

Market Price

1. the price at which the seller and the buyer agree to trade on the open market.

2. in a transfer pricing context, the best transfer price in the sense that it will maximize the profits of the company as a whole, if it meets the following two conditions: (1) a competitive market price exits, and (2) divisions are independent of each other. If divisions are free to buy and sell outside the company, the use of market prices preserves divisional autonomy and leads divisions to act in a manner that maximize the profits of the company as a whole.

Market Research a systematic approach to gathering and accessing quantitative and qualitative market information. Serves as a basis for policy and decision making concerning new programs or the evaluation of existing ones.

Market Segmentation individuals clustered into recognizable groupings based on common characteristics such as age, sex, income, or geographic location. Products or services are designed to satisfy that segment of the total market.

Market Share that percentage of total sales by any single firm in a given market.

Market Share Elasticity the percentage change in a firm's market share resulting from a percentage change in the price. *See also* Elasticity of Demand.

Market Timing

1. an abusive practice where big stock market traders move in or out of funds at the end of the trading day, exploiting stale price data. The practice is not illegal, but it can be damaging to the interests of other investors in the funds. Regulators are currently studying ways to thwart timing-related trades in mutual fund shares.
2. an ideal investing strategy of switching into stocks before they rise and switching out of them before they decline.

Market Value the price at which an asset can be sold; also called *Fair Market Value*.

Marketing basically a bridge between production and consumption that directs the flow of goods and services to the consumer. It also contributes to the recognition of consumer needs and their eventual satisfaction.

Marketing Expenses *see* Selling Expenses.

Marketing Information System a process for making marketing decisions using computers, in which marketing information is collected, analyzed, and disseminated or distributed.

Marketing Mix the four Ps in marketing decisions—product, price, place, and promotion.
- **Product** – an item or service that is offered to the customer.
- **Price** – what the customer pays for the product or service you offer.
- **Place** – the product's channels of distribution or how the product is conveyed to the end user.
- **Promotion** – advertising, sales promotions, and public relations.

The marketing mix is the set of choices that determine a company's offer to its target market(s). *See also* Four Ps.

Marketing Strategy a selected combination and predetermined mix of the four Ps as applied to any marketing function, good, or service.

Marketing Intelligence the systematic collection, analysis, and evaluation of publicly available information about competitors and developments in a marketing environment.

Markov Analysis a method of analyzing the current behavior of some variable to predict the future behavior of that variable. One important application of this method in accounting is the estimation of that portion of the accounts receivable that will eventually become uncollectible. It is used for marketing analysis as well.

Markup the difference between what a retailer pays and what it charges a customer.

Markup Pricing *see* Cost-Plus Pricing.

Maslow's Hierarchy of Needs a list of individual needs from low to high proposed by psychologist Abraham Maslow. These needs are (from lower levels to higher levels): (a) physiological needs–for food, clothing, and shelter; (b) safety needs–for safety and for protection from possible harm; (c) social needs –for belonging and group relatedness; (d) ego needs–for self-esteem and competence; and (e) self-fulfillment needs–for self-development and creativity. These types constitute a hierarchy of needs. The first group (physiological) is the first to be satisfied. After these are satisfied, the next higher needs (safety) are of chief importance, followed, in turn, by social needs, ego needs, and self-fulfillment needs. It is important to note that after a need is satisfied, it ceases to motivate until it is again felt.

Mass Marketing a marketing method that essentially assumes "one size fits all," i.e., particular product mix will satisfy everyone in a particular market, and it is not necessary to identify and service different aspects of the overall market. It is a simple strategy of selling products or services throughout the entire country with one strategy ignoring regional or segment differences.

Master (Comprehensive) Budget a plan of activities expressed in monetary terms of the assets, equities, revenues, and costs that will be involved in carrying out the plan. Simply put, a master budget is a set of projected or planned financial statements. It consists basically of a pro forma income statement, pro forma balance sheet, and cash budget. A budget is a tool used for both planning and control. At the beginning of the period the budget is a plan or standard; at the end of the period it serves as a control device to help management measure its performance against the plan so that future performance may be improved.

Master Production Schedule (MPS) time-phased statement of how many finished items are to be manufactured. It is obtained by disaggregating the production plan and is the primary input to material requirements planning (MRP).

Matching Grant a contingent grant given by some other body. A governmental unit must invest its own resources for the originally intended purpose to enable this type of matching grant by some other body to be realized and received by the governmental unit.

Material
1. raw material; direct or indirect; a noun. An example is steel to make a car.
2. as an adjective; relatively important and significant in dollar amount.

Material Requirement Planning (MRP) a computer-based information system designed to handle ordering and scheduling of dependent-demand inventories (such as raw materials, component parts, and subassemblies, which will be used in the production of a finished product). MRP begins with a schedule for finished goods, which is converted into a schedule of requirements for the subassemblies, component parts, and raw materials that will be needed to produce the finished items in the specified time frame. Thus, MRP is designed to answer three questions: What is needed? How much is needed? and When is it needed? The primary inputs of MRP are a bill of materials, which tells of what a finished product is composed; a master schedule, which tells how much finished product is desired and when; and an inventory-records file, which tells how much inventory is on hand or on order. This information is processed using various computer programs to determine the net requirements for each period of the planning horizon. Outputs from the process include planned-order schedules, order releases, changes, performance-control reports, planning reports, and exception reports.

Matrix a rectangular array of numbers, usually in large parentheses, with the horizontal numbers referred to as rows and the vertical numbers as columns.

Matrix Management; Matrix Structure an organizational structure as a grid with intersecting responsibilities. This is a dual rather than a single chain of command and some managers report to two bosses rather than one boss. For instance, in matrix management, marketing in Asia may report to both a functional manager (marketing) and a geographical manager (Asia) in terms of hierarchical relationships.

Maturity
1. the period when a financial obligation, such as a loan, mortgage, or bond matures and must be paid. The original maturity is the time period from the effective date of issue to the maturity date.
2. a term describing a stage of growth or a company. The maturity stage of growth describes a company that has passed through the inception and growth stages and is now well established, has good credit, and is a major factor in its market segment.
3. an individual who has matured in a personal sense. Typically, a person matures with age and experience.

Maximin Strategy a decision rule in game theory; also called *maxmin strategy.* The rule states that a player with a number of possible strategies to adopt considers first the worst or minimum possible pay-offs that could be gained from each depending on the reaction of his opponent. The player should then choose the strategy that corresponds to the maximum of all the minimum pay-offs to him that are possible. Thus, the maximin strategy is the one that maximizes the minimum gain.

Maximization a behavior that attempts to maximize such performance measures as revenue, profits, contribution margin, or expected net present value. For example, a marketing manager wishes to maximize sales revenue or market share of the firm's product or service. Profit maximization has been the traditional goal of the firm in classical economic theory.

Maximum Tax the maximum tax rate that would apply to the various tiers of income subject to tax.

Mazur Plan an organizational format that divides retail functions into four categories: (1) merchandising, (2) accounting, (3) management, and (4) control.

M-Commerce mobile commerce, spawned by advances in technology for mobile communication devices.

Mean a measure of central tendency, that is a measure of the center of the data; also called an *average*. Mean and standard deviation are the two most widely used statistical measures that summarize the characteristics of the data.

Mechanic's Lien a claim on property by an unpaid workman or contractor. The property may be sold to recover the money owed.

Median the value of the midpoint variable when the data are arranged in ascending or descending order. For example, in the following data set: 2, 3, 4, 8, 8, the median is the value of the third variable since there are two variables above it and two variables below it. Therefore, the median of the five variables is 4.

Medicare a program enacted under Title XVIII of the Social Security Amendments of 1965 providing medical benefits for those 65 years of age and over. Medicare coverage is also available for those under 65 years of age who are disabled and have been receiving Social Security disability benefits for the past 24 months. The program is funded through Social Security taxes.

Medicare, Part A the first part of the Medicare program by which retired employees over the age of 65 who are currently receiving Social Security benefits also qualify for hospital insurance coverage. It pays 80% of all allowable hospital costs. In addition, the first day of hospital admission has a substantial deductible amount.

Medicare, Part B the second part of the Medicare program, by which retired employees over the age of 65 who are currently receiving Social Security benefits are provided supplementary medical insurance coverage on a voluntary basis for physicians' services. It pays 80% of all allowable physician costs.

Medigap Coverage private health insurance to cover all or part of the 20% of hospital and medical costs not covered by Medicare.

Meeting of the Minds an agreement of all parties to the terms of a contract. In order for there to be a meeting of the minds there must be:
1. an offer and acceptance
2. an evaluation of the property under consideration
3. a financial consideration
4. financial and related terms

Megabyte (M, MB, MEG) roughly one million bytes.

Megahertz (MHz) the measurement of speed of the transmission of the computer's electronic devices. One MHz represents one million cycles per second. The speed of microprocessors, called the *clock speed*, is measured in megahertz. For example, a microprocessor that runs at 200 MHz executes 200 million cycles per second.

Member, Appraisal Institute (MAI) member of the American Institute of Real Estate Appraisers.

Memory the space within a computer where information and program are stored while being actively worked on, also called *core*. It is expressed in terms of the number of characters (bytes) that can be retained. The memory of the computer is in the form of read-only (ROM) and random-access memory or read/write memory (RAM). It is this memory facility that distinguishes the computer from devices such as calculators and bookkeeping machines, which, although they have input, output, and processing capabilities, cannot store programs internally within the processing unit.

Merchandising efforts by (1) manufacturers and wholesalers to encourage sales promotion activities by retailers, (2) marketers to influence consumers at the point of sale by other than personal selling, and (3) marketers to plan the best marketing mix to stimulate consumption.

Merger the combining of two or more entities into one through a purchase acquisition. It differs from a consolidation in that no new entity is created from a merger.

Merit Increase a salary increase often given once a year due to continued successful performance.

Metes and Bounds Description a legal description that gives the boundaries of a property as defined by different landmarks on the property.

Methods-Time Measurement (MTM) system of predetermined motion-time data used to develop standards for highly repetitive tasks.

Metropolitan Statistical Area (MSA) *see* Standard Metropolitan Statistical Area (SMSA).

Mezzanine Debt that part of the capital structure between the first mortgage and the equity of a property.

Microcomputer a small, low cost computer whose CPU consists of a single integrated circuit known as the microprocessor. It has a RAM for storing programs during their execution and usually a ROM for permanent storage of required programs. Microcomputers are basically 8, 16, or 32 bit microprocessors. They are typically used by one individual at a time. Small, personal, desktop computers are microcomputers.

Microeconomics the study of the individual units of the economy–individuals, households, firms, and industries. It zeros in on such economic variables as the prices and outputs of specific firms and industries, the expenditures of consumers, wage rates, competition, and the markets. *See also* Macroeconomics.

Micromarketing the practice of tailoring products and marketing programs to the needs and wants of specific individuals and local customer groups. Includes local marketing and individual marketing.

Microprocessor a general, all-purpose circuit, placed on a silicon chip; also called *CPU*, or the *processor*. It is a power source of microcomputers. The microprocessor is at the heart of the micro-electronics revolution. This chip is used in calculators, watches, video games, microwave ovens, and, of course, computers. CPUs are given names such as 286, 386, and 486, Pentium, or P6, which refer to how quickly the brain can think.

Microsoft Network (MSN) one of the major commercial online services.

Mid-Caps stocks from mid-sized companies, smaller than blue chips, but larger than small caps.

Middle Management managers who are in the middle between the bosses who make important decisions and the people who actually do the work. These middle managers are often eliminated in case of downsizing.

Middleware the system that stands between the user interface and the database access software.

Miller-Orr Model a model to determine the optimum amount of transaction cash under conditions of uncertainty. It is a stochastic approach used when uncertainty exists regarding cash payments. *See also* Baumol Model.

Minimax Strategy a decision rule in game theory. The rule involves the following steps: (1) to each possible strategy that he may adopt, the decision maker can assign the greatest possible loss and (2) he would then select the strategy that minimizes the maximum loss. *See also* Maximin Strategy.

Miranda Rule reading of a person' rights at the time of an arrest.

MIS *see* Management Information System (MIS).

Misery Index an index that tracks economic conditions including inflation and unemployment. It was particularly referred to in the economically depressed period of 1977 through 1981 in the United States. The inflation rate was in the double digits at that time. Misery Index = inflation rate + unemployment rate + prime rate. The index typically is negatively correlated to the current condition of the stock market. The misery index has little value as a predictor of future stock prices. The index may be found in the Bureau of Labor Statistics publications and *The Wall Street Journal*.

Misleading leading to an interpretation that is not factual or is unrealistic–includes facts or statements that may be misstated, distorted, augmented, omitted, and arranged in such a manner as to obscure and conceal material aspects of an item. The accountant carefully prepares, based on the reliance on accepted standards of auditing practice and statement presentation, financial information to avoid misleading inferences.

Mission Statement a formal statement by top management of an organization's mission. Mission defines an organization's line or lines of business, identifies its products and services, and specifies the markets it serves at present and in a time frame of three to five years. It typically reflects a company's past achievements, its distinctive competencies (what the company and its businesses do best), and the environments in which it operates.

Missionary Salespeople (Selling) salespeople who are "selling goodwill" by offering technical or service assistance that aids the buyer in selling that firm's products. Used extensively in the marketing of cosmetics.

Mixed Costs costs that vary with changes in volume but, unlike variable costs, do not vary in direct proportion; also called *semivariable costs* or *semifixed costs*. In other words, these costs contain both a variable and a fixed component. Examples are (a) the rental of a delivery truck, where a fixed rental fee plus a variable charge based on mileage is made or (b) power costs, where the expense consists of a fixed amount plus a variable charge based on consumption. A further example is salespersons' compensation including, salary and commission. *See also* Fixed Costs; Variable Costs.

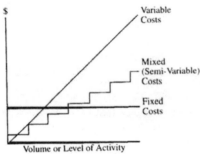

Mixed Economy Certain sectors of the economy are left to private ownership and free market mechanisms, while other sectors have significant government ownership and government planning.

MNC *see* Multinational Company (MNC).

Mode The mode is determined by observation, usually in a graphic form. On such a graph, the modal value is the value of the point of highest density of activity. Example: The simple mode is shown in Figure 1. Bimodal distribution occurs in certain cases. For example, if a retailer wishes to find the modal values of the distribution of weekly sales volume, the graph may be drawn as shown in Figure 2. There are a wide variety of economic applications for modal analysis; including the evaluation of a product's selling periods when there are two clear distinctions. Modal analysis is useful with any financial or other data graph to display the most commonly occurring value. Modal analysis can be applied to sales, income, utilization rates, population, and other data where there is a clearly occurring value. Use of a mode graph can be extremely effective in making business presentations.

Figure 1 & Figure 2

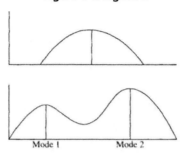

Mode 1   Mode 2

Model a representation or an abstract of a real life system. It may take any of a variety of forms: a diagram, graph, physical, or mathematical. The objective of a model is to generate forecasts and perform a variety of What-If analyses. *See also* Economic Model.

Modified Accelerated Cost Recovery System (MACRS) a method of accelerated depreciation permitted by tax codes, as modified by recent changes. It classifies depreciable assets into one of several recovery periods, each of which has a designated pattern of allowable depreciation (double-declining balance, 150% declining balance, or straight-line with a half-year convention). *See also* Accelerated Cost Recovery System (ACRS).

Modified Du Pont Formula the second version that ties together the return on investment (ROI) and the degree of financial leverage as measured using the equity multiplier, which is the ratio of total assets to stockholders' equity to determine the return on equity (ROE):

$$\text{ROE} = \frac{\text{Net profit after taxes}}{\text{Stockholders' equity}} = \frac{\text{Net profit after taxes}}{\text{Total assets}} \times \frac{\text{Total assets}}{\text{Stockholder's equity}}$$

$$= \text{ROI} \times \frac{\text{Equity}}{\text{Multiplier}}$$

Example: Consider the following financial data:

Total assets	$100,000
Net income after taxes	18,000
Sales	$200,000
ROI =	$18,000/$100,000 = 18%

Assume stockholders' equity is $45,000.

$$\text{Then, equity multiplier} = \frac{\text{Total assets}}{\text{Stockholder's equity}} = \frac{\$100,000}{\$45,000} = 2.22$$

$$\text{ROE} = \frac{\text{Net profit after taxes}}{\text{Stockholder's equity}} = \frac{\$18,000}{\$45,000} = 40\%$$

$$\text{ROE} = \text{ROI} \times \text{equity multiplier} = 18\% \times 2.22 = 40\%$$

If the company used only equity, the 18% ROI would equal ROE. However, 55%

of the firm's capital is supplied by creditors ($45,000/$100,000 = 45% is the equity-to-asset ratio; $55,000/$100,000 = 55% is the debt ratio). Since the 18% ROI all goes to stockholders, who put up only 45% of the capital, the ROE is higher than 18%. This example indicates the company was using leverage (debt) favorably. The use of the equity multiplier to convert the ROI to the ROE reflects the impact of the leverage (use of debt) on stockholders' return. It enables the company to break its ROE into a profit margin portion (net profit margin), an efficiency-of-asset-utilization portion (total asset turnover), and a use-of-leverage portion (equity multiplier). Managers have the task of determining just what combination of asset return and leverage will work best in the business' competitive environment. Most businesses try to keep at least a level equal to what is considered "normal" within the industry.

Modified Phillips Curve the curve that plots the change in the inflation rate against the unemployment rate; also called an *expectations-augmented Phillips curve* or an *accelerationist Phillips curve*. *See also* Phillips Curve.

Modular Design design of components that can be assembled in a variety of ways to meet individual consumer needs.

Momentum

1. a measure of how fast a market or stock is rising or falling, incorporating both price levels and trading volumes.
2. a technique used to construct an overbought/oversold oscillator. Momentum measures price differences over a selected span of time. To construct a 10-day momentum line, the closing price 10 days earlier is subtracted from the latest price. The resulting positive or negative value is plotted above or below a zero line.
3. the underlying power or thrust behind all upward or downward price movement. Momentum is represented on a graph as a line that is continually fluctuating above and below a horizontal equilibrium level, which represents the halfway point between extreme readings. Momentum is a generic term embracing many different indicators, such as rate of change (ROC), relative strength indicators (RSIs), and stochastics.
4. the rate of acceleration of an economic, price or volume movement. An economy with strong growth that is likely to continue is said to have momentum.

Monetarism a school of economic thought arguing that monetary growth is a more significant factor than fiscal activities as the primary cause of price instability in the economy. It postulates that changes in the monetary growth rate are the primary cause of changes in the price level, and hence changes in nominal GDP.

Monetary Aggregates (M1, M2, M3) *see* Money Supply.

Monetary Assets assets held in cash, marketable securities, accounts receivable, or checks that can easily be converted to cash. Property, machinery, and inventory are nonmonetary assets.

Monetary Indicators economic indicators that tell about money and credit market conditions. Most widely reported in the media are money supply, consumer credit, the Dow Jones industrial average, and the Treasury bill rate.

Monetary Policy a deliberate exercise of the Federal Reserve's power to induce changes in the money supply in order to achieve price stability, to help smooth out business cycles, and to bring the economy's employment and output to desired levels. Monetary policy is essentially directed at regulating the economy's overall money supply, credit availability, and, to a lesser degree, the level of interest rates by the Federal Reserve System.

Money
1. cash.
2. a term broadly used to refer to a medium of exchange and unit of value.
3. currency and coins that are designated as legal tender by the government. Money retains its value because individuals are willing to receive it in exchange for merchandise or services provided. The value of money can be affected by the rate of inflation, which cheapens its worth. The value of money relative to other currencies is determined by the international monetary exchange markets.

Money Magazine a popular magazine for individual investors, covering such topics as investments, money management, and personal finance.

Money Markets the markets for short-term (less than 1 year) debt securities. Examples of money market securities include U.S. Treasury bills, federal agency securities, bankers' acceptances, commercial paper, and negotiable certificates of deposit issued by government, business, and financial institutions.

Money Market Deposit Accounts (MMDA) a federally insured money market account offered through a depository institution, such as a bank, credit union, or savings and loan association. It usually pays a higher interest rate than a traditional passbook savings account, since it earns interest at rates competitive with money market funds. If the account balance falls below the minimum deposit required, the interest rate drops to a traditional passbook account.

Money Market (Mutual) Funds an open-ended mutual fund that pools the deposits of many investors and invests exclusively in short-term debt securities (maturing within one year) such as U.S. government securities, commercial paper, and certificates of deposit. These funds provide more safety of principal than other mutual funds since net asset value (NAV) never fluctuates. Typically shares are quoted at $1 each.(Each share has a net asset value of $1). Through a unique accounting treatment, all returns are paid as interest so the share price does not change. The yield, however, fluctuates daily. Examples are Fidelity Spartan Money Market Fund and Merrill Lynch CMA Money Fund.

Money Management a branch of personal finance and financial planning. It studies management of money in general, covering banking, credit management, consumer loans, budgeting, and tax savings.

Money Market Instruments *see* Money Markets.

Money Order check drawn upon the bank where the bank makes it out to a payee. It is issued when an individual gives the bank funds in exchange. Payees sometimes require a money order since it is in effect guaranteed payment. An example is where a person gives American Savings Bank $1,000 asking American Savings Bank to make out its own check payable to an auto dealer.

Money Purchase Plan a pension annuity is acquired by giving a specified payment (typically based on salary) at regular intervals.

Money Supply the stock of money in the economy, consisting of currency in circulation and deposits in checking and savings accounts. The nation's money supply is divided into the categories: M1, M2, M3, and L.

- M1 = narrowest measure of basic money supply, immediately spendable forms: traveler's checks, other checkable deposits (now, share draft, and other accounts), demand deposits, currency.
- M2 = M1 + money that cannot be used directly for payments but can be converted easily into spendable forms: savings (time) deposits, repurchase agreements (overnight), money market mutual fund shares, Eurodollars (overnight).
- M3 = broader measure of money supply = M1 and M2 plus the financial instruments of large institutions, which are not converted easily into spendable forms: large-denomination time deposits, term repurchase agreements.
- L = M3 + other liquid assets.

Monopolistic Competition a market situation with many sellers, each of which differentiates its products or services, physically and/or conceptually, and which has some degree of control over prices.

Monopoly or cartel. A situation in which all production and distribution is totally dominated by one firm or group of firms colluding. In this situation, consumers and suppliers are at an extreme disadvantage since the monopolist can dictate price as well as demand for supplies. Antitrust legislation, including the Sherman Anti-Trust Act, the Clayton Anti-Trust Act, and the Robinson-Patman Act have been passed to prevent the rise of abusive monopolies. The Federal Trade Commission is an independent regulatory agency charged with the responsibility of administering Antitrust legislation.

Monopsony a market with a single buyer. An example is milk producers selling to a grocery chain.

Monte Carlo Technique (Method, Simulation, or Analysis) a special type of simulation where the variables of a given system are subject to uncertainty. The technique gets its name from the famous Mediterranean resort often associated with games of chance. In fact, the chance element is an important aspect of Monte Carlo simulation: the approach can only be used when a system has a random, or chance component. Under this approach, a probability distribution is developed that reflects the random component of the system under study. Random samples taken from this distribution are analogous to observations made on the system itself. As the number of observations increases, the results of the simulation will tend to more closely approximate the random behavior of the real system, provided an appropriate model has been developed. Sampling is accomplished by the use of random numbers. Simulation applications include testing alternative inventory policies and simulating a cash budget. *See also* Simulation.

Monthly Treasury Average (MTA) average of the previous 12 monthly values of the one-year "Constant Maturity Treasury" index. This is one of the most common indexes used to determine the interest rate of an adjustable-rate mortgage. A borrower's fluctuating interest rate is determined by adding the MTA to a preset margin (typically from 2 percent to 3 percent).

Moody's Investor Service a financial services company owned by Dun & Bradstreet and located in downtown Manhattan. Moody's is probably one of the best-known investment rating services, with Standard & Poor's being the other. Moody's rates corporate as well as governmental securities with ratings ranging from AAA for highest investment quality to D for default.

Morningstar Mutual Fund Service a popular mutual fund reporting and rating service for individual investors.

Mortgage a long-term loan secured by property. The borrower, the mortgagee, pledges not only the property but also his or her personal credit to repay the loan. If the mortgagee defaults on the loan, the property can by foreclosed by the mortgagor in repayment of the loan. The mortgagee retains use of the property during the terms of the loan.

Mortgage Banker an individual or company that originates mortgages and collects payments on them. The mortgage banker usually sells these mortgages to long-term investors and obtains service fees for the loans. The mortgage banker is a major originator of FHA- and VA-insured mortgages and also plays a substantial role in the conventional mortgage markets.

Mortgage Banking Association (MBA) (*www.mbaa.org*) a national trade association of people engaged in the mortgage banking business, dedicated to the betterment of the mortgage banking industry through education, legislation, and high ethical standards for its members. It is located at 1125 Fifteen Street, N.W., Washington, D.C. 20005.

Mortgage Bonds bonds secured by real assets. There are two types of mortgage bonds: senior mortgages, which have first claim on assets and earnings, and junior mortgages, which have a subordinate lien. A mortgage bond may have a closed-end provision that prevents the firm from issuing additional bonds of the same priority against the same property or may be an open-end mortgage that allows the issuance of additional bonds having equal status with the original issue.

Mortgage Broker an individual or company that obtains mortgages for others by finding lending institutions, insurance companies, or private lenders. The mortgage broker sometimes makes collections and handles disbursements. The mortgage broker is usually compensated in the form of a percentage of the amount financed.

Mortgage Insurance a form of life or disability insurance where a mortgagor insures a mortgage in the event of death or disability. The principal covered by mortgage insurance declines as the mortgage is amortized. Thus, mortgage insurance is a form of decreasing term insurance. For example, Smith purchased a home for $150,000 and obtained a $100,000 30-year mortgage to finance the purchase. He then obtained a $100,000 mortgage insurance policy with decreasing terms of coverage corresponding to the amortization rate.

Mortgage Interest Deduction a tax deduction allowed for interest paid or accrued within the taxable year with respect to mortgage indebtedness. Under the Tax Reform Act of 1986, interest is deductible on mortgages secured by principal and second homes. A taxpayer may not write off interest on any part of the mortgage that exceeds the original purchase price plus improvements of property, unless the taxpayer uses the money for medical or educational purposes.

Mortgage-Backed Securities a share in an organized pool of residential mortgages. Some are pass-through securities whose principal and interest payments are passed through to shareholders, usually monthly. There are several kinds of mortgage-backed securities. They include the following:
- Government National Mortgage Association (GNMA — Ginnie Mae) Securities
- Federal Home Loan Mortgage Corporation (FHLMC — Freddie Mac) Securities
- Federal National Mortgage Association (FNMA — Fannie Mae) Securities
- Collateralized Mortgage Obligations (CMOs)

Mortgagee/Mortgagor a legal term for the one who has the mortgage and the one who is giving the mortgage.

Mortgages lines securing notes payable that have as collateral real assets and require periodic payments. For personal property, such as machines or equipment, the lien is called a *chattel mortgage*. Mortgages can be issued to finance the acquisition of assets, construction of plants, and modernization of facilities. The bank will require that the value of the property exceed the mortgage on that property. Mortgages have a number of advantages over other debt instruments, including favorable interest rates, less financing restrictions, and extended maturity date for loan repayment.

Moving Average
1. an average that is updated as new information is received. With the moving average, an accountant employs the most recent observations to calculate an average, which is used as the forecast for the next period.
2. a rolling average of the stock market performances for a specified number of days, often around 200 days. It is intended to show a general trend in the market.

MRP *see* Material Requirement Planning.

MTA *see* Monthly Treasury Average (MTA) .

MTM *see* Methods-Time Measurement.

Multinational Company (MNC) a company operating in two or more countries. Its ownership is in only one country. Special features of a multinational corporation (MNC) are as follows: (1) Multiple-currency problem. Sales revenues may be collected in one currency, assets denominated in another, and profits measured in a third. (2) Various legal, institutional, and economic constraints. There are variations in such things as tax laws, labor practices, balance of payment policies, and government controls with respect to the types and sizes of investments, types and amount of capital raised, and repatriation of profits. (3) Internal control problem. When the parent office of a multinational company and its affiliates are widely located, internal organizational difficulties arise.

Multiple Correlation a measure of the goodness of fit of an estimated multiple regression model. *See also* Correlation Coefficient (r), Regression Analysis.

Multiple Listing Service (MLS) an information and referral network among real estate agents that pools all properties offered into a common offering list. If a sale results, the listing broker and the selling broker split the commission. The members of a MLS receive the advantage of greater sales exposure, which, in turn, means a better price and a quicker sale.

Multiple Regression Analysis statistical procedure that attempts to assess the relationship between the dependent variable and two or more independent variables.

Multiplier the fact that changes in an economic variable can bring about magnified changes in another performance-related economic variable. There are various multipliers in economics, depending on what we try to measure.

Multitasking simultaneous execution of two or more computer functions.

Municipal Bonds (MUNIS) bonds issued by local governments and their agencies on which interest is exempt from federal income taxation, provided they qualify as public purpose bonds; simply called *munis*. Interest may also be exempt from state and local income taxation in the state of issue. Note: you may consider municipal bonds for tax or income reasons. If you do, you may face three investment choices for diversification: (1) buying them on your own, (2) muni unit investment trust (UIT), and (3) muni mutual funds. If the preservation of capital is of primary importance, the UIT may be a better investment than a mutual fund.

Municipals ("MUNIES") a short term for municipal bonds.

MUNIES *see* Municipal Bonds.

Murphy's Law "If anything can go wrong, it will."

Mutual Fund portfolio of securities professionally managed by the sponsoring management company or investment company that issues shares to investors. Ownership is in the form of proportionate shares. Mutual fund investing is characterized by:

1. **Diversification:** Your investment money may be used to buy a broad range of equity, debt, and other securities. Diversification reduces your risk.

2. **Automatic reinvestment:** Dividends, interest, and capital gains may be reinvested into the fund, usually at no charge.
3. **Automatic withdrawals:** Funds may be withdrawn, usually at no charge.
4. **Liquidity:** You can redeem your shares at any time.
5. **Switching:** You can go from one fund type to another in a family of funds.
6. **Small minimum investment:** Some mutual funds can be bought into initially for less than $1,000.

A major reason for the attractiveness of mutual funds is the many convenient services offered to their shareholders. Some can be used in your investment strategy. Types of Mutual Funds:

- **Growth.** The purpose is capital appreciation. The stocks invested in have growth potential, but greater risk.
- **Income.** The objective is to obtain current income (e.g., dividends, interest income). Typically, the portfolio comprises high-dividend common stock, preferred stock, and debt securities. Generally, high-quality securities are bought.
- **Balanced.** These funds provide capital gains and current income. A high percentage of the portfolio is in high-quality common stock to achieve capital appreciation with a lower percentage in fixed income securities. There is a safe return with minimal risk. It is a hybrid between growth and income funds.
- **Bonds.** An investment is made in different types and qualities of bonds. Interest income is the paramount concern. The funds provide liquidity, safety, and diversification. Some bond funds invest only in municipal securities to obtain tax-free income.
- **Money market.** These funds invest in short-term money market securities such as commercial paper, so there is liquidity with low risk. Usually the return on the fund exceeds what can be earned on a bank account.

Mutual Fund Fees the variety of fees charged by mutual funds, such as exchange fees, management fees, and redemption fees.

Mutual Insurance Company an insurance company that is owned by its policyholders and operates on a nonprofit basis.

Nn

NAFTA *see* North American Free Trade Agreement.

Naked Option an uncovered option strategy. It is the opposite of a covered option. A naked option is an investment in which the written options are not matched with a long stock position or a long option position that expires no earlier than the written options. The loss potential with such a strategy is thereby unlimited.

Nanosecond a measure of how fast computers execute functions. One nanosecond is one billionth of a second.

National Apartment Association (NAA) association of apartment owners across the country. It publishes monthly *Apartment News,* which carries educational articles and new developments in apartment-related activities.

National Association of Home Builders (NAHB) founded in 1942 and located in Washington, D.C., the NAHB has 155,000 members with 824 local groups. Its membership consists of single, multifamily, and commercial home builders. The NAHB serves as a public interest group to support legislation for the home building industry.

National Association Of Securities Dealers (NASD) a self-regulatory organization that has jurisdiction over certain broker-dealers who handle over-the-counter (OTC) securities. The NASD requires member broker-dealers to register and conduct examinations for compliance with net capital requirements and other regulations.

National Association of Security Dealers (NASDAQ) a self-policing organization of brokers and dealers who handle the over-the-counter (OTC) market securities. The NASD functions principally along five lines: (1) it has developed a written code of fair practices dealing with such matters as the appropriateness of prices quoted to customers, (2) it has promulgated standard procedures in transactions between members, (3) it has improved the quality of service that the OTC market gives the investing public, (4) it undertakes to investigate and arbitrate disputes between parties and to take disciplinary measures when justified, and (5) it undertakes to study and make recommendations on pending legislation in the security field. It also owns and operates a computerized system providing price quotations for OTC and some exchange-listed securities.

NASDAQ *see* National Association of Security Dealers (NASDAQ).

NASDAQ 100 Index Tracking Stock (QQQ)-stock symbol an Exchange Traded Fund (ETF) that allows investors to basically invest in all of the stocks that compose the NASDAQ 100 in a single security.

National Association of Manufacturers (NAM) the nation's largest industrial trade association (*www.nam.org*). The NAM represents 14,000 members (including 10,000 small and mid-sized companies) and 350 member associations serving manufacturers and employees in every industrial sector and all 50 states. Headquartered in Washington, D.C., the NAM has 10 additional offices across the country. The NAM was founded in Cincinnati, Ohio, in 1895. Fortune magazine rates the NAM as one of the 10 most influential advocacy groups in the United States.

National Association of Realtors (NAR) (*www.realtor.com*) founded in 1908 and located in Chicago, IL, a federation of 50 state associations and 1,848 local real estate boards, termed either Realtors or Realtor-Associates. With over 800,000 members, the National Association of Realtors promotes education, professional standards, and updates brokerage appraisal techniques, property management and land development practices, industrial real estate and farm brokerage, and counseling methods.

National Debt the money that the federal government owes, usually in the form of Treasury bills, Treasury notes, and Treasury bonds.

National Do Not Call Registry managed by the Federal Trade Commission (FTC), the government's consumer protection agency, the registry will limit the telemarketing calls you receive. On Oct. 1, 2005, when the registry was enforced most telemarketers were required to remove the numbers on the registry from their call lists.

National Federation of Independent Business (NFIB) (*www.nfib.com*)the largest advocacy organization representing small and independent businesses in Washington, D.C., and all 50 state capitals. NFIB was ranked the most influential business organization (and 3rd overall), in "Washington's Power 25" survey conducted by *Fortune* magazine. NFIB's purpose is to impact public policy at the state and federal level and be a key business resource for small and independent business in America. NFIB also gives its members a power in the marketplace. By pooling the purchasing power of its 600,000 members, the National Federation of Independent Business gives members access to many business products and services at discounted costs. NFIB also provides timely information designed to help small businesses succeed. The NFIB's well-known, small-business optimism index is based on responses from 1,221 members' firms.

National Flood Insurance insurance based on the National Flood Insurance Program, enacted by Congress in 1968. The intent of this legislation is to provide insurance coverage for those people suffering real property losses as a result of floods. To encourage the buying of national flood insurance, any real property located in a flood plain area cannot be financed through a federally regulated lender unless flood insurance is purchased.

National Income Accounting a necessary step in learning how macroeconomic variables–such as the economy's total output, the price level, the level of employment, interest rates, and others–are determined. The national income accounts give us regular estimates of Gross Domestic Product (GDP), the basic measure of the performance of the economy in producing goods and services. They are also useful because they provide us with a conceptual framework for describing the relationships among three key macroeconomic variables: output, income, and spending.

Near Money liquid assets readily convertible into cash as needed, such as marketable securities, money market funds, and time deposits.

Negative Amortization increase in the outstanding loan balance that occurs when the mortgage payment does not fully cover the required interest charge on the loan. This situation generally occurs under indexed loans for which the indexed rate change may not affect the periodic debt service payments.

Negative Cash Flow
In general: a situation in which a business spends more money than it takes in within a given time period. This is an unfavorable situation that may result in liquidity or solvency problems.
Real estate: a situation in which operating expenses and mortgage payments exceed rental income; also called *alligator*.

Negligence an act resulting from the omission of prudence that a reasonable person would exercise in a particular situation. A legal delinquency resulting when an individual fails to pursue a considerate and responsible course of action.
Contributory negligence: the failure to provide prudent care, resulting in an injury.
Criminal negligence: the failure to render proper care, resulting in the killing of an individual (manslaughter).
Gross negligence: the intentional failure to take legally due and proper care, having a serious personal or property outcome.
Ordinary negligence: any situation in which an individual fails to exercise proper responsibility, resulting in an outcome that has a seriously detrimental effect.

Negotiable
1. a security, title to which, when properly endorsed by the owner, is transferable by delivery.
2. a registered security that has an assignment and a power of substitution signed by the registered owner, either on the certificate or by an accompanying stock or bond power.
3. a price that can be bargained about and further adjusted.
4. a matter that is resolved between two or more parties through discussions in which common interests are redefined. For example, broker commissions are

now negotiable and clients may seek to negotiate the rate of commission being charged.

Negotiable Instrument any instrument that can easily be converted into cash. *See also* Negotiable. For an instrument to be negotiable, it must meet certain criteria:

1. It has to be signed by the maker.
2. It cannot have conditions.
3. It must promise to pay a certain sum of money.
4. It must be payable on demand by the bearer or to the order of a named party.
5. It cannot contain any other promise or restriction.

Nepotism hiring someone related to another employee, such as a husband and wife. The company policy may prevent two related people from being in the same department, in particular, a boss and a subordinate. The rationale is that the relationship may prevent the full exercise of authority.

Nest Egg an amount of money put aside and saved by an individual for a serious purpose, such as retirement, purchase of a home, or an emergency. Such money is also termed *serious money* and is invested conservatively.

Net

1. the amount remaining after all deductions have been subtracted.
2. the net amount of the proceeds of a sale, taking into account the acquisition cost and any additional investments made.
3. the difference between plus amounts and minus amounts, or the difference between additions and subtractions.
4. the net income or loss of a business.
5. a term used to describe a network.
6. the conclusive bottom line or end result.

Net Asset Value (NAV)

1. measure of the market value of a mutual fund share, which reveals what each share of the mutual fund is worth. Net asset value equals:

$$\frac{\text{Fund's total assets less total liabilities}}{\text{Number of shares outstanding in the fund}}$$

2. book value of a company's different classes of securities such as net book value per common share.

Net Earnings *see* Net Profit.

Net Income *see* Net Profit.

Net Income Multiplier a method of determining the price of income producing property. It is calculated as

$$\frac{\text{Purchase price}}{\text{Net Operating Income (NOI)}}$$

NOI is the gross income less allowances for vacancies and operating expenses, except depreciation and debt payments. *See also* Gross Income Multiplier (GIM); Gross Rent Multiplier (GRM); Capitalization Rate (Cap Rate).

Net Lease a lease in which the lessee pays not only a fixed rental charge but also expenses on the rented property, including maintenance; also called *Triple Net Lease.*

Net Operating Income (NOI) gross income of a rental property less allowance for vacancies and operating expenses, except depreciation and debt repayments.

Net Present Value (NPV) the difference between the present value of cash inflows generated by the project and the amount of the initial investment. The present value of future cash flows is computed using the cost of capital (minimum desired rate of return, or hurdle rate) as the discount rate.

Net Proceeds
1. amounts received from the sale or disposal of property less all relevant deductions (direct costs associated with the sale or disposal).
2. amounts received from issuance of securities less floatation costs.

Net Profit
1. the difference between the total price you paid for a security, with the brokerage commission you paid, and the net proceeds from the sale. It will show either a profit or a loss.
2. sales revenue minus total expenses; also called *earnings* or *net income.*

Net Working Capital the excess of current assets over current liabilities; also called *working capital.*

Net Worth
1. the difference between total assets and total liabilities.
2. a measure of personal or family wealth determined by subtracting total debts from total assets.
3. the owner's equity.

Netiquette short for network etiquette; good etiquette on the Internet or online service.

Netscape Navigator one of the popular web browsers.

Network
1. interconnected nodes (points where working units interact (link) with others.
2. connection of computers and devices.

Networking making and using professional contacts to get work. It is a popular tool in business where exchange of information and establishing contacts is an important part of expanding your business.

Neural Networks technology in which computers actually try to learn from the database and operator what the right answer is to a question. The system gets positive or negative response to output from the operator and stores that data so that it will make a better decision the next time. While still in its infancy, this technology shows promise for use in accounting, fraud detection, economic forecasting, and risk appraisals. The idea behind this software is to convert the order-taking computer into a "thinking" problem solver.

New Economy the new, digital economy driven by industrial information technology, much of which is related to telecommunications such as the Internet– a technology that, many argue, has a huge potential to transform the engineering industry. In the new economy, production and distribution systems are automated, computer-based systems. The old economy, classical or traditional, is undergoing sweeping changes through the speed and efficiency brought by applications of information technology and the Internet.

Niche Market; Niche Marketing the marketing strategy that targets a narrow market segment, usually a market not served by bigger companies.

Nielsen Ratings the number of people viewing a particular television show as measured by the A.C. Nielson Company

No Par or, No Par Value Stock. A stock that does not have a par or stated value assigned to it. There is no value stated on the stock certificate. When the stock is issued, the company credits the capital stock account for the entire amount received.

Nobel Economists distinguished economists who won the Nobel prize for making unsurpassed contributions to the development of economic theory and policy.

No-Fault a legal concept whereby the parties affected do not have to prove fault or no-fault in an action. No-fault takes a constructive view by seeking to redress the harm caused rather than to determine fault or blame for an action.
Divorce: a concept used in certain states allowing a marriage to be terminated by proclaiming it to be irretrievably broken because of irreconcilable differences. Thus, it is not incumbent upon the parties to determine who is at fault.
Insurance: a concept widely used in automobile insurance when the law permits an aggrieved party in a traffic accident to recover all expenses from insurance without determining fault in the accident. Often, there are restrictions on the right of third parties to sue in order to discourage frivolous suits.

No-Load; No-Load Fund commission-free mutual fund that sells its shares at net asset value, either directly to the public or through an affiliated distributor, without the addition of a sales charge. Most no load funds permit switching money among its funds with no transfer fee. In the financial newspaper, the designation of a no-load fund is NL.

Nominal Income the value of income expressed in current dollars. No adjustment is made for changes in the purchasing power of the dollar.

Nominal GDP the total domestic output in current dollars, not adjusted for inflation. *See also* Real GDP.

Nominal Interest Rate
1. the stated rate of interest on a debt security or loan. It may not be the true

rate earned. In the case of bonds, the terms *nominal interest rate* and *coupon rate* are synonymous. The interest received on a bond investment equals the nominal interest rate times the face value of the bond. For example, on an 8%, $10,000 bond, the investor would receive annual interest income of $800 ($10,000 x 8%). *See also* Effective Interest Rate (Effective Annual Yield).

2. the interest rate without adjusting for inflation. *See also* Rental Interest Rate.

Nongoods Services music, education, or nonproduct services.

Nonlinear Function a mathematical relationship between variables that is not directly proportional. For example, a per unit cost may decrease as production increases due to economies of scale. The diagram below shows a comparison between a linear (top) and a nonlinear (bottom) cost function. *See also* Linear Function.

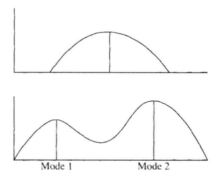

Mode 1   Mode 2

Nonparametric Statistics type of statistics applied to problems for which rank order is known but the specific distribution is not; also known as *distribution-free statistics*. Thus, various metals may be ranked in order of hardness without having any measure of hardness. Nonparametric tests include rank correlations, sign tests for paired data, one-sample runs tests, and rank sum tests (often called the *Mann-Whitney U Test*).

Nonprice Competition competition based on service, location, depth of assortment, or other nonprice factors.

Nonprofit Organization an organization that doesn't pay taxes. "Nonprofits" for short (such organizations as churches, hospitals, colleges, and charities) may also receive tax-deductible contributions.

Non-Value-Added Activity activity that increases the time spent on a product or service but does not increase its worth to the customer. The designation "non-value-added" reflects a belief that the activity can be redesigned, reduced, or eliminated without reducing the quantity, responsiveness, or quality of the output required by the customer or the organization.

Non-Zero Sum Game a type of game in which the amount that one player wins is not equal to that his opponents have lost, so that the total payments made as a result of the game is not zero.

Normal Curve; Normal Distribution a probability distribution that has the following important characteristics:

1. The curve has a single peak.
2. It is bell-shaped.
3. The mean (average) lies at the center of the distribution and the distribution is symmetrical around the mean.
4. The two tails of the distribution extend indefinitely and never touch the horizontal axis.
5. The shape of the distribution is determined by its mean and standard deviation.

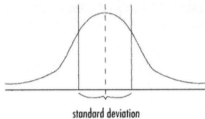

standard deviation

North American Free-Trade Agreement an agreement among the United States, Canada, and Mexico in which all trade restrictions will eventually be eliminated. A goal is for the three countries to improve employment from increased trade. In the free trade area there should be equal treatment, free transfer of funds, arbitration of disputes, and complying with international law.

Notary Public a professional who is authorized by the government to certify affidavits and acknowledgments called *notarizing*.

Note a legally transferable debt instrument by which the insurer resolves to pay the payee within a specified period of time. Notes normally pay a stated rate of interest dependent upon the market rate of interest. An individual may sign his or her note payable, promising to pay money to another party, such as a bank or creditor, at a future date. The payment consists of principal and interest. Governmental notes normally have a maturity of from two to ten years, whereas municipal notes commonly have shorter term maturities ranging from one to four years with two-year maturities being the most common. Often notes are issued on the basis of the full faith and credit of the issuer carrying no collateral.

Collateral note: A note by which the promise to pay is secured by a pledge of property such as securities, real estate, or other assets.

Demand note: A note payable on demand by the payee rather than on a specific maturity date.

Joint note: A note by which two or more individuals are mutually indebted for payment.

Mortgage note: *See* Mortgage.

Secured note: *See* Collateral.

Time note: As opposed to a demand note, a note payable at a definite time in the future.

Unsecured note: A note of indebtedness not pledging any collateral or security to guarantee payment.

Notebook a portable computer smaller than a laptop.

Notes Payable; Notes Receivable accounts showing either the amounts due or the amount to be paid by a company.

Notice of Tax Due and Demand for Payment the official notice by the IRS stating that the tax has not been fully paid and there's no more discussion on the subject. This is the beginning of collection.

Notice to Pay Rent or Quit notice by a landlord to a tenant to either pay rent due or vacate the premises; also called a *three-day notice to quit*. If the tenant has a long-term lease, the notice may list penalties.

Not-Sufficient-Funds Check (NSF) or, bounced check. Notification by a bank to a drawee that a check cannot be negotiated because the drawer's account does not have sufficient funds to cover it. Often a bad check processing fee will be charged to both the drawee and to the drawer by the respective banks.
In preparing one's bank reconciliation, one deducts the NSF check from the book balance.

NOW Account (Negotiable Order of Withdraw) a checking or savings account earning slightly higher interest.

NPV *see* Net Present Value (NPV).

Nuisance an activity by a property owner that annoys or seriously disturbs other property owners, making it discomforting to use their own property.

Null and Void in law, something that is not permitted or binding and, as such, is not legally enforceable. An example is an unlawful clause in a contract such as prohibiting the rental of property based on sex, race, or religion.

Number Cruncher an act that involves primarily calculations, computer work, or accounting all day.

Oo

Obsolescence a major factor in depreciation, resulting from technological or market changes. Wear and tear from use and natural deterioration through interaction of the elements are other factors that cause depreciation in assets. It is also a big factor in inventory risk.

Occupational Safety and Health Act (OSHA) a federal law concerned primarily with the regulation of working conditions in commerce and industry. It contains guidelines and regulations issued by the Department of Labor mandating standards with respect to occupational safety and health of workers involved in interstate commerce. The Act was enacted in 1970 by the Occupational Safety and Health Review Commission.

OCR *see* Optical Character Recognition (OCR).

Odd-Lot any exception to the standard trading unit. For example, a standard unit of stock is 100 shares, called *round lot*. Any amount other than 100 shares or multiples thereof would be an odd-lot. An example of an odd-lot is 25 shares. The commission rate on an odd-lot transaction typically includes an odd-lot differential, usually one-eighth of a point. The commission rate on an odd-lot transaction is relatively higher than on a round-lot transaction.

Odd-Number Pricing a pricing practice, noticeable in retailing, that set prices in such a way that they end in an odd number. The assumption is made that it is possible to sell a great number of items priced at 31 cents rather than 30 cents, or at 99 cents rather than $1.00. The idea applies to higher-priced merchandise as well.

Off-Balance Sheet Financing a description often referring to a long term, noncancelable lease accounted for as an operating lease.

Offer
1. the price for which one is willing to sell a security; also called *ask* or *sell*. Opposed to bid, it is the price at which one is ready to buy.
2. the bid and asked prices for over-the-counter securities are published in newspapers.
3. a proposal to perform some activity or to pay some money. Once an offer is

accepted, a contract exists.

4. to offer a good or service for sale.

Offer Price the price at which a market maker is willing to sell a security; also called *Ask Price*.

Office of Management and Budget (OMB) an agency within the Executive Office of the President. The OMB has broad financial management power as well as the responsibility of preparing the executive budget. Among the other duties assigned OMB are (1) to study and recommend to the president changes relative to the existing organizational structure of the agencies, their activities and methods of business, etc.; (2) to apportion appropriations among the agencies and establish reserves in anticipation of cost savings, contingencies, etc.; and (3) to develop programs and regulations for improved data gathering pertaining to the government and its agencies.

Offshore; Offshore Banking

1. term to describe a financial institution (e.g., bank) headquartered outside of the country in question. For example, a U.S. company having an account in a bank in another country would say it has offshore deposits. Another example is a U.S. mutual fund having a legal domicile in the Cayman Islands. Major reasons for offshore deposits or other transactions is to save on taxes in a lower (or no) tax area or to circumvent stringent regulation in the U.S. A mutual fund legally domiciled outside of the U.S. must follow all federal and state laws to operate in the U.S.

2. an offshore finance subsidiary of a company located outside the United States to conduct financing, banking, or some other financial related function.

Offshore Assembly the overseas production of goods whose inputs are constructed or processed in one country and then the final products are shipped to the target market for sale.

Offshore Production either offshore sourcing or offshore assembly.

Okun's Law law that describes the relationship between changes in the rate of economic growth (measured by changes in GDP) and changes in the unemployment rate. This law is attributed to Arthur Okun, chairman of the Council of Economic Advisors under President Johnson. The law states that for every 2 1/2 percentage points of growth in real GDP above the trend rate that is sustained for a year, the unemployment rate declines by 1 percentage point. It means that the economy must continue to grow considerably faster than its trend (long-term average) rate in order to achieve a substantial reduction in the unemployment rate.

Old Economy *see* New Economy.

Oligopoly a situation where sellers are few and offer similar products. The supply offered by any single producer materially affects the market price and all are extremely sensitive to another's actions. Sometimes called *partial* or *competitive monopoly.*

Oligopsony a market structure in which few companies are buyers, as opposed to oligopoly in which few companies are sellers.

One-Year Treasury Constant Maturity Index an index of rates on U.S. Treasury borrowings that determines the changes in many adjustable-rate mortgages. The index is released by the Federal Reserve Board, which recalculates yields on a variety of Treasury securities as if each would mature in one year.

Online to be captivated to a network of computers, such as the Internet or a commercial service such as MSN.

Online Advertising advertising that appears while consumers are surfing the Web, including banner and ticker ads, interstitials, skyscrapers, and other forms.

Online Analytical Processing (OLAP) powerful tools that take a complex, multi-dimensional view of aggregated data to quickly yield strategic information. The power of OLAP tools is predictive, in answering "why" and "what-if" questions.

On-Line Database information transmitted by telephone, microwaves, or other means that may be accessed with a modem and displayed on a monitor or as a printout. To take advantage of a database, typically stored on a mainframe, one needs a personal computer, telecommunications software, a modem, and a telephone. A database may consist of information on tax laws and regulations, investment information, financial data on companies, and other information.

Online Networking getting people together online, as opposed to face-to-face networking. This is great for business development, market research, publicity, and knowledge sharing. The greatest value is the easy access to expertise, usually for free. Examples of online networking service are *www.onlinebusinessnetworks. com* and *www.ryze.com.*

Online Searching using a computer retrieval system to obtain information from a database such as on the Internet.

On-The-Job Training learning on the job rather than taking a training course. It can be the quickest way to learn the job.

OPEC *see* Organization of Petroleum Exporting Countries (OPEC).

Open Architecture a computer system that can be used by third-party designers to develop programs for its use.

Open Book Management management philosophy that gets all employees involved in increasing financial performance and ensures that all workers have access to operational and financial information necessary to accomplishing performance improvements. For example, a project manager can meet with a group of employees working on the project to discuss return on the project's investment and its impact on the firm's return on equity.

Open Door Policy a business practice that allows employees to see the boss with just about any problem or question.

1031 Exchange *see* Exchange, 1031.

Open Interest the number of futures contracts that have not been closed.

Open Market Operations the activity of the Federal Reserve Bank in buying and selling of government securities so as to influence bank reserves, the interest rates, the volume of credit, and the money supply. It is an instrument of monetary policy. If securities are bought, the money paid out by the Fed increases commercial bank reserves and the money supply increases. If securities are sold, the money supply contracts. *See also* Monetary Policy; Money Supply.

Open Outcry a trading practice in the commodity exchange by which dealers stand in a "pit" on the trading floor and yell out bid and offer prices for commodities.

Open Shop a work place in which employees are free to decide whether to join the union.

Open Source Software a category of computer programs that are not controlled by a single company but are developed by the group efforts of volunteers. The best-known open-source program is the Linux operating system. Open-source software developers allow other users to make improvements with as few restrictions as possible

Open-End (Mutual) Funds a mutual fund that an investor buys shares from and sells these shares back to the fund itself. This type of fund offers to sell and redeem shares on a continual basis for an indefinite time period. Shares are purchased at net asset value (NAV) plus commission (if any), and redeemed at NAV less a service charge (if any).

Open-end Investment Company *see* Open-End (Mutual) Funds.

Open-End Mortgage additional financing the borrower may obtain from the lender according to the mortgage agreement that usually specifies a maximum amount that can be borrowed.

Operational (Operating) Budget a budget that embraces the impacts of operating decisions. It contains forecasts of sales, net income, the cost of goods sold, selling and administrative expenses, and other expenses. The cornerstone for preparing an operational budget is forecasted sales. Therefore, the sales budget is the basic building block for the operational budget. Once the sales budget is prepared, then the production budget can be formulated. The operational budget also consists of the ending inventory budget, direct material budget, direct labor budget, factory overhead budget, selling and administrative budget, and budgeted income statement.

Operations Management (OM) design, operation, and improvement of the productions/operations system that creates the firm's primary products or services; also called *Production/Operations Management*.

Operations Strategy is concerned with setting broad policies and plans for using the production resources of the firm to best support the firm's long-term competitive strategy. There are four basic operations strategies: cost, quality, speed of delivery, and flexibility. These four strategies translate directly into

characteristics used to direct and measure manufacturing performance. Typical operations strategy issues include:
- *Capacity requirements*: amount, timing, and type.
- *Facilities*: size, location, and specialization.
- *Technology*: equipment, automation, and linkages.
- *Vertical integration*: extent of use of outside suppliers and distributors.
- *Workforce*: skill level, wage policies, and employment security.
- *Quality*: defect prevention, monitoring, and intervention.
- *Production planning/materials control*: sourcing policies, centralization, and decision rules.
- *Organization*: structure, control/reward systems, and role of staff groups.

Operating Cycle average time period between buying inventory and receiving cash proceeds from its eventual sale. It is determined by adding the number of days inventory is held and the collection period for accounts receivable.

Operating Decisions decisions that involve routine tasks, such as planning production and sales, scheduling of personnel and equipment, adjusting production rates, and controlling the quality of production.

Operating Expense Ratio total operating expenses divided by effective gross income.

Operating Expenses
1. those costs associated with the selling and administrative activities of a company. They are subdivided into selling expenses and general and administrative expenses.
2. those expenses incurred in association with managing an investment property, including repairs and maintenance, legal, and management fees.

Operating in the Red a vernacular term describing a business sustaining a loss from current operations. The income statement shows an imbalance between expenses and revenues.

Operating Leverage a measure of operating risk that arises from fixed operating costs. A simple indication of operating leverage is the effect that a change in sales has on operating income. The formula is:

$$\text{Operating leverage at a given level of sales} = \frac{\text{Percent change in operating income}}{\text{Percent change in sales}}$$

$$\text{Or} = \frac{(\text{unit selling price} - \text{unit variable cost}) \times \text{sales}}{(\text{unit selling price} - \text{unit variable cost}) \times \text{sales} - \text{fixed costs}}$$

Example: Assume a unit selling price of $25, a unit variable cost of $15, and fixed costs of $50,000. The company is selling 6,000 units per year. Its operating leverage is:

$$\frac{(\$25 - \$15)(6,000)}{(\$25 - \$15)(6,000) - \$50,000} = \frac{\$60,000}{\$10,000} = 6$$

which means if sales increase by 10 percent, the company can expect its income to increase six times that amount, or 60 percent.

Operating leverage may also be measured by the ratio of fixed operating costs to total costs. A higher ratio indicates greater risk.

Operating Loss a loss incurred by a business. Gross expenses exceed gross sales.

Operating Risk the risk that is caused by fluctuations of operating income. This type of risk depends on variability in demand, sales price, input prices, and amount of operating leverage. A business with a high degree of risk in its operations will have greater instability often resulting in lower market price of stock and increased cost of financing. *See also* Operating Leverage.

Operating System system software that manages the operations of the computer.

Operations Research often used interchangeably with management science or quantitative methods, a scientific method of providing the decision maker with a quantitative basis for decisions regarding the operations under his/her control. Operations research (OR) is divided broadly into two categories of techniques (models): optimization models (mathematical programming) and simulation models. Optimization models attempt to provide an optimal solution (or prescriptive solution) to a problem, while simulation models produce a descriptive (or "what-if" type of) solution. It, for example, covers such quantitative techniques as inventory models, linear programming, queuing theory, Program Evaluation and Review Technique (PERT), and Monte Carlo simulation.

Opinion Polling a subjective method of economic forecasting, amounting largely to a weighted or unweighted averaging of attitudes and expectations; also called *Sample Survey Techniques. See also* Blue Chip Economic Indicators; Index of Consumer Confidence; Purchasing Manager's Index; University of Michigan's Index of Consumer Sentiment.

Opportunity Cost the net revenue foregone by rejecting an alternative use of time or facilities. For example, assume a company has a choice of using its capacity to produce an extra 10,000 units or renting it out for $20,000. The opportunity cost of using that capacity is $20,000. A further example is the return foregone from having money tied up in accounts receivable for a longer time because of a collection problem. If the extra funds tied up in receivables were $400,000 for a three-month period the firm could earn 10% per annum, the opportunity cost is $10,000 ($400,000 x 3/12 x 10%). A concept that all investment or business options have some risk.

Optical Character Recognition (OCR) the software that involves reading text from paper and translating the images into a form that the computer can manipulate.

Optimal Capacity the optimal level of output for a firm to produce, which corresponds to the minimum point of the average total cost schedule.

Optimal Capital Structure capital structure with a minimum weighted-average cost of capital and thereby maximizes the value of the firm's stock, but it does not maximize earnings per share (EPS). Greater leverage maximizes EPS but also increases risk. Thus, the highest stock price is not reached by maximizing EPS. The optimal capital structure usually involves some debt, but not 100% debt. Ordinarily, some firms cannot identify this optimal point precisely, but they should attempt to find an optimal range for the capital structure. The required rate of return on equity capital (R) can be estimated in various ways, for example, by adding a percentage to the firm's long-term cost of debt. Another method is the Capital Asset Pricing Model (CAPM).

Optimism Index the index prepared by the National Federation of Independent Business, a Washington-based advocacy group, based on small-business owners' expectations for the economy.

Optimization maximization or minimization of a special goal.

Optimization Models prescriptive techniques for finding the best solutions to the problem at hand. Linear programming is an example.

Optimize to find the best result given the circumstances; usually to find a minimum or maximum solution to a problem.

Option contract giving you the right, not the obligation, to buy or sell a specified number of shares of an asset at a set price for a given time period. The value of an option is typically a minor percentage of the underlying value of the asset. It has three basic features. It allows an investor to reserve the right to buy or sell (1) a specified number of shares of stock (2) at a fixed price per share (3) for a limited length of time. There are two types of option contracts: call options and put options.

Optional Arm a mortgage in which borrowers typically pick from four payment choices each month. The options are a minimum payment, which is like borrowing money to cover the payment (causing the loan principal to grow); an interest-only-payment (in which the principal remains unchanged); a normal payment based on a 30-year loan schedule (the principal shrinks some); and a bigger payment based on a 15-year loan, for quicker payoff (causing the principal to shrink a lot).

Oral Contract a contract that is not in writing or signed by the parties. In most cases, oral contracts are legally enforceable except for those related to the sale of real estate.

Ordinary Annuity an insurance contract designed to pay an income to the annuitant on a monthly, quarterly, or semiannual basis. While annuities do have death benefits, they differ from life insurance in that they are intended to provide income for the annuitant during his or her lifetime rather than simply provide a lump-sum distribution to the beneficiaries on the insured's death.

Ordinary Income income from the usual activities of an individual or business as distinguished from capital gains. Such income includes wages, salaries, fees, commissions, tips, bonuses, prizes and awards, director's fees, earned interest, and others. Subsequent to current tax law, long-term and short-term capital gains are also treated as ordinary income for tax purposes.

Organizational Behavior (OB) the actions and attitudes of people in organizations. The field of organizational behavior (OB) is the body of knowledge derived from these actions and attitudes. It can help managers understand the complexity within organizations, identify problems, determine how to correct them, and establish whether the changes would make a difference.

Organization Chart an illustration of the functions, divisions, and positions in a company and how they are related. A sample organization chart is shown below:

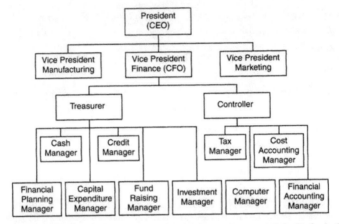

Organizational Culture the collective assumptions and beliefs held by an organization's employees that shape the behavior of individuals and groups in the organization.

Organization for Economic Cooperation and Development (OECD) *(www.oecd.org)* a forum set up to discuss, develop, and refine economic and social policies. It is an international organization that encourages economic growth, high employment, and financial stability among its members.

Organization of Petroleum Exporting Countries (OPEC) a group of Arabic countries that produce oil and engaged sometimes in dramatic increases in the price of oil, such as in the 1970s.

OSHA *see* Occupational Safety and Health Act (OSHA).

Other People's Money (OPM) the use of borrowed funds by individuals to increase the return on an invested capital. Examples are a mortgage to buy real estate and buying stock on margin. *See also* Financial Leverage; Leverage.

Outlay Costs expenditure by cash to carry on a particular activity. They are the explicit costs that go into a firm's formal accounting records to arrive at a measure of earnings.

Outlier in statistics, a data value that is far outside the normal range.

Out-Of-Pocket Cost actual cash outlays made during the period for payroll, advertising, and other operating expenses. Depreciation is not an out-of-pocket cost. since it involves no current cash expenditure.

Out-Of-The-Money the term used when the striking price of an option is less than the market price of the underlying stock for a call option or greater than the price of the underlying stock for a put option.

Outplacement Service a group of services provided to displaced employees to give them support and assistance. It is often used with those involuntarily removed because of plant closings or elimination. The service usually done by outside firms, provide counseling in writing resumes, networking, and interviewing skills.

Output Gap the difference between the nation's gross domestic product (GDP) and the potential according to economists.

Outside Directors non-employees/officers who serve on the board of directors of a company.

Outsourcing the practice of purchasing either products or services from outside the company as opposed to producing or performing these services in-house. Outsourcing can be up and down the service chain from software programming, engineering, and design as well as accounting and other professional service jobs.

Outstanding Shares all the shares a company has issued. They are shares held by company's insiders as well as shares owned by the public, including institutional and individuals investors. Insiders often are traded infrequently while shares in public hands, known as float, tend to be traded more often. *See also* Float.

Overdraft negative balance in a checking account caused by payment of checks drawn against insufficient funds.

Overhead indirect costs that cannot be specifically charged to a product or project, but instead are lumped together and charged to all units of the company. *See also* Factory Overhead.

Overextension
Banking: the extension of more credit to an individual or company than can reasonably be expected to be repaid.
Business: the condition of a business that has overly expanded itself and is having financial and management difficulties because of it.
Financial: the situation of a person who is excessively in debt beyond his or her ability to pay. An example is the result of using charge accounts beyond one's financial limits.
Physical Labor: an individual's doing more physically than he or she can realistically handle.
Securities: the situation of an individual whose stock margin purchases exceed his or her financial resources to repay.

Over-the-Counter (OTC) Stocks stocks traded electronically via a network of dealers across the nation. OTC stands for over-the-counter, but these days, over-the-computer would be more appropriate. Stocks listed on exchanges are traded face-to-face at one location, such as the New York Stock Exchange (NYSE). All others are OTC stocks. The NASDAQ stock market is the OTC system in the U.S., listing over 5,000 companies. In the U.S., OTC usually applies to smaller or newer companies that do not meet the stringent listing requirements of one of the major stock exchanges like the AMEX or NYSE. In recent years, however, this has changed as many companies have elected to keep their shares trading on NASDAQ even after they have grown large, rather than moving to an exchange. A good example of this is Microsoft. As for foreign companies, ADRs are largely available to U.S. investors.

Owner's Equity the interest of the owners in the assets of the business represented by capital investments and accumulated earnings less any dividends. It is total assets minus total liabilities of an individual or company; also called *net worth* or *shareholders' equity*.

Pp

P2P *see* Peer-To-Peer Networking.

Paasche Price Index a price index that measures the cost of purchasing the given-year quantities at given-year prices relative to their cost at base-year prices. It is a given year weighted price index. *See also* Lasperyes Price Index; Price Indexes.

PAC Man a defensive tactic to a tender offer where the firm under attack becomes the attacker.

Pacific Rim Countries those countries that literally rim the Pacific Ocean and enjoy dynamic economies, such as Japan, South Korea, Malaysia, and Indonesia.

Paid Inclusion an alternative to paid listings. Paid listings can be pricey, particularly for companies whose product lines are so complex and fluid that they would have to buy listings for a multitude of keywords and continually buy new ones to cover their inventory. For these companies especially, an alternative, paid inclusion, can be an effective way to increase visibility on the web. In paid inclusion, a company pays a search engine for the right to submit the entire content of its web site, or selected pages, directly to the search engine's database. *See also* Paid Listings; Search-Engine Optimization.

Paid Listings the hottest category in search marketing. It is short text advertisements, with links to the advertiser's site, that appear on the pages that display the results of an Internet search. Marketers refer to these ads as pay for *placement, pay for performance, pay per click* or *cost per click*—terms that reflect how the system works for advertisers. *See also* Paid Inclusion; Serach-Engine Optimization.

Paper Profit or Loss an unrealized profit or loss on a security still held. A paper (unrealized) profit occurs when the market price of a security exceeds the original purchase price, while an unrealized loss occurs when the market price of a security declines from the initial purchase price. Such profits or losses have no tax effect except upon the actual sale of the security when it becomes a realized profit or loss.

Par Value

1. amount arbitrarily assigned by the corporate charter to one share of stock and printed on the stock certificate. The par value represents the legal capital per share. There can be no dividend declared that would cause the stockholders' equity to go below the par value of outstanding shares. Par value may be a minimum cushion of equity capital existing for creditor protection. The par value is the amount per share entered in the capital stock account. It is usually significantly lower than the market price per share.
2. for preferred issues, the value on which the issuer promises to pay dividends. Preferred dividends are typically expressed as a percentage of the preferred stock. For example, a 12%, $500,000 par value stock would pay annual dividends of $60,000.
3. nominal, face value, maturity value of a bond. For example, the face value of a bond is in $1,000 denominations. Interest paid on a bond is the nominal (stated, coupon) interest rate multiplied by the face value of the bond.
4. for a country's currency, the value established by the government for it relative to other currencies.

Paradigm a model or theory of business practices.

Parameter a constant or the coefficient of a variable in an equation or a system of equations. For example, in a cost volume formula of the form of $y = a + bx$, the constant a and the slope b are parameters. The total fixed costs, the unit variable cost, and the unit selling price are examples of parameters.

Parametric Statistics a branch of statistics in which the parameters of a population distribution are predetermined. It makes restrictive assumptions about the populations from which samples are drawn. For example, samples drawn are either large or from normally distributed populations. A majority of statistical analyses use this method. *See also* Nonparametric Statistics.

Parent Company a company that owns one or more companies and that may oversee and manage them.

Pareto Analysis analysis used to differentiate between the vital few and the trivial many. It is based on the concept that about 80 percent of the problems come from 20 percent of the items. Pareto analysis can be used to identify cost drivers or activity drivers that are responsible for the majority of cost incurred by ranking the cost drivers in order of value.

Pareto Rule

1. the 80-20 rule that suggests that 80 percent of the business comes from 20 percent of customers.
2. a rule-of-thumb that, for the typical product category, 80 percent of the products sold will be consumed by 20 percent of the customers.
3. the concept that about 80 percent of the problems come from 20 percent of the items.

See also Pareto Analysis.

Pareto's Optimality condition that exists in an economy when no change in the combination of resources or of output can be implemented that will make someone better off without making someone else worse off; also called *economic efficiency*. Perfect competition is considered Pareto-optimal. *See also* Efficiency.

Parkinson's Law laws advanced by C. Northcote Parkinson in satirical accounts of the administration procedures of business and public organizations. The laws are (1) work always expands so as to fill the time available for its completion and (2) expenditure rises to meet income.

Partnership a form of business organization created by an agreement between two or more persons who contribute capital and/or their services to the organization. Its advantages are (1) It is easily established with minimal organizational effort and costs. (2) It is free from special government regulation. Its disadvantages are. (1) It carries usually unlimited liability for the individual partners. (2) It is dissolved upon the withdrawal or death of any of the partners. (3) Its ability to raise large amounts of capital is limited. General partners are those who are responsible for the day-to-day operations of the partnership and who are responsible for the partnership's total liabilities, while limited partners are those who contribute only money, who are not involved in management decisions, and whose liability is limited to their investment.

Passive Income; Passive Losses sources of income or losses resulting from any businesses in which one is not an active participant.

Pass-Through Securities securities supported by a pool of mortgages. The principal and interest are due monthly on the mortgages and are passed through to the investors who bought the pool. Examples are the mortgage-backed securities guaranteed by the GNMA and Freddie Mac securities. However, Freddie Mac securities are not federally guaranteed.

Password a secret character string that is required before one can log onto a computer system, thus preventing unauthorized persons from obtaining access to the computer. The primary reason for using a password is to protect confidential information from modification, destruction, misuse, and other security-related dangers by unauthorized persons.

Patent an exclusive right conferred on an inventor for the use of an invention, for a limited time (usually 17 years). It creates a temporary monopolistic power and is intended as a device for promoting invention.

Payback Period the length of time required to recover the initial amount of a capital investment. If the cash inflows occur at a uniform rate, it is the ratio of the amount of initial investment over expected annual cash inflows, or Payback period = initial investment/annual cash inflows. For example, assume projected annual cash inflows are expected to be $3,000 a year for five years from an investment of $18,000. The payback period on this proposal is 3 years, which is calculated as follows: Payback period = $18,000/$6,000 = 3 years. If annual cash inflows are not even, the payback period would have to be determined by trial and error. Assume instead that the cash inflows are $4,000 in the first year, $5,000 in the second year, $6,000 in the third year, $6,000 in the fourth year, and $8,000 in the fifth year. The payback period would be then 3.5 years. In three years, all but $3,000 has been recovered. It takes one-half year ($3,000/$6,000) to recover the balance. When two or more projects are considered, the rule for making a selection decision is as follows: Choose the project with the shorter payback period. The rationale behind this is that the shorter the payback period, the greater the liquidity, and the less risky the project. Advantages of the method include (1) it is simple to compute and easy to understand and (2) it handles investment risk effectively. Disadvantages of the method include (1) it does not recognize the time value of money and (2) it ignores profitability of an investment.

Paycheck Withholding the amount taken out of an employee's salary for taxes and other items (e.g., union dues) to be remitted by the employer to other parties (e.g., Internal Revenue Service, union).

Payment in Kind payment for goods, services, or satisfaction of liabilities with similar or identical mediums of exchange and value (e.g., money for money, goods for goods, and services for services). It also connotes a transaction where one medium of exchange is satisfied with another. For example, I fixed your roof whose service has a value of $200. You pay me with (maybe your are a lawyer) one hour's worth of legal services.

Payoffs
1. complete satisfaction of a debt.
2. an unethical or illegal payment made to obtain otherwise unobtainable goods or favors. examples of a payoff would be a bribe or a kickback.

Payout Ratio the dividends per share divided by the earnings per share. For example, if a company pays out dividends per share of $2 and earnings per share is $10, the payout ratio is 20%. In general, stockholders prefer companies with higher payout ratios.

Payroll Costs employer costs incurred for employees' services. Payroll costs consist of the actual cash paid to the employees and the withheld amounts (liabilities) for employee's federal income taxes, FICA, and various voluntary health and benefit plans. Employer's payroll costs also consist of its matching share of employee's FICA taxes and contributions to the state and federal unemployment insurance programs.

Payroll Tax taxes levied because of employee's salaries and net income of self-employed individuals. Social Security taxes are imposed upon employees and self-employed individuals, and employers are responsible for a matching amount. Unemployment taxes are only levied upon the employer.

PC Cards credit card sized expansion cards for portable computers, also known as *PCMCIA* (Personal Computer Memory Card International Association) *cards*.

PDA *see* Personal Digital Assistant (PDA).

P/E RATIO *see* Price-Earnings (PE) Ratio.

Peak Load Pricing a pricing method of charging a differential (higher) price for demand during the peak period. The idea is based on the fact that price elasticities of demand for certain products (such as public utilities) differ at certain times. This pricing scheme will allow firms to allocate their limited facilities during periods of high demand in an equitable manner. For example, telephone companies charge higher long-distance rates during the weekdays (a peak period) and lower rates during the weekend (an off-peak period).

Peer Review a performance review by those who are at your level. This is sometimes done at companies to obtain comments from those who work side-by-side.

Peer-to-Peer Networking networking that allows all computers to communicate and share resources as equals. Music-file sharing, instant messaging, and other applications rely on P2P technology.

Pending House Sales Index a new index to serve as a leading economic indicator for the nation's housing market. The index is based on pending sales of existing homes, including single-family and condo. An index of 100 is equal to the average level of contract activity during 2001. National Association of Realtors put it together from a national sample representing about 20 percent of transactions for existing-home sales.

Penetration Pricing a method of pricing a standard product. It sets a low initial price for a product in order to gain quick acceptance in a broad portion of the market. It calls for a sacrifice of short-term profits in order to establish a certain amount of market share. One objective is to obtain a committed customer. *See also* Skimming Pricing.

Penny Stock a stock usually selling for less than $1 a share but may rise above it after being promoted. Companies issuing penny stocks usually have low revenue and profitability, short lives, or past instability in operations. As such, the companies are financially weak and very speculative. These stocks typically experience volatility in price relative to the stocks of established companies on the major stock exchanges. Many brokerage firms are very careful when they recommend penny stocks because the Securities and Exchange Commission mandates that they should only be bought by investors who are financially and intelligently suited for these high risk securities. Many brokerage houses will ask for written statements from investors that they are aware of the high speculation and the investors find the penny stocks suitable for them. Most penny stocks are traded in the over-the-counter market.

Pension Benefit Guarantee Corporation (PBGC) a federal government corporation established by a provision of the Employee Retirement Income Security Act of 1974 (ERISA). This organization guarantees to eligible workers certain benefits payable to them even if their employer's pension plan has insufficient assets to fulfill its commitments. Payment is financed through premiums paid by insured plans. This agency currently guarantees payment of basic pension benefits for more than 44 million U.S. workers and retirees. PBGC insures defined benefit plans, such as a traditional pension that promises to pay a specific monthly benefit at retirement. It does not cover "defined contribution plans," such as your 401-k or profit-sharing. PBGC gets its money from insurance premiums paid by companies that sponsor pension plans.

Pension Plan a legal agreement in which the employer agrees to provide retirement benefits to employees. Plans vary among employers. The employee may or may not contribute to the fund depending on the terms of the agreement. The deposited pension monies accumulate a return (dividends, interest income) over time. At retirement, the individual typically receives the funds in an annuity. The amounts received from the employer's contributions or originally non-taxed employee contributions are subject to income tax when withdrawn. A self-employed individual may have his or her own pension plan. *See also* Defined Benefit Plan; Defined Contribution Plan; Keogh Pension Plan (HR-10); Individual Retirement Account (IRA).

Pentium Chip the name Intel has given to its 586 microprocessor. It contains 3.3 million transistors, nearly triple the number contained in its predecessor, the 80486 chip.

Per Capita per person. For example, the per capita income of the United States is arrived at by dividing the entire population by the total personal income of everyone in the country including children and others who do not earn any income at all.

Per Diem per day. The term is used most frequently in connection with payment by the day for work done. As an example, an accountant may work on a per diem basis for a CPA firm.

Percentage Statement an approach by which items in the financial statements are shown as percentages of a total; in the income statement, each item is shown as a percentage of sales; in the balance sheet, each item is shown as a percentage of total assets or equities. *See also* Common Size Statements.

Percent-of-Sales Method
1. a way to determine the amount of external financing needed. Under this method, the various expenses, assets, and liabilities for a future period are estimated as a percentage of sales for the present period. These percentages, together with the projected sales for the upcoming year, are then used to construct pro forma (planned or projected) balance sheets.
2. method of determining the advertising budget based on an analysis of past sales, as well as a forecast for future sales.

Perfect Competition market structure possessing the following characteristics: (1) large number of small firms, (2) homogeneous products, (3) free entry and exit, and (4) perfect communication between buyers and sellers.

Perfect Market a market structure characterized by a very large number of buyers and sellers of a homogeneous (nondifferentiated) product. Entry and exit from the industry is costless, or nearly so. Information is freely available to all market participants, and there is no collusion among firms in the industry.

Performance Bond surety bond given by one individual or company to another so as to safeguard the second party from loss if the contractual provisions are not carried out. The surety company is mainly responsible with the principal (contractor) if nonperformance occurs. For example, a company having a new office constructed may ask for a performance bond from the contractor so that the company would be compensated if the office is improperly done within the specified time provided for.

Performance Budget a medium- to short-range budget used in governmental accounting. It is typical of the type incorporated by a program planning budgeting system (PPBS) but without references to long-range goals.

Performance Evaluation a cumulative consideration of factors (that may be subjective or objective) to determine a representative indicator or appraisal of an individual or entity's activity, or performance in reference to some subjective (or standard) over some period of time. Factors to consider may include degree of goal attainment, how items are measured, and what standards are to be applied. *See also* Cost Center; Investment Center; Profit Center.

Performance Report a statement that displays measurements of actual results of some person or entity's activity over some time period. These results are ideally compared with budgeted or standard measurements obtained under some conditional assumptions over the same period. Variations from such budget or standards are known as variances and may be favorable or unfavorable depending upon lower or higher measurements relative to the standards. Corrective action is taken for unfavorable performance. *See also* Variance.

Peril in insurance, a condition or situation that may result in future damages or loss. There may be exposure to harm or injury. An individual is sometimes warned to "proceed at your own risk."

Period Certain Annuity an annuity that guarantees payments to the annuitant–or a beneficiary if the annuitant should die early–for a fixed time period.

Periodic Inventory System an inventory system that does not require a day-to-day record of inventory changes. Costs of materials used and costs of goods sold cannot be calculated until ending inventories, determined by physical count, are subtracted from the sum of opening inventories and purchases (or costs of goods manufactured in the case of a manufacturer).

Peripherals auxiliary equipment used in computer systems, including printers, card readers, tape and disk drives, and other input-output and storage devices. Peripherals do not include the central processing unit (CPU).

Permanent File a separate file of working papers, documents, and schedules that will be used for ensuing audits. It usually covers copies or summaries of various documents such as minutes of the board meetings, lease agreements, schedules of capital assets including fixed assets and capital stock, the charter of the corporation, and descriptions of accounting methods, policies, and internal controls of the company.

Perpetual Inventory System an inventory system that keeps continual track of additions or deletions in materials, work in process, and cost of goods sold on a day-to-day basis. Physical inventory counts are usually taken at least once a year in order to check on the validity of the books' records. Cost of goods sold therefore is kept on a day-to-day basis rather than being determined periodically. *See also* Periodic Inventory System.

Perpetuity an annuity that goes on indefinitely. An example of a perpetuity is a preferred stock that yields a constant dollar dividend indefinitely. The present value of a perpetuity is A/i where A is the periodic payment (the amount of an annuity) and i is the discount rate per period. For example, assume that a perpetual bond has an $80 per-year interest payment and that the discount rate is 10%. The present value of this perpetuity is $800 ($80/0.10).

Perquisite (Perk) various forms of executive compensation, such as corporate jets, fancy offices, company cars, entertainment expenses, company credit cards, support staff, club memberships, cellular phones, sport tickets, and the like. These are part of a firm's agency costs. *See also* Agency Costs; Agency Problem; Golden Parachute.

Personal Computer (PC) a computer built around a microprocessor for use by an individual, as in an office, or home, or school. *See also* Microcomputer.

Personal Consumption Expenditures the spending by households in goods (durable and nondurable) and services. This is a major component of gross domestic product (GDP).

Personal Consumption Expenditure Price Index (PCEPI) a measure of inflation preferred by the Federal Reserve. It is a measure of price changes in consumer goods and services. It consists of the actual and imputed expenditures of households, and includes data pertaining to durables, non-durables, and services. This measure (year 2000=100) excludes food and energy costs. *See also* Inflation.

Personal Digital Assistant (PDA) little portable device for electronic computing purposes. It has a variety of features including wireless communications to phones or computers.

Personal Disposable Income *see* Disposable Income.

Personal Financial Planning a field of financial planning for individuals. It involves (1) analyzing a client's personal finances and (2) recommending how to improve the client's financial condition. Personal financial planning covers the following specific areas:

Analysis of current financial position	Long-term accumulation plans
Investment strategies	Life insurance
Estate planning	Tax planning
Cash flow analysis	Disability insurance
Retirement income	

See also Financial Planner.

Personal Financial Statements financial statements prepared for a person or family to reflect their financial condition. They list assets, such as cash, securities, and real estate and liabilities, such as credit cards and mortgages payable. Some uses of the statements include computation of net worth, obtaining a mortgage, and investment planning.

Personal Identification Number (PIN) a personal password for identification.

Personal Income the before-tax income received by individuals and unincorporated businesses, such as wages and salaries, rents, and interest and dividends, and other payments such as unemployment and social security. Personal income represents consumers' spending power. When personal income rises, it usually means that consumers will increase their purchases, which will in turn affect favorably the investment climate. In government statistics, it is the national income less undivided profits, corporate taxes, and social security tax contributions, plus transfer payments from government or business including social security benefit payments and military pensions. Personal income data are released monthly by the Commerce Department.

Personal Property property, other than real estate, owned by an individual; also called *Chattel*.

Personal Spending spending by consumers accounts for about two-thirds of the U.S. economy.

Personnel the traditional function that oversees hiring, training, compensation, benefits, and other related activities. It is now more commonly referred to as Human Resources or HR.

Personnel File the file on the company personnel, such as their job application, resume, and performance reviews.

PERT/cost technique designed to assist in the planning, scheduling, and controlling of project costs; also known as the Critical Path Method (CPM).

Peter Principle a theory that employees within an organization will advance to their highest level of competence and then be promoted to and remain at a level at which they are incompetent.

Petro-Dollars dollar-denominated deposits generated by oil-producing countries.

Petty Cash a small amount of cash for incidental and miscellaneous expenses, as in an office.

Phillips Curve a graph showing a trade-off between inflation and unemployment. It is theorized that when unemployment is high, inflation is low, and when unemployment is low, inflation is high. Figure 1 illustrates a conventional Phillips Curve and indicates the nature of the trade-off between lower unemployment and high rates of inflation. Every point on a curve denotes a different combination of unemployment and inflation. A movement along the curve reflects the reduction in one at the expense of a gain in the other.

Figure 1

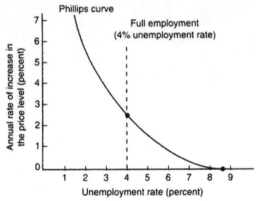

The Phillips Curve

PIN *see* Personal Identification Number (PIN).

Pink Sheets publication put out for each trading day published by the national quotation bureau listing bid and asked prices of over-the-counter stocks not shown in the financial newspapers for the NASDAQ Stock Market including the national NASDAQ and small capitalization NASDAQ listings. The pink sheets present the current prices of NASDAQ stocks not listed along with their market makers. Generally, the companies listed are very small and extremely risky. Note: yellow sheets are used to list debt securities.

Pink Slip notices of termination of employees written on pink slips of paper.

Pixel the smallest element addressable on a computer monitor.

PkZip/UnZip shareware software that compresses and uncompresses files.

Place one element in the "four Ps" in the marketing mix. Place is the means of physically distributing the product to the customer. It includes production, transportation, storage, and distribution on both the wholesale and retail levels. Where to deliver the product to the customer, and how to get the product to this location, are the principal concerns of place analysis subsystems. Typically, a distribution chain starts at the manufacturing plant and ends at the final consumer. In the middle is a network of wholesale and retail outlets employed to efficiently and effectively bring goods and services to the final consumer. But where are the best places to locate manufacturing facilities, wholesale outlets, and retail distribution points? Factors such as manufacturing costs, transportation costs, labor costs, and localized demand levels become factors that are critical to answering this issue.

Plan A, Plan B the primary plan of action and the fall-back plan if plan A doesn't work.

Plan-Do-Check Act Cycle (PDCA) "management by fact" or scientific method approach to continuous improvement (the Deming Wheel). PDCA creates a process-centered environment because it involves studying the current process, collecting and analyzing data to identify causes of problems, planning for improvement, and deciding how to measure improvement (Plan). The plan is then implemented on a small scale if possible (Do). The next step is to determine what happened (Check). If the experiment was successful, the plan is fully implemented (Act). The cycle is then repeated using what was learned from the preceding cycle.

Planned Economy an economy that is planned and controlled mostly by the government; also called *command economy*, as opposed to market economy in which individuals and businesses make most of the economic decisions.

Planned Giving gifts to be made to nonprofit organizations in the form of wills, bequests, and as a beneficiary of the donor's life insurance policy.

Planning the selection of short- and long-term objectives and the drawing up of tactical and strategic plans to achieve those objectives. In planning, managers outline the steps to be taken in moving the organization toward its objectives. After deciding on a set of strategies to be followed, the organization needs more specific plans, such as locations, methods of financing, hours of operations, etc. As these plans are made, they will be communicated throughout the organization. When implemented, the plans will serve to coordinate, or meld together, the efforts of all parts of the organization toward the company's objectives.

Platform either the standard hardware or the standard operating system that the organization uses.

PMI U.S. Market Risk Index a quarterly report that measures the probability that home prices will decline in the nation's top 51 metro areas. The index is based on statistics from a variety of sources: home-price appreciation, employment figures, median household income, and local mortgage costs.

Point
1. in the case of shares of stock, a point means $1. For example, if Xerox shares rise 2 points, each share has risen $2.
2. in the case of bonds, a point means $10, since a bond is quoted as a percentage of $1,000. A bond that rises 2 points gains 2 percent of $1,000 or $20 in value.
3. in the case of market averages, the word *point* means merely that and no more. It is not equivalent to any fixed sum of *money*. In banking, a loan service fee; each point equals 1% of the amount of the total Mortgage Loan, which must be paid in full when a home is bought. It is a one-time, immediate charge that increases the effective cost of borrowing. Example: $50,000 X .01 = $500. Costs can be added to the mortgage and paid over the lifetime of the contract.

Point Estimation an estimate that specifies a single value for a population parameter, as contrasted with internal estimation, involving the establishment of confidence intervals for the true parameter value.

Point of Purchase Display (POP); Point of Purchase; Point-of-Sale (POS)

1. a system that uses a computer terminal located at the point of sales transaction so that the data can be captured immediately by the computer system.
2. the general point for revenue recognition. Generally accepted accounting principles (GAAP) require the recognition of revenue in the accounting period in which the sale is deemed to have occurred. For services, the sale is deemed to occur when the service is performed. In the case of merchandise, the sale takes place when the title to the goods transfers from seller to buyer. In many cases, this coincides with the delivery of the merchandise. As a result, accountants usually record revenue when goods are delivered.

Point-to-Point Protocol (PPP)

1. a protocol for communication between two computers, as opposed to a network.
2. a protocol that allows a computer to be its own Internet host.

Poison Pill a company about to be bought by another company seeks to block the acquisition by taking some step, such as issuing excessive preferred stock or borrowing heavily, to be less attractive financially. An objective is to make the cost of the acquisition prohibitive to deter the takeover bid. A threat sometimes used to block the acquisition is that the whole management team says they will resign immediately if the acquisition becomes effective.

Policy

Procedures: a specific course of predetermined procedures. Policies are rules and regulations to be followed in certain specific events. For example, a parent may develop a policy that a child can watch television only after all homework is finished.

Insurance: a written agreement that defines coverage against specified perils and the limits of that coverage.

Policy Loan in insurance, the amount a policyholder of a life insurance policy can borrow at interest against the cash surrender value. If the interest is not paid, it is deducted from the cash surrender value of the policy. If the policy owner dies the death benefit is adjusted by any outstanding loans or unpaid interest payments. If the cash value of the policy is exhausted through loans, the policy ceases.

Policyholder/Policyowner an individual who owns an insurance policy.

Political Risk risk associated with political or sovereign uncertainty; also called *sovereign risk*. Political factors are a major determinant of the attractiveness for investment in any country. Countries viewed as likely candidates for internal political upheaval or with a pronounced trend toward elimination of the private sector will be unattractive to all investors, foreign and domestic alike. There is no reason to believe that local investors will be systematically optimistic regarding their country's future. When political risks increase significantly, such investors will attempt to diversify from the home market as rapidly as will foreigners. As a result, prices will fall until someone will be satisfied to hold the securities of a risky country. Political instability, limited track records, poor statistics–they all make gauging risk a risky business. Several companies try to evaluate the risk in some of the countries that are receiving the most attention from foreign investors. An example is Euromoney magazine's annual *Country Risk Rating*, which is based on a measure of different countries' access to international credit, trade finance, political risk, and a country's payment record. The rankings are generally confirmed by political risk insurers and top syndicate managers in the Euromarkets.

Polycentric Staffing a staffing policy in a multinational company in which host-country nationals are recruited to manage subsidiaries in their own country, while parent-country nationals occupy key positions at corporate headquarters.

Ponzi Scheme a dishonest and bogus investment scam where money from new investors is used to pay off earlier investors.

Population in statistics, the whole range of whatever is being studied, as opposed to sample, which is only a part of the population.

Pop-Up Ad an ad that displays in a new browser window.

Port a socket on the outside of the system unit that is connected to an expansion board on the inside of the system unit. A port allows you to plug in a cable to connect other devices such as a monitor, a keyboard, or a printer. In general, they are categorized into two types:
- **Parallel ports**: a parallel port allows a line to be connected that allows many bits to be transmitted at one time. Since many bits can be transmitted, the transmission speed is higher. Printers, monitors and keyboards use parallel ports.
- **Serial ports**: a serial (or RS-232) port, enables a line to be connected that will send one bit at a time. The serial port is usually used for data communication purposes.

Porter's Five-Forces Model the most widely used techniques of competition analysis. It states that the state of competition in an industry is a composite of five competitive forces:
- rivalry among competing sellers in the industry
- threats from potential entrants
- suppliers' bargaining power
- buyers' bargaining power
- threats from potential substitute products

Portfolio combining assets to reduce risk by diversification. An example of a portfolio is a mutual fund, which is a popular investment vehicle that consists of a variety of securities or assets that are professionally managed. A major advantage of investing in mutual funds is diversification. Investors can own a variety of securities with a minimal capital investment. Since mutual funds are professionally managed, they tend to involve less risk. To reduce risk, securities in a portfolio should have negative or no correlations to each other.

Portfolio Diversification the process of selecting alternative investment instruments that have dissimilar risk-return characteristics. The rationale behind portfolio diversification is the reduction of risk. The main method of reducing the risk of a portfolio is the combining of assets that are not perfectly positively correlated in their returns. *See also* Asset Allocation; Portfolio.

Portfolio Theory theory advanced by H. Markowitz in attempting a well-diversified portfolio. The central theme of the theory is that rational investors behave in a way that reflects their aversion to taking increased risk without being compensated by an adequate increase in expected return. Also, for any given expected return, most investors will prefer a lower risk, and for any given level of risk, they will prefer a higher return to a lower return. Markowitz showed how quadratic programming could be used to calculate a set of "efficient" portfolios. An investor then will choose among a set of efficient portfolios the best that is consistent with the risk profile of the investor. *See also* Beta Coefficient; Capital Asset Pricing Model (CAPM); Diversification.

POS *see* Point-of-Purchase Display (POP); Point-of-Purchase; Point-of-Sale (POS).

Positioning a market strategy of presenting and packaging products in a certain way in order to influence customers.

Positive Leverage when borrowed funds cost less than the return earned on those funds. It is using other people's money to make money.

Positive Yield Curve a condition in which the interest rates on long-term debt securities are higher than the interest rates on short-term debt securities of similar quality. This is typical, as an investor usually receives a higher interest rate when investing in long-term debt securities because of the longer time period involved, which results in greater uncertainty and risk. For example, the yield curve is positive when the interest rate on 30-year Treasury bonds is higher than the interest rate on 6-month Treasury bills.

Post Date placing on a document or check a date that follows the date of initiation or execution. An example is buying something on January 10th and dating the check January 25th, so the check cannot be cashed until later.

Power Function any functional form where the independent variable is raised to a power greater than one.

Power Marketing a tool that helps a business exploit gaps (market segments) in the marketplace.

Power of Attorney a legally executed and witnessed document giving another the power to act as one's attorney or agent in handling all personal affairs. The power may be general or specific. The power of attorney is revoked upon the death of the principal.

PPGC see Pension Benefit Guaranty Corporation (PPGC).

PPO *see* Health Insurance; Preferred Provider Organization (PPO).

PPP *see* Point-to-Point Protocol (PPP).

Pre Authorized Check (PAC) a check written by the payee on the payor's account and deposited on the agreed date.

Pre Authorized Debit (PAD) authorization given by the customer to the seller to routinely and automatically charge his or her account.

Preemptive Right right of a current stockholder to maintain the percentage ownership interest in the company by buying new shares on a pro rata basis before they are issued to the public. It prevents existing stockholders from dilution in value or control. The typical procedure is that each existing stockholder receives a subscription warrant indicating how many shares can be bought. Usually, the new shares are issued to the current stockholder at a lower price than the going market price so they are attractive to exercise. In addition, brokerage commissions do not have to be paid. For example, if an individual owns 2% of the shares of a company that is coming out with a new issue of 100,000 shares, the individual is entitled to buy 2000 shares at a favorable price to maintain the proportionate interest. Many states allow companies to payoff stockholders to waive their preemptive rights.

Pre-Existing Condition in insurance, a condition already in existence at the date an insurance policy is issued and that is typically excluded from coverage under that policy. However, some policies may waive exclusion from coverage of that item after a period of time has elapsed. For example, a medical insurance policy may exclude coverage for a preexisting thyroid problem.

Predatory Dumping dumping that is practiced to force domestic manufacturers out of business so that the foreign competitor is the primary source of supply and can raise prices.

Predatory Pricing the practice of setting prices below cost for the purpose of injuring competitors and eliminating competition. A large grocery chain could enter a small market, price small competitors out of business, and then raise prices to regain losses. Predatory pricing on the international market is called *dumping*.

Preferred Provider Organization (PPO) a group of medical providers (doctors, hospitals, etc.) who contract with a health insurance company to provide services at a discount to policyholders if the policyholders choose to be served by PPO members.

Preferred Stock a class of capital stock generally issued at its par value that has preference over common stock in the event of corporate liquidation and in the distribution of earnings. However, in liquidation, corporate bondholders come before preferred stockholders. Preferred stockholders represent a pseudo-equity interest in the corporation, but their risk of loss is limited to the liquidation value of the preferred stock in the event the company declares bankruptcy and makes a distribution of the corporate assets. Preferred stock is considered a hybrid security because it has features of both common stock and corporate bonds. It is like common stock because it represents equity ownership, is issued without stated maturity dates, and pays dividends. Preferred stock does have certain risks, preferences, or restrictions not existent with common stock. Preferred stock is also like a corporate bond in that it provides for previous claims on profit and assets, its dividend is fixed for the life of the issue, and it can carry call and convertible features and sinking fund provisions. The preferred dividend is stated in dollars per share or as a percentage of par (stated) value of the stock. For example, 6% preferred stock means that the dividend equals 6% of the total par value of the outstanding shares.

Premium
1. the purchase price of a bond or preferred issue higher than the par or face value.
2. purchasing or selling price of an option contract.
3. amount in excess of market value of an entity in a tender offer.
4. fee paid by a short seller to the lender of a security that is sold short.
5. the amount at which a closed-end fund trades above its net asset value.

Prepaid Expenses an expense paid in advance, such as rent or insurance.

Prepayment Clause a clause in a loan that allows the borrower to pay more than the monthly amount and to retire the loan early without a penalty.

Prepayment of Principal payment of a debt before its due such as a mortgage payment or insurance premiums.

Prepayment Penalty a penalty charge levied by a lender when a borrower repays a loan before a specified time.

Prerequisite an event or action that has to be satisfied before the next event or action can occur. For example, an accounting student must take intermediate accounting before advanced accounting can be taken.

Present Value (PV) the present worth of future sums of money. The process of calculating present value, or discounting, is actually the opposite of finding the compounded future value. *See also* Discounting.

Press Release a short article that can get an organization's name mentioned, and even featured, in a newspaper or magazine.

Prestige Pricing a method of pricing pursued by a firm with the intention of exploiting the consumer that enjoys social status and a high level of taste and judges the quality of a product by its price; also called *Status Pricing*.

Preventive Costs a category of quality costs incurred to prevent defects of products and services. Examples are the costs of new product review, quality planning, supplier capability surveys, process capability evaluations, quality improvement team meetings, quality improvement projects, and quality education and training.

Price Discrimination the charging of different prices to different customers for essentially the same product.

Price Elasticity the ratio of a percentage change in quantity demanded to a percentage change in price. We classify the price elasticity of demand (e_p) into three categories:

Price elasticity of demand	Degree of elasticity
$e_p > 1$	Elastic
$e_p = 1$	Unitary
$e_p < 1$	Inelastic

Whether price cutting is desirable or not depends largely on the price elasticity of demand for the product. Economists have established the following relationships between price elasticity (e_p) and total revenue (TR), which can aid a firm in setting its price.

Price	$e_p > 1$	$e_p = 1$	$e_p < 1$
Price rises	TR falls	No change	TR rises
Price falls	TR rises	No change	TR falls

See also Elasticity of Demand.

Price Fixing a practice in which firms conspire to set the price of a good or service at a specified level.

Price Indexes various price indexes that are used to measure living costs, price-level changes, and inflation. They include Consumer Price Index (CPI), Producer Price Index (PPI), GDP Deflator (Implicit Price Index), personal consumption expenditure price index, and Employment Cost Index. *See also* Inflation.

Price To Sales Ratio the current price divided by the sales per share for the trailing twelve months. If there is a preliminary earnings announcement for a quarter that has recently ended, the revenue (sales) values from this announcement will be used in calculating the trailing twelve month revenue per share.

Price-Earnings (P/E) Ratio statistic that equals market price per share divided by current year earnings per share. It is a tool for investors to see if a stock has been evaluated by the market at higher or lower than other stocks in the same industry. Example: If market price per share is $50 and earnings per share is $10, the price-earnings ratio equals 5. The P/E ratio may also be computed using an analysts' expected earnings per share for next year (referred to as forward P/E). The higher the P/E ratio, the better because more earnings growth is expected. The price-earnings ratios of certain companies are given below:

P/E ratios

Company	Industry	2006
Boeing	Aerospace	23.40
Ford	Cars & Trucks	7.00
Reynolds	Cigarettes	19.80
Nordstrom	Retailing	21.30
Intel	Semiconductor	14.50
Safeway	Food	19.20

Pricing Decisions decisions faced by top management and marketing managers. How much to charge for a product or service depends on a multitude of factors such as competition, cost, advertising, and sales promotion. Economic theory suggests that the best price for a product or service is the one that maximizes the difference between total revenue and total costs. However, in reality, the price charged is usually some form of cost-plus, which is later adjusted for market conditions and competition.

Primary Beneficiary
1. the person identified as the major beneficiary(ies) of an insurance policy. Secondary beneficiaries may also be nominated if the primary beneficiary dies before the policyholder.
2. the person(s) to receive the benefits of a trust when distribution occurs. Secondary beneficiaries may be nominated if the primary beneficiary(ies) predecease the trust distribution.

Primary Market a market that trades new issues of securities, as distinguished from the secondary market, where securities of old issues are traded. The term also applies to auctions of government securities such as treasury bills.

Prime Cost the sum of direct materials costs and direct labor costs of a product. Prime costs tend to vary with the level of output.

Prime Rate the loan rate charged by commercial banks to their best customers. The borrowers are large, well-known firms with high credit ratings. These companies often have access to the commercial paper market and often can borrow below the prime interest rate. *See also* Interest Rate.

Principal
1. the person for whom a broker executes an order, or a dealer buying or selling for his own account
2. face amount of a bond
3. basic amount invested
4. owner of a privately held business

Principal, Interest, Taxes and Interest Payment (PITI) used to indicate what is included in a monthly payment on rental property. Principal, interest, taxes, and interest payment (PITI) are the four major portions of a usual monthly payment.

Prisoner's Dilemma a fundamental concept in game theory suggesting the impact of non-cooperation. The concept illustrates that behaviors differ when decisions are made individually as opposed to collectively. For example, it shows how rational behavior at the micro level leads to an obviously irrational macro outcome.

Private Offering *see* Private Placement.

Private Placement the sale of securities by the issuing company directly to an investor (generally a large institutional investor), also called a private offering or direct placement, rather than an offering through the public exchange markets. A private placement does not have to be registered with the SEC, as a public offering does, if the securities are not purchased for resale.

Private Sector the part of all economic activities that are independent of government control (or outside the so-called public sector), carried on principally for profit but also including nonprofit organizations directed at satisfying private needs, such as private hospitals and private schools. Included are enterprises owned individually or by groups (such as corporations with numerous stockholders) as well as the self-employed.

Private Trading Networks (PTNs) B2B trading networks that link a particular seller with its own trading partners.

Privately-Held Company a company owned by a few people and is distinguished from a publicly-held corporation, which is also a private company, but whose shares are traded in the public market; also called a *closed corporation* or *private corporation*. A publicly-held company can either be closely held (meaning most of the public shares are owned or controlled by a few people) or widely held, as with a company whose shares are listed on a national stock exchange.

Privatization the process of shifting government responsibilities into the private sector. Many municipalities privatized the removal of garbage, among other services.

Pro Forma Statement a summary of various component projections of revenues and expenses and a schedule for expected assets, liabilities, and stockholders' equity under a hypothetical situation.

Probabilty the degree of likelihood that something will happen. Probabilities are expressed as fractions (1/2, 1/4, 3/4), as decimals (.5, .25, .75) or as percentages (50%, 25%, 75%) between 0 and 1. For example, when you assign a probability of 0, it means that something can never happen; when you assign a probability of 1, it means that something will always happen.

Probability Distribution a table or graph showing the relative frequency of each of various outcomes. Widely known probability distributions include the Binomial distribution and the normal distribution. A probability distribution of a possible number of tails from two tosses of a fair coin may look like this:

Number of tails	Probability of this outcome
0	.25
1	.50
2	.25

Probate a judicial procedure to test the authority and validity of an estate, will guardianship, or trust agreement.

Probate Court the court that resolves wills, estates, and trusts.

Proceeds the funds received from the sale of assets or issuance of securities, such as capital stock or bonds.

Process sequence or arterial network of logically related and time-based work activities to provide a specific output for an internal or external customer. For example, the assembly of a television set or the paying of a bill or claim entails several linked activities.

Process Planning planning involving a total analysis of the product and its processing requirements, decisions concerning the purchase of items outside versus their internal manufacture, and techniques for selecting among competing processes.

Producer Price Index (PPI) a measure of the cost of a given basket of goods priced in wholesale markets, including raw materials, semifinished goods, and finished goods. The PPI is published monthly by the Bureau of Labor Statistics of the Department of Commerce.

Product Bundling Pricing combining several products and offering the bundle at a reduced price.

Product Costs inventoriable costs, identified as part of inventory on hand. They are therefore assets until the products are sold. Once they are sold, they become expenses, i.e., cost of goods sold. All manufacturing costs are product costs. Examples are direct material, direct labor, and factory overhead.

Product Financing Arrangement an agreement to finance the acquisition of a product through debt. Another entity may buy a product on behalf of the purchaser. At the time of acquisition, the purchaser debits inventory and credits a liability for the amount owed to the other entity. When payment of the obligation is made the liability is debited for the principal, interest expense is debited for the interest, and cash is paid for the total amount.

Product Life Cycle stages in the life cycle of a good. The product life cycle charts the development of the product from introduction, or birth, through various growth and development stages, to deletion or death. Names have been given to four stages in the life cycle: introduction, growth, maturity, and decline. It guides marketing managers in developing marketing strategy and decisions.

Product Life Cycle

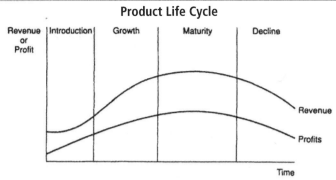

Product Mix the relative proportions of different products or services offered by a firm. Improving the product mix is a key to profit making. Generally, shifting the emphasis from low margin products to high margin products will magnify total profits of the firm. Contribution margin analysis can be applied for this purpose.

Product Mix Decisions decisions that concern the relative amounts of each type of product or service that, given demand and resource constraints, will maximize total profits. For example, if the firm can sell as much as it can produce and has a single resource constraint, the decision rule is to maximize the contribution margin per unit of the constrained resource. However, given multiple constraints, the decision is more difficult and more sophisticated techniques must be used, such as linear programming.

Product Planning the activities of manufacturers and intermediaries that are designed to adjust the merchandise produced, or offered for sale, to consumer demand.

Product Positioning the perception consumers have regarding a market offering(s) relative to its competitors. Product positioning is the act of analyzing and managing consumer product position perceptions.

Product Stewardship the practice of designing, manufacturing, maintaining, and recycling products to minimize adverse environmental impacts. Life-cycle assessment is the means for improving product stewardship.

Production Function a schedule, table, or mathematical relationship showing the maximum amount of output that can be produced from any specified set of inputs, given the existing technology or state of the art. It is a catalogue of output possibilities.

Production Possibilities Curve a curve illustrating the various combinations of goods that a society is capable of producing at any given time if its technology and resources are fixed and all its resources are fully and efficiently employed.

Productivity the measured relationship between the quantity of output and the input. For example, labor productivity is the output of employees expressed in terms of the quantity produced per labor hour—in other words, the average output per hour of work. Getting more worker output is vital to increasing the standard of living without inflation. Productivity measures reflect the joint effects of many influences, including changes in technology; capital investment; level of output; utilization of capacity, energy, and materials: the organization of production: managerial skill; and the characteristics and effort of the work force. The data are published in a press release and in Bureau of Labor Statistics journals. Computer users can visit *www.stats.bls.gov* on the Internet for this data. Productivity statistics mainly cover manufacturing, not the large service sector.

Professional Corporation a company established by professionals, including medical doctors, accountants, attorneys, and architects. Although a professional corporation still has unlimited liability for malpractice, there are certain tax advantages to being treated as an S Corporation. A key tax benefit is the avoidance of double taxation since only personal tax is paid, (not corporate tax), on the income. The professional corporation files Form 1120-S, which passes the income and the resulting tax onto the individual's Form 1040. Another important benefit is that greater contributions can be made to a pension plan.

Professional Liability Insurance an insurance policy taken out by a professional for malpractice coverage. The policy covers legal fees and possible damages. Medical doctors, accountants, and attorneys typically take out such policies.

Profit and Loss Statement *see* Income Statement.

Profit Center a responsibility center of an organization. It is the unit in an organization that is responsible for revenues earned and costs incurred. A manager of a profit center has control over both revenues and costs and attempts to maximize profit. Examples include a college book division of a publishing company, a housewares department in a retail store, and a product division. A profit center has the following characteristics: (1) its goal is to earn a profit; (2) its management is evaluated by means of contribution income statements, in terms of meeting sales and cost objectives; and (3) its management has the authority to make decisions regarding factors that determine the amount of profit (may include selection of sales outlets, advertising policy, and selection of sources of supply). *See also* Cost Center; Investment Center.

Profit Impact Marketing Strategies (PIMS) a model for estimating the impact on profit from a change in the marketing mix.

Profit Margin ratio of income to sales. (1) Net profit margin equals net income divided by net sales. If a company's net income was $800,000 and its sales were $8,000,000, the profit margin would be 10%. It indicates the entity's ability to generate earnings at a particular sales level. By examining a company's profit margin relative to previous years and to industry norms, one can evaluate the company's operating efficiency and pricing strategy as well as its competitive status with other companies in the industry. (2) Gross profit margin equals gross profit divided by net sales. Net sales equals gross sales less sales returns and allowances. Gross profit equals net sales less cost of goods sold. A high gross profit margin is desirable since it indicates the company is earning a good return over the cost of its merchandise sold.

Profit Maximization the hypothesis that the goal of a firm is to maximize its profit. This is the traditional theory of the firm, which is distinguished from the behavioral theory of the firm.

Profit Planning a process of developing a profit plan that outlines the planned sales revenues and expenses and the net income or loss for a time period. Profit planning requires preparation of a master budget and various analyses for risk and "what-if" scenarios. Tools for profit planning include the cost-volume-profit (CVP) analysis and budgeting.

Profit-Sharing Plan a plan instituted by a company in which employees receive a stipulated percentage of the profits of the firm. The terms of profit-sharing plans differ widely, however, there is usually a stated amount above which profit-sharing proceeds will be distributed, based on a predetermined formula. In those periods when the company does not produce a qualified profit for the profit-sharing plan, there are no distributions to employees. The basic intent is to provide an incentive to improve productivity, as well as loyalty to the firm.

Program
1. an organized system for completing objectives. For example, a company may develop and use a management development program for developing and improving its managerial staff.
2. to arrange, classify, categorize, or systematize any area of concern, such as entertainment, music, management strategy, and governmental actions.
3. in computers, to produce a sequence of software instructions to be executed by the central processing unit of a computer to accomplish a particular objective action. A set of instructions that tells a company how to process the information it gets. A programmer is the person who designs the program.

Program Evaluation And Review Technique (PERT) a useful management tool for planning, coordinating, and controlling large complex projects such as formulation of a master budget, construction of buildings, installation of computers, and scheduling the closing of books. The development and initial application of PERT was done in connection with the development of the Polaris submarine by the U.S. Navy in the late 1950s. The PERT technique involves the diagrammatical representation of the sequence of activities comprising a project by means of a network consisting of arrows and circles (nodes). Questions to be answered by PERT include:
• When will the project be finished?
• What is the probability that the project will be completed by any given time?

Program Trading the term used to describe the use of computer-based buying or selling programs. The software has built-in guidelines that instantaneously trigger buy and sell orders when differences in the prices of the securities are great enough to produce profit. Program trading is used by institutional investors, who place buy and sell orders in large blocks of ten thousand or more units. This type of large trade tends to significantly impact the prices of securities in the market.

Programmed (Fixed) Costs *see* Discretionary (Fixed) Costs.

Programming the process of writing instructions for a computer to carry out. The program has to be turned into machine-readable form and inputted into the computer. The program must be tested to assure accuracy, and supporting documentation must be prepared.

Program-Planning-Budgeting System (PPBS) a planning-oriented approach to developing a program budget. A program budget is a budget wherein expenditures are based primarily on programs of work and secondarily on character and object. It is a transitional type of budget between the traditional character and object budget on the one hand and the performance budget on the other. The major contribution of PPBS lies in the planning process, i.e., the process of making program policy decisions that lead to a specific budget and specific multi-year plans.

Progressive Tax a tax that requires a higher percentage payment on higher income. The personal income tax structure in the United States with its multiple brackets has traditionally been an example of a progressive tax although the Tax Reform Act of 1986 introduced two broad brackets and is generally considered a modified flat tax system.

Project broad, complex, multidisciplinary approach to the production of a good or service.

Project Management the set of activities that is performed to ensure the timely and successful completion of a project within the budget. Project management includes planning activities, hiring and managing personnel, budgeting, conducting meetings, and tracking technical and financial performance. Project management software can help to facilitate these activities.

Project Planning making planning decisions for capital investments, many of which may extend over long periods. For example, the decision to buy a particular piece of machinery and equipment is the result of project planning. Project planning has long-term effects on the company's future profitability. Capital expenditure analysis or cost-benefit analysis is a technique needed for project planning. *See also* Capital Budgeting.

Promissory Note a formal, written, unconditional promise in writing to pay on demand or at a future date a definite sum of money. The person who signs the note and thereby promises to pay is called the maker of the note. The person to whom payment is to be made is called the payee of the note; also called *note*.

Promotion all the means of marketing the sale of the product, including advertising and personal selling. Product success is a direct function of the types of advertising and sales promotion done. The size of the promotions budget and the allocation of this budget to various promotional mixes are important factors in deciding the type of campaigns that will be launched. Television coverage, newspaper ads and coverage, promotional brochures and literature, samples, public appearances, and training programs for salespeople are all components of these promotional and advertising mixes.

Promotional Mix a strategic combination of advertising, personal selling, sales promotion, publicity, and other promotional tools employed to achieve sales objectives.

Property Tax a tax assessed on real property. A property tax is determined by its land use classification (ranging from rural farmland to heavy industry), improvements made on the property, its assessed valuation, and the mileage rate.

Proprietary Technology technology that is unique and owned or controlled by particular individuals or organizations. It may be held as a trade secret, or it may be published as a patent.

Proprietorship
1. assets minus liabilities of an organization. It equals contributed capital plus accumulated earnings.
2. a form of business organization. *See also* Sole Proprietorship.

Proration to allocate or assign an amount in proportion to some base to an activity, department, or product. Service costs are frequently allocated to user departments based on the base allocation formula/procedure (e.g., number of employees, machine hours spent). *See also* Allocation.

Prospectus a document that must accompany a new issue of securities and that contains the same information appearing in the registration statement, such as a list of directors and officers, financial reports certified by a CPA, underwriters, the purpose and use for the funds, and other reasonable information that prospective buyers of a security need to know. A preliminary prospectus, red-herring, (so named because of a red stamp indicating the tentative nature of the document during the period in which it is being reviewed for fraudulent or misleading statements by the Securities and Exchange Commission [SEC]) is issued prior to the final, statutory prospectus, which also contains offering instructions.

Protectionism the government's placing of duties or quotas on imports to protect domestic industries from global competition.

Protective Covenants
1. an agreement restricting specified financial transactions. For example, a covenant may be agreed to in a loan agreement that a person may not borrow additional monies from another lending institution against a certain collateralized property.
2. statement in a deed that specified actions, or improvements, can or cannot take place on a given property. The covenants may stipulate the use of the property, (e.g., residential, business), restrict the number of occupants, and prohibit certain actions (e.g., early morning parties, animals).

Protocol guidelines and principles associated with the workings of a network. Rules surround data and electrical signals on the network, manner of information transmissions, accessing the network, and processing applications on the network.

Provision

1. the amount of an expense that must be recognized currently when the exact amount of the expense is uncertain. An example is an expense, such as a provision for income taxes.

2. a contra asset account, such as allowance for bad debts and allowance to reduce securities from cost to market value.

3. making an appropriation of retained earnings for a specified purpose.

Proxy

1. power of attorney by which the holder of stock transfers the voting rights to another party. Sometimes proxy fights erupt wherein outside groups compete in the solicitation of proxies that would give them voting control.

2. short for proxy statement, a written document that the SEC requires be provided to shareholders before they vote by proxy on corporate matters. It typically contains proposed members of the board of directors, inside directors' salaries, and any resolutions of minority stockholders and of management.

Proxy Fights (Battles) fights that erupt when outsiders attempt to gain control of a company's management. This requires soliciting a sufficient number of votes by proxy to unseat the existing management. The fights (battles) generally occur when the present management is performing poorly. However, the odds of outsiders winning a proxy fight are generally slim.

Proxy Statement *see* Proxy.

Prudent Investment

1. investment made prudently and intelligently as would be expected by a professional person. A reasonable degree of safety and return are expected. *See also* Fiduciary; Prudent Man Rule.

2. a rule that allows an uninstructed trustee considerable discretionary authority to purchase investments of any type that an ordinarily prudent person would find suitable in the case at hand.

Prudent Man Rule an investment standard. In some states, the law requires that a fiduciary, such as a trustee, may invest the fund's money only in a list of securities, called the *legal list*, designated by the state. A reasonable degree of safety and return are expected. In other states, the trustee may invest in a security if a prudent man of discretion and intelligence, who is seeking a reasonable income and preservation of capital, would buy it.

Public Assistance Programs government programs aimed at providing assistance to people, such as the aged, the handicapped, and the sick who for reasons beyond their control are unable to find employment.

Public Company Accounting Oversight Board (PCAOB) established in 2002 as a result of the Sarbanes-Oxley Act, a private sector, non-profit corporation set up to oversee the audits of public companies and ensure that accountancy firms should no longer derive non-audit revenue streams, such as consultancy, from their audit clients.

Public Expenditure spending by local and federal governments. *See also* Government Expenditure.

Public Offerings offering of new securities to the investing public, after registration requirements have been filed with the SEC. The securities are usually made available to the public at large by a managing investment banker and its underwriting syndicate. In the public offering, unlike private placement, the corporation does not deal directly with the ultimate buyers of the securities. The public market is an impersonal one. *See also* Private Placement.

Public Sector all economic activities–mostly services–that are carried out directly by government agencies (or outside the private sector), largely for the public benefit rather than for profit. Included are the entire machinery of government offices and agencies (on the local, state, and national levels) and all the various enterprises they support (police and fire protection, military payrolls, highway maintenance, public education, and so on).

Public Spending spending at the federal, state, and local levels.

Publicly-Held Company an enterprise whose ownership is held by the general public, including individuals, officers, employees, and institutional investors. A publicly held company has stock listed on the exchange and must file financial statements and reports with the SEC. *See also* Privately-Held Company.

Pull Strategy a marketing strategy emphasizing mass media advertising as opposed to personal selling.

Punitive Award; Punitive Damages or exemplary damages. Damages, awarded by a court of law to a plaintiff in an action, over and above the actual financial loss incurred by the plaintiff. Such damages are awarded by the court when a wrong doing by the defendant in the action was judged to be the result of malice, fraud, violence, or evil intent. The concept of punitive damages is to set an example by punishing the defendant.

Purchase Discounts cash discounts or trade discounts. A cash discount is intended for prompt payments by the purchaser, whereas a trade discount represents a reduction in list price in return for quantity purchases. *See also* Trade Discount.

Purchase Order a form or document used by the purchasing department to order goods or merchandise. Several copies are usually prepared, each on a different color paper. The original is sent to the supplier. The purchase order is an authorization to deliver the merchandise and to submit a bill based on the prices listed. Carbon copies of the purchase order are usually routed to the purchasing, accounting, receiving, and finance departments.

Purchasing Manager's Index the monthly index released by the National Association of Purchasing Management that tells you about buying intentions of corporate purchasing agents. The Association conducts a survey that polls purchasing managers from 20 industries. Since the purchasing managers are responsible for buying the raw materials that feed the nation's factories, their buying patterns are considered a good indication of the direction of the economy. A reading of 50 or more percent indicates that the manufacturing economy is generally expanding. A reading above 44.5 percent over a period of time indicates that the overall economy is augmenting.

Purchasing Power Parity (PPP) thesis stating that exchange rates adjust to inflation differentials between two countries.

Purchasing System the procedures, manual or computerized, followed by an organization to achieve the following basic objectives: (1) to determine the quality and quantity needed and when an item is needed, (2) to obtain the best possible price, and (3) to maintain the information on sources of supply. The system should utilize such concepts as economic order quantity, optimal reorder point, quantity discounts, and material requirement planning (MRP).

Pure Competition *see* Perfect Competition.

Push Strategy a marketing strategy emphasizing personal selling rather than mass media advertising.

Put
1. an option to sell a specific security at a specified price within a designated period for which the option buyer pays the seller (writer) a premium or option price. Contracts on listed puts (and calls) have been standardized at date of issuance for periods of three, six, and nine months, although as these contracts approach expiration, they may be purchased with a much shorter life.
2. bondholder's right to redeem a bond prior to maturity.

Pyramiding
1. a classical illegal investment plot in which an operator promises hefty returns but only distributes money contributed from new investors, while the operator uses and spends most of the money.
2. adding further positions to stocks, bonds, or commodities as the market continues in the right direction.
3. a structure of low-, medium-, and high-risk investments. In a financial pyramid, money is invested from most to least, as follows: liquid and safe investments, income and long-term growth investments, and speculative and high risk investments.
4. holding gains from a securities or commodities position as collateral to buy additional positions with funds borrowed from a broker. The use of leverage results in higher profits in a bull market. But in a bear market, there is potential for larger losses arising from margin calls.

Qq

Q-Ratio the market value of all securities (not just equity) divided by the replacement cost (not book value) of all assets. The q-ratio reflects the market's valuation of new investment. A ratio greater than one means that a firm is earning returns greater than the amount invested. For this reason, a company with a ratio exceeding one should attract new resources and competition; also called *Tobin's Q*. The higher the Q-ratio, the greater the industry attractiveness and/or competitive advantage. The notion of this ratio holds that a firm's market value ultimately equals the replacement cost of its tangible assets. Some argue that calculating the replacement cost of assets is subject to enormous measurement errors and thus the Q-ratio is useless as a valuation tool.

Quadratic Equation an equation in which the highest power term is a squared term. It takes the form: $ax^2 + bx + c = 0$.

Qualified Opinion an auditor's opinion of a financial statement for which some limitations existed, such as an inability to gather certain information or a material upcoming event that may or may not occur. It is the opposite of unqualified opinion.

Quality Assurance all of the activities necessary to ensure that the customer receives satisfactory performance.

Quality at the Source responsibility of every employee, work group, department, or supplier to inspect the work.

Quality Benchmarking *see* Benchmarking (Best Practices). The measuring of your company's products and services against the best quality products or services in the field.

Quality Circle tapping employees for ideas concerning quality and productivity improvement. The circles are a voluntary group of workers who meet regularly to identify and solve problems of quality and productivity. It is usually a small group of 6 to 12 employees doing similar work.

Quality Control

1. to ensure that manufactured products and services conform to specifications of design. This includes the prevention of defects, detecting them when they occur, and applying corrective action. In this sense, quality control is an activity that must be carried out on a day-to-day basis. It covers the entire range of production, beginning with product or service design, continuing through the transformation process, and extending to service after delivery.

2. in computers, standards and other procedures that maintain program writing, systems development, and documentation standards at a higher level.

Quality Costs the sum of the appraisal costs, failure costs, and prevention costs. It represents the difference between the actual cost of a product or service and what the reduced cost would be if there was no possibility of substandard service, failure of products, or defects in their manufacture.

Quality Training familiarizing all employees with the means for preventing, detecting, and eliminating nonquality. The educational processes are tailored to the appropriate groups.

Quantity Discounts discounts realized when buying in bulk, or volume.

Quasi Contract a legal duty or obligation imposed by the law to pay for a benefit received as though a contract had actually been made. This will be done in a limited number of situations in order to attain an equitable or just result. For example, when a homeowner permits repairs to be made with the knowledge that they are being made by a stranger who would expect to be paid for such repairs, there is quasi-contractual duty to pay for the reasonable value of the improvement in order to avoid the homeowner's unjust enrichment at the expense of the person making the repair.

Query an instruction in a database management system to retrieve records that meet certain conditions or criteria.

Queue waiting line that forms wherever there is more than one user of a limited resource.

Queuing Theory the quantitative approach to determine the facilities to be provided when the need for them varies at random. It attempts to establish the best way of handling a sequence of events (grocery checkouts, gas pumps) to avoid bottlenecks and minimize costs. Other business applications are:

- How many shipping docks and receiving docks should be built for incoming and outgoing shipments?
- How many lift trucks should be provided to move products?
- How should machines be arranged to minimize waiting lines of products in process?
- How many teller windows should be open in a bank?
- How many checkout counters should be made available at retail or supermarket stores?

Quick Asset current asset that can be converted into cash in a short time. Examples are cash, marketable securities and accounts receivable. Certain current assets, such as inventory and prepaid expenses, are excluded.

Quick Ratio a stringent measure of a company's liquidity; also called *Acid-Test Ratio*. It equals quick assets divided by current liabilities.

Quickbooks Pro a leader in accounting software for small business, which brings complete financial management capabilities to small business owners who do not want to deal with the hassle of trying to understand accounting jargon or debit/credit accounting. QuickBooks users can easily set up their business with QuickBooks, making it easy to create custom invoices, enter sales, perform electronic banking and bill payment, track customer contracts, track time, perform job costing, manage inventory, handle payroll and even prepare for tax time.

Quitclaim Deed a deed that conveys whatever present right, title, or interest the grantor may have. It does not warrant that the grantor actually has any particular title or interest in the property. It is customarily used to clear some cloud on the title, such as deed restrictions that are no longer enforceable, or an unused easement. In addition, it frequently is used by a spouse to convey his or her half of community or joint tenancy property to the other spouse.

Quota

1. an allotment or limited amount. It is the amount of sales needed to reach a company's sales goal.

2. a proportional share assigned to a group or to each member of a group, such as import quota, minority hiring quota, or immigration quota.

Quotation the highest bid to buy and the lowest offer to sell a security in a given market at a given time; also called *quote*. For example, if you ask your broker for a quotation on a stock, he/she may say,"26.25 to 26.50." This means that $26.25 was the highest price any buyer wanted to pay (bid) at the time the quotation was given on the exchange and that $26.50 was the lowest price at which any holder of the stock offered to sell.

Quote an estimate of the cost of insurance based on information supplied to the agent, broker, or insurance company.

Qwerty a computer-nerd word for the standard American-English keyboard. The letter keys in the top row from left to right are "Q-W-E-R-T-Y," hence the name.

Rr

R *see* Correlation Coefficient.

Rack Jobber a wholesaler who sets up and maintains merchandise displays in retail outlets. In word processing, the common non-even right margins.

Raider an individual or a firm that takes over a publicly owned firm, or threatens to do so in an unfriendly manner; also called *corporate raider.*

Random Access File file constructed in a manner in which record may be placed in a random order; also called *direct access file.* Each record in a random access file has associated with it a relative index number. Whenever a record is read from a random access file, a computer program must produce a relative index number for this record in order to locate the record in the file. This type of file design offers the following advantages: (1) It provides rapid access to the desired information. In a decision making environment where information is needed quickly, random access is a requisite to rapid retrieval. (2) It is efficient for retrieving a relatively few records at a time. (3) It provides a method of keeping files up to date as transactions or events occur.

Random Access Memory (RAM) a computer's main memory where it can store data, so the size of the RAM (measured by kilobytes) is an important indicator of the capacity of the computer, also called read/write memory. RAM chips can be added to your computer to increase its memory. The characteristics of the RAM are:
1. Usable memory programmed into the computer by the user.
2. Where application software is being run.
3. Altered by user programs.
4. Easily accessed or altered.
5. Restricted capacity.
6. Complicated software programs can normally be run with a minimum of 64K of RAM.

Random Numbers a set of numbers that follow no systematic pattern or distribution. These numbers can be generated either by a computer programmed to scramble numbers or by a table of random numbers, called a table of *random digits*. They are widely used to select a random sample of observations from a population.

Random Sample a probability sample allowing for the equal probability that each item will be chosen. It is obtained by choosing items in such a way that each unit in the population has an equal chance of being selected. To assure this, a table of random numbers could be used. In other words, we assign the identification number of each item and use a table of random numbers for its selection.

Random Walk Theory a theory of stock market price movements suggesting that the prices of stocks are random and that it is futile to try to predict future prices based upon past price movements. Individual stock prices are affected by a whole range of random events including overall direction of the stock market, government rulings, changes in earnings, new product releases, competitive developments, interest rates, the money supply, and the rate of unemployment.

Range the difference between the highest and lowest observed values in the set. It is a measure of the degree of dispersion of a sample of observations or of a frequency distribution.

Rank Correlation a measure of the correlation that exists between the two sets of ranks, a measure of the degree of association between the variables that cannot be calculated otherwise. The measure begins with the assigning of a rank to each of the observations on each of the variables according to their descending value.

Rate of Exchange the rate at which one currency (or commodity) can be exchanged for another. For example, one British pound may be equivalent to a 1.50 in U.S. dollars. One Japanese Yen may equal $.0065 in American currency.

Rate of Return on Investment (ROI)
1. for the company as a whole, net income divided by invested capital. Invested capital may be total assets or stockholders' equity. Depending upon which is used as a measure of invested capital, there is the rate of return on total assets (ROA) and the rate of return on stockholder's equity (ROE). For example, assume that net income is $18,000 and total assets are $100,000. The ROA is then $18,000/$100,000=18%. If the stockholder's equity is $90,000, the ROE would be $18,000/$90,000=20%.
2. for the segment of an organization, net operating income divided by operating assets.
3. for capital budgeting purposes, also called *simple*, *accounting*, or *unadjusted rate of return*, expected future net income divided by initial (or average) investment.

Rate of Return Pricing method of pricing targeted for a certain percentage rate of return on capital. Regulatory agencies frequently impose this type of pricing method on utility firms. *See also* Target Return Pricing.

Rate Structure a set of prices that may be charged to various users of a regulated utility's services so as to produce the target revenue, assuming that users purchase estimated quantities of output.

Rating

Credit: a process used by the lender to decide on the soundness of making a loan. It systematically assigns ranks to individuals or businesses in terms of their financial soundness. The lower the rating, the higher the interest rate. *See also* Credit Rating; Credit Scoring.

Securities: evaluation of investment grade and credit risk of a security as derived by rating services, such as Moody's, Fitch Investors Service, and Standard & Poor's. *See also* Bond Ratings.

Insurance:

1. a valuation of insurance risks, using such methods as probability theory and mortality rates, so as to establish the premium rates for varying rating categories.

2. annual ratings of financial stability and claim service given to insurance companies by A. M. Best Company.

Rating Services an agency that publishes credit ratings for securities such as preferred stock and bonds. These rankings are arrived at by looking at a variety of balance sheet data. Three major rating services are S&P, Moody's and Fitch. They are very influential, and an upgrade or downgrade can affect their borrowing costs greatly.

Rational Behavior consistent behavior that maximize an individual's satisfaction. The individual is called an *economic man*.

Rational Expectations an approach to economics that claims that anticipations are based on both past experience and a reasoned analysis of available information. For example, if inflation starts to fall, consumers will not immediately adjust to it because they have come to expect higher inflation.

Read-Only Memory (ROM) the memory that contains instructions that do not need to be altered. The computer can read instructions out of ROM, but no data can be stored in ROM. It is the permanent memory of the computer put in by the manufacturers that cannot be altered.

Reaganomics the economic program, better known as the 1981 Economic Recovery Act (ERA), originally implemented by the Reagan administration in 1981. The main features of the program are (1) tax cuts to stimulate economic growth (*see also* Supply-Side Economics), (2) deregulation to reduce government interference in the economy, and (3) a tight money policy to control inflation.

Real Assets tangible assets having physical substance that one can touch (e.g., real estate, collectibles, and precious metals).

Real Estate something permanently affixed or attached to the land, such as buildings, walls, fences, and shrubs; also called *real property*. It is contrasted from personal property, which is movable.

Real Estate Investment Trust (REIT) a type of investment company that invests money (obtained through the sale of its shares to investors) in mortgages and various types of investments in real estate, in order to earn profits for shareholders. Shareholders receive income from the rents received from the properties and receive capital gains as properties are sold at a profit. REITs have been formed by a number of large financial institutions, such as banks and insurance companies. The stocks of many of them are traded on security exchanges, thereby providing investors with a marketable interest in a real estate investment portfolio. REITs that distribute all of their income generally pay no entity-level tax. However, in exchange for this special tax treatment, REITs are subject to numerous qualifications and limitations including: (1) Shareholder qualifications. Generally, REITs are not permitted to be closely held and must have a minimum of 100 shareholders. (2) Qualified asset and income tests. REITs are required to have at least 75% of their value represented by qualified real estate assets and to earn at least 75% of their income from real estate investments.

Real Estate Taxes the dominant form of property taxes paid by the owner of real estate. It is typically collected by the county and distributed among other governmental bodies to finance schools and other services. The tax is normally based on the assessed value of the property. The assessed value varies by states.

Real GDP GDP adjusted for inflation.

Real Income income measured in constant prices relative to some base period. It is the income adjusted for changes in purchasing power caused by inflation. Real wages is an example of real income.

Real Interest Rates interest rates adjusted for inflation.

Real Property rights, interests, and benefits inherent in the ownership of real estate, as distinguished from personal property; frequently thought of as a bundle of rights. Real estate may be loosely defined as land (including air rights) and other properties that are permanently attached to land such as houses, fences, and landscaping. The terms *real property* and *real estate* are often used interchangeably.

Real Time the calculation of data as quickly as they are inputted. A real-time stock, bond, option, or futures quote is one that reports the most current price available when a security changes hands. A delayed quote shows a security's price 15 or sometimes 20 minutes after a trade takes place.

Real-Time System a system that uses a nonsequential processing method. This differs from batch processing, which employs sequential processing. It provides access to any piece of information and finds that piece of datum in the same amount of time as any other piece. Real-time processing systems are more expensive than batch processing, but provide decision-making information on a current basis, that is, when the decision needs to be made or while a customer waits for a response.

Rebates
1. synonymous with abatements.
2. amounts paid back or credit allowed because of an overcollection or on account of the return of an object sold, also called *refunds*.

3. unearned interest refunded to the borrower if the loan is paid off prior to maturity.
4. payment made to a customer upon completion of a purchase as an inducement or sales promotion tactic.

Recapitalization the process of changing a firm's capital structure by altering the mix of debt and equity financing without changing the total amount of capital. This process often occurs as part of reorganization under the bankruptcy laws. In defeasance, the total capital amount can change.

Recapture

In general: return of an investment or payments made through a contractual agreement or by a depreciation provision.

Real estate: the return by owners of a property investment usually through a depreciation allowance.

Possession: a provision in a contract allowing the previous owner of an asset to take it back under certain conditions. For example, if an individual sells a business to someone on an installment purchase agreement and the buyer does not make the payments, the previous owner could recapture the business by taking possession of it.

Government: a legal seizure by the government of profits beyond a fixed amount.

Recapture of Depreciation the portion of a capital gain (the amount of a gain on depreciable assets) representing tax benefits previously taken and is taxed as ordinary income. Under the Tax Reform Act of 1986, the distinction between capital gain and ordinary income has no monetary meaning since capital gain is treated as ordinary income.

Recession a lower phase of a business cycle, in which the economy's output (GDP), income, corporate profits, and employment are declining, coupled with a declining rate of business investment and consumer spending. Two to three successive quarterly declines in GDP is usually the sign of a recession. Economists, however, have never made the distinction between a recession and a depression clear. It is the old rule of thumb that if your neighbor loses his/her job, it is a recession, and if you lose yours, it is a depression. *See also* Business Cycle; Depression.

Here are three primary ways economists define a recession:
1. Three or more straight monthly drops of the Index of Leading Economic Indicators are generally considered a sign of recession.
2. Two consecutive quarterly drops of Gross Domestic Product (GDP) signals a recession.
3. Consecutive monthly drops of durable goods orders that most likely results in less production and increasing layoffs in the factory sector signals a recession.

Reciprocal Arrangement an agreement where one party will perform a certain act if the other agrees to perform a specified act as well. An example is where company X agrees to buy certain goods from company Y if company Y orders merchandise from some division of company X.

Reciprocity a mutual or cooperative interchange of favors or privileges, especially the exchange of rights or privileges of trade between nations.

Record a collection of related data items. A collection of records is called a file. For example, a company may store information regarding each employee in a single record consisting of a field representing the name, a field representing the Social Security number, etc.

Red Flag a sign for immediate attention.

Red Herring a slang term for a preliminary prospectus that outlines the important features of a new security issue. This does not contain selling price information or offering date. It is so named since it is stamped in red ink telling the reader that the document is not an official offer to sell the securities.

Redemption

1. the right to call or redeem a firm's outstanding preferred stock by paying the preferred stockholders the par value of the stock plus a premium.
2. repayment of bonds by a call before maturity, usually involving a call premium.
3. repayment of mutual funds at net asset value when a shareholder's holdings are liquidated.

Redemption (Exit) Fees fees that a mutual fund charges when an investor sells his/her share of a fund. These fees can range from a flat $5 to 2% of the amount withdrawn. The redemption fee may decline on a sliding basis depending on how long the funds were invested. For example, 3% after one year, 2% after two years, 1% after three years, and no fee thereafter.

Reduction In Force (RIF) the formal term for downsizing, that is, when the company has reduced its workforce.

Reengineering the process by which an organization takes a fresh look at a business process and reorganizes it to attain efficiency; also called *Business Process Reengineering (BPR)*.

Refinance a revised schedule of debt payments, including a mortgage. Creditors may be willing to refinance a person's debts if he or she cannot meet the original payments or if interest rates have fallen since a borrower took out a loan. Whether refinancing is worthwhile depends on the costs of refinancing and the time required to recoup those costs through low mortgage payments. The costs of refinancing are the closing costs.

Refund amount paid back or credit given due to an overcollection or the return of merchandise. Examples are a tax return for the overpayment of taxes during the year and a cash refund given for clothing returned to the store that was originally bought for cash.

Regional Stock Exchanges organized securities exchanges other than the New York Stock Exchange (NYSE) and the American Stock Exchange (AMEX) that deal primarily in securities having a local or regional flavor.

Registered Security

1. a security whose owner is recorded by the issuing corporation or its registrar. In the case of a registered bond, principal of such a bond and interest, if registered as to interest, is paid to the owner of the bond listed on the record of the issuing company. It contrasts with bearer (coupon) bonds, where detachable coupons must be presented to the issuer for interest payment.
2. a public issue registered with the SEC.

Registrar

In general: person responsible for keeping and securing official records. For example, a college registrar maintains official student records and transcripts.

Real estate: the individual holding official real estate records, including deeds, mortgages, and surveys. This is often the clerk of the governmental jurisdiction. For example, the county or town clerk.

Securities: the trustee for all new issued bond and stock certificate records. Often this function is accomplished by a bank. The registrar maintains the corporation's or jurisdiction's security register and takes possession of transferred security certificates from the transfer agent as well as newly issued certificates. A function of the registrar is to substantiate the uniformity between old and new security registration numbers.

Registration

1. an act or fact of making an entry of any class of transactions or statements for the purpose of documentation for future reference. Such documentation may be in the form of financial information noted in registers, such as a cash register.
2. process set up by the Securities and Exchange Acts of 1933 and 1934 that requires publicly-issued securities to be reviewed by the SEC.
3. recording of stocks or bonds in the owner's name as opposed to bearer's name.

Registration Statement a document that must be submitted to the SEC disclosing all facts relevant to the new securities issue that will permit an investor to make an informed decision. It is a lengthy document containing (1) historical, (2) financial, and (3) administrative facts about the issuing corporation. *See also* Prospectus.

Regression Analysis a statistical procedure for estimating mathematically the average relationship between the dependent variable and the independent variable(s). Simple regression involves only one independent variable, such as price or advertising in a demand function. Multiple regression involves two or more variables, such as both price and advertising in the prediction of sales. Regression analysis is used to do the following: (1) To find the overall association between the dependent variable and a host of explanatory variables. For example, foreign exchange rates are explained by such things as inflation rates, interest rates, and the balance of payment. (2) To attempt to identify the factors that influence the dependent variable. For example, factors critical in affecting sales include price, advertising, taste, and competition. (3) To use it as a basis for providing sound forecasts of the dependent variable. For example, sometimes cash collections from receivables are forecasted from credit sales of prior months since cash collections lag behind sales. *See also* Least-Squares Method.

Regression Line the linear line that best fits or passes through the scatter graph. *See also* Least-Squares Method.

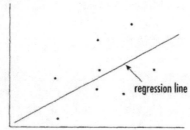

regression line

Regressive Tax a tax in which the percentage of income that is paid in taxes declines as income rises. Under a regressive system, as income rises from $15,000 to $100,000, the tax rate would fall—from 20 to 10 percent, for example. In this sense, a regressive tax is the opposite of a progressive tax. The term is also used generally to refer to any tax system that favors the rich at the expense of the poor. In this sense, the general sales tax with its fixed rate is considered regressive, because lower income groups tend to spend a higher percentage of their incomes on goods and services than higher income groups.

Regulation Q the Federal Reserve Bank's regulation that sets deposit interest rate ceilings and regulates advertising of interest on savings accounts. This regulation applies to all commercial banks. It is a rule, first instituted in the Banking Act of 1933.

Regulation S-X a Securities and Exchange Commission (SEC) regulation specifying the specific format and content of the financial reports required to be submitted. It also requires the companies that intend to offer their securities to the public to provide adequate disclosure so that the investing community can evaluate the merits of the issue.

Regulation T the Federal Reserve Bank's regulation governing the amount of credit that may be advanced by brokers and dealers to customers for the purchase of securities. *See also* Initial Margin.

Regulation U the Federal regulation governing the amount of credit which may be advanced by a bank to its customers for the purchase of securities.

Regulation W the Federal Reserve Bank's regulation that establishes guidelines for down payments and repayment schedules of installment credit loans. This regulation affects all institutions offering consumer credit and money market mutual funds.

Regulation X the Federal Reserve Bank's regulation that establishes guidelines for down payments and repayment schedules for U.S. mortgage loans.

Regulation Z the Federal Reserve Bank's regulation that regulates consumer and mortgage credit transactions. A lender must specify the annual percentage rate (APR) of the loan and other key information in consumer and mortgage credit contracts.

Regulations an authoritative body of rules specifying details of procedure and conduct to be followed in accordance to such criteria as uniformity, efficiency, control, ethics, and legal considerations.

Reinsurance an agreement whereby one insurer indemnifies another insurer for all or part of the risk of a policy originally issued and assumed by that other insurer.

Reinvent The Wheel to do something on one's own even though it has already been done before.

Reinvestment shareholders of mutual funds can decide to reinvest the money they earn, take it in cash, or do a little of each.

REIT *see* Real Estate Investment Trust.

Relational Database database consisting of relationships between datum items.

Release
In general: voluntarily to quit, abandon, or give up any further legal right against another. For example, exercising a prepayment of a loan clause would release the borrower from any further financial loan obligations.
Real estate: to free real estate from a mortgage by paying the mortgage. When a mortgage is paid in its entirety, often a confirming release of record is issued, legally attesting to the retirement of the debt.
Finance: the creditor's forgiveness of the debtor's obligation.

Relevant Costs the expected future costs that differ between the decision alternatives. Therefore, the sunk costs are not relevant to the decision at hand, because they are past and historical costs. The incremental or differential costs are relevant since they are the ones that differ between the alternatives. Not all costs are of equal importance, and managers must identify the costs that are relevant to a decision. For example, in a decision on whether to sell an existing business for a new one, the cost to be paid for the new venture is relevant. However, the initial cost of the old business is not relevant to the decision because it is a sunk cost.

Relevant Range the span of activity over which a certain cost behavior holds true. It is risky to extrapolate beyond the relevant range because there are no observations outside the range. For example, fixed costs will not change only for a specified range of volume of activity, called the *relevant range*. Beyond this, fixed costs are not constant. Break-even analysis and analysis of mixed costs are most useful only in this range of activity; that is, the volume zone in which the behavior of variable costs, fixed costs, and selling prices can be predicted with reasonable accuracy. *See also* Fixed Costs; Variable Costs.

Renewable Term a contract that can be renewed at its expiration for another specified time period. An example may be a bank loan or insurance policy.

Renminbi Chinese currency that literally translates as " The People's Currency." The popular unit of renminbi is the yuan.

Reorder Point the inventory level at which it is appropriate to replenish stock. Reorder point is calculated as follows:

Reorder point = average usage per unit of lead time x lead time + safety stock.

First, multiply average daily (or weekly) usage by the lead time in days, (or weeks), yielding the lead time demand. Then, add safety stock to this to provide for the variation in lead time demand to determine the reorder point. If average usage and lead time are both certain, no safety stock is necessary and should be dropped from the formula. For example, assume that annual demand is 35,000 dozen baseballs, lead time is constant at two weeks, and there are 50 working weeks in a year. Then reorder point is 1,400 dozen = (35,000 dozen/50 weeks) x 2 weeks. Therefore, when the inventory level drops to 1,400 dozen, the new order should be placed. Suppose, however, that the store is faced with variable usage for its baseballs and require a safety stock of 300 additional dozens to carry. Then the reorder point will be 1,400 dozen plus 300 dozen, or 1,700 dozen. *See also* EOQ Model; Safety Stock.

Reorganization the process of restating a company's assets to reflect their current market value and restating its financial structure downward to reflect reductions on the asset side of the balance sheet. A financially troubled firm usually goes through reorganization. Under a reorganization, the firm continues in existence. Chapter 11 of the bankruptcy law provides for reorganization. Chapter 7 provides for liquidation.

Replacement Cost

In general: the cost of replacing one item with another for the purpose of providing the same function with the same useful life.

Insurance: the cost of replacing an insured's property with comparable property less the cost of depreciation (fair wear and tear). In this context, replacement cost is equivalent to the current cash value of an insured item. The purpose is to restore the insured's property without suffering a financial loss or enjoying a profit.

Real estate: the cost of replacing an existing structure with another exact replica. The current construction costs of replacing buildings and homes built years ago are substantially more than the original construction costs.

Replacement Demand demand resulting from obsolescence, depreciation, or wear of capital or durable goods.

Replication to duplicate methods or processes in order to gather data to confirm or deny a standing assumption or set of circumstances. Results may be replicated (if such methods are employed independently and these results are verified under similar conditions), thus providing two independent checks upon the data gathered and their implied assumptions. An example is when two accountants independently add the total of daily cash receipts and find agreement.

Report Form
1. format of an income statement that reads from top to bottom. It begins with sales or revenues at the top, leading to net income at the bottom, with significant totals in between.
2. an auditor's report format, either in short or long form.

Report on Current Economic Conditions ("The Beige Book") the report, informally known as the *Beige Book*, is released about every six weeks by the Federal Reserve Board. It provides the most recent assessment of the nation's economy, with a regional emphasis. It is used to help the Fed decide on its monetary policies such as changes in interest rates.

Repurchase Agreement (REPO) the temporary sale of securities (such as U.S. treasury or government agency securities, bankers' acceptances, certificates of deposit, commercial paper, and other marketable securities) to the investor (lender) accompanied by an agreement to repurchase them at some point in the near future. There is a provision for interest to be paid to the investor at the end of the transaction. Theoretically, the funds borrowed are collateralized by securities.

Request for Information (RFI) a request to vendors for general, somewhat informal, information about their products.

Request for Proposal (RFP) a request or document specifying all the system requirements and soliciting a proposal from vendors who might want to bid on a project or service.

Required Rate of Return the rate of return required by the investor, above which an investment makes sense and below which it does not. It is based on the firm's cost of capital plus or minus a risk premium to reflect the project's specific risk characteristics; also called *Hurdle Rate*.

Rescind the act of canceling, nullifying, abrogating, or dishonoring a contractual obligation. The Truth-in-Lending Act provides the right of recission whereby an individual can annul a contract without penalties, including the refund of any deposits within three business days. Other types of co-contracts may also be rescinded when they are improperly executed. For example, a minor may rescind a contract with no penalties since children cannot make legal contracts.

Research and Development (R&D) activity responsible for creating new products and doing the research for marketing and manufacturing needs.

Reserves funds put away by an individual or company to meet a particular contingency, such as a pending lawsuit or likely bad debts.

Residential Property an owner-occupied property (includes not only the single-family dwelling but almost any type of structure) designed for habitation–condominiums, cooperatives, town houses, and "plexes" where the owner can live in one but rents the others, as opposed to commercial or office space.

Residual Income (RI) the operating income that an investment center is able to earn above some minimum return on its assets. It is a popular alternative performance measure to return on investment (ROI). RI is computed as:

RI = Net operating income - (minimum rate of return on investment x operating assets).

Residual income, unlike ROI, is an absolute amount of income rather than a rate of return. When RI is used to evaluate divisional performance, the objective is to maximize the total amount of residual income, not to maximize the overall ROI percentage figure. For example, assume that operating assets is $100,000, net operating income is $18,000, and the minimum return on assets is 13 percent. Residual income is $18,000 - (13% x $100,000) = $18,000 - $13,000 =$5,000. RI is sometimes preferred over ROI as a performance measure because it encourages managers to accept investment opportunities that have rates of return greater than the charge for invested capital. Managers being evaluated using ROI may be reluctant to accept new investments that lower their current ROI although the investments would be desirable for the entire company. Advantages of using residual income in evaluating divisional performance include (1) it is an economic income taking into account the opportunity cost of tying up assets in the division, (2) the minimum rate of return can vary depending on the riskiness of the division, (3) different assets can be required to earn different returns depending on their risk, (4) the same asset may be required to earn the same return regardless of the division it is in, and (5) maximizing dollars rather than a percentage leads goal congruence.

Residual Value
1. the value of leased property at the end of the lease term.
2. at any time, the actual or estimated value (that is, proceeds minus disposal costs) of an asset, also called *salvage value* or *scrap value*.
3. value of a depreciable asset after all allowable depreciation has been taken.

Resolution the degree to which the image on a computer monitor is sharp. Higher resolution means a sharper image. Resolution depends on the number of pixels on the screen and the dot pitch.

Resource Allocation the distribution of factors of production such as money, plant and equipment, and skilled labor among alternative uses.

Responsibility obligation to perform. In the classical view, this obligation formally comes down from a superior position and is inherent in any job (it has its origins in the rights of private property as defined by the appropriate laws). In the behavioral view, responsibility must and should be delegated; a successive dividing and passing down of obligation occurs. The appropriate amount of authority or power must be delegated with the responsibility. However, a higher position can never rid itself of ultimate responsibility.

Responsibility Accounting the collection, summarization, and reporting of financial information about various decision centers (responsibility centers) throughout an organization; also called *activity accounting* or *profitability* *accounting.* It traces costs, revenues, or profits to the individual managers who are primarily responsible for making decisions about the costs, revenues or profits in question and taking action about them. Responsibility accounting is appropriate where top management has delegated authority to make decisions. The idea behind responsibility accounting is that each manager's performance should be judged by how well the manager manages those items under the manager's control. *See also* Responsibility Center.

Responsibility Center a unit in the organization that has control over costs, revenues, or investment funds. For accounting purposes, responsibility centers are classified as cost centers, revenue centers, profit centers, and investment centers, depending on what each center is responsible for. A well-designed responsibility accounting system should clearly define responsibility centers in order to collect and report revenue and cost information by areas of responsibility.

Responsibility Centers within a Company

Restatement to reiterate or republish a financial statement or document, such as a balance sheet or income statement, in a manner that incorporates revisions and changes based on accounting principles or policies.

Restrictive Covenant

1. language in a loan agreement by which the borrower agrees to do certain things but refrains from others. An example of an affirmative covenant is a borrower's agreement to maintain proper insurance. An example of a negative covenant is a prohibition against the borrowers selling assets.
2. a provision in a bond agreement protecting bondholder interests, such as the debtor's promise to maintain timely payments of principal and interest.
3. a provision in a contract that denies or limits the full rights of the purchaser or lessor to the property. For example, a landlord may stipulate in the lease that the tenant may not put up paneling unless written permission is obtained.

Retail Sales the estimate of total sales at the retail level. It includes everything from bags of groceries to durable goods such as automobiles. It is used as a measure of future economic conditions: A long slowdown in sales could spell cuts in production. The data are issued monthly by the Commerce Department. Retail sales are a major concern for analysts because they represent about half of overall consumer spending. Consumer spending, in turn, accounts for about two-thirds of the nation's Gross Domestic Product (GDP). The amount of retail sales depends heavily on consumer confidence in the economy. *See also* Economic Indicators; Personal Income; Consumer Confidence Index; University of Michigan's Index of Consumer Sentiment.

Retained Earnings that proportion of total earnings not distributed in the form of dividend payments to stockholders or paid in the form of tax payments. These funds are important internal sources of financing for capital expenditure plans.

Retirement

1. removal of a fixed asset from operative service with the appropriate adjustments to the fixed asset and accumulated depreciation accounts. Retirement may be due to a variety of reasons, such as the asset has reached the end of its useful life or it has been disposed of by sale.
2. repayment of a debt.
3. cancellation of reacquired shares of stock or bonds by a corporation. *See also* Redemption; Treasury Stock.
4. Permanent withdrawal of an employee from employment.

Retirement Plan a plan provided by the employer and/or employee to pay retirement benefits when the employee retires. The plan normally consists of developing various financial options in the retirement fund, such as the extent of the contribution to the plan, choice of beneficiaries, and payment options. In addition to financial considerations, retirement planning also includes considerations of housing arrangements, possible relocation, and a possible second career.

Return the reward for investing. The investor must compare the expected return for a given investment with the risk involved. The return on an investment consists of the following sources of income: (a) Periodic cash payments, called *current income,* or (b) appreciation (or depreciation) in market value, called *capital gains* (or *losses*). Current income, which is received on a periodic basis, may take the form of interest, dividends, rent, and the like. Capital gains or losses represent changes in market value. A capital gain is the amount by which the proceeds from the sale of an investment exceeds its original purchase price. If the investment is sold for less than its purchase price, the difference is a capital loss. *See also* Bond Yields; Holding Period Return (HPR); Total Return; Yield (Rate of Return).

Return on Assets (ROA) net income after taxes divided by total tangible assets and measures the effectiveness of assets to create profits:

$$\text{ROA} = \frac{\textbf{Net income after taxes}}{\textbf{Average total assets}}$$

where

$$\text{Average total assets} = \frac{\text{beginning total assets} + \text{ending total assets}}{2}$$

Intangibles (e.g., goodwill) are usually not included in total assets because they are a problem to measure and do not contribute to operating profits. However, an exception might be trademarks that do contribute to profits. *See also* Du Pont Formula; Return on Investment (ROI).

Return on Assets Pricing pricing method in which the objective of price determination is to earn a profit equal to a specific rate of return on assets employed in the operation.

Return on Equity (ROE) return on stockholders' investments. It is a variant of the Du Pont formula, which equals total assets (investment) turnover, times the profit margin, times the equity multiplier.

Return on Investment (ROI) a traditional and important calculation made by taking the net profits, after taxes, divided by the total assets of a company; also called *return on assets* (ROA).

Returns to Scale the relationship between output of a product and the quantities of factor inputs used to produce it. It refers to how output changes when all inputs are increased by the same multiple. If output increases by a greater multiple than that by which the inputs are increased, then increasing returns to scale are present. If output increases by the same multiple, constant returns to scale are present. Finally, if output increases by a smaller multiple, decreasing returns to scale are present. Returns to scale play an important role in economic decisions. They affect the optimal scale, or plant size of a firm and its production facilities. They also affect the nature of competition in an industry and thus are important in determining the profitability in a particular sector of the economy.

Revaluation a rise in the foreign exchange value of a currency that is pegged to other currencies or gold.

Revenue
1. amount of money earned from selling goods or services rendered for a specified period of time. Under an accrual system revenue is recognized and recorded when the business earns it (whether money is collected or not). Earned revenues result in an increase in assets.
2. earnings from dividends, rents, wages, and interest.
3. gross receipts and receivables of a governmental unit resulting from taxes and other sources.

Revenue Anticipation Note notes issued by a municipality in expectation of future revenues to be received from given sources, such as sales taxes.

Revenue Bonds bonds whose principal and interest are payable exclusively from earnings of the project built with proceeds, such as a stadium, toll bridge, hospital, or other enterprise. Revenue bonds are issued normally by municipalities. In addition to a pledge of revenues, such bonds sometimes contain a mortgage on the enterprise's property and are known as mortgage revenue bonds.

Revenue Center a unit within an organization that is responsible for generating revenues. A revenue center is, virtually in all cases, a profit center since for all practical purposes there is no revenue center that does not incur some costs during the course of generating revenues. A favorable variance occurs when actual revenue exceeds expected revenue.

Reverse Annuity Mortgage (RAM) a mortgage that allows a borrower to receive monthly receipts against the equity in his or her home. It is designed for older people who own their homes and need additional funds to meet current living expenses but do not want to sell their homes. At the end of the payment term, often 10 or 15 years, the mortgage on the borrower's home equals a predetermined amount so that the value of the equity is reduced by the amount.

Reverse Discrimination a situation in which an employer favors minorities at the expense of others, such as in hiring and promotion. This may arise from a quota that has not been approved as an affirmative action policy.

Reverse Leverage or negative leverage. The interest rate on debt is higher than the rate of return generated from investing the borrowed funds. This magnifies losses. *See also* Positive Leverage.

Reverse Split a decision by the board of directors of a public company to reduce the total number of shares outstanding by some specified amount. The decision is usually intended to price shares higher so investors can think better of it.

Revocable Trust an arrangement that deeds income-generating assets to heirs. The grantor may change the terms of the trust, if desired. The grantor also has the right to terminate the trust. It is different from an irrevocable trust because assets may be transferred permanently while the grantor is alive; thus, it avoids estate taxes.

Revolving Fund a fund whose amounts are repeatedly expended, replenished, and then expended again. An imprest petty cash fund is an example. Vouchers are paid daily and the petty cash fund is usually replenished at the end of each month.

Rider a written modification to an insurance policy that changes its provisions. The rider may update the policy and add or delete specified coverage.

Right
1. something to which a just claim exists having a moral or legal nature. An example is the right of a common stockholder to vote in a corporate election.
2. a privilege to subscribe to new stock issues. One right attached to existing shares may provide the opportunity to purchase a fractional share or particular number of shares of a new capital stock issue. A preemptive right allows a shareholder the opportunity of maintaining a proportionate share of the enterprise by subscribing to an appropriate amount of newly issued shares. *See also* Rights Offering.

Right-Hand Side

1. the right-hand side of the balance sheet that covers liabilities and stockholders' equity.
2. typically the amount of resources or capacities available to a firm for a given period, which appears on the right-hand side of a linear programming problem. *See also* Linear Programming.

Rights Offering an offering of rights to current stockholders to buy new common shares in the company at a specified subscription price that is less than what the offering price will be to the public. It enables existing stockholders to maintain their proportionate ownership in the company when the new issues are made, which are called *preemptive rights*.

Rightsizing the process of making a company leaner and smaller, reducing its workforce.

Risk

1. variation in earnings, sales, or other financial variable.
2. probability of a financial problem affecting the company's operational performance or financial position, such as economic risk, political uncertainties, and industry problems. *See also* Uncertainty.
3. a peril insured against.
4. possibility of losing value.
5. a state of knowledge in which each alternative leads to one of a set of specific outcomes, each outcome occurring with a probability that is known to a decision maker.

Risk-Adjusted Discount Rate riskless rate plus a risk premium. It is a rate adjusted upward as the investment becomes riskier. By increasing the discount rate from 10% to 15%, for example, the expected flow from the investment must be relatively larger or the increased discount rate will generate a negative NPV, and the proposed acquisition/investment will be rejected. Although difficult to apply in extreme cases, this technique has much intuitive value.

Risk Analysis the process of measuring and analyzing the risks associated with financial and investment decisions. Risk refers to the variability of expected returns (earnings or cash flows). Statistics, such as standard deviation and coefficient of variation, are used to measure various risks. Beta coefficient is used to measure a stock's relative volatility in relation to the market and to analyze a portfolio risk. Risk analysis is important in making capital investment decisions because of the large amount of capital involved and the long-term nature of the investments being considered. The higher the risk associated with a proposed project, the greater the return that must be earned to compensate for that risk. There are several methods for the analysis of risk, including: risk-adjusted discount rate, certainty equivalent, Monte Carlo simulation, sensitivity analysis, and decision trees.

Risk Averse opposed to risk. It is a subjective attitude against risk taking. An investor not willing to take risk may place his/her funds into U.S. treasury bills.

Risk Management

1. the analysis of and planning for potential risks and their subsequent losses. The objective of risk management is to try to minimize the financial consequence of random losses.
2. the business activity that assesses the risks a company is faced with and a plan for the potential coverage or payment of those risks.

Risk Measures quantitative measures of risk. They attempt to assess the degree of variation or uncertainty about earnings or return. There are several measures, including the standard deviation, coefficient of variation, and beta coefficient. The standard deviation is a statistical measure of dispersion of the probability distribution of possible returns. The smaller the deviation, the tighter the distribution, and thus, the lower the riskiness of the investment. One must be careful in using the standard deviation to compare risk since it is only an absolute measure of dispersion (risk) and does not consider the dispersion of outcomes in relationship to an expected return. In comparisons of securities with differing expected returns, we commonly use the coefficient of variation. The coefficient of variation (CV) is computed simply by dividing the standard deviation for a security by its expected value. The higher the coefficient, the more risky the security. The coefficient of beta measures a stock's or mutual fund's volatility relative to the general market.

Risk Neutral an adjective describing an individual who neither fears nor enjoys risk but views it in an objective rational manner with a view toward its control when beneficial.

Risk Premium the amount by which the required return on an asset or security exceeds the risk-free rate. The risk premium is the additional return required to compensate investors for assuming a given level of risk. The higher this premium, the more risky the security and vice versa.

Risk Taker a person who is not fearful of uncertainty and may even enjoy risky, speculative situations. He/she is a person who will take a chance or gamble in hopes of winning.

Risk Transfer an individual transferring a given risk to another, such as taking out fire and theft insurance policies so the insurance company will bear much of the risk of loss.

Risk-Free Rate the interest rate that would exist on a riskless security if no inflation were expected, and it may be thought of as a rate of interest on short-term U.S. Treasury securities in an inflation-free world.

Risk-return Trade-off the concept that the higher the return or yield, the larger the risk; or vice versa. All financial decisions involve some sort of risk-return trade-off. The greater the risk associated with any financial decision, the greater the return expected from it. Proper assessment and balance of the various risk-return trade-offs available is part of creating a sound financial and investment plan. For example, the less inventory a firm keeps, the higher the expected return (since less of the firm's current assets are tied up). But there is also a greater risk of running out of stock and thus losing potential revenue. In an investment arena, you must compare the expected return from a given investment with the risk associated with it. Generally speaking, the higher the risk undertaken, the more ample the return, and conversely, the lower the risk, the more modest the return. In the case of investing in stock, you would demand a higher return from a speculative stock to compensate for the higher level of risk. On the other hand, U.S. T-bills have minimal risk, so a low return is appropriate. The proper assessment and balance of the various risk-return trade-offs is part of creating a sound investment plan.

Robinson-Patman Act legislation that forbids quoting different prices to competing customers unless such price discrimination is justified by differences in costs of manufacturing, sales, or delivery.

Rollover
1. a renewal of a short-term obligation by mutual agreement of debtor and creditor. This short-term debt appears under current liabilities. Footnote disclosure of the arrangement is made along with major provisions.
2. movement of funds from one investment to another. For example, when a certificate of deposit or bond matures, the funds may be rolled over into another certificate of deposit or bond.

Rollover IRA *see* IRA Rollover.

ROM *see* Read-Only Memory.

Rothschild Index measure of the sensitivity to price of a product group as a whole relative to the sensitivity of the quantity demanded of a single firm to a change in its price.

Rough-Cut Capacity Planning analysis of the master production schedule (MPS) to determine the feasibility with respect to capacity limitations (warehouse facilities, equipment, labor, etc.).

Round Lot or even lot. A unit of trading on a securities exchange. For example, a round lot on the New York Stock Exchange is 100 shares of stock or one $1,000 face-value bond (although brokers may have their own higher round lot requirements in the case of bonds).

Royalty monies paid to use property, such as the use of copyrighted materials and natural resource extractions. The royalty payment is usually based upon some percentage of the income or fee for substances generated from the use of such property.

R-Squared (r-Squared) *see* Coefficient of Determination.

Rule
1. a statement governing procedures, interpretations or inferences belonging to sets of operations or decisions. *See* Decision Rule.
2. a directive, instruction, or order detailing something to be done. Requiring the cash receipts to be counted at the end of the day to assure that the physical cash received agrees with the recorded book amount is an example of a rule.

Rule of 69 very similar to the rule of 72, a rule stating that an amount of money invested at r percent per period will double in 69/r (in percent) + .35 periods. Example: You bought a share of ADR yielding an annual return of 25%. Then the investment will double in a little over three years (69/25 + .35 = 2.76 + .35 = 3.11 years).

Rule of 72 a rule of thumb method used to determine how many years it takes to double investment money at a given growth or interest rate. Under the method, dividing the number 72 by the fixed rate of return equals the number of years it takes for annual earnings from the investment to double. That is, 72/r (as a percentage). Example: You bought a share of ADR yielding an annual return of 25%. The investment will double in less than three years (72/25 = 2.88 years). The rule can be reversed, too. Example: If you know that your money doubled in four years, you can divide 72 by 4. You will see that you earned roughly 18% per year. Note: The Rule of 72 does not work, however, when dealing with extreme numbers. For example, dividing 72 by a 72% return indicates that you expect to double your money in one year. It is not true. It would rather take a 100% return. Furthermore, it is more accurate when dealing with somewhat higher returns to use 76, not 72.

Rule of 78 or the rule of the sum of the digits. A method that banks use to develop a loan amortization schedule. It results in a borrower's paying more interest in the beginning of a loan when she has the use of more of the money, and less interest as the debt is reduced. Therefore, it is important to know how much interest can be saved by prepaying the loan after a certain month and how much of the loan is still owed.

Rulings an expression of the official interpretation of the Internal Revenue Service (IRS) tax laws as they were applied to specific situations; also called *revenue rulings*. Unlike a Treasury Department issued regulation, the IRS interpretation does have complete authoritative significance and, as such, is more limited in application. Rulings of interest to the general public have been published subsequent to 1976 and are available as references for taxpayers.

Russell 2000/3000 two useful indexes of small cap stocks, calculated by Frank Russell Co. of Seattle (*www.russell.com*). The Russell 2000 consists of smaller capitalization stocks. The Russell 3000 consists of the largest 3,000 publicly traded stocks of U.S. domiciled corporations and includes large, medium, and small capitalization stocks. It represents about 98 percent of the total capitalization of the New York, American, and NASDAQ markets.

Ss

S Corporation (Subchapter S Corporation) a form of corporation whose stockholders are taxed as partners; also called *Subchapter S Corporation.* Distributes its income directly to shareholders; avoids corporate income tax while enjoying the other advantages of the corporate form. However, unlike a partnership, shareholders cannot receive allocations disproportionate to their interests. To qualify as an S corporation, a corporation must:
• Have fewer than 75 shareholders; none may be nonresident aliens.
• Have only one class of stock.
• Properly elect Subchapter S status.

Sabbatical Leave authorized leave, paid or unpaid. It is usually taken every seventh year.

Safe Deposit Box a secured lock box available for rent in banks and used as a storage place for keeping valuables such as jewelry, contracts, stock certificates, titles, and other special documents.

Safety Stock extra units of inventory a firm must carry as protection against possible stockouts. The safety stock must be carried when the firm is not sure about either the demand of the product or lead time or both. In the case where the demand is uncertain, safety stock is the difference between the maximum usage and the average usage multiplied by the lead time.

Salami Slicing a program designed to siphon off small amounts of money from a number of larger transactions, so the quantity taken is not really apparent.

Salary a regular form of compensation an employee receives from an employer.

Salary Reduction Plans *see* 401(k) Plan.

Salary Review an appraisal by an employer of an employee's performance over a period of time, usually yearly, to determine whether an adjustment should be made to the employee's salary. Often, the reasons for the employer's decision are given to the employee.

Sales Force Automation equipping traveling salespeople with notebook computers, PDAs, telecommunication devices, and other devices that allow them to communicate with the home office, retrieve and store information from and to other computers remotely, and fax information.

Sales Forecasting a projection or prediction of future sales. It is the foundation for the quantification of the entire business plan and a master budget. There are two primary approaches to sales forecasting: qualitative and quantitative. Qualitative approaches include sales people polls and consumer surveys. Quantitative methods include moving average, exponential smoothing, trend analysis, and regression analysis. Sales forecasts serve as a basis for planning. They are the basis for capacity planning, budgeting, production and inventory planning, manpower planning, and purchasing planning:

Sales Forecasts and Managerial Functions

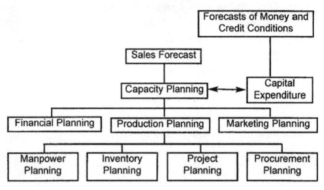

Sales Management the activity of directing the sales effort. It includes hiring, training, motivating, and coordinating the sales force in accordance with a firm's objectives.

Sales Mix the relative proportions of the products sold. For example, a company has three products and their respective sales are as follows:

	A	B	C	Total
Sales	$30,000	$60,000	$10,000	$100,000

Then the sale mix ratio for A, B, and C are 30%, 60%, and 10%, respectively.

Sales Promotion selling aids, often at point-of-purchase, which reinforce other types of promotion.

Sales Quota an assigned volume or target for a given marketing unit. An important component in sales forecasting.

Sales Tax a state or local tax based on a percentage of the selling price of a good or service that the buyer pays. The seller collects the tax and remits it to the sales tax agency. For example, if goods have a selling price of $5,000 are bought and the sales tax is 8%, the amount of sales tax is $40 ($5,000 x 8%). Thus, the total purchase price is $5,040. The sales tax, if any, varies among states. The sales tax is not deductible on an individual's tax return.

Sales-Force Polling use of sales people who have continual contacts with customers as a forecast source. They believe that the sales force who are closest to the ultimate customers may have significant insights regarding the state of the future market.

Salomon Brothers Bond Index a highly quoted index of fixed-income securities that combines U.S. treasury and agency securities, corporate bonds, and mortgage-backed securities.

Same-Store Sales used when analyzing the retail sector. It is considered the best measure of a retailer's performance. It compares sales in stores that have been open for a year or more. This allows you to compare what proportion of new sales have come from sales growth rather than resulting from just the opening of new stores.

Sample a part of the population. It is often impossible or impractical to observe the population if it is large. A decision maker relies on a sample of it. And then he tries to draw conclusions or make inferences about the population. An example of a sample is counting selected inventory items in performing an audit to verify the total inventory balance. *See also* Population.

Sampling the process of selecting items from a population to reach a conclusion about the population. *See also* Statistical Sampling.

Sampling Distribution a probability distribution that gives the probability of each possible value of a statistic, computed from a sample of n items, for all possible samples of size n from a particular population. For example, we can compute a statistic, such as the mean, standard deviation, etc., which will vary from sample to sample. In this manner, we obtain a distribution of a statistic that is its sampling distribution.

Sampling Error the difference between the value obtained by sampling and the value that would have been obtained if the entire population had been investigated. The auditor is concerned that such a sampling error is minimized.

Samurai Bond yen-denominated bonds issued in Japan by a foreign borrower. This contrasts with Shogun bonds. *See also* Foreign Bonds; Shogun Bonds.

S&P 500 *see* Standard & Poor's 500 Stock Composite.

Sarbanes-Oxley Act wide-ranging U.S. corporate reform legislation, coauthored by the Democrat in charge of the Senate Banking Committee, Paul Sarbanes, and Republican Congressman Michael Oxley. The Act, which became law in July, 2002, lays down stringent procedures regarding the accuracy and reliability of corporate disclosures, places restrictions on auditors providing non-audit services and obliges top executives to verify their accounts personally.

Satellite Office a secondary office of a company.

Satisficing a concept of managerial behavior where a firm does not seek to maximize profit but to achieve a satisfactory level of profit. For example, a firm tries to achieve a certain level of profit or a specified level of market share of its product.

Saturation the point of a product life cycle where the market has been completely filled so that no more sales for goods and services can be taken up; also called *Market Saturation.*

Savings funds set aside, commonly in interest-bearing form, to accomplish financial or investment goals.

Savings and Loan (S&L) a financial institution that channels the savings of its depositors mostly into mortgage and home improvement loans. It concentrates in originating, servicing, and holding mortgage loans. Traditionally, they have been the largest supplier of single-family owner-occupied residential permanent financing, although S&Ls are not limited solely to this type of financing. Savings and loan associations also make home-improvement loans and loans to investors for apartments, industrial property and commercial real estate. An S&L is either federally or state charted.

Savings Bonds *see* Series HH Savings Bonds; Series EE Savings Bonds.

Say's Law an assertion, made by the French economist Jean Baptiste Say, that supply creates its own demand. That is, the total demand for goods and services must equal the total value of goods and services produced. Under this law, no overproduction is possible, and thus the economy would automatically tend toward full employment equilibrium without government interference.

Scalability
1. a client server's capability to handle more and more users.
2. the ability to adapt applications as business needs grow.

Scan to read through a document rather hastily. In a desk-top publishing computer system, a document can be quickly examined through a scanner so that the document can be edited later by the system.

Scanner a device that scans pictures and text and transforms them into digitized files.

Scatter Diagram; Scattergraph; Scatter Plot a graph or plot of data usually in the form of dots. It is a visual aid in detecting a relationship between variables such as revenue and advertising. See chart on next page for example.

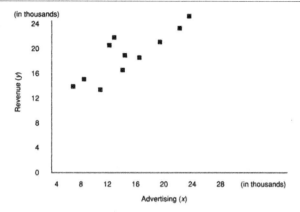

Schedule

1. a supporting set of calculations, data, information, or analysis that shows or amplifies upon how figures in primary statements are derived. An example is a schedule for an aging of accounts.
2. an auditor's set of working papers for an audit.
3. used as a verb, to prioritize, arrange or position with respect to a finite time period.

Scheduling assignment of work to a facility and the specification of the sequence and timing of the work.

Scroll movement of the window on a computer up or down relative to the contents of a file in order to reach parts of the file that were not originally seen on the screen.

S-Curve one of the most common curves used in technological forecasting. The S-curve is indicative of many technological developments, such as incandescent and fluorescent lighting efficiency, the maximum speed of aircraft, and the efficiency of commercial electric power plants, as well as the sales of many new products including color TVs, CB radios, and small calculators.

SDR *see* Special Drawing Rights (SDR).

Seamless having no seams.

Search the finding of an occurrence of a particular sequence of characters, working through a file on the screen. It is a function of an editor which is a computer program, that enables the user to sit at a terminal or a keyboard, view the contents of a file, scroll, add material, or make other changes.

Search Engine software tools to find information on the Internet. Popular search engines are Google, Yahoo, Alta Vista, and Lycos.

Search-Engine Optimization the act of altering a company's web site so that it may rank well for particular terms used in web searches. The idea is to get the company's site to the top of the results of a web search, or at least on the first page of the results. One relatively easy change to make is to use simple terms or words that everyone would understand to describe your products—and therefore be more likely to use in a search—instead of industry jargon. *See also* Paid Inclusion; Paid Listings.

Seasonal Index a number that indicates the seasonality for a given time period. For example, a seasonal index for observed values in July would indicate the way in which that July value is affected by the seasonal pattern in the data. Seasonal indexes are used to obtain deseasonalized data. *See also* Deseasonlized Data; Time Series Analysis.

Seasonal Unemployment unemployment caused by seasonal variations in certain industries such as weather and custom (e.g., unemployment in off-season for holidays such as Christmas and Easter). *See also* Unemployment.

Seasonality a fluctuation in business or economic conditions that occurs on a regular basis. It may be caused by such factors as weather and vacations. An example is the sales volume of the toy industry in November and December, the months in which it records its highest sales. Seasonality affects individuals, such as an accountant who is extremely busy during tax season.

Second Mortgage a mortgage debt with a subordinated claim to that of the first mortgage. However, a second mortgage is senior to subsequent liens. A second mortgage may be used to reduce the amount of a cash down payment or in refinancing to raise cash for some purpose (e.g., home improvement, investment in a business) The interest rate on a second mortgage is higher because of the increased risk. The second mortgage typically has a repayment term significantly shorter than the first mortgage with a fixed amortization schedule. There may also be a balloon payment. By illustration, a home costs $200,000 and a first mortgage is taken out for 70%, totaling $140,000. Thus a $60,000 down payment is needed. If a second mortgage is available for $40,000, then the required cash down payment will be $20,000.

Secondary Distribution an "off the board" offering of a previously issued and listed security from an investment institution, acting as an underwriter or as a selling investor, to other members of the exchange on which the security is listed. Sales of this nature are usually block sales. Allowing such a sale to take place on the exchange floor might have the effect of severely lowering the price of the stock. Certain block dispositions are required to have SEC sanction.

Secondary Market the market in which previously issued securities are traded between investors. It is equivalent to a used-car market. *See also* Primary Market.

Secondary Mortgage Market a market where mortgage loans can be sold to investors. The availability of funds for financing real estate is affected by economic conditions, both local and national. The result is that at certain times or in certain geographic locations little or no capital is available for mortgages; consequently, few if any loans are made. From the viewpoint of the lender, another problem is that real estate loans can be highly illiquid; thus, the supplier of funds can have a difficult time converting loans into cash. For these reasons, the need exists for some means by which a lender can sell a loan prior to its maturity date. The secondary mortgage market attempts to meet these needs.

Section 403(B) Plan an individual retirement plan specified in the Internal Revenue Code (IRC) Section 403(b) in which employees of certain nonprofit organizations may set aside funds, thus deferring current taxation until retirement.

SECTION 501(C) the IRS code under which nonprofit organizations are organized. Section 501(C) entities are exempt from federal and usually state income taxes.

Sector Fund or specialized fund. A mutual fund that invests in one or two fields or industries (sectors). These funds are risky in that they rise and fall depending on how the individual fields or industries do. An example is Prudential Bache Utility Fund.

Secular Trend a long-term change (growth or decline) in an economic time-series variable. For example, in empirical demand analyses, such factors as increasing population changes in its makeup or changing consumer tastes may result in general changes of a demand over time. The term *secular* signifies that it is the trend computed from a long run of data.

Secured Liability an obligation secured by a pledge of assets that can be sold, if necessary, to ensure payment.

Securities financial instruments of issuers that provide investors with ownership rights and return in the form typically of periodic payments (dividends, interest) and appreciation (or decline) in market price. Examples of securities are stocks, bonds, and options.

Securities Act of 1933 landmark legislation that provided governmental regulation over the initial issuance of securities. It covered registration and disclosure. The Securities and Exchange Act of 1934 dealt with the trading of already outstanding securities. It covered enforcement. The regulating body set up to enforce and promulgate regulations, as well as mandate policies and standards within the accounting and auditing disciplines is the Securities and Exchange Commission (SEC).

Securities Act of 1934 *see* Securities Act of 1933.

Securities & Exchange Commission (SEC) a federal agency that regulates the U.S. financial markets. Established by Congress to help protect investors, the SEC administers the Securities Exchange Act of 1933, the Securities Exchange Act of 1934, the Trust Indenture Act, the Investment Company Act, the Investment Advisers Act, the Public Utility Holding Company Act, and the amendments to some of these contained in the Securities Acts Amendments of 1964.

Securitization

1. development of financial markets for various new negotiable instruments so that borrowers and lenders are matched up.
2. process of converting nonmarketable financial assets, such as loans or mortgages, into negotiable securities issued in capital markets.
3. spreading risk by combining debt securities in a pool, and then selling new securities backed by the pool.

Security

1. a certificate of ownership in a company (e.g., stock), an evidence of a debtor's obligation (e.g., bond), or other ownership rights.
2. collateral issued to support a borrowing. An example is a house that serves as security for the mortgage.
3. means of protecting property from unauthorized access or use, such as posting a security guard in an apartment building.

Security Interest an interest "in personal property or fixtures which secure payment or performance of an obligation." The property that secures the interest is the collateral (tangible-physical property and non-tangible-non-physical property).

Seed Capital the initial money necessary to start a business or project.

Seed Money funds put up by venture capitalists to finance a new business. Often, seed money involves a loan or investment in preferred stock or convertible bonds. A major purpose of seed money is to form a basis for additional financing to aid in a firm's growth.

Segment Margin contribution margin less direct (traceable) fixed costs.

Segmental Reporting; Segmented Reporting the presentation of financial information, such as profitability, by a major business segment; including the product, major customer, division, department, and responsibility centers within the department.

Self Insurance insurance borne by the person or company itself against the risk of loss that may occur if property is destroyed or damaged from some cause (e.g., fire). A company that self-insures cannot establish an estimated liability. It can appropriate retained earnings and footnote the nature of the self-insurance.

Self-Employment Income the net taxable income of a self-employed individual from the operation of a trade or business. The income is reported on Schedule C of Form 1040. If there is more than one business, self-employment income is the total earnings of all businesses. A loss in one business is deductible from the profits of another. A self-employed individual pays a higher social security tax than a regular employee.

Self-Liquidating Loan a seasonal loan that is used to pay for a temporary increase in accounts receivable or inventory. As soon as cash is realized from the assets, the loan is repaid. The borrowed money is used to acquire resources that are combined for later sale, and the proceeds from the sale are used to repay the loan. Most short-term unsecured loans are self-liquidating. This kind of loan is recommended for use by companies with excellent credit ratings for financing projects that have quick cash flows.

Sell on the News the practice of selling a security when the actual earnings news came about after buying on the anticipated earnings expectations.

Sellers' Market a market in which the seller has the advantage because demand for the product, property, or security exceeds supply. In addition, the seller has a strong influence over the terms of sale. This will drive up the price.

Selling Expenses all the expenses associated with obtaining sales and the delivery of the product and service to customers. Examples are advertising, sales commissions, and freight-out. Selling expenses are one of the categories under operating expenses.

Selling Short Against the Box short sale undertaken to protect a profit in a stock and to defer tax liability to another year. For example, an investor owns 100 shares of ABC Company, which has gone up and which he thinks may decline. Consequently, he sells the 100 shares "short" and keeps them. If ABC Company stock declines, the profit on his short sale is exactly offset by the loss in the market value of the stock he owns. If the ABC Company's stock advances, the loss on his short sale is offset by the gain in the market value of the stock he has retained.

Selling Syndicate security dealers or brokers united for the purpose of distributing a new or secondary security issue to the public; also called *selling group*. The group is chosen by a syndicate manager (managing underwriter). This group usually has an established reputation for the disposition of the type of securities to be issued. If the disposition of securities comes under the supervision of the SEC, then the appointment of such a group does not occur until filing and SEC confirmation takes place. A member of the selling syndicate may have to take a position in securities that have not yet been resold to the public.

Semifixed Costs costs that rise in steps with increased levels of production; also called *Stepped Costs*.

Semivariable Costs costs that vary with changes in volume but, unlike variable costs, do not vary in direct proportion; also called *mixed costs*. In other words, these costs contain both a variable and a fixed component. Examples are the rental of a delivery truck (where a fixed rental fee plus a variable charge based on mileage is made) and power costs (where the expense consists of a fixed amount plus a variable charge based on consumption).

Sensitivity Analysis

1. in linear programming a technique for determining how the optimal solution to the linear programming problem changes if the problem data such as objective function coefficients or right-hand side values change; also called *post-optimality analysis*. To an alert accountant, the optimal solution not only

provides answers (given assumptions about resources, capacities, and prices in the problem formulation) but should raise questions about what would happen if conditions would change. Some of these changes might be imposed by the environment, such as changes in resource costs and market conditions. Some, however, represent questions raised by the manager because they are changes that the manager can initiate, such as enlarging capacities or adding new activities.

2. a form of simulation that enables decision makers to experiment with decision alternatives using a "what-if" approach. The manager might wish to evaluate alternative policies and assumptions about the external environment by asking a series of "what-if" questions. *See also* What-If Analysis.

SEP *see also* Simplified Employee Pension (SEP).

Separate Return a tax return filed by married individuals who chose to state their own income and deductions, exemptions and credits. A return filed in this manner forces both couples to either itemize deductions or use the zero bracket amount. Tax rates are generally unfavorable in comparison with joint return rates. *See also* Filing Status.

Separately Managed Accounts (SMAs) managed accounts with customized investment products in search of a performance edge or just the ability to brag about having a personal money manager. The allure of SMAs stems from their flexibility and transparency. Don't like semiconductor stocks? No problem. Your religious beliefs ban owning "sin stocks"? They're out. As for transparency, you get a list of this week's trades, the website address and the password so you can check up on your holdings. SMAs can be pricy, especially for smaller investors. While US stock mutual funds charge an average of 1.4 percent in fees, SMA fees can top 3 percent. There is disagreement on the point at which they become "fee-efficient."

Sequencing determination of the order in which a facility is to process a set of jobs.

Sequential Access the storing of records based upon some sequence determination, such as alphabetic or numeric order. Direct access file processing requires a direct access device, such as magnetic disk unit, where retrieval time can be in milliseconds as compared with several seconds or even minutes in a sequential file utilizing a tape unit. A majority of today's computerized information systems that use the direct access method also use sequential processing for some portion of the processing activities in the same information system.

Serial Port an outlet that accepts a cord for serial transmission. Different things, such as a mouse, a modem, a printer, and other assorted peripherals, can be plugged into this.

Series EE Savings Bond a U.S. government bond purchased for 50% of its face value. It pays no periodic interest, since the interest accumulates between the purchase price and the bond's maturity value. For example, a Series EE bond can be purchased for $100 and redeemed at maturity for $200.

Series HH Savings Bond a U.S. government bond issued only in exchange for Series E and EE savings bonds. It is purchased at face value and pays interest semiannually until maturity five years later. The bond can be redeemed after six months and has a maturity period of ten years.

Server a computer connected to networks of several less powerful computers that can utilize its databases and applications.

Service Bureau a service business that makes its facilities available to outsiders at a fee. An example is a service offering payroll processing. Because of economies of scale, the user will incur a lower cost from using the service than by doing it himself or herself.

Service Department a responsibility center within a factory that performs a class of service distinct from operating departments of the factory. Examples are purchasing, building and ground, personnel, and power departments. All of these activities are necessary parts of the manufacturing process and primarily supportive of production departments. Service department costs must be allocated to production departments before factory overhead rates are determined.

Service Inseparability a major characteristic of services—they are produced and consumed at the same time and cannot be separated from their providers, whether the providers are people or machines.

Service Intangibility a major characteristic of services—they cannot be seen, tasted, felt, heard, or smelled before they are bought.

Service Level the percentage of time that all orders arriving during the reorder period can be satisfied. It is computed as 1 minus the probability of being out of stock. For example, assume that a company establishes the probability of being out of stock it is willing to live with as 5 percent. Then the service level is 95 percent.

Service Perishability a major characteristic of services—they cannot be stored for later sale or use.

Service of Process the delivery of a notice or document in a suit to the opposite party to effectuate a charge against him or her with receipt of charge and to subject that person to its legal effect. The service of process gives a defendant reasonable notice of the proceedings against him or her to afford ample opportunity to appear and be heard.

Service Providers companies that give online access. There are commercial service providers and Internet service providers.

Service Sector the business sector in the economy, based on services, not manufacturing. Services are businesses such as airline travel, hotel, hospital, water parks, movies, and Disneyland.

Settlement Options the options available to the life insurance beneficiary and/or the insured concerning the form of payment of the death benefit of a life insurance policy: over fixed periods, in fixed amounts, interest only, or as income for life.

Setup Cost the cost incurred each time a batch is produced. It consists of the engineering costs of setting up the production runs or machines, paperwork costs of processing the work order, and ordering costs to provide raw materials for the batch.

Severance Pay employer compensation to an employee who has been laid off. It is supposed to help bridge the gap of the income lost while the former employee is looking for a new job. For example, a laid-off executive may receive one month's pay.

Sexual Harassment any unwelcomed sexual advances, requests for sexual favors, or other verbal or physical contact of a sexual nature existing under one of three conditions:
- Where such activity is a condition of employment.
- Where such activity has an employment consequence (promotion or dismissal).
- Where the activity creates a hostile environment.

Shadow Price not the actual price, but imputed value; that is, maximum price that management is willing to pay for an extra unit of a given limited resource.

Shakeout
> **Business:** a condition in which businesses, often in the same industry, experience a significant loss of profitability through a combination of increased competition and lower product demand. In a business shakeout, some businesses often fail.
> **Securities:** a situation in which a market suddenly experiences rapidly falling prices, accompanied by high volume, until it reaches a new trading range.

Shamrock Team a team composed of a core of members, resource experts who join the team as appropriate, and part-time/temporary members as needed.

Share one unit of ownership interest in a company, mutual fund, limited partnership, or other. In the case of ownership in a company, a stock certificate is issued including the company's name, stockholder's name, number of shares, and such information. For example, the owner of 200 shares of a company's common stock that has 10,000 shares outstanding has a 2% equity interest.

Shareholder an investor owning stock in a company.

Shares Outstanding *see* Outstanding Shares.

Shareware software that is distributed usually by modem on the honor system. It can be tried out, and if you like the program, you are asked to send the developer a fee.

Sharpe Ratio *see* Sharpe's Risk-Adjusted Return.

Sharpe's Risk-Adjusted Return risk-adjusted grades that compare five-year, risk-adjusted returns, developed by Nobel Laureate William Sharpe. The fund manager is thus able to view his excess returns per unit of risk. This measure combines standard deviation and mean total return to show a risk-adjusted measure of the fund's performance. The higher this number is, the better. Note: As a rule of thumb, a Sharpe ratio of more than 1.00 is pretty good.

Sherman Antitrust Act the act, passed in 1890, after a series of major corporate mergers. It outlaws any form of monopoly. It also outlaws acts or contracts to create monopoly and any attempt to acquire monopoly power. *See also* Antitrust Laws.

Shift in Demand increase or decrease in demand for a good brought about by a change in any factor other than the price of the product (see the following graph). These factors include (1) consumers' incomes, (2) the prices of substitute or complementary goods, and (3) consumers' tastes.

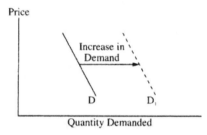

Shift in Supply increase or decrease in supply of a good brought about by a change in any factor other than the price of the product (see the following graph). These factors include (1) prices of factors of production, (2) the prices of related goods, and (3) the state of technology. A leftward (rightward) shift, or an increase (decrease) in supply implies that more (less) product is supplied than before the increase (decrease) at every price.

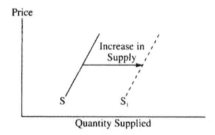

Shogun Bonds
1. foreign currency-denominated bonds issued within Japan by Japanese companies.
2. bond issued and distributed solely in Japan by a non-Japanese firm and denominated in a currency other than yen.

Shopping-Cart Analysis a process of primary marketing research in which you observe purchases in a supermarket, drugstore, or other mass-market arena. You basically analyze the contents of a shopping cart, play detective, and make some deductions about lifestyles as you observe the behaviors of shoppers.

Short

1. a stock is sold by an investor who does not have title to it. The seller anticipates a drop in price and at that time will buy the stock back. A profit is realized between the higher selling price and the lower purchase price. To sell short, an individual must have a brokerage account.
2. having insufficient funds to complete a purchase.

Short Sale a trading technique in which one sells securities investors do not own (by borrowing it from a broker) and later buying a like amount of the same security. This technique is used to make a profit from a fall in stock price. The rationale behind short selling goes as follows. We all know that the simplest way to make money in the stock market is to buy a stock at a low price and sell it later at a higher one. In a short selling situation, investors are reversing the sequence; they are selling high, expecting to buy back the stock later at what they hope will be a lower price. If the stock price falls, they make money. If it rises and they have to buy back their stocks for more than they sold it, they lose money.

Short Selling *see* Short Sale.

Shortage Costs those costs incurred when an item is out of stock, also called *stockout costs*. These costs include the lost contribution margin on sales plus lost customer goodwill.

Short-Term Capital Gain or Loss the profit or loss from selling an investment that is held one year or less. Short-term profits are considered ordinary income, while short-term losses are deducted from current income. Short-term gains or losses do not qualify for any special tax treatment.

Short-Term (or Short Run) Decisions the decisions usually involving idle capacity; a time period of a year or less during which certain factors of production are fixed and cannot be changed.

Shrinkage an excess of inventory shown on the books over actual quantities on hand. It can result from theft, evaporation, or general wear and tear.

Shutdown Costs those costs that would be incurred in the event of a temporary suspension of activities and which could be saved if operations are allowed to continue. The concept is important because of an economic principle that as long as a firm is at least covering its variable costs, it will not discontinue operations in the short run since any surplus, known as contribution margin, will be applied to the recovery of its fixed costs. *See also* Contribution Margin (CM); Contribution Margin Analysis.

Sick Leave the amount of days accumulated for possible illness based on the service period with the employer. The employee will be paid for the days he or she is sick. For example, an employer may give one sick-leave day per month to employees. Thus, 12 sick-leave days are earned per year. The employer may place a limit of 180 on total sick-leave days that can be accrued so the employee will not accumulate more. Some employers give retired people payment for all or part of their accumulated sick-leave days.

Sight Draft a written order signed by the drawer asking the drawee to pay the amount due the payee upon demand. In many cases, the drawer and payee are the same.

Sigma in statistics, the symbol for standard deviation or summation.

Signature Loan an unsecured personal loan. It requires only a borrower's signature if supported by satisfactory credit history, employment, and income.

Significance Level a value indicating the percentage of sample values that is outside certain limits, assuming the null hypothesis is correct, i.e., the probability of rejecting the null hypothesis when it is true. *See* Hypothesis Testing.

Significant important, essential, distinctive, or of sufficient nature to warrant special notice relative to a standard or norm. The deviation may be of such magnitude that its occurrence is probably not due to chance. Significant events often require disclosure in the body or footnote in the financial statements. An example of a material happening mandating disclosure is a significant lawsuit filed against the company.

Significant Testing a methodology incorporating probability theory to investigate the possible outcomes of events or population parameters to determine whether or not their occurrence is associated with chance. A popular approach entails the use of the null hypothesis (i.e., there is no difference between groups or variables). At a chosen level of significance (alpha), a sample statistic is compared with the specified population. If there is found to be a difference, the null hypothesis is rejected and the finding is significant at the given alpha level. If the null hypothesis is retained, the relationship is referred to as nonsignificant.

Silent Partner a partner in a partnership who provides funds but has no direct operational management role. A silent partner shares the net income equally with other general partners. While a silent partner is often unknown, he or she has equal liability with the partnership.

Simple Interest interest computations based only on the original principal. Compound interest is applied to the original principal and accumulated interest. For example, $100 deposited in a savings account at 10% simple interest would yield the interest of $10 per year (10% of $100). The same $100 at 10% interest compounded annually would yield $10 interest in the first year. In the second year, however, the interest will be $12.10 (10% of $110, the first year's principal and interest).

Simple Rate of Return a measure of profitability obtained by dividing the expected future annual net income by the required investment; also called *accounting* or *unadjusted rate of return*. Sometimes, the average investment rather than the original initial investment is used as the required investment, which is called *average rate of return*.

Simple Regression a regression analysis that involves one independent variable. For example, total factory overhead is related to one activity variable (either direct labor hours or machine hours). Also, the demand for automobiles is a function of its price only. *See also* Regression Analysis.

Simplex Method the technique most commonly used to solve a linear programming (LP) problem. It is an algorithm, which is a step-by-step procedure for moving from corner point to corner point of the feasible region in such a manner that successively larger (smaller) values of the objective function in a maximization (minimization) problem are obtained at each step. The procedure is guaranteed to yield the optimal solution in a finite number of steps. The simplex method is capable of solving large-scale problems while the graphical method can typically solve a two-variable problem. In practical applications of LP, computer software packages that employ the simplex method are available for obtaining optimal solutions.

Simplified Employer Pension Plan (SEP) a pension plan whereby an employer makes annual contributions on the employee's behalf to an Individual Retirement Account (IRA) set up by the employee.

Simulation an attempt to represent a real life system via a model to determine how a change in one or more variables affect the rest of the system, also called *What-If analysis*. Simulation will not provide optimization except by trial and error. It will provide comparisons of alternative systems or how a particular system works under specified conditions. It is a technique used for "what-if" scenarios. The advantages of simulations are (1) when a model has been constructed, it may be used over and over to analyze different kinds of situations, (2) it allows modeling of systems whose solutions are too complex to express by one or several mathematical relationships, (3) it requires a much lower level of mathematical skill than do optimization models, and (4) it is usually cheaper than building the actual system and testing it in operation. Financial planning models that are used to generate pro forma financial statements and help answer a variety of "what-if" questions are examples of simulations. Simulation is usually done with the help of a computer.

Simulation Models What-If models that attempt to simulate the effects of alternative management policies and assumptions about the firm's external environment. They are basically a tool for management's laboratory. It is a detailed representation of the real world. Most financial models are simulation models that are designed primarily for generating projected financial statements, budgets, and special reports, and for performing a variety of What-If analyses in an effort to find the best course of action for the company. Due to technological advances in computers (such as spreadsheets, financial modeling languages, graphics, database management systems, and networking), more and more companies are building and using modeling for their planning and decision-making efforts. Another version of simulation is Monte Carlo simulation that is used when a system has a random, or chance component.

Simultaneous Equations a set of two or more equations in an economic model which have variables in common and whose values must satisfy all of the equations simultaneously, such as demand and supply.

Sin Tax a slang term for taxes on cigarettes or alcohol.

Single Life Annuity an annuity that covers the life of a single annuitant.

Single Premium Annuity Contract an annuity purchased with a lump-sum payment, often just prior to retirement.

Sinking Fund a fund set aside for periodic payments, aimed at reducing or amortizing a financial obligation. A bond with a sinking fund provision is an example. The issuer makes periodic payments to the trustee. The trustee can retire part of the issue by purchasing the bonds in the open market. The trustee can invest the cash deposited periodically in the sinking fund in income-producing securities. The objective is to accumulate investments and investment income sufficient to retire the bonds at their maturity. A sinking fund may be established for other purposes such as for plant expansion.

Six Sigma a statistical measurement of six standard deviations from the mean. Its aim is to reduce radically the number of errors in a given production cycle. Six Sigma is a structured and disciplined, data-driven process for improving business performance.

Skewed Distribution a probability distribution that is not centered but tilted to one side or another.

Skills Inventory a listing of the skills of all employees in a company. It should consist of (1) Individual employee demographics (age, length of service); (2) Individual career progressions (jobs held, time in each job, promotions; pay rates); and (3) Individual performance data (growth in skills, accomplishments).

Skimming Pricing a pricing strategy that is used when a new product is introduced. It involves setting a high initial price primarily in order to recoup the investments in many years' research and development efforts with a progressive lowering of the price as time passes and competition sets in. The objective is to maximize short-term profits. *See also* Penetration Pricing.

SKU *see* Stock Keeping Unit.

Slide an error caused by a misplacing of a decimal point. 35.9750 recorded incorrectly as 3597.50 would be an example of a slide.

Slope the steepness and direction of the line. More specifically, the slope is the change in y for every unit change in x.

Small Business a business employing less than 100, according to the U.S. Department of Commerce. *The Small Business Review*, a quarterly newsletter published by BankOne, reports that small businesses of 2,000 or fewer employees make up 99.7% of all business in the U.S. and employ more than 50% of the nation's private sector workforce.

Small Business Corporation

1. under Internal Revenue Code section 1244, a corporation that enables the shareholders of the corporation to claim an ordinary loss (rather than a capital loss).
2. a Subchapter S corporation. For legal purposes, an S corporation is no different from other corporations. For tax purposes, however, an S corporation is a partnership. That is, corporate income and losses pass through to the shareholders' individual tax returns. To qualify as an S corporation, a company must meet the following requirements: (1) it cannot have more than thirty-five shareholders, (2) it cannot have more than one class of stock, (3) it cannot have any nonresident foreigners as shareholders, and (4) it must properly elect S corporation status.

Small Claims Court a special court designed to provide swift, inexpensive, and informal settlement of normally small financial claims between parties. Typically, the parties represent themselves. An owner of a retail store might sue a customer for nonpayment of a bill in this court.

Smart Card small plastic card resembling a credit card with a unique embeddiment of an integrated circuit of electronic data. It provides security on who uses it, how it is used, and what data are contained or stored on it.

Snail Mail any mail that is physically delivered by the postal service, as distinct from electronic mail.

Social Choice Investing investment practice that puts funds in companies investors believe have favorable environmental, social, workplace, or ethical practices. These investors hope to meet their twin goals of investing with their conscience and achieving competitive returns. In recent years, issues such as environmental concerns, gambling, employment practices, and community relations have emerged as critical issues for socially concerned investors. Social choice investing–particularly in accounts that use screens to eliminate offending companies from portfolios–has grown in popularity.

Social Engineering deceptive methods that computer hackers use to entice people to release information, such as access codes and passwords. Frequently, the crooks misrepresent themselves as technicians who need one's password for fixing a problem in a network.

Social Security the federal social security act passed in 1935 to provide supplemental retirement insurance benefits to its beneficiaries as supervised by the Social Security Administration. Employees and employers pay an equal share of the social security tax, up to a maximum level of annual income, which is then pooled in social security trust funds. Upon retirement, the employee can qualify for supplemental Social Security income depending upon the number of years worked, amounts paid into the fund, and retirement age.

Social Security Tax a tax on employers and employees on a stated percentage of salary charged by the federal government to fund the social security program and other benefits, which permits payments to currently eligible retired persons or their survivors. The social security tax is withheld from the employee's pay and, with the employer's payroll tax share, is remitted to the government periodically. *See also* FICA.

Soft Dollars

1. a financial arrangement in which services are exchanged for certain hard dollar transactions. For example, a brokerage firm may agree to provide free institutional security research to an investment adviser who performs a certain level of security trades for his or her clients with the brokerage firm.

2. indirect payments for services.

Soft Landing term used to describe, in Fed language, the economy slowing enough to eliminate the need for the Fed to further raise interest rates to dampen activity–but not enough to threaten a recession, which is what results when the economy contracts instead of expands. Hard landing, on the hand, could mean a recession.

Soft Market situation in which supply exceeds demand for securities and property. It may be characterized by one or more of the following: low trading volume, significant decline in price, and increasing spreads between bid-ask prices.

Software the instructions given to a computer to perform. Software is needed to make hardware operate. Two specific terms in connection to software are:

1. **Program**–a set of instructions that tells a computer how to perform a particular task. An example is a program for calculation of depreciation.

2. **Packages**–sets of programs to do specialize tasks, such well-known packages as Excel, QuickBooks, Peachtree, and Quicken. The term *software* applies to application programs, specialized system programs, or operating system utilities. It generates the screen menus and stores the data in a given order. Software may interact with the user.

Software Piracy the phenomenon of copying software illegally.

SOHO (Small Office/Home Office) the fastest growing type of business, thanks to the availability of inexpensive information technology, such as PCs and fax/modems; also called *TOHO* (*Tiny Office/Home Office*).

Sole Proprietorship a business or other financial venture in which a single person is the managing owner bearing full financial liability for the enterprise.

Solvency ability of long-term assets to pay long-term debt. Excessive debt may make it difficult for the company to borrow funds at reasonable interest rates during tight money markets. Solvency also relates to corporate earning power.

Sovereign Risk *see* Political Risk.

SPAM a computer term for unwanted e-mail. In a Monty Python television skit, a group of Vikings in a restaurant sing about the meat product, "Spam, spam, spam, spam, spam, spam, spam, spam, lovely spam! Wonderful spam!" until told to shut up. As a result, something that keeps being repeated to great annoyance was called *spam*, and computer programmers picked up on it. Tips to avoid getting spam:

- **Protect your e-mail address.** Spammers either buy lists of e-mail addresses or use software programs that mine the addresses from the Internet. If your address is posted in discussion groups, on websites, chat rooms, etc., chances are it will end up on one or more of these lists. Only post your address publicly when absolutely necessary.
- **Set up multiple e-mail accounts.** If you do participate regularly in online activities where you post your address, set up another e-mail account. Reveal it only to close friends and family.
- **Use spam filters.** Many e-mail programs, such as Outlook Express, have built-in tools that block messages sent from certain addresses or that filter messages based on key words you define. Check the online help files for your e-mail software.
- **Use anti-spam software.** You can install software designed to eliminate spam. Some work by matching incoming messages against a list of known spammers; others block messages that don't match an approved list of acceptable addresses. Check out the latest anti-spam programs at *Download.com*.
- **Report violators.** A number of government agencies and private groups accept complaints. Whether they can do anything to stop the deluge is an unanswered question. Forward spam to the Federal Trade Commission at *uce@ftc.gov*. Source: *about.com*.

Span of Authority, Span of Control how many subordinates a manager can effectively and efficiently supervise. Typically no more than six is recommended in order to main close control. The span of control determines how many levels and managers a company will have.

Special Drawing Rights (SDR) an artificial official reserve asset held on the books of the International Monetary Fund (IMF). Unlike gold, SDRs have no tangible life of their own and take the form of bookkeeping entries in a special account managed by the Fund. They are used as the instruments for financing international trade.

Special Purpose Entity (SPE) a type of corporate entity or limited partnership created for a specific transaction or business, especially one unrelated to a company's main business; also called *special purpose vehicle (SPV)*. Their losses and risks generally aren't recorded on a company's balance sheet. This is a separate company, usually established as a charitable trust, set up to take legal rights over assets sold to it by the parent company.

Special Purpose Vehicle (SPV) *see* Special Purpose Entity (SPE).

Specialist

In *general:* an individual who develops and is recognized for an area of expertise within a business, profession, or any other field of interest.

Securities: an individual member of a stock or commodity exchange representing one or more securities to floor brokers for a portion of their commission. It is the specialist's responsibility to maintain an orderly trading market. The specialist executes limit orders as well as buying or selling securities when prices begin to fluctuate rapidly. Such a trading environment could become disorderly without the specialist's market management. All specialists operate under the governance of their respective market's rules.

Specialty products or services that are either unique in the marketplace, are in limited supply, or have brand identification for which a significant group of buyers is willing to make a special purchase effort.

Specialty Shop, Store any retailer that carries a narrow product line with a deep assortment within that line.

Speculation investing capital in any type of property or security with the anticipation of making a fast, significant, short-term profit through a price change. Speculation often involves a high degree of risk.

Speech Recognition Software program in which verbal commands activate the computer to perform functions.

Speed Limit the rate at which the economy can grow without triggering inflation.

Spillover any effect, negative or positive, that a business can have on its neighboring businesses.

Spinoff a type of corporate reorganization in which the original corporation transfers some of its assets to a newly formed corporation in exchange for all of the latter's capital stock, which it then distributes to its shareholders as a property dividend.

Split the amendment of a firm's charter to increase (split up) or decrease (split down) the number of authorized shares. It requires stockholder approval. If a company with one million shares did a two-for-one split, the company would have two million shares. An investor, for example, with 100 shares before the split would hold 200 shares after the split. The investor's percentage of equity in the company remains the same. Note: For a stock split announcements, go to *www.stocksplits.net/*.

Split Dollar Life Insurance an insurance policy whose premiums, rights, and death proceeds are split between parties (e.g., employer and employee, husband and wife, parent and child). The employer pays part of the premiums at a minimum equal to the increase in cash value. The employee may pay the balance of the premium, or it may be paid in full by the employer. If the increase in cash value equals or exceeds the yearly premium, the employer pays the entire premium.

Spoilage production that does not result in good finished goods. The amount of spoilage can be considered either normal or abnormal. Spoilage can be classified into the following categories:

1. **Spoiled goods**–goods that do not meet production standards and are either sold for their salvage value or discarded.
2. **Defective units**–goods that do not meet standards and are sold at a reduced price or reworked and sold at the regular or a reduced price.
3. **Waste**–material that is lost in the manufacturing process by shrinkage, evaporation, etc.
4. **Scrap**–by-product of the manufacturing process that has a minor market value.

Spot Market cash market for immediate delivery, as opposed to a futures market that provides the delivery at a future date.

Spot Rate the exchange rate of one commodity for another for immediate delivery; also called *Cash Rate*.

Spot Transaction transaction involving the purchase and sale of commodities, currency, and financial instruments for immediate delivery; also called *Cash Transaction*. This contrasts with a forward transaction which provides the delivery at a future date.

Spread
1. the difference between the bid and ask prices of a security; also called *Bid/Ask Spread*.
2. the difference between the purchase price paid by an investment banking firm and expected resale price of a new issue of securities.
3. the difference in yield between various grades of securities at comparable maturity dates.

Spreadsheet a table of numbers arranged in rows and columns. Spreadsheets have long been used for accounting and financial calculations. However, manual spreadsheet calculations can be time consuming and tedious, especially when changing a single number can affect the results in many different rows and columns. Therefore, it helps greatly to have a computer program perform the spreadsheet calculations. Many software packages are now available that turn the computer into an electronic spreadsheet. Some of the popular spreadsheet packages are Lotus 1-2-3, QuatrroPro, and Excel. These programs are excellent tools for a variety of "what-if" experiments, financial projections, and various accounting applications. It is one of the four popular applications of software programs: spreadsheets, word processing, desktop publishing, and database management.

Spyders *see* Standard & Poor's Depositary Receipts (SPDR).

Staff Authority the authority to give advice, support, and service to line departments. Staff managers do not command others. Examples of staff authority are found in personnel, purchasing, engineering, and finance. The management accounting function is usually "staff" with responsibility for providing line managers and also other staff people with a specialized service. The service includes budgeting, controlling, pricing, and special decisions. *See also* Line Authority.

Stagflation the incidence of rising prices during a slowdown in business activity. It is a combination of stagnation and inflation; the existence of high unemployment and recession at the same time as high rates of inflation. *See also* Inflation; Recession.

Stagnation a situation where output does not grow over a period of time. Such an economy is in a prolonged slump of the business cycle.

Stakeholder any group or individual that has an interest in a company.

Standard a quantitative expression of a performance objective, such as standard hours of labor allowed for actual production or a standard purchase price of materials per unit. Sometimes the terms *standard* and *budget* are used interchangeably. For example, budgeted sales revenue could be used as a standard in evaluating the performance of the marketing department. A standard is set for the following three reasons: (1) to measure performance of a responsibility center, (2) to simplify recordkeeping, and (3) to improve performance by taking appropriate remedial action on an unfavorable deviation from the standard.

Standard & Poor's 500 Stock Composite (S&P 500) the 500 Stock Composite Index calculated by Standard & Poor's. It differs from the Dow Jones Industrial Average (DJIA) in several important ways. First, it is a value-weighted, rather than price-weighted, index. This means that the index considers not only the price of a stock but also the number of shares outstanding. That is to say, it is based on the aggregate market value of the stock; i.e., price times number of shares. An advantage of the index over the DJIA is that stock splits and stock dividends do not affect the index value. A disadvantage is that large capitalization stocks–those with a large number of shares outstanding–heavily influence the index value. The S&P 500 actually consists of four separate indexes: the 400 industrials, the 40 utilities, the 20 transportation, and the 40 financial. *See also* Market Indexes and Averages.

Standard & Poor's Depositary Receipt (SPDR) shares of a security designed to track the value of the S&P 500; also called *SPDRs* or *Spiders*. Spiders trade on the American Stock Exchange under the symbol SPY. One SPDR unit is valued at approximately one-tenth of the value of the S&P 500. Dividends are distributed quarterly, and are based on the accumulated stock dividends held in trust, less any expenses of the trust.

Standard Deduction a deduction allowed to an individual taxpayer if the taxpayer does not elect to itemize deductions; previously called the *zero bracket amount* (*ZBA*). This standard deduction is incorporated into the tax rate and table schedules. A taxpayer who elects to itemize deductions may deduct only the excess over the standard deduction amount to determine taxable income.

Standard Deviation a statistic that measures the tendency of data to be spread out. Accountants can make important inferences from past data with this measure. It is commonly used as an absolute measure of risk. The higher the standard deviation, the higher the risk.

Standard Error a measure of the degree to which a calculated statistic is dispersed around its mean value.

Standard Industrial Classification Code (SIC) a digital coding system that classifies industry types and firms into groups and subgroups.

Standard Metropolitan Statistical Area (SMSA) socioeconomic census areas defined by population and economic-geographic characteristics. This designation by the U.S. Census Bureau of a geographic area is helpful to businesses particularly for advertising.

Standard of Living
Nationally: the degree of prosperity enjoyed in a country. Measures of the standard of living include diet, housing conditions, quality of medical care, educational system, transportation communication systems, and others.
Personally: the quality of life enjoyed by an individual. This is determined by the amount of disposable income, housing conditions, clothing, education, personal automobile, and similar measures.

State Unemployment Compensation compensation, paid to eligible unemployed individuals, financed by a payroll tax levied on employers by the various states. Some variation exists as to the filing and payment requirements among different states.

Stated Capital
1. amount of capital contributed by stockholders of a corporation. It may also refer to the method of valuating no-par-value stock where the portion of the amount contributed is credited to the capital stock account and the balance is credited to paid-in-surplus.

2. legal capital.

Stated Liability the amounts listed for liabilities in the various financial records and statements without audit or verification. They are subject to future adjustment or correction. It is basically a face value observation of liabilities.

State-Directed Economy an economy in which the state plays a proactive role in influencing the direction and magnitude of private sector investments.

Statement
1. a formal document presenting the financial condition and operating performance of an enterprise. These include the income statement, balance sheet, statement of changes in financial position, and may include documents for internal use, such as performance appraisals, budgets, etc.
2. a summary statement documenting the terms, conditions, or status of an account. An example is a statement of retail credit account status.
3. a verbal utterance or proposition.

Statement of Cash Flows a required statement prepared by a company in its annual report showing cash flow from operating, investing, and financing activities. The statement shows the cash receipts and cash payments of the company, and can be analyzed by the investor to appraise the firm's liquidity posture. Cash is defined in this statement as cash plus short-term marketable securities having a maturity of three months or less. Note the following example:

GOLD MEDAL ATHLETIC APPAREL CO. Statement of Cash Flows For the Year Ended December 31, 20x6			
Cash flows from operating activities:			
Net income, per income statement		$125,800	
Add: Depreciation	$92,000		
Increase in accounts payable	25,500		
Decrease in accounts receivable	34,700	152,200	
		$278,000	
Deduct: Increase in merchandise inventory	$13,900		
Increase in prepaid expenses	2,000	(15,900)	
Net cash flow from operating activities			$262,100
Cash flows from investing activities:			
Cash paid for equipment		($244,500)	
Net cash flow used for investing activities			(244,500)
Cash flows from financing activities:			
Cash received from sale of common stock		$250,000	
Less: Cash paid for dividends	$88,000		
Cash paid to retire mortgage note	205,000	(293,000)	
Net cash flow used in financing activities			(43,000)
Decrease in cash			($25,400)
Cash at the beginning of the year			257,900
Cash at the end of the year			$232,500

Statement of Functional Expenses a statement of the nonprofit organization's expenses designated by object classifications (e.g., legal fees, salaries, supplies, etc.). These expenses are allocated into three functions: program services, management and general, and fundraising.

Statement of Revenue, Expenses, and Changes in Net Assets; or Fund Balances a required financial statement of nonprofit organizations showing operating performance.

Static Budget a budget based on one level of activity (e.g., one particular volume of sales or production). It has two characteristics: (1) a flexible budget is geared toward only one level of activity, and (2) actual results are compared against budgeted (standard) costs only at the original budget activity level. A flexible budget differs from a static budget on both scores. First, it is not geared to only one activity level, but rather, toward a range of activities. Second, actual results are not compared against budgeted costs at the original budget activity level. Managers look at what activity level was attained during a period and then turn to the flexible budget to determine what costs should have been at that actual level of activity. *See also* Flexible Budget.

Statistic numerical characteristic of a sample (taken from a population) computed using only the elements of a sample of the population. For example, the mean and the mode are statistics of the sample.

Statistical Control Chart a management control tool that shows results of measurements over a period of time, with statistically determined upper and lower limits; or simply a control chart. Control charts provide a visual means of determining whether a specific process is in control (i.e., staying within predetermined bounds).

Statistical Significance meaning "meaningful or material" statistically instead of intuitively or subjectively. A variety of statistical tests are available to test statistical significance of a particular hypothesis. *See also* Hypothesis Testing; Significance Level; t-Test.

Statistical Inference the process of making inferences about populations from information contained in samples.

Statistical Software computer software that applies statistics to economic and business analysis, specifically for market analysis, business and economic forecasting, and statistical modeling. Popular packages include SAS, Minitab, and SPSS.

Statistics field of study concerning information calculated from sample data. The field is divided into two categories: descriptive statistics and inferential statistics. Both are widely used in business.

Status Pricing *see* Prestige Pricing.

Statute of Limitations a statutory time limitation for assessing or prosecuting an infringement, improper act, or civil or criminal offense. Notification or proceedings must be brought prior to the expiration date of the applicable federal, state, or local statute of limitations. For example, except for tax fraud, the internal revenue service must assess income taxes within three years after the tax return was filed. In the case where income is underreported by 25% or more, the statute of limitations is six years. Most states allow up to six years to file a claim for violation of a written contract and five years for civil (tort) liability claims.

Step Costs costs that are approximately fixed over a small range of volume, but are variable over a large volume of range. For example, supervision costs are fixed for a given range of production volume, but increased production often requires additional work shifts leading to added supervisory costs in a lump sum fashion.

Stepwise Regression a form of multiple regression analysis in which explanatory variables are added one at a time to the regression equation until some goodness-of-fit criterion (usually in terms of explanatory power and statistical significance) is satisfied.

Stereotyping the process of categorizing or labeling people on the basis of a single attribute or characteristic. Common attributes from which people often stereotype are race and gender. Of course, stereotypes along these lines are inaccurate and can be harmful.

Stock
1. shares of capital of a publicly traded corporation. The two types of stock include common stock and preferred stock. Stock is traded in a stock exchange.
2. certificate of one unit of ownership in a company. It is the capital a company raises by selling shares.

Stock Appreciation Rights rights given to employees to receive cash or stock, in any combination thereof (determined at grant date or when exercised), in an amount equivalent to the excess of market price on a specified number of shares of the corporation's stock above an option price.

Stock Buyback a company's buying of its own stock on the open market. This is done for several reasons: (1) to increase the price of the remaining stock, (2) to make it more difficult for the company to be taken over by another company, and (3) to use excess cash so as to increase its asset turnover.

Stock Company a firm having capital that is in the form of shares with transferable ownership rights.

Stock Dividend pro rata distribution of additional shares of a corporation's own stock to its stockholders (or a subsidiary's shares being spun off) instead of cash. A stock dividend may be declared when the cash position of the firm is inadequate and/or when the company wishes to prompt more trading by reducing the market price of stock. A small stock dividend (less than 20%-25% of the shares outstanding at the date of declaration) decreases retained earnings and increases the capital accounts (capital stock and paid-in capital) for an amount equal to the fair value of the shares issued. A large stock dividend (in excess of 20%-25% of shares outstanding) decreases retained earnings and increases capital stock at the par or stated value only. If a company with 500,000 shares outstanding declares a 10% stock dividend, the total shares for the stock dividend will be 50,000. From a tax perspective, the stockholder is not taxed on the stock received until the time it is sold whereas a cash dividend is taxable income in the year received.

Stock Exchange a marketplace in which buyers and sellers are brought together to trade securities, such as the New York Stock Exchange (NYSE).

Stock Keeping Unit (SKU) a specific item that a reseller stocks (for example, a 5,000-watt Dayton professional duty, portable, gasoline power generator is an SKU). It refers to a specific identifying stock number for each separate product carried out by store.

Stock Market a market in which securities are traded. All stock markets are ruled by boards of governors. Securities traded include common stock, convertibles, preferred stock, rights, and warrants. The principal stock markets in the United States are the New York Stock Exchange, the American Stock Exchange, and the NASDAQ (over-the-counter) market.

Stock Option the right to buy or sell a stock at a particular price within a given time period. A stock option enables one to speculate in stocks with a minimal investment. There is great potential for return. However, the entire investment may be lost if the stock does not move sufficiently in the right direction. Stock options can also be used to hedge one's position in other securities. *See also* Call; Put.

Stock Right a privilege giving a current stockholder the first right to buy shares in a new offering below the market price, thus maintaining the stockholder's proportionate ownership interest; also called *preemptive right*. Assume an investor owns 1% of Company ABC. If the company issues 10,000 additional shares, the investor may receive a stock rights offering—an opportunity to buy 1%, or 100 shares, of the new issue. The right enables the investor to buy new common stock at a subscription price for a short time, typically no more than several weeks. The subscription price (exercise price) is typically lower than the public offering price of the stock. A single right is the privilege applicable to the holder of one old share of capital stock to purchase a certain number of shares of new capital stock.

Stock Split issuance of a substantial amount of additional shares, thus reducing the par value of the stock on a proportionate basis. A stock split also means that dividends per share will also fall proportionately. No journal entry need to be made, because the company's accounts do not change. However, there should be a memorandum entry describing the stock split. A stock split is often prompted by a desire to reduce the market price per share in order to stimulate investor buying.

Stockholder/Shareholder a term describing those individuals or organizations owning an interest in a publicly held corporation by owning shares of stock issued by the company. The shares of ownership are certified by stock certificates in the owners' names. A stockholder/shareholder has limited liability and is not legally responsible for corporate liabilities while still enjoying full corporate ownership privileges and rights. Stockholders share in the financial success of the company in the form of dividends and appreciation in the market price of the stock.

Stockholders of Record holders of stock as of the date of record and who are entitled to receive a cash dividend already declared. For example, on January 8, the board of directors of a company declared a $.30 per share cash dividend on its common stock payable on February 18 to stockholders of record on January 20. The common stockholders who are on the company's records on January 20 will receive the $.30 dividend per share on February 18 (date of payment). Stockholders of record are also entitled to rights, voting privileges, and dividends in other than cash.

Stockholder's Equity the sum of all outstanding stock, common and preferred shares, and retained earnings. Equity is a residual claim against the assets of the business after the total liabilities are deducted. Example: The equity of the owners of the business is quite similar to the equity commonly referred to with respect to home ownership. If you were to buy a house for $150,000 by putting down 20 percent, i.e., $30,000 of your own money and borrowing $120,000 from a bank, you would say that your equity in the $150,000 house was $30,000.

Stockout Cost those costs incurred when an item is out of stock, also called *stockout costs*; also called *shortage costs*. These costs include the lost contribution margin on sales plus lost customer goodwill.

Stop Payment instruction to the bank not to honor a check when presented. As long as the check has not been cashed, the maker has up to six months to present a stop payment notice. However, a stop payment right does not apply to electronic funds transfers.

Stop-Loss Protection

Securities: a stop limit order that is triggered when a security's price falls below the stop price whereupon the order becomes a market order to sell. The purpose of stop-loss protection is to preserve a profit or prevent a loss.

Reinsurance: protection for a reinsurance company against a maximum level of losses from an insurance company when losses exceed a certain percentage of the premium.

Stores
1. raw materials, supplies, and parts.
2. a control account for all purchases of materials and supplies. All purchases of materials, parts, and supplies are charged to Stores as purchased because the storekeeper is accountable for them. The Stores Control account is supported by an underlying subsidiary ledger, called *store cards*.
3. retail outlets.

Straddle to combine a call and put on the identical stock with the same expiration date and strike price. It is employed to take advantage of significant variability in stock price. High beta (a measure of volatility) stocks might be most suited for this. A significant price movement on one side will cover the cost of obtaining the options.

Straight Bankruptcy known as Chapter 7, a legal proceeding that results in "wiping the slate clean and starting anew." It aims at providing individual debtors a fresh start, calling for liquidation of all but essential assets such as, (with some exceptions) house, car, and household belongings. Businesses using this option are closing down. Protection under Chapter 7 cannot be sought again for six years.

Straight Life (Pure) Annuity an annuity that pays a fixed amount every month until the annuitant's death, with no refund to any other person.

Straight Rebuy a business buying situation in which the buyer routinely reorders something without any modification.

Straight-Line Depreciation the depreciation method where an equal amount of depreciation expense is allocated to each full period of the asset's useful life. The amount of depreciation expense by straight-line is computed as follows:

Annual depreciation = (Original cost - salvage value)/ Useful life

For example, assume that the asset costs $1,000 and has an estimated useful life of five years. The estimated salvage value at the end of the five-year period is $100. Then the straight-line depreciation per year is ($1,000 - $100)/5 years = $180/year.

Strategic Alliance an agreement of two or more companies with complementary core competencies to jointly contribute to the value chain.

Strategic Business Units (SBU) an operating unit in an organization that sells a distinct set of products or services to an identified group of customers in competition with a well-defined set of competitors. SBUs operate within the objectives and strategy set by top management. Within the framework, each SBU performs its own strategic management process. For example, SBUs of General Electric are aircraft engines, appliances, broadcasting, industrial, materials, power systems, technical, and capital services.

Strategic Cost Management managerial use of cost information for the purpose(s) of establishing organizational strategy, controlling the methods to achieve the strategies, and evaluating the level of success in meeting the proclaimed strategies. Its goal is to develop and identify superior strategies that will produce a sustainable competitive advantage.

Strategic Decision Making choosing among alternative strategies with the goal of selecting a strategy, or strategies, that provides a company with reasonable assurance of long-term growth and survival.

Strategic Human Resource Planning the process by which an organization ensures that it has the right number and kinds of people, capable of effectively and efficiently completing those tasks that are in direct support of the company's mission.

Strategic Management the process by which top management determines the long-run direction and performance of the organization by ensuring that careful formulation, effective implementation, and continuous evaluation of the strategy takes place.

Strategic Planning the implementation of an organization's objectives. In any organization, strategic planning occurs in two phases: (1) deciding on the products to produce and/or the services to render and (2) deciding on the marketing and/or manufacturing strategy to follow in getting the intended product or service to the proper audience. Strategic planning decisions will have long-term impacts on the organization while operational decisions are day-to-day in nature.

Strategy the determination and evaluation of alternatives available to an organization for achieving its objectives and mission and the selection of the alternative to be pursued.

Strategy Formulation making decisions to define an organization's philosophy and mission, establish objectives, and select the strategy to be used in achieving the objectives.

Strategy Implementation making decisions to match strategy and organizational structure and developing budgets, functional strategies, and motivational systems.

Street Smart intelligence gained from field experience rather than from formal education.

Strike Price the price at which a call option or a put option can be exercised, normally at a price set close to the market price of the stock at the time the option is issued; also called *Striking Price* or *Exercise Price*. It is the exercise price for an option.

STRIPS (Separate Trading Registered Interest and Principal of Securities) zero-coupon bonds sold by the U.S. Treasury and created by stripping the coupons from a Treasury bond and selling them separately from the principal; also called *Strip*.

Strong Dollar *see* Appreciation of the Dollar.

Structural Inflation a general rise in prices that arise when producers are unable to adjust production quickly to changes in the structure of the economy. The causes for this type of inflation include changes in the demand for a product, in the technology of its production, and in the competition facing the producers. *See also* Inflation.

Structural Unemployment unemployment resulting from changes in the long-term demand for products or technology, which lead to an over-supply of labor with particular skills and education or in particular regions. For example, NASA engineers were left unemployed at the end of the race to the moon. *See also* Unemployment.

Structured Data that subset of a company's data that is stored electronically in databases and thus can be accessed by data field.

Student Loan Marketing Association (Sallie Mae) Securities purchases by the Student Loan Marketing Association (Sallie Mae) of loans made by financial institutions under a variety of federal and state loan programs. Sallie Mae securities are not guaranteed, but are generally insured by the federal government and its agencies. These securities include floating rate and fixed rate obligations with maturities of five years or more as well as discount notes with maturities from a few days to 360 days.

Student's T a statistical test between the means of two distributions to see how alike or not they are.

Subchapter S Corporation form of corporation whose stockholders are permitted by the Internal Revenue Service to be taxed as partners. That is, income is taxed as direct income of the shareholders, regardless of whether it is actually distributed to them. To qualify as an S corporation, a company cannot have more than thirty-five shareholders, cannot have more than one class of stock, cannot have any nonresident foreigners as shareholders, and it must properly elect S corporation status. The key advantage of this form of organization is that the shareholders receive all the organizational benefit of a corporation while escaping the double taxation of a corporation.

Suboptimization optimization of the goals of different departments of the entire organization. Suboptimization occurs when different subunits each attempt to reach a solution that is optimal for that unit but that may not be optimum for the organization as a whole. For example, the quality control department of a factory may want to introduce a program that would guarantee every bulb that is produced is perfect. However, the higher cost and the resulting high price would lead to a disaster for the overall company in the form of lower sales.

Subordinated Debt debt whose holders have a claim on the firm's assets only after the claims of holders of senior debt (the debt to which the subordinated debt is junior) have been satisfied. The subordinated debt holder is in a much riskier position than the senior debt holders.

Subscript and Superscript in math or footnoting, small numbers or letters just a little lower or higher than normal.

Subscription
1. agreeing to purchase a security.
2. making a pledge to give a contribution to an organization for a cause (e.g., charity).
3. subscribing to periodicals.

Subsidiary Company a company in which a controlling interest in its stock is owned by another company, called the *parent company*. After acquisition, the parent company accounts for its investment in the subsidiary company, including intercompany eliminations. *See also* Consolidation.

Substitution
Securities:
1. the exchange of securities. For example, a security analyst recommends replacing one stock in an industry by another in that same industry.
2. the replacement of a different security of the same value for another security serving as collateral in a margin account.
Law: replacement of one party to a contract by another.
Banking: replacement of the original collateral by another collateral.

Subsystem any system that is a part of a larger system. For example, the financial, marketing, accounting, and production systems are subsystems or components of a management information system (MIS).

Suite a group of general software applications packaged together as a combined unit, such as spreadsheets, word-processing, and database management all in one.

Sum-of-the-Year's-Digits Depreciation (SYD) an accelerated depreciation method where the amounts recognized in the early periods of an asset's useful life are greater than those recognized in the later periods. That fraction is formed with the numerator being the year in question and the denominator being the sum of the asset's years of useful life.

Sunk Cost the cost of resources that have already been incurred at some point in the past whose total will not be affected by any decision made now or in the future. Sunk costs are usually past or historical costs. For example, suppose you acquired a machine for $50,000 three years ago that has a book value of $20,000. The $20,000 book value is a sunk cost that does not affect a future decision that involves replacement of this machine.

Sunset Provision a provision in the law that ends at a specific time.

Supercomputer the most powerful class of computers, used by large organizations, research institutions, and universities for complex scientific computations and the manipulation of huge databases.

Supplementary Statement schedules or statements that amplify, elaborate on, or detail the income statement, balance sheet, and statement of changes in financial position. An example is an inflation-adjusted statement.

Supply the amounts of a good or service that producers are willing and able to offer to the market at various prices during a specified period of time.

Supply Chain interdependent collection of organizations that supply materials, products, or services to a customer.

Supply Chain Management (SCM) managing upstream and downstream value-added flows of materials, final goods, and related information among suppliers, the company, resellers, and final consumers. It is a set of programs undertaken to increase the efficiency of distribution systems that move products from the producer's facilities to the end user. By sharing information, production lead times and inventory holding costs are reduced, while on-time deliveries to customers are improved. SCM software systems support the planning of the best way to fill orders and help the tracking of products and components among companies in the supply chain. Example: Wal-Mart and Procter & Gamble (P&G) are two companies that have become well known for their cooperation in the use of SCM. When P&G products are scanned at a Wal-Mart store, P&G receives information on the sale via satellite and, thus, learns when to make more products and to which specific Wal-Mart stores the products should be shipped. Related cost savings are passed on, at least in part, to Wal-Mart customers.

Supply Chain Management (SCM) Software software that facilitates supply chain management function seamlessly. SCM is the organization of activities between a company and its suppliers in an effort to provide for the profitable development, production, and delivery of goods to customers. By sharing information, production lead times and inventory holding costs are reduced, while on-time deliveries to customers are improved. SCM software systems support the planning of the best way to fill orders and help tracking of products and components among companies in the supply chain. Wal-Mart and Procter & Gamble (P&G) are two companies that have become well known for their cooperation in the use of SCM. When P&G products are scanned at a Wal-Mart store, P&G receives information on the sale via satellite and, thus, learns when to make more product and to which specific Wal-Mart stores the product should be shipped. Related cost savings are passed on, at least in part, to Wal-Mart customers.

Supply Curve a graphical representation of the quantity of a good or service supplied at different price levels, holding other things equal, (normally with price on the vertical axis and quantity supplied measured along the horizontal axis). The positive relationship between these two variables is reflected by the fact that the supply curve slopes upwards from left to right.

Supply Shock disturbance caused by events external to the economy, such as changes in commodity prices (e.g., oil, coffee, or gold) and exchange rates.

Supply-Side Economics an approach to economics that aims at achieving efficiency through policies designed to stimulate production. It involves cutting taxes on individuals and businesses so there will be greater stimulus to produce more goods and services. Unlike demand-side economics that focuses on regulating aggregate demand, supply-side economics relies heavily on the direct use of incentives. For example, reductions in marginal tax rates—the taxes paid on the last dollar of taxable income—provide direct incentives to work, save, and invest, thereby stimulating aggregate supply rather than aggregate demand. Tight monetary control to curb inflation is another principal prescription of supply-side economics.

Supply-Siders followers of the supply-side economic principles.

Surplus
1. earned surplus or retained earnings reflecting the accumulated net income less dividend distributions.
2. capital surplus, the stockholders' equity in a corporation in excess of par or stated value of capital stock.

Surtax an additional tax applied to income above some specified figure resulting in a higher effective tax rate.

Survey of Current Business a publication by the Bureau of Economic Analysis of the U.S. Department of Commerce, which is published monthly and contains monthly and quarterly raw economic data. It presents a monthly update and evaluation of the business situation, analyzing such data as GDP, business inventories, personal consumption, fixed investments, exports, labor market statistics, financial data, and much more.

Sushi Bonds Eurodollars, or other non-yen denominated, bonds issued by a Japanese company for sale to Japanese investors.

Sustainable Growth

1. the rate of growth in earnings that needs to be sustained to keep the market value of the firm (or to maintain its shareholder value).
2. a steady rate of economic growth that can continue for a long period of time.

Swap

1. an agreement by two parties to exchange a series of cash flows.
2. the selling of one security and buying of another security for the purpose of improving overall yield with little or no market or credit risk.

Sweat Equity the equity in property created by the investment of work in it by the buyer or holder, which directly increases the value of the asset.

Sweep Account a bank account in which excess funds are automatically transferred into an interest-earning account at the same bank.

SWOT an acronym for a company's strengths (S), weaknesses (W), opportunities (O), and threats (T).

SWOT Analysis analysis of a company's strengths (S) and weaknesses (W) in light of the threats (T) and opportunities (O) presented by the environment. A SWOT analysis stresses that the organizational strategies must result in a proper fit between the organization's internal and external environments. For example, as the usage of the Internet and electronic commerce continues to rise, a software company tries to extend its exploitation of this market by acquiring and merging with companies with specialized web expertise, such as an Internet service provider, makers of a web page creation system, makers of object-oriented programming software, and makers of Internet commerce software.

SYD *see* Sum-of-the-Year's-Digits Depreciation (SYD).

Syndicated Loan a big size loan made by a group of banks to a large multinational corporation or government. It allows the group to spread the risk of loan default.

Syndicates

Securities: a group of investment bankers brought together for the purpose of underwriting a large block of an outstanding issue.

Real estate: a limited partnership that invests in various types of real estate and is professionally managed. It is registered with the SEC and includes a great number of limited partners.

Synergy, Synergism from Greek: "to work together." A merger of comparable companies resulting in operational efficiencies and cost reduction such as by eliminating duplication. It is an idea that " 2 plus 2 is greater than 4."

System Software software that consists of utilities, device drivers, language translators, and operating systems. Operating systems manage resources, provide user interface, and run applications.

Systematic Risk a risk that results from forces outside of a firm's control, also called *nondiversifiable, noncontrollable risk*. Purchasing power, interest rate, and market risks fall in this category. This type of risk is assessed relative to the risk of the market portfolio or of a diversified portfolio of securities. It is measured by the beta (b) used in the Capital Asset Pricing Model (CAPM). The systematic risk is simply a measure of a security's volatility relative to that of an average security. For example, b=0.5 means the security is only half as volatile, or risky, as the average security; b=1.0 means the security is of average risk; and b=2.0 means the security is twice as risky as the average risk. The higher the beta, the higher the return required.

Systems Analyst one who is engaged in systems analysis that involves identification, measurement, and recommendation of system alternatives to management for final selection. After an intensive investigation of the information needs of the different levels of management, the systems analysts should identify the available system alternatives. These include (1) the acquisition of a new system; (2) the modification of the old system; and (3) the use of a third party's services, such as a timeshare outside service bureau, which could eliminate or continue the use of the old system. For each available alternative, feasibility studies should be conducted before a recommendation is made to management for final selection.

t Distribution a probability distribution that closely approximates the normal distribution; also called *Student's distribution*. In general, the t-distribution is flatter than the normal distribution and fat in tail areas, and there is a separate t distribution for each of the possible sample sizes (or degrees of freedom). The t-distribution is used to establish confidence intervals when using small samples (30 or less) to estimate a true population mean.

T-Account a typical accounting form resembling a capital T. The account name is given on the top (e.g., cash), the left side of the account is called a debit, and the right side is called a credit. Each item on the income statement and balance sheet has its own account. A T-account takes the following form:

Cash

debit	credit
(left side)	(right side)

Tactical Planning covering a relatively short period of time, is primarily concerned with how to attain objectives, and is usually very specific in nature.

Taft-Hartley Act legislation enacted in 1947 to amend the National Labor Relations Act to limit some of the more aggressive union labor activities.

Taguchi Method of Quality Control a method of controlling quality, developed by Genichi Taguchi, a past winner of the Deming Award, that emphasizes robust quality design and the quality loss function (QLF). Taguchi claims that quality is greatly determined at the design level. In addition to quality control in production, he emphasizes quality control in four other functions: (1) product planning, (2) product design, (3) process design, and (4) production service after purchase. Further, Taguchi's QLF quantitatively measures the success or failure of quality control. The traditional view is that any product that measures within the upper and lower specification limits is "good," and a product outside the limits is "bad." In contrast, the QLF presumes that any deviation from the target specification is important since it means economic losses for the customer. Furthermore, the economic losses increase quadratically as the actual value deviates from the target value.

Takeover a form of acquisition usually followed by a merger. Takeover can be hostile or friendly. The public tender offer is a means of acquiring a target firm against the wishes of management. A friendly takeover is when the acquiring firm negotiates with the targeted company and common agreement is reached in an amiable atmosphere for subsequent approval by shareholders. *See also* Proxy Fight.

Tangent (Line) the straight line that passes through the point on a curve and that has a slope that is the same as the slope of the curve at that point:

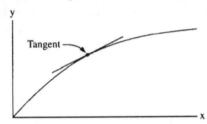

Tangible Assets tangible items of real and personal property that generally have a long life, such as housing and other real estate, automobiles, jewelry, cash, and other physical assets.

Target Costing
1. a method of determining the cost of a product or service based on the price that the customers are willing to pay. It is a Japanese method of determining the maximum available cost of a product before it is designed, engineered, or produced by subtracting an acceptable rate of profit margin from a projected selling price.
2. the target price minus desired profit margin.
3. sometimes used interchangeably with *standard costing.*

Target Income the amount of income an organization is trying to achieve during a particular period. The specification of target income may be based upon a desired rate of return on invested money (for example, 20% return on investment) or a growth in earnings per share (EPS). The target income may be also specified as a percentage of sales (for example, 15% of sales).

Target Marketing breaking a total market into market segments representing smaller homogeneous markets. Once these segments are identified, they are targeted for a particular product or service based on conformity of their homogeneous characteristics to the product or service specifications. Target marketing involves tailoring a marketing mix (product, price, place, and promotion) to their needs and preferences.

Target Price expected market price for a product, given the company's knowledge of its customers and competitors.

Target Pricing a pricing method that involves (1) identifying the price at which a product will be competitive in the marketplace, (2) defining the desired profit to be made on the product, and (3) computing the target cost for the product by subtracting the desired profit from the competitive market price. The formula is as follows:

$$\text{Target Price - Desired Profit} = \text{Target Cost}$$

Target cost is then given to the engineers and product designers, who use it as the maximum cost to be incurred for the materials and other resources needed to design and manufacture the product. It is their responsibility to create the product at or below its target cost.

Target Return Pricing method of pricing that seeks to achieve a targeted rate of return on a firm's capital for specific products, product groups, and divisions. The pricing formula can be stated as follows:

$$\text{Price} = \frac{\text{Total cost + (Target rate of return x Total capital employed)}}{\text{Sales volume in units}}$$

Most firms tend to use stockholders' equity plus long-term debt in measuring return on capital. Example: A single-product firm's total cost is $350,000, total capital employed is $1,250,000, the planned sales volume is 50,000 units, and the target rate of return is 20%. Then the price would be:

$$\text{Price} = \frac{\$350,000 + (20\% \times \$1,250,000)}{50,000 \text{ units}} = \frac{\$60,000}{50,000} = \$12$$

See also Rate of Return Pricing.

Targeted Stock *see* Tracking Stock.

Tariff

1. a tax on imports or exports, most often calculated as a percent of the price charged for the good by the foreign supplier. The money collected is duty. A tariff may be imposed as a source of revenue for the government. However, a more common purpose of tariffs is protection against foreign competition. By raising prices of imported goods relative to the prices of domestically goods, tariffs encourage domestic consumers to buy domestic rather than foreign products.

2. schedule of rates or fares in the transportation industry.

Tax Anticipation Bill (TAB) short-term obligation issued by the U.S. Treasury to raise funds during a period when tax receipts are not large enough to cover current disbursements. TABs mature approximately one week after quarterly corporate tax payments are due. The attractiveness of TABs is that the government will accept them in payment for taxes at their face value.

Tax Anticipation Note (TAN) a short-term debt instrument issued by a municipality in order to raise funds to cover shortages prior to tax receipts. TAN debt is retired once individual and corporate tax revenues are received.

Tax Avoidance paying the least tax possible by using legal tax planning opportunities such as estate planning. Engaging in tax avoidance measures is not in any way construed as betraying or shirking a public or patriotic duty. In fact, a majority of court decisions have supported this assertion. Tax evasion, in contrast, utilizes illegal methods to achieve this end.

Tax Benefit Rule the rule that amounts received in one period representing a recovery of an amount deducted in a prior year are to be included in income to the extent that the prior deduction resulted in a decrease in taxable income in that year.

Tax Credit an amount that is deducted directly from a taxpayer's tax liability, as opposed to a deduction, which simply reduces the base amount subject to the tax. A tax credit is dollar for dollar offset against a tax liability. Tax credits include foreign tax credit, residential energy credit, earned income credit, child and dependent care credit, and credit for the elderly. For example, assume a taxpayer is single with a 33 percent marginal tax rate. An additional $300 tax deduction would result in a tax reduction to the taxpayer of $99 (33% x $300). If the $300 qualified as a tax credit, however, the taxpayer would have a $300 tax reduction--the equivalent of a $447.76 tax deduction ($300/(1 - .33)). *See also* Deductions.

Tax Deed a document evidencing the passage of title to a purchaser of property sold for taxes. The tax deed is issued upon foreclosure of the property lien. Typically, there is a grace time period permitting the owner to make good on the delinquent taxes in order to redeem the property.

Tax Deferral a feature available in certain investments, including tax-deferred annuities, in which the payment of taxes on income occurs only after the benefit is received. Other examples of tax-deferred investments include Individual Retirement Accounts (IRA), Keogh Plans, Series EE and HH U.S. savings bonds, stock purchase or dividend reinvestment plans, and universal, variable, or whole life insurance policies.

Tax Effect

1. a general term describing the consequences of a specific tax scenario with respect to a particular tax paying entity. Many factors are considered, such as time elements, projections and estimates of revenues, expenses, deductions, acquisitions, disposals, the like, and their relationship upon present and future tax liability.

2. the impact on taxes of a taxable revenue or expense item. For instance, an interest expense itemized deduction of $2,000 will result in tax savings of $560 at the 28% tax bracket.

Tax Election a choice of an option or options with respect to tax treatments of specified situations, transactions, report forms, and timing of reports. Some elections must have the Commissioner's approval (such as certain changes in accounting method), and some may be done without approval, on an annual basis (such as the filing of a joint tax return).

Tax Evasion or Tax Fraud. An illegal practice of avoiding the payment of taxes. Tax evasion methods include unreported income, fraudulently claiming tax exemptions, and overstating deductions. Tax fraud is a criminal offense.

Tax Exempt a tax-free status granted to certain organizations and governmental entities. Most registered charitable organizations and tax-exempt bonds are free from taxation from other governmental entities. However, governmental entities can, if they so choose, tax the interest on their own securities. For example, interest paid on federal government securities is taxable by the federal government, but not by state or local governments. Normally, most state and local government jurisdictions do not tax the interest payments on their own securities as an incentive for individuals living in the jurisdiction to purchase them. However, outside states and jurisdictions can and often do tax other state and local government security interest payments.

Tax Preference Item under Section 57 of the Internal Revenue Code, certain items that may result in the imposition of the alternative minimum tax. These items of otherwise exempt income or deductions or of special tax benefit were targeted to ensure that taxpayers who benefit should pay at least a minimum amount of tax. Items include tax-exempt interest on nonessential municipal bonds and contributions of appreciated property.

Tax Shelter any legal methodology or device an individual can use to reduce his or her tax liability legally. Tax shelters function by providing credit or deductions to income. Most tax shelters were eliminated under the Tax Reform Act of 1986.

Tax Shield deductions that result in a reduction of income tax payments. The tax shield is computed by multiplying the deduction by the tax rate itself. For example, assume an annual depreciation deduction is $3,000 and the tax rate is 40%, the tax shield or tax savings on depreciation is $3,000 x .4= $1,200. The company saves $1,200 annually in taxes from the depreciation deduction. The higher the deduction, the larger the tax shield. Therefore, an accelerated depreciation method produces higher tax savings than the straight-line method. Note that the term applies to other non-cash charges (e.g., amortization and depletion) as well.

Tax Software computer software specifically designed to help in tax planning. Tax-planning software provides "what-if" spreadsheet capabilities with which the impact of various tax strategies can be calculated. Examples of tax-planning applications are timing the sale of a security, ascertaining how many years to take out funds at retirement from a pension plan, and deciding on the timing of investments.

Tax Table a table accompanying the tax return for computing taxes payable based on taxable income. If the income exceeds $50,000, the taxpayer must use a tax rate schedule that provides a percentage calculation of taxable income based on filing status.

Tax Write-Off an item that is deductible for tax purposes. An example is the depreciation on a self-employed taxpayer's computer and car used for business purposes, deducted as a business expense on Schedule C of Form 1040.

Taxable Income adjusted gross income (AGI) less itemized deductions and personal exemptions. Taxable income is the basis for determining the tax owed by reference to the tax tables or tax rate schedules.

Tax-Deferred Annuities (TDAs) a defined contribution plan available to teachers, hospitals, and nonprofit organizations; also called the *403(B) Plan.*

Tax-Equivalent Yield the yield on a tax-free municipal bond on an equivalent before-tax yield basis. The formula used to equate interest on tax-free municipals to other taxable investments is shown below:

Tax-equivalent yield = Tax-exempt yield/ (1 - tax rate)

If an individual has a marginal tax rate of 28% and is evaluating a municipal bond paying 10% interest, the equivalent before-tax bond yield on a taxable investment is:

10%/(1 - .28) = 13.9%

Thus, she could choose between a taxable investment paying 13.9% and a tax-exempt bond paying 10% as their yields are the same.

Tax-Exempt Bonds municipal bonds where interest income is not subject to federal tax, although the Tax Reform Act (TRA) of 1986 imposed restrictions on the issuance of tax-exempt municipal bonds. Municipal bonds may carry a lower interest than taxable bonds of similar quality and safety. However, after-tax yield from these bonds are usually more than a bond with a higher rate of taxable interest. Municipal bonds are subject to two principal risks; interest rate and default.

Taxpayer Identification Number (TIN) usually the same as your Social Security number.

Tax-Tree Exchange *see* Exchange, 1031.

TCP/IP *see* Transfer Control Protocol/Internet Protocol (TCP/IP).

Technical Analysis as the antithesis of fundamental analysis, investment analysis that concentrates on past price and volume movements, while totally disregarding economic fundamentals, to forecast a security price or currency rates.

Technological Forecasting projecting the effects of technology changes into the uncertain future. The primary incentive for growing importance and use of technological forecasting can be found in the increased rate of technological innovation and the decreasing time between discovery and commercial use, such as bio-medical research, fusion reactor research, or developments in computer technology, the information superhighway, or aviation.

Technology Costs category of cost associated with the development, acquisition, implementation, and maintenance of technology assets. It can include costs such as the depreciation of research equipment, tooling amortization, maintenance, and software development.

Telecommunications the transmission of messages by computer, fax, telephone, telegram, or television. Modern technological developments have ushered in an age of telecommunications in which faxed messages and computer telecommunication networks make a whole world of data and information instantly available. The majority of telecommunications use a telephone line or radio waves. However, satellite transmission is assuming greater importance in this function. Computer telecommunications allows the transmission of machine readable data as well as executable programs to any other computer, using a modem and a serial port on the computer. This enables one to do extensive data analysis as quickly as the data are developed and transmitted.

Telemarketing systematic and continuous program of communicating with customers and prospects via telephone and/or other person-to-person electronic media.

Template
1. a mechanical aid in drawing flowcharts and flowchart symbols.
2. a worksheet that includes the relevant formulas for a particular application but not the data. It is a blank worksheet that we save and fill in the data as needed for a future accounting application. Templates are guides in preparing the spreadsheet and are predefined files, including cell formulas and row or column labels for specific applications. In effect, they are worksheet models designed to solve specific types of problems. Templates allow for the referencing of cells and formulations of interrelated formulas and functions. They are reused to analyze similar transactions.

Temporary Investments investments in marketable securities typically using seasonal excess of cash that the company intends to convert back into cash within one year. The investments produce dividend and/or interest income, as well as possible capital appreciation for the company. Temporary investments are considered short-term investments and are classified as current assets under the heading "marketable securities" on the balance sheet.

Tenancy
1. the time period a tenant may occupy the premises; it may be a fixed term lease (e.g., 3 years) or a period tenancy (e.g., month to month).
2. the right or interest to possess real estate, whether by title or by lease.

Tenancy by the Entirety a form of ownership by husband and wife, recognized in certain states, in which the rights of the deceased spouse automatically pass to the survivor. It is the same as joint tenancy, except that one spouse cannot dispose of his or her share without permission of the other spouse.

Tenancy in Common

Real estate: ownership of property by any two or more persons in undivided interests (not necessarily equal) without the right of survivorship. If one tenant dies, his or her share is transferred to the estate rather than to the other common tenants. An example of this arrangement is partners in real property.

Securities: ownership of a brokerage account by at least two individuals, each having a separable equity.

Tenant

1. the person renting a residential unit.
2. a business renting commercial space.

Tender Offer an offer to buy the stock of a firm at a specified price (usually at a premium over the market price). The objective of a tender offer is to take control of the target company. Sometimes the offer is submitted for approval to the board of directors of the target company, or the offer may be made directly to the shareholders of the company. The SEC requires that any corporate suitor accumulating 5% or more of a target company make disclosures to the SEC, the target company, and the pertaining exchange. *See also* Takeover.

10-K Report annual filing with the SEC for publicly traded companies. Financial statements and supporting information are furnished. Form 10-K typically includes more financial information than that contained in the annual report. Included are the audited basic financial statements consisting of the balance sheet, income statement, and statement of cash flows. Examples of disclosures are sales, operating income, segmental sales by major product line for the last five years, and general business information.

10-Q Report a quarterly filing with the Securities and Exchange Commission by publicly traded companies. It contains interim financial statements and related disclosures and may cover one particular quarter or be cumulative. It should present comparative figures for the same period of the previous year. The statements may or may not be audited. Form 10-Q is less comprehensive than Form 10-K.

Terabyte (T, TB) a trillion bytes.

Term Bond a bond issue whose component bonds mature at the same time.

Term Life Insurance a form of life insurance that covers the insured only for a given period of years, such as 5, 10, 20, or until a given age, such as 65, and does not provide for the accumulation of any cash values. Term insurance comes in several varieties:

level term: The face amount (the amount of coverage) remains fixed for the life of the contract.

declining, decreasing, or reducing term: The face amount periodically drops according to a fixed schedule over 10, 15, or more years.

convertible term: The policy can be converted into a Cash Value policy with no need to meet medical standards at the time of conversion. Most insurance companies offer policies that are both convertible and renewable up to specified ages or for a fixed period.

Term Loans intermediate- to long-term (typically, two to ten years) business loans with provisions for systematic repayments (amortization during the life of the loan). The repayment or amortization schedule is a particularly important feature of such loans. The feature of amortization protects both the lender and borrower against the possibility that the borrower will not make adequate provisions for retirement of the loan during its life. The term loan sometimes ends with a balloon payment.

Term Structure of Interest Rates the relationship between length of time to maturity and yields of debt instruments; also known as a *yield curve*. Other factors, such as default risk and tax treatment, are held constant. An understanding of this relationship or yield curve is of major interest to (1) corporate treasurers who must decide whether to borrow by issuing long or short-term debt, (2) investors who must decide whether to buy long- or short-term bonds and (3) fixed income security analysts who must make judgments about the direction of interest rates.

Terminal an input-output device whereby a user is able to communicate directly with a computer. A terminal must have a keyboard, so that the user can type in instructions and input data, and a means of displaying output, such as a CRT screen or a typewriter. This type is called a *dumb terminal*. When a terminal includes a microprocessor, or when it is actually a microcomputer, it can perform certain operations independent of the CPU. This type is known as an intelligent (or a smart) terminal.

Test Market a specific geographical area that is deemed a representation of the national market as a whole.

Test Marketing the practice of testing a new product or service. It can generate valuable feedback for predicting the success or failure of a potential new product. It can also indicate how a product should be modified to be successful.

Testament the disposition of personal property; also called *will*. Common usage uses the terms *will*, *testament*, and *last will and testament* interchangeably.

Testamentary Trust a trust created by a will taking effect upon the death of the donor, also termed *settlor*. It empowers a trust administrator to implement the terms of the testamentary trust.

Theory of Constraints approach to continuous improvement (reducing operating expenses and inventory and increasing throughput) based on a five-step procedure: (1) identifying constraints, (2) exploiting the binding constraints, (3) subordinating everything else to the decisions made in the second step, (4) increasing capacity of the binding constraints, and (5) repeating the process when new binding constraints are identified. It seeks to identify a company's constraints or bottlenecks and exploit them so that throughput is maximized and inventories and operating costs are minimized.

Theory X the traditional style of management with strong control, concern for the job to the exclusion of concern for the individual; motivation derived primarily from external incentives.

Theory Y the newer and developing style of management with a balance between control and individual freedom. As the individual matures, the need for external motivation decreases; concern of management is for the individual first and the job second.

Theory Z a theory advanced by William Ouchi; often referred to as the "Japanese" management style. Theory Z essentially advocates a combination of all that's best about theory Y and modern Japanese management, which places a large amount of freedom and trust with workers, and assumes that workers have a strong loyalty and interest in team-working and the organization. Theory Z also places more reliance on the attitude and responsibilities of the workers whereas Mcgregor's XY theory is mainly focused on management and motivation from the manager's and organization's perspective.

Three-Sigma Limits in statistical quality control charts, three standard deviations from the mean are used as the upper and lower control limits. There are about three in one thousand chances that a variation that falls outside the control limits will be only random in character.

Throughput rate of production of a defined process over a stated period of time. Throughput can be measured in either financial or nonfinancial terms. For example, cash flows generated from selling products or services to customers, units of products, batches produced, dollar turnover, or other meaningful measurements.

Tick and Closing Tick a tick is a measure of movement in closing stock prices; a positive (+) tick means prices were rising at the end of the day, while a negative (-) tick means prices were falling. Tick closing prices provide insight into how strong the market was near the close. These tick statistics show the number of stocks whose last price change was an increase, less those whose last move was a downtick.

Tight Money
1. fewer funds available to borrowers from lending institutions and creditors. This is a situation in which credit is difficult to obtain.
2. a reduction in the dollars available for individual spending because of a decrease in the money supply. *See also* Easy or Loose Money.

Tight Money Policy a monetary policy designed to curb inflation by way of restricting the supply of money and credit. *See also* Monetary Policy.

TIGR *see* Treasury Investment Growth Receipts (TIGR).

Time and Motion Study the systematic study of the time and human motions used to perform an operation. The purpose is to eliminate unnecessary motions and to identify the best sequence of motions for maximum efficiency. Therefore, time and motion study can be an important source of productivity improvements.

Time Deposit savings account at a financial institution that earns interest, but it is not legally subject to withdrawal on demand or transfer by check. The depositor can withdraw only by giving notice. A certificate of deposit (CD) is a special type of time deposit.

Time is of the Essence a contract clause that makes it essential that the provisions be carried out at the specified time or the contract is voidable.

Time Sharing

1. an information system that services many users from one computer; these users are served simultaneously until the volume of work to be processed forms a waiting line. Time-sharing is a multi-user environment whereby many terminals are usually logged-on to a mainframe computer. All of the users are able to access the computer to upload information, to download information, obtain electronic mail, use programs on the computer, etc.
2. in real estate the division of ownership or use of a resort unit or apartment on the basis of time periods.

Time Series a chronologically arranged sequence of values of a particular variable, the time periods being monthly, quarterly, or yearly. Graphically, time is plotted along the horizontal axis, and other data of interest are plotted along the vertical axis.

Time Series Forecasting; Time Series Analysis the application of statistical and econometric methods to time series data to forecast the future. Time series analysis breaks data into components and projects them into the future (see Figure 2). The four commonly recognized components are trend, seasonal, cycle, and irregular variations.

1. The trend component (T) is the general upward or downward movement of the average over time. These movements may require many years of data to determine or describe them. The basic forces underlying the trend include technological advances, productivity changes, inflation, and population change.
2. The seasonal component (S) is a recurring fluctuation of data points above or below the trend value that repeats with a usual frequency of one year, e.g., Christmas sales.
3. Cyclical components (C) are recurrent upward and downward movements that repeat with a frequency that is longer than a year. This movement is attributed to business cycles (such as a recession, inflation, unemployment, and prosperity), so the periodicity (recurrent rate) of such cycles does not have to be constant.
4. The irregular (or random) component (R) is a series of short, erratic movements that follow no discernible pattern. It is caused by unpredictable or nonrecurring events such as floods, wars, strikes, elections, environmental changes, and the passage of legislation.

Figure 2

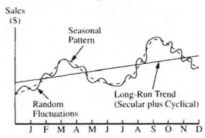

Time Software a computer program that tracks hours worked by employees by function, operation, or activity. It prepares an analysis of the variance between budgeted and actual hours as well as trends in actual hours over a stated time period (e.g., quarterly comparisons).

Time Standard amount of time required to perform a task by a trained operator working at a normal pace and using a prescribed method.

Time Study development of standards through stopwatch observation.

Time to Market how long it takes to get a product or service to the market.

Time Value of Money the fact that a dollar you have today is worth more than a dollar tomorrow. The reason is that the dollar today can earn interest from putting it in a savings account or placing it in an investment. The longer it takes to get $1, the less it is worth today because you are losing interest on that money. Time value of money is a critical consideration in business and economic decisions. For example, compound interest calculations are needed to determine future sums of money resulting from an investment. Discounting, or the calculation of present value, which is inversely related to compounding, is used in the valuation of stocks, bonds, business ventures, real estate, and capital expenditure projects. *See also* Future Value (FV); Present Value (PV).

Times Interest Earned Ratio earnings before interest and taxes (EBIT)/interest expense. A ratio that measures the firm's ability to meet its interest payments from its annual operating earnings.

Timing a good time to do something to achieve an optimal benefit. An example is selecting a suitable time to invest in stocks before they rise (also called *timing the market*) or entering into a lease transaction before rental rates rise. The choice of the right time for an action is based on judgment.

Tip

1. supposedly "inside" information on corporation affairs.

2. money directly paid to a waiter, taxi driver, or bell hop as compensation for service.

TIPS *see* Treasury Inflation-Protected Securities (TIPS).

Title the legal right of an ownership interest in a property. It is evidence of ownership and lawful possession.

Title Insurance insurance required of home buyers by lenders, to protect against loss due to defective titles. The policies are written by a title insurance company.

Tobin's Q *see* Q-Ratio.

TOHO (Tiny Office/Home Office) *see* SOHO (Small Office/Home Office).

Tokens string of digits for an amount of a particular currency. Each token is digitally stamped by the bank for authentication purposes.

Tombstone also called *Tombstones*. Advertisement that states the borrower's name, gives the conditions of an issue, and lists the various banks taking part in the issue.

Top Down establishing company objectives from the top rather than from the bottom up.

Top Line a term referring to the first line in an income statement that reflects a firm's sales revenue.

Tort Liability a legal obligation arising from a civil wrong or injury for which a judicial remedy can occur. A tort liability arises as a result of any combination of a direct violation of an individual's rights, the transgression of a public obligation resulting in damage to an individual, or a private wrongdoing to another individual. For example, if an individual is struck and injured by a municipal bus as he or she is legally crossing the street, this would be a direct violation and a wrongdoing to the individual. This is a violation of the municipality's obligation to preserve and protect the safety and welfare of the public. The injured individual may sue the municipality for damages.

Total Cost the sum of the various costs incurred. For example, total manufacturing costs are the sum of direct materials, direct labor, and factory overhead. By management function, the total costs of a manufacturing business are the sum of manufacturing costs and selling and administrative expenses. By behavior in relation to fluctuations in activity, the total costs are the sum of variable costs and fixed costs. *See also* Unit Cost.

Total Leverage that portion of the fixed costs that represents a risk to the firm, which is divided into operating leverage, a measure of operating risk and financial leverage, a measure of financial risk. Total leverage is a measure of total risk.

Total Quality Management (TQM) an approach to quality that emphasizes continuous improvement, a philosophy of "doing it right the first time," striving for zero defects, and elimination of all waste. It is a concept of using quality methods and techniques to strategic advantage within firms. A comparison between TQM and business process reengineering (BPR) is presented on the next page.

	TQM	Business Process Reengineering (BPR)
Goals	Small-scale improvements at all levels of management with cumulative effects	Outrageous
Case for action	Assumed to be necessary	Compelling
Scope and focus	Attention to tasks, steps, and processes across the board	Select but broad business processes
Degree of change	Incremental, evolutionary, and continual	Order of magnitude and periodic; revolutionary
Role of information technology (IT)	Incidental	Cornerstone
Senior management involvement	Important up front	Intensive throughout

Total Return the return received on an investment over a specified period of time. It is composed of two basic elements: (1) the current yield such as dividend, interest, and rental income and (2) capital gains or losses. It is usually expressed as an annual percentage. Return is measured considering the relevant time period (holding period), called a *holding period return*.

Tracking Stock a stock created by a company to follow, or "track" the performance of one of its divisions, typically one that is in a line of business that is fast-growing and commands a higher industry price-to-earnings ratio than the parent's main business. Also called *letter stock* or *targeted stock*. The objective is to increase value to shareholders, and thereby lower a company's cost of capital. Some companies distribute tracking stock to their existing shareholders. Others sell tracking stock to the investing public, raising additional cash for themselves. Some companies do both. Tracking stock, however, does not typically provide voting rights. Issuing tracking stock is an increasingly popular corporate-financing technique.

Trade
1. the exchange of securities or commodities taking place on organized exchanges (e.g., stock exchange, commodity exchange) or informally (e.g., over-the-counter market).
2. the exchange of goods and services. An exchange usually requires the payment of money and/or financial instruments. A barter arrangement is also possible.
3. an occupation, profession, or business. A trade usually refers to a skilled occupation such as the plumbing trade.
4. those who merchandise, sell, or manufacture a particular product line.

Trade Advertising advertising targeted at retailers and wholesalers and not at the final consumer of goods and services.

Trade Balance the balance of a country's exports and imports. Statistics on trade deficits are available on numerous websites such as *www.economy.com.*

Trade Credit credit extended by one business to another business, allowing the latter to buy goods from the former without making an immediate full payment by check or with cash. It is credit obtained through open-account purchases represented by an accounts payable by the buyer and an accounts receivable by the seller. Trade credit is an important external source of working capital for a business, although it can be very expensive. For example, a credit of 2/10 net 30 (2% cash discount if paid within 10 days, otherwise due in 30 days) translates into a 36 % annual interest rate if the cash discount is foregone.

Trade Deficit an unfavorable balance of trade; that is, the excess of imports of goods (raw materials, agricultural and manufactured products, and capital and consumer products) over the exports of goods, resulting in a negative balance of trade. Trade surplus is the reverse. The balance of trade is distinguished from the balance of payments that consists of the current account, which includes services as well as merchandise trade and other invisible items such as interests and profits earned abroad. Factors that affect a country's balance of trade include (1) the strength or weakness of its currency value in relation to those of the countries with which it trades and (2) a comparative advantage in key manufacturing areas.

Trade Discount discounts that reduce the list or regular price given by a supplier in return for the purchase of large quantities; also called *quantity discounts* or *price discounts.* For example, a schedule of trade discounts would look as follows:

Order Quantity	Unit Price
0 to 500	$40,00
501 to 1,000	39.90
1,001 or greater	39.80

Sales are recorded at the net amount after taking into account the trade discount. For example, a $100,000 sale with a trade discount of 4% would be shown in the financial records only at $96,000 ($100,000 x 96%).

Trade Magazine or Publication any newspaper or magazine specifically directed to the members of a specific industry.

Trade Secret information, such as a formula, pattern, device, or process, that is not known to the public and that gives the person possessing the information a competitive advantage. It may include customer lead lists, marketing and/or business plans, and suppliers.

Trade Show a large show in which goods and services in a specific industry are exhibited and demonstrated.

Trademark an exclusive right of a company. It is a distinctive name or symbol that legally identifies a company or its products and services, and sometimes prevents others from using identical or similar marks.

Trade-Through Rule a regulation approved in April, 2005, by the SEC requiring that stock trades, with few exceptions, be sent to whatever market has the best available price for immediate execution, rather than allowing investors to choose faster execution.

Trading Band the range a country's finance officials will let the currency trade before intervening. For example: the Chinese currency's trading band is currently 0.3 percent. *See also* Revaluation.

Trading on Equity financial leverage or the use of borrowed funds, particularly long-term debt, in the capital structure of a firm. Trading profitably on the equity, also known as *positive* (favorable) *financial leverage*, means that the borrowed funds generate a higher rate of return than the interest rate paid for the use of the funds. The excess accrues to the benefit of the owners because it magnifies, or increases, their earnings.

Trading Pit, Post trading locations at which stocks assigned to that location are bought and sold on the exchange floor.

Trailing Earnings the actual reported earnings over the past year. Trailing earnings claim the virtue of certainty, but forward earnings are more relevant for investors assessing current stock market valuations. *See also* Forward Earnings.

Tranches slices or pieces of a security issue, such as a bond or stock sold to investors. They are related securities that are offered at the same time, but have different risks, rewards, and/or maturities. For example, a CMO tranch might have mortgages that are 1 year, 2 year, 5 year, and 20 year maturities.

Transaction Cycle the repetitive flow of the activities of an ongoing enterprise described in terms of three major transaction cycles as follows: (1) revenue cycle, relating to sales, shipping, receivables, and collections, (2) buying cycle, referring to purchases, payables, and payments, and (3) production cycle relating to manufacturing products and storage.

Transactions events or happenings in a business that change its financial position and/or earnings. Transactions are recorded in a journal and then posted to a ledger. Examples of business transactions are investing in the business, buying supplies, paying bills, withdrawing money from the business, buying equipment, and paying rent.

Transcribe
1. to take audio representation and transform manually into typed copy.
2. an act that serves to transfer an amount from one financial record to another. Transferring an original source document amount to a journal or posting to a ledger is an example of this act.

Transfer
1. moving something from one location to another, such as withdrawing savings from one bank account and putting the money into another bank account offering a higher interest rate.
2. the switching of ownership to property. An example is the delivery of a stock

certificate from the seller's broker to the buyer's broker so that there may be a legal transfer of ownership.

3. a change of ownership recorded on the books, such as a transfer agent's listing the name of the new owner of a bond.

Transfer Agent usually a bank or trust company designated by a corporation to make legal transfers of stocks and bonds and may then, if appointed, distribute dividends. In this case the agent keeps the current stock-transfer books, ledger, and payment lists. Transfer agent and registrar duties may be performed by the same agent.

Transfer Control Protocol/Internet Protocol (TCP/IP) protocol explaining the subdivision of information into packets for transmission, and the way in which applications involve transmitting e-mail and file transfer.

Transfer Payments

Government finance: payments made to an individual (usually by a government body) who does not perform any service in return. Transfer payments would include disability payments, social security retirement payments, unemployment compensation, veterans' benefits, and welfare payments.

Current accounts: disbursements of interest and dividends to foreign entities and governments as recorded in the balance of payments.

Transfer Price the price charged when one division of a company provides goods or services to another division of the company. A good transfer price will help us evaluate the performance of the divisions. Under ideal circumstances, the transfer price will promote congruence between the goals of divisions and the company as a whole. Unfortunately, there is no single transfer price that may accomplish all these goals. Because the divisions are evaluated as independent investment centers, their managers may use transfer prices that are not in the best interest of the company as a whole.

Transfer Pricing pricing the goods or services that are exchanged between various divisions (or subsidiaries) of a decentralized organization. A major goal of transfer pricing is to enable divisions that exchange goods or services to act as independent businesses. Various transfer pricing schemes are available, such as market price, cost-based price, or negotiated price.

Transfer Tax

1. a state levied tax upon the transfer or sale of a security or property. Some states base the tax on selling price (e.g., New York) while other states base the tax on the par value (e.g., Texas).

2. federal tax on the sale of stocks and bonds.

3. federal tax on gifts made, inheritance, and estate proceeds.

Transparent Market a market in which (1) there is open communication between stakeholders, investors, and company officials and (2) current trade and quote information is readily available to the public.

Travel and Entertainment (T&E) Account a separate account through which the employer agrees to reimburse employees, often salespeople, for expenses incurred in traveling and entertaining in the performance of their duties. In many cases, the employees use separate credit cards to charge for travel and entertainment so specific records may be kept for tax purposes.

Treasurer a person in a firm who deals with financial and money problems. The treasurer is engaged in (1) obtaining capital, (2) investor relations, (3) short-term financing, (4) banking and custody, (5) credits and collections, (6) investments, and (7) insurance and employee benefits. The treasurer's functions are distinguished from those of the controller, who supervises the accounting activities of the firm.

Treasuries; T-Bills; T-Bonds; T-Notes debt obligations issued and backed of the full credit and faith by the U.S. government. Depending on their denominations and maturities, they are classified into three types: Treasury bills, Treasury notes, and Treasury bonds. The income earned on Treasuries is exempt from state and local taxes. Treasuries, backed by the government, are considered riskless. Note: They carry the lowest markup, and you can even buy them without commission directly from Federal Reserve branches (for information, go to *www.publicdebt. treas.gov*). Treasury yields are published daily in the larger newspapers and there are numerous websites.

Treasury Bill a short-term obligation of the federal government, commonly called *T-bill*. Treasury bills are auctioned through competitive bidding weekly by the Treasury with maturities of 91 days and 182 days. In addition, nine-month and one-year bills are sold periodically. Treasury bills carry no coupon but are sold on a discount basis. Denominations range from $10,000 to $1 million. *See also* Treasuries; T-Bills; T-Bonds; T-Notes.

Treasury Bond
1. a long-term debt instrument issued by the U.S. Treasury department with maturities of 10 years or longer issued in minimum denominations of $1,000. *See also* Treasuries; T-Bills; T-Bonds; T-Notes.
2. a bond issued by a corporation and then repurchased. Such a bond is considered as retired when repurchased.

Treasury Direct an account established to buy and hold Treasury bonds directly through the Federal Reserve System (*www.treasurydirect.gov/*). Retail investors can buy Treasuries without paying a fee to a broker/dealer.

Treasury Inflation-Protected Securities (TIPS) securities identical to treasury bonds except that principal and coupon payments are adjusted to eliminate the effects of inflation.

Treasury Investment Growth Receipts (TIGR) a trademarked security of Merrill Lynch providing a stripped treasury bond.

Treasury Notes intermediate government obligations with maturities of one to ten years. Denominations range from $1000 to $1 million or more. Due to the existence of a strong secondary market, they are very attractive marketable security investments. Like Treasury bills, Treasury notes have a low yield because of their virtually risk-free nature. *See also* Treasuries; T-Bills; T-Bonds; T-Notes.

Treasury Stock issued shares that have been reacquired by the company. Treasury stock, although issued, is not outstanding. Treasury shares may be held indefinitely, resold, or cancelled. Dividends are not paid on treasury shares nor are voting rights associated with them. The company receives no dividends and has no voting rights because a company cannot own itself.

Trend the general upward or downward movements of the average over time. These movements may require many years of data to determine or describe them. They can be described by a straight line or a curve. The basic forces underlying the trend include technological advances, productivity changes, inflation, and population change. It is a long-term directional change, up or down in time-series data, aside from seasonal, cyclical, and irregular components. *See also* Trend Analysis.

Trend Analysis a forecasting technique that relies primarily on historical time series data to predict the future. The analysis involves searching for a right trend equation that will suitably describe trend of the data series. The trend may be linear or it may not.

Trial Balance a listing of all accounts to determine if they balance, i.e., whether the debits equal the credits.

Trickle-Down Economics the concept that if you give tax breaks and benefits to big business and the wealthy, it will find its way down to the middle-class and poor, through capital expansion, increased productivity, and increased employment. It was a popular concept in the Reagan years and espoused by Prime Minister Margaret Thatcher. The trickle-down concept was used in *Reaganomics* as a means to fight inflation. However, during times of inflation it tended to have the reverse effect. The newspapers and journals labeled it the "horse and sparrow theory," that is, "feed a horse oats and the sparrow could live off of the dropping." It tended to increase the tax burden on the middle-class and the poor working class in order to cover the lost taxes from the wealthy, thus having the effect of reducing discretionary spending.

Triple A a bond or preferred stock that is rated with three As. *See also* Bond Ratings.

Triple Net Leases a lease that requires tenants to pay all utilities, insurance, taxes, and maintenance costs.

Triple Witching Hour *see* Program Trading.

Trojan Horse an illegal program (virus), contained within another program, that "sleeps" until some specific event occurs, then triggers the illegal program to be activated and cause damage.

Trust an agreement in which the trustee takes title to the property (referred to as the corpus) owned by the grantor (donor) to protect or conserve it for either the grantor or the trust's beneficiary. The trust is established by the grantor. The trustee is usually given authority to invest the property for a return. Trusts may be revocable or irrevocable.

Trust Company

1. an entity that serves as a trustee, fiduciary, or agent of funds for people. The funds may be in trust for children, an estate, or others. The trust company performs a custodial function. The trust may also invest funds held in conformity with state law. Many trust functions are conducted by commercial banks.
2. a trust company may also serve as a fiscal agent for a company, paying dividends and bond interest.

Trust Fund
a fund used to account for a government's fiduciary responsibilities and activities in managing trusts. There are basically three types of trust funds: expendable trust funds, nonexpendable trust funds, and pension trust funds.

Trustee

1. the third party to a bond indenture. The trustee's function is to make sure the issuer lives up to the numerous provisions in the indenture. A trustee is usually a trust department of a commercial bank. The trustee is paid a fee and acts to protect the interests of the bondholders.
2. the third party to a bankruptcy proceeding. The trustee's responsibility is to value and recapitalize the firm if it is to be reorganized. *See also* Trustee in Bankruptcy.

Joint trustees: two or more individuals being entrusted with property for one or more beneficiaries.

Judicial trustee: a trustee appointed by a court for the purpose of administering the terms of a trust.

Testamentary trustee: a trustee appointed by a will for the purpose of administering a trust created by the will. The executor of the will is separate from the testamentary trustee who is charged with the responsibility of administering the terms of the established trust.

Trustor
the individual who holds/the person who creates the trust.

Truth-in-Lending Act (TILA)
or Consumer Credit Protection Act of 1969; Regulation Z. A major federal law designed to protect credit purchasers. The most important provision is the requirement that both the dollar amount of finance charges and the annual percentage rate (APR) charged must be disclosed before credit is extended.

t-statistic *see* t-Test.

t-Test

1. in regression analysis, a test of the statistical significance of a regression coefficient. It involves basically two steps: (1) compute the t-value of the regression coefficient as follows: t-value = coefficient/standard error of the coefficient and (2) compare the value with the t table value. High t-values enhance confidence in the value of the coefficient as a predictor. Low values (as a rule of thumb, under 2.0) are indications of low reliability of the coefficient as a predictor.
2. a general statistical test for hypotheses, based on t-distribution, known as a small sample distribution. The t-test is used to estimate and test hypotheses about

population means, the difference between two means, a population variance, and a comparison of two population variances. For example, an accounting instructor wishes to test to determine if the use of a new and old textbook had anything to do with the difference in performance of the two classes.

Turnkey Projects a project in which a firm agrees to set up an operating plant for a foreign client and hand over the "key" when the plant is fully operational. The firm receives a fee for setting up the facility.

Turnover
1. the number of times merchandise is sold and then replaced over a specific period of time, often on a monthly, quarterly, or annual basis. It measures the speed of product movement.
2. the volume of business in a security or the entire market. For example, if turnover on the New York Stock Exchange is reported at 3,000,000 shares on a particular day, 3,000,000 shares changed hands.

Two Sets of Books keeping two sets of financial records: one set of books for regular financial reports and another for credit or tax purposes. Both sets of books are accurate and legitimate, but are kept differently for different purposes. Often this is not legitimate, such as when a company tries to mislead investors, creditors, and others by cooking figures for public statements, while keeping accurate figures for private use. *See also* Cook the Books.

Two-Bin System an inventory control system in which there are physically two bins or parts for manufacturing, one for regular inventory, and the other to be used when the first bin is empty. As soon as the first bin is empty, inventory is reordered.

Two-Part Pricing pricing that charges a per unit price that equals marginal cost, plus a fixed fee for the right to buy the good or service. With two-part pricing, a firm charges a fixed fee for the right to buy its products or services, plus a per unit charge for each unit purchased. This pricing strategy is commonly used by such establishments as athletic clubs, golf courses and health clubs. They typically charge a fixed "initiation fee" plus a charge (either per month or per visit) to use the facilities. Buying clubs are another good example. By paying a membership fee in those clubs, members get to buy products at "wholesale cost."

Tying Contract an agreement between seller and buyer that requires the buyer of one good or service, as a condition for purchasing the desired good or service, to purchase some other product or service. This practice was declared illegal in the Clayton Act. For example, the United Shoe Machinery Company once required shoemakers to buy other materials as a condition for purchasing their shoe machinery.

Uu

U-Form Enterprise an enterprise in which decision-making is centralized around top management. This form of organization is common to small and medium-sized firms; large firms are usually decentralized.

Ultra Vires an action outside the proper authority or power of a corporation or corporate officer as established in the corporate charter. (Latin for "beyond the power.")

Umbrella Policy a policy providing an extra liability insurance with regular insurance.

Unavoidable Costs costs that must be continued regardless of the decision as to whether to make or buy a certain part or as to whether to keep or drop a certain product line and thus cannot be recovered or saved. Much or all of fixed costs in those cases are unavoidable costs. Examples of unavoidable costs are property taxes and rent which cannot be avoided or saved no matter what decision you choose.

Uncertainty a state of knowledge in which one or more alternatives result in a set of possible specific outcomes, but where the probabilities of the outcomes are neither known nor meaningful. Unlike risk, therefore, uncertainty is not objective and does not assume complete knowledge of alternatives. In most practical cases, decision makers tend not to distinguish between uncertainty and risk. *See also* Decision Making Under Uncertainty.

Undercapitalized a company not having enough capital to carry out its business.

Underemployment a condition in which the best available technology and resources are not fully utilized in a production process; also called *resource misallocation*.

Underground Economy a variety of economic activities unreported or unaccounted for in national product accounts. Examples include legal activities unreported, such as garage sales, and illegal activities, such as the prostitution and drug trade.

Underlying refers to a security on which a derivative contract is written. It is a commodity price, interest rate, share price, foreign exchange rate, index of prices, or other variables applied to an amount specified in the contract so as to compute cash settlement or other exchange per the contract provision. While an underlying may be the price of an asset or liability, it is not itself an asset or liability.

Underwrite; Underwriter; Underwriting the act of buying the securities from the issuing company, thus guaranteeing the company the capital it seeks, and in turn selling the securities, at a markup, to the investing public or institutions.

Undistributed Profit the earnings of a business entity, such as a syndicate, joint venture, or partnership, preceding the allocation of profit according to the member's profit distribution agreement. *See also* Retained Earnings.

Unearned Income income from sources other than salary or wages, such as income from investments.

Unemployment the state of being out of work. To be considered unemployed by the Department of Labor, an individual must satisfy three conditions: She (1) must have been previously employed, (2) must be actively seeking employment, and (3) cannot be unemployed longer than 26 weeks, after which unemployment benefits expire. Unemployed individuals are entitled to receive unemployment benefits from the state unemployment compensation division of the Department of Labor. There are different types of unemployment:
1. **Frictional unemployment** is the amount of unemployment due to the normal workings of the labor market, e.g., approximately 4% at "full" employment according to policy definition.
2. **Structural unemployment** exists when aggregate demand is sufficient to provide full employment, but the distribution of the demand does not correspond precisely to the composition of the labor force, e.g., NASA engineers that were unemployed at the end of the race to the moon.
3. **Cyclical unemployment** is caused by a downturn in the business cycle, specifically by lack of demand for labor. Generally the lowest-paid, least skilled workers are the first to be laid off, but in a prolonged period of business contraction layoffs gradually affect all groups.
4. **Seasonal unemployment** occurs periodically owing to seasonal variation in particular industries. It is particularly evident in jobs affected by weather, either in terms of the ability to perform any work at all (construction, agriculture) or in terms of consumer demand for the end-product (Christmas ornaments, air conditioners, summer and winter resorts).

The effect of unemployment on the economy is summarized in the figure on the next page.

Unemployment Effects

a. Less Tax Revenue: Fewer jobs mean less income tax to the state and nation, which means a bigger U.S government deficit and forces states to make cuts in programs to balance their budgets.

b. Higher Government Costs: When people lose jobs they often must turn to the government for benefits.

c. Less Consumer Spending: Without a job, individuals can't afford to buy cars, computers, houses, or vacations.

d. Empty Stores: Retailers and homebuilders can't absorb lower sales for long. Soon they have to lay off workers, and in more serious shortfalls, file for bankruptcy.

e. Manufacturing Cuts: The companies that make consumer products or housing materials are forced to cut jobs, too, as sales of their goods fall.

f. Real Estate Pain: As companies fail and as individuals struggle, mortgages and other bank loans go unpaid. That causes real estate values to go down and pummels lenders.

Unemployment Insurance a payment received from the government after being unemployed for a certain number of weeks.

Unemployment Rate the number of unemployed workers divided by total employed and unemployed who constitute the labor force. Because unemployment-insurance records relate only to people who have applied for such benefits, and because it is impractical to actually count every unemployed person each month, the government conducts a monthly survey of 55,000 households. A second survey of employers counts the loss or gain in payrolls, hours, and earnings. The government replaced the outdated Standard Industrial Classification system with the North American Industry Classification System. It has new categories such as "Information," incorporating Internet providers, publishing, telecommunications, and broadcasting. The government compiled the three-year phasing-in of probability-based sampling, this time in the services sector, to better reflect shifts in the economy. It updated seasonal adjustments using monthly estimates. And it changed the way government jobs are counted to include civilian Defense Department employees in the payroll tabulation.

Unfunded no funds have been provided for a specified obligation or liability. Such may be the case for a pension plan where part of pension expense has not been funded (cash paid) by the employer. This will result in a deferred pension credit.

Unicode an international standard to enable the storage and display of characters of a vast variety of languages on computers, such as Arabic, Hebrew, and Asian.

Uniform Commercial Code (UCC) the code that standardizes business law in this country. The Code was formulated in 1952 by the National Conference of Commissioners on United State Laws. The Code was offered to the state legislatures, and all states except Louisiana adopted it. For example, the Code covers regulations on commercial paper, warranties, uncertified checks, written agency agreements, security agreements, and bankruptcy. The Uniform Commercial Code is followed by practicing lawyers.

Unified Gift and Estate Tax a federal tax charged on the net value of an estate and on gifts above a certain amount. The transferrer is liable for gift taxes. However, if the transferrer for some reason does not pay them, the transferee will be held liable for payment.

Uniform Gifts Minors Act (UGMA) a uniform act establishing rules for transferring and administering assets to a minor. A custodian is designated to act on the behalf of the minor, making all related investment decisions, including buying and selling assets for the minor. All earned income is taxed to the minor. The custodianship ends when the child reaches the age of majority.

Uniform Resource Locator (URL) an address system used for the Internet. The http prefix is used for the WWW. For example, *http://www.barnesandnoble. com* is the full address for the Barnes & Noble online bookstore.

Some common prefixes	
http://	World Wide Web
ftp://	FTP server
Gopher://	Gopher server
mailto://	e-mail
News://	Newsgroup
wais://	Wide Area Information Server

Uninsured Motorist Coverage automobile insurance that provides reimbursement to the owner of a vehicle for losses caused by an uninsured motorist. Its objective is to protect the insured driver and passengers from bodily injury losses and, in some states, property damage losses resulting from an auto accident caused by an uninsured motorist.

Union Shop a work place where all employees, except management, are required to belong to the union.

Unique Visitor Pages the number of different pages at a website that a single visitor accesses.

Unique Visitors Per Month the number of people who visits a website each month; each person is counted only once, even if that person visits the site more than once during the month.

Unit Cost the cost of producing one unit of a product or service, usually based on averages; total costs divided by total units. For example, if total manufacturing costs are $100,000 and the production volume for a given period is 10,000 units, the unit production cost is $10 per unit ($100,000/10,000 units). Unit costs may be stated in terms of gallons, feet, tons, individual units, etc. Unit costs must be available for comparison of varying volumes and amounts and for the purpose of establishing unit sales price of the product or service. If volume of activity increases, the variable cost per unit remains the same but the fixed cost per unit drops.

Unit Investment Trust a closed-end investment company in which the proceeds from the sale of original shares are invested in a fixed portfolio of taxable or tax-exempt bonds and held until maturity. Like a mutual fund, a unit investment trust offers to small investors the advantages of a large, professionally selected and diversified portfolio. Unlike a mutual fund, however, its portfolio is fixed; once structured, it is not actively managed. Therefore, fees are very low. Unit investment trusts are also available for money market securities, corporate bonds of different grades, mortgage-backed securities, preferred stocks, utility common stocks, and other investments. Unit trusts are most suitable for people who need a fixed income and a guaranteed return of capital. They disband and pay off investors after the majority of their investments have been redeemed.

Unit Labor Cost labor cost per unit of output. For the economy, the data on unit labor costs are released by the Department of Labor. Unit labor cost increases at the rate of wage increase minus the rate of increase in labor productivity. It is a key gauge of future price inflation along with the Consumer Price Index (CPI), Producer Price Index (PPI), and Gross Domestic Product (GDP) Deflator.

Unit Trust *see* Unit Investment Trust.

Unitary Elasticity a price elasticity of demand equal to one. The percentage change in price leads to the percentage change in quantity demanded. A change in price therefore does not alter consumer expenditures. *See also* Price Elasticity.

Unitary Tax a taxing system under which the state taxes the percentage of a multinational corporation's (MNC's) worldwide income that reflects the proportion of payroll, property, and sales attributable to activities within the state. Under this accounting method, a MNC is required to account to the state for the earnings of all affiliates that make up its unitary business, even those that do no business in the state or in the United States. This system is distinct from arm's length accounting.

Universal Life a variation of whole life insurance that combines investment features with term life insurance. The savings yields are substantially higher than for whole life. It provides both the pure death protection and cash value buildup of whole life insurance but with variability in the face amount, death benefit, rate of cash value accumulation, premiums, and rate of return.

Universal Product Code (UPC) a bar coding system for visual scanners used at check-out or point-of-purchase locations to electronically record price and content information.

University of Michigan's Index of Consumer Sentiment an index that measures consumers' personal financial circumstances and their outlook for the future. The index is compiled through a telephone survey of 500 households by the University of Michigan Survey Research Center. The index is used by the Commerce Department in its monthly *Index of Leading Economic Indicators (LEI)* and is regularly charted in the Department's *Business Conditions Digest.* Many economists pay close attention to the index, which provides insight into consumer attitudes toward spending and borrowing, since consumers account for two-thirds of the nation's economic activity (i.e., gross domestic product) and thus drive recovery and expansion. *See also* Index of Consumer Confidence and Index of Leading Economic Indicators (LEI).

Unlimited Liability in a sole proprietorship or a general partnership, the liability of owners is not limited to the owner's investment. In a corporation, stockholders usually have limited liability. They risk their investment in the enterprise but not their personal assets.

Unlimited Marital Deduction the absence of estate tax regardless of the amount transferred if a deceased spouse leaves his or her estate to the other spouse.

Unsecured Loan loan that is not secured by a mortgage on a specific property. It is backed only by the borrower's credit rating. Unsecured loans are typically short term. The disadvantages of this kind of loan are that, because it is made for the short term and has no collateral, it carries a higher interest rate than a secured loan and payment in a lump sum is required.

Updesk a term that refers to the real estate agent on hand who answers questions when someone calls to ask about buying or selling a piece of real estate. If a person who calls does not have a real estate agent, the agent on the updesk can claim the caller as his or her own new agent.

Upload in telecommunications, the transmission of a file or program from one computer to a network. The opposite of uploading is downloading, which is to receive binary programs or data from another computer. For example, it is possible to upload one's income tax return to the IRS to facilitate an income tax refund.

Upswing a widespread upward movement in unemployment or total output or both.

URL *see* Uniform Resource Locator (URL).

Useful Life the typical operating service life of an asset for the purpose it was acquired. The term usually applies to fixed assets. The useful life used for depreciation accounting does not necessarily coincide with the actual physical life or any commonly recognized economic life. *See also* Depreciation.

U.S. Savings Bond *see* Series HH Savings Bonds; Series EE Savings Bonds.

U.S. Series I Savings Bond a U.S. savings bond designed to protect the purchasing power of your principal and guarantees a real fixed rate of return above inflation for the life of the bond (10 to 30 years). The current series I savings bond, called *I-bond* for short, guarantees 3% above inflation. You can purchase up to $30,000 worth of the bonds each year, you can never lose principal, earnings are free from state and local taxes, and federal taxes are deferred until you redeem the bond. Plus, there are no fees when you buy or sell these bonds. Although you can cash an I-bond six months after the issue date, there is a three-month earnings penalty if you redeem them in less than five years. I-bonds are sold in denominations of $50 to $10,000 at most banks and also online at *www.savingsbonds.gov*.

Utilities Software a set of computer programs in an operating system that performs all that file management stuff like sorting, deleting, copying files, formatting disks and diskettes, and renaming stored files.

Utility

1. an economic and highly subjective term describing satisfaction of a specified want. *Utility* and *usefulness* are not necessarily synonymous terms. Artwork may be functionally useless but yet provide great utility to an art lover.

2. the value of a certain outcome or payoff to someone; the pleasure or displeasure that person would derive from that outcome.

Utility Function a preference function stating that a consumer's satisfaction is dependent upon the goods he or she consumes and their amounts. Economic theory postulates that consumers behave in such a way as to maximize their utility.

Utility Program program supporting the processing of a computer, such as diagnostic and tracing programs.

Vv

Valuation the process of determining the intrinsic value of an asset, such as a security, business, or a piece of real estate. The process of determining security valuation involves finding the present value of an asset's expected future cash flows using the investor's required rate of return.

Value

1. a highly subjective term, usually an expression of monetary worth applied to a particular asset, group of assets, business entity or services rendered. It should not be confused with the term cost even though it is frequently measured, equated, and identified by it. Thus the term should be used with an appropriate modifying adjective.
2. the amounts at which items are stated in financial records and statements. Value is expenditures or amounts that are deemed to benefit future periods. *See also* Book Value; Market Value.
3. represented by the amount of goods, services, or money necessary to complete an exchange for a specific commodity. In economic terms, value of goods equals price multiplied by quantity.

Value Added the difference, at each stage of production, between the cost of a product and the cost of all the materials purchased to make the product.

Value Added Tax (VAT) an indirect percentage tax levied on products or services at various stages of production and distribution. The actual value added to the product, including raw materials, labor and profit, is determined at each stage or state of production and the tax is computed upon the increase in value. It is basically a tax allocated among the economic units responsible for the production and distribution of goods and services. Collection of VAT takes place at the product's ultimate destination, therefore VAT is not charged on export sales. VAT is charged on all domestically sold products regardless of the country of origin. Thus, VAT is designed to provide an incentive to export and of course a disincentive to import.

Value Analysis process of trying to reduce product costs by substituting less-costly materials, redesigning nonessential parts, and the like; also called *Value*

Engineering. It involves asking questions such as the following: What is the function of the item? Is the function necessary? Can a lower cost part that serves the purpose be identified? Can the item be simplified to achieve a lower price?

Value Chain the linked set of value-creating activities beginning with the basic raw material sources and concluding with delivery of the ultimate end-use product to the final consumer.

Value Creation performing activities that increase the value of goods or services to consumers.

Value Engineering a systematic effort to reduce the cost or improve the performance of items either purchased or produced; also called *Value Analysis*. This is used to rethink the design of a part, product, or service in order to eliminate anything that does not add value. It attempts to define as simply as possible the purpose or function of the item, then search for the simplest way to accomplish that function. Good "partnership" suppliers often initiate value analysis, suggesting ways to make an item better and cheaper, thereby benefiting both buyer and supplier, and ultimately the final customer.

Value of the Firm present value of the firm's expected future cash flows or profits, discounted back to the present at an appropriate interest rate.

Value Stock a stock perceived by the marketplace to be undervalued based on criteria such as its price-to-earnings ratio, price-to-book ratio, dividend yield, etc.

Value-Added Activity activity that increases the worth of a product or service and for which the customer is willing to pay.

Variable something whose magnitude can change, i.e., something that can take on different values. For example, quantity of a good demanded will vary according to its price.

Variable Annuity an annuity whose periodic payments are dependent on some undetermined or uncertain outcome such as the value of a securities portfolio. A contract between an investor and insurance company may take this form, and, subsequently, the periodic payments would change as a function of the changes in applicable securities prices or rates of return. A variable annuity may also consist of payments that vary depending on changes in money market interest rates.

Variable Costs costs that vary in total in direct proportion to changes in activities, such as machine hours and labor hours within a relevant range. Examples are direct materials and gasoline expense based on mileage driven. Variable cost per unit is constant. *See also* Fixed Costs; Mixed Costs.

Variable Life a type of cash value life insurance that allows the policyholder to choose the investments made with his or her cash value accumulations and to share in the gains and losses of those investments. Like universal life insurance, variable life insurance promises higher investment yields than traditional whole life. It is similar to whole life insurance except that the policyholder can specify how the premiums are to be invested. Since the insured decides where his or her money is invested and bears the risk of those investments, variable life is considered a security by the government and is the only kind of life insurance sold by prospectus.

Variable Rate Loan loan carrying an interest rate that may move either up or down, depending on the movements of an outside standard such as the rate paid on U.S. Treasury securities; also called an *adjustable rate loan.* The lender can increase or decrease the interest rate on this type of loan at specified intervals to keep pace with changing market conditions. The frequency of the interest rate changes and the limit, if any, on the amount of change is set by the lender and must be specified in the loan document.

Variable Rate Mortgage a mortgage for which interest rates are not fixed. The rate applicable to the mortgage goes up or down, depending on the movement of an outside index, such as the rate paid on U.S. Treasury Securities or the cost of funds.

Variance

1. in statistics, the square of the standard deviation. For example, if the standard deviation is 20, the variance is 400. *See also* Standard Deviation.
2. in cost accounting the deviation between the actual cost and the standard cost. If actual cost exceeds standard cost, an unfavorable variance exists. A variance can be calculated for different cost items such as manufacturing costs (i.e., direct material, direct labor, and overhead), selling expenses, and administrative expenses. The reasons for a variance should be identified and corrective action taken. For example, actual production is 80 units. Standard cost per unit is $5 while actual cost per unit is $6. The unfavorable variance equals $80 ($400 vs. $480).

Variance Analysis analysis and investigation of causes for variances between standard and actual. A variance is considered favorable if the actual cost is less than the standard cost; it is unfavorable if the actual cost exceeds the standard. Unfavorable variances are the ones that need further investigation for their causes. Analysis of variances reveal the causes of these deviations. This feedback aids in planning future goals, controlling costs, evaluating performance, and taking corrective action. Management by exception is based on the analysis of variances, and attention is given to only the variances that require remedial actions.

Using variance analysis to control costs

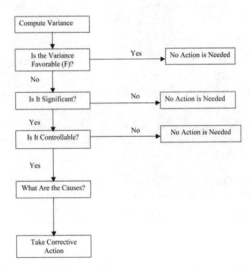

Vendor Performance Index index that represents the percentage of companies reporting slower deliveries. As the economy grows, firms have more trouble filling orders. This is one component of the Index of Leading Indicators.

Venture Capital funds invested in companies that normally do not have access to conventional sources of capital; usually for a new, risky, start-up, business venture. Providers usually demand significant control of the equity ownership.

Venture Capitalists investors interested in supplying capital to particularly high-risk situations, such as start-ups or firms denied conventional financing.

Vertical Analysis preparation of common-size statements. Key changes and trends can also be highlighted by the use of common-size statements. A common size statement is one that shows the separate items appearing on it in percentage terms. This is known as vertical analysis. In vertical analysis, a material financial statement item is used as a base value, and all other accounts on the financial statement are compared with it. In the balance sheet, for example, total assets equal 100%. Each asset is stated as a percentage of total assets. Similarly, total liabilities and stockholders' equity are each assigned 100% with a given liability or equity account stated as a percentage of the total liabilities and stockholders' equity, respectively. *See also* Horizontal Analysis.

Vertical Integration the extension of activity by a firm into business directly related to the production or distribution of the firm's end products. It typically combines a parent firm and the suppliers of its raw materials or purchasers of its finished product. Vertical merger involves extending the lines of distribution or production, either backward toward the source or forward toward the end-user. A firm controlling the entire production process is considered totally integrated vertically. This compares with horizontal integration.

Vertical Marketing System (VMS) a distribution channel structure in which producers, wholesalers, and retailers act as a unified system. One channel member owns the others, has contracts with them, or has so much power that they all cooperate.

Vertical Merger the combination of a parent firm and the suppliers of its raw materials or purchasers of its finished product. A vertical merger involves extending the lines of distribution or production, either backward toward the source or forward toward the end-user. A firm controlling the entire production process is considered totally integrated vertically.

Vested the rights of an individual to benefits from employment, such as pension, sick leave, and vacation. Pension benefits are vested when the employee has worked a specified number of years. The person may then leave the employer for another one and still collect the accumulated amount at retirement. For example, an employee might be 100% vested after five years of service.

Veterans Administration (VA) a federal government agency that helps veterans of the armed forces obtain housing. For example, it guarantees a home loan for up to a specified dollar amount or percentage of the loan balance, whichever is less.

Viral Marketing the Internet version of word-of-mouth marketing-e-mail messages or other marketing events that are so infectious that customers will want to pass them along to friends.

Virtual a computer term meaning without boundaries or a representation of reality.

Virtual Memory storage space on a disk that is treated by the operating system as if it were part of the computer's RAM. It is a technique of organizing computer memory so that it appears to have more memory than in actuality, allowing larger programs to run.

Virtual Office an office that requires very little office space. It has devices such as a cellular phone, pager, access to the Internet, and a fax.

Virtual Reality a set of hardware and software that creates images, sounds, and the sensation of touch that gives the user the feeling of a real environment and experience. The user may use devices such as helmets and gloves in order to artificially interact with simulated 3-D reality.

Virus a rogue computer program that, like a real-life biological virus, infects any computer it is entered into.

Voice over Internet Protocol a technological innovation that requires us to pay telecoms service providers to make phone calls. This technology transfers voice traffic across the internet; a medium designed primarily for data traffic.

Voice Recognition technology that enables computers to recognize human voice, translate it into program code, and act upon the voiced commands.

Voidable descriptive of a contract that may be annulled by a party to it because of some illegality (e.g., fraud), incompetence, or the existence of some provision to rescind it.

VoIP *see* Voice over Internet Protocol.

Volatility the yardstick for risk of a security—a stock or the market itself—both up and down. It is a measure of the amount by which a security is expected to fluctuate in a given period of time. Volatility in stock prices may be due to many factors, such as instability in earnings, economic uncertainty, thinly traded security, and erratic economic or political conditions.

Voucher System a type of internal system used to control the cash (checks) being spent (written). The voucher system consists of vouchers; voucher files (paid and unpaid); voucher register, which takes the place of the purchase journal; cash register, which takes the place of the cash disbursement journal; and the general journal. This system ensures to the person paying the bills that these bills are proper and should be paid. On the due date, a voucher is removed from the "unpaid voucher" file and forwarded to the firm's disbursing officer for final approval of payment.

Vouching the process of recognizing obligations and authorizing the disbursement of cash.

W-2 Form a statement or form, called *Wage and Tax Statement*, sent to an employee of a business which shows the gross earnings and deductions (such as FICA, Federal, State, and local income taxes) for a calendar year, which is used for income tax purposes. The business sends a copy of the W-2 to the Internal Revenue Service and other tax jurisdictions as needed. The employee attaches a copy of the W-2 to the employee's Federal, State, and local income tax returns.

W-4 Form a form (Employee's Withholding Allowance Certificate), filled out by a new employee or an employee who wishes to change the figures in the form, that provides the information needed by the employer to calculate an employee's pay, net of exemptions and other tax deductions. The W-4 form does not provide information for deductions for union dues, medical insurance, pension, etc.

Wage Earner Plan known as *Chapter 11*, an arrangement that schedules debt repayment over future years; that is, an alternative to straight bankruptcy (or Chapter 7) when a person has a steady source of income and there is a reasonable chance of repayment within three to five years. It is for wage earners who have less than $100,000 in unsecured debts and less than $350,000 in secured debts, and allows for a full or partial payoff of debts. *See also* Chapter 13; Straight Bankruptcy.

Wage Garnishment a court order that requires a borrower's employer to pay a lender a regular sum in order to reduce a debt. It is a legal action taken only after a credit user has defaulted. The consumer credit Protection Act limits the amount of disposable income subject to garnishment and prohibits the dismissal of an employee for garnishment of any indebtedness.

Waiver of Premium a clause or an option in an insurance policy that provides for automatic payment of premiums should the policyholder be ill or disabled. This option may be included in an insurance policy or be purchased separately. With this option, the insurer waives premium if the insured becomes permanently disabled. All policy benefits remain in force during the waiver period.

Wall Street a street in lower New York City surrounded by the entire financial district. Both the New York Stock Exchange and the American Stock Exchange are located there. Wall Street has become the sign of capitalism throughout the world.

Wall Street Journal a leading financial newspaper covering financial markets and news of company activities.

Warehouse Receipt a document listing goods or commodities (e.g., gold) that have been stored in a warehouse that shows retention of title to the goods. Warehouse receipts may be negotiable or non-negotiable. Negotiable receipts allow transfer without endorsement and may act as a security for a loan. Non-negotiable receipts must be endorsed upon transfer. Warehouse receipts allow the sale of the good without having to physically deliver them. Warehouse receipts are regulated by the Uniform Warehouse Receipts Act.

Warrant a paper giving its holder the right to buy a security at a price, either within a specified period or perpetually. A warrant is generally offered with another security as an added inducement or sweetener to buy. Warrants are like call options, but with much longer time spans—sometimes years. Note: When you buy a warrant, you're paying a small price now for the right to buy a certain number of shares at a fixed price when the stock is finally issued. Consequently, you pay now and own later. You do this only if you think the price of the stock will rise.

Warranty an assurance by a seller to a buyer to satisfy for a stated period of time deficiencies in the quality or performance of items, such as an automobile or appliance. Typically, there is no additional charge for correcting deficiencies during the warranty period.

Wash Sale
1. a transaction or sale that is nullified by its reversal or offset within a short time of its initiation. Wash sales typically were used to induce trading activity by artificially inflating activity and price. Such sales are now forbidden by rules of the stock exchange.
2. losses on a sale of stock that, for federal income tax purposes, may not be recognized if the same stock is purchased within 30 days preceding or following the date of sale.

Wasting Asset
1. any fixed asset with limited life and subject to depreciation. It therefore excludes land.
2. natural resource such as oil, coal, timber, having a limited useful life and subject to depletion. Such assets decrease in worth primarily due to the extraction of the valued commodity held by these assets. *See also* Intangible Assets.
3. security whose value expires at a specified time in the future. An option contract (put or call) is an example of a wasting asset.

Watered Stock capital stock issued in exchange for assets with a fair market value less than its par or stated value. In this manner, assets are recorded at overstated values. This practice is illegal if the Board of Directors acted in bad faith or fraudulently with respect to knowledge of such circumstances surrounding the issue. Watered stock got its name from the cattlemen's practice of encouraging their stock to drink large quantities of water, induced by salt, before taking them to market. Thus the stock would appear larger and perhaps become more comparatively valuable.

Weak Dollar *see* Appreciation of the Dollar.

Wealth

1. an accumulation of assets that an individual or other entity has developed over a period of time, often a lifetime in the case of an individual.

2. stockholders' value or market value of a firm's stock.

Welfare Maximization a firm's goal that considers the risk associated with alternative decisions, as opposed to profit maximization, which is a short-term goal and provides no explicit way of incorporating the degree of uncertainty into the analysis. The wealth-maximization criterion requires that a firm evaluate the expected future costs and benefits associated with a decision, by explicitly accounting for the timing of these flows as well as the risk associated with them.

Web see World Wide Web (www).

Web Browser browsers for the World Wide Web (www), enabling one to hook up with network servers to obtain HTML documents and web pages. It provides a linkage among pages and documents. The server may physically be on the Internet or a private network. The browser may contain "help" applications for special files.

Web Communities websites upon which members can congregate online and exchange views on issues of common interest.

Web Conferencing software supporting video, audio, document, and data conferencing on the World Wide Web. It is used in business applications.

Web Page a screenful of text, pictures, sounds, and animation that the user faces when using a web browser.

Web Server software that manages and controls information on the website. The program enables responses to be made to requests for information from Web browsers.

Webcasting the automatic downloading of customized information of interest to a recipient's PCs, affording an attractive channel for delivering internet advertising or other information content.

Webmaster/Webmistress the person in charge of constructing and managing a website.

Website Traffic the amount of visitors and visits a website receives.

Websites the electronic presence of an organization or individual on the World Wide Web that have homepage information.

Weekly Jobless Claims *see* Jobless Claims.

Weighted Average average of observations having different degrees of importance or frequency, rather than treating each component equally, which is the case of simple average or mean.

Weighted Average Cost of Capital *see* Cost of Capital.

Weighted Mean *see* Weighted Average.

Wellness Programs health promotion initiatives in an organization. These programs are known to prevent and combat job stress. More than 81 percent of U.S. businesses with over 50 employees have wellness programs.

Wells Notice an alert from the SEC that the agency might bring an enforcement action against an individual or company. The notice provides the officers of a company under investigation with an opportunity to submit to the SEC written statements explaining why an enforcement action should not be brought.

West Texas Intermediate Crude the price per barrel of a benchmark of crude oil produced in West Texas. It is reported on the New York Mercantile Exchange and used by oil traders to set the price of other grades of crude. Rising oil prices boost prices for gasoline, air travel, shipped products, and petroleum-base products and may be a sign of future inflation.

What-If Analysis *see* Simulation.

Whistleblowing the process of alerting the proper authorities (such as the tax authority, SEC, and the environmental agency) of a firm's improper or illegal action.

White Collar Crimes crimes committed by white collar employees. Examples are bribery, money laundering, insider trading, and RICO (Racketeer-Influenced and Corrupt Operations).

White Knight a slang term for an individual or company who saves a corporation from an unfriendly takeover by taking it over himself or itself. This way the targeted corporation is rescued from the unwanted bidder's control.

White Paper
1. a government report; bound in white; also called a *white book*.
2. an authoritative report on a major issue, as by a team of journalists.
3. a short treatise whose purpose is to educate industry customers.

Whole Life Insurance a cash value life insurance policy that provides level protection for a fixed premium for the lifetime of the insured and includes a savings feature. The policy remains in force as long as the insured continues to pay the insurance premiums. The premiums remain level and fixed. It has loan privileges, optional riders, and surrender and exchanges rights.

Wholesale Banking banking that deals in a significant volume of transactions typically with large depositors, such as major corporations. There may also be dealings with other financial institutions. This is in contrast to retail banking, which applies to regular smaller accounts of people and small businesses.

Wholesale Money money borrowed in large amounts from banks, large firms or financial organizations, in contrast to retail money, which is acquired by attracting deposits from individuals and small companies.

Wholesaler a marketing intermediary located in the channel between the original supplier and the buyer-user. Jobber and distributor are other wholesalers.

Wholly Owned Subsidiaries a subsidiary in which the firm owns 100 percent of the stock.

Wide Area Network (WAN) network comprising of a large geographic area. The connected LANs to derive a WAN may be in the same building, different buildings near each other, or distantly apart. WANs are essential in the client/server environment because the applications in client/server usually apply to accessing data stored in separate locations.

Widows and Orphans
1. in word processing software, a widow is the last line of a paragraph that appears on the next page. An orphan is the first line of a paragraph that appears as the last line in a page.
2. secure stock with a record of high dividends. It is typically fairly stable in market price. In most cases, the company is very cyclical in nature. An example would be a large and mature utility.

Wi-Fi *see* Wireless Fidelity.

Wildcat Strike a strike called spontaneously by workers at a company, without the sanction of union headquarters.

Will a written document specifying that a person, called a testator, is disposing of his or her property, upon death, to the parties named. The will may also specify other conditions that have to be met before the property may be fully disposed of. To be enforceable, the will must be signed and witnessed.

Wilshire 5000 Index the broadest weighted index of all common stock issues on the NYSE, AMEX and the most active issues on the over-the-counter market. Approximately 85% of the securities are traded on the NYSE. The index's value is in billions of dollars. It includes about 6,000 stocks (not 5,000 as its name would suggest) so it is representative of the overall market.

Windfall Profits profits of an unexpected nature and generally not due to the efforts and expenditures of the entity that benefits. The Crude Oil Windfall Profits Tax of 1980 placed a tax on such profits on the production and sale of crude oil. The windfall profits figure is derived from complex calculations defined in the Code, based on the difference between selling price less state severance taxes and a defined base price.

Window a portion of a computer display screen. Some programs allow the user to divide the screen into two or more windows, making it possible to work on two different tasks simultaneously.

Windows Mobile a new version of its Windows operating system for mobile devices that adds such features as PowerPoint viewing while making it easier for gadget makers to equip phones and handheld computers with typewriter keyboards and iPod-sized hard drives. Windows Mobile 5.0, introduced in May 2005, also marks an about-face in marketing by eliminating the distinct Pocket PC and Smartphone brands of the operating system. Other feature enhancements include updates to the mobile versions of Microsoft Word and Excel that better maintain the formatting of documents created on a computer and allow charts to be created from a spreadsheet. The elimination of the 5-year-old Pocket PC brand for PDAs and the separate Smartphone label puts Windows Mobile on the same page as rival mobile-device platforms such as Symbian and BlackBerry.

Wireless *see* Wireless Technology.

Wireless Fidelity (Wi-Fi) the popular term for a high-frequency wireless local area network. The consumer-friendly name for the 802.11b engineering standard. It lets home and office users create wireless local networks, which connect two or more computers to each other and a faster Internet line. This way there is no more poking holes in walls or tripping over bulky Ethernet cables. The Wi-Fi technology is rapidly gaining acceptance in many companies as an alternative to a wired local area network. It can also be installed for a home network.

Wireless Lan (WLAN) one in which a mobile user can connect to a local area network (LAN) through a wireless (radio) connection. A standard, 802.11 specifies the technologies for wireless LANs.

Wireless Technology a variety of technologies to communicate without wires, namely radio transmissions. Examples are cellular, microwave, infrared, and satellite.

Withholding Tax deductions by an employer from employee salaries for the payment of federal and state income taxes. It is paid in a prescribed manner to the taxing authority. Withholding tax is remitted by the employer to the IRS or deposited into the designated bank on a periodic basis as prescribed by the IRS. *See also* FICA.

WLAN *see* Wireless LAN (WLAN).

WOM *see* Word-of-Mouth (WOM) Advertising.

Word popular word-processing software by Microsoft.

Word Processing; Word Processing Software a method that involves the use of computerized equipment to automatically produce written letters and documents, reports, memorandums, reminder letters, audit bid proposals, contracts, confirmations, representation letters, and billings. Typically, the word processing programs allow for insertion, deletion, rearrangement, search and replace, writing style sheets, and moving text from one document to another. A table of content may be prepared from headings and subheadings. A glossary and index may also be furnished. Windows can display different portions of the same document or of completely independent but related documents. Examples of word processing programs that are in wide use include WordPerfect and Word.

Word-of-Mouth (WOM) Advertising advertising that occurs when people share information about products or promotions with friends. It is informal communications between consumers about products and services they like or dislike.

WordPerfect Software a popular word processing software.

Work Measurement the determination of the length of time it should take to complete the job. Job times are vital inputs for manpower planning, estimating labor costs, scheduling, budgeting, and designing incentive systems. In addition, from workers' standpoint, time standards provide an indication of expected output. Time standards used under standard cost systems reflect the amount of time it should take an average worker to do a job under typical operating conditions. The standards include expected activity time plus allowances for probable delays. The most commonly used methods of work measurement are (1) stopwatch time study, (2) historical times, (3) predetermined data, and (4) work sampling.

Work Sampling work measurement technique involving the sampling of the nature of the activity in which the worker is involved; used for the broader problem of determining production standards.

Worker's Compensation a program providing payments, without regard to a finding of negligence of either party, to workers involved in specific job-related injuries. These laws were enacted so that the employee would not have to go through a long and arduous lawsuit and possibly not recover due to the employer's advantageous financial standing. Payments are specifically exempt from taxation.

Working Capital a concept traditionally defined as a firm's investment in current assets. Net working capital refers to the difference between current assets and current liabilities.

Work-in-Progress Inventory (WIP) inventory of goods that are started but not finished. That is, partially completed units, not ready for sale.

World Bank created by Bretton Woods in an agreement in 1944 that lends money to countries who have difficulty getting loans from private sources. It is an integrated group of international institutions that provides financial and technical assistance to developing countries. The World Bank (*www.worldbank. org*) includes the International Bank for Reconstruction and Development and the International Development Association. World Bank affiliates, which are legally and financially separate, include the International Center for Settlement of Investment Disputes, the International Finance Corporation, and the Multilateral Investment Guarantee Agency. World Bank headquarters are in Washington, D.C.

World Class the best, or among the best, in the world.

World Knowledge Competitiveness Index collated by Robert Higgins Associates (*www.hugginsassociates.com/*) an integrated and overall benchmark of the knowledge capacity, capability and sustainability of 125 regions across the globe, and the extent to which this knowledge is translated into economic value, and transferred into the wealth of the citizens of these regions, utilizing 19 knowledge economy benchmarks, including employment levels in the knowledge economy, patent registrations, R&D investment by the private and public sector, education expenditure, information and communication technology infrastructure, and access to private equity. The World Knowledge Competitiveness Index is the only existing instrument that benchmarks such regional performance at a global level, with the index comprising of 55 North American regions, 45 from Europe, and 25 from Asia-Pacific.

World Wide Web (www) Internet system for world-wide hypertext linking of multimedia documents, making the relationship of information that is common between documents easily accessible and completely independent of physical location.

Worldatwork (*http://www.worldatwork.org/*), the world's leading not-for-profit professional association dedicated to knowledge leadership in compensation, benefits, and total rewards. Founded in 1955, WorldatWork focuses on human resources disciplines associated with attracting, retaining, and motivating employees. In addition to serving as the membership association of the profession, WorldatWork provides education programs, the monthly *workspan®magazine*, online information resources, surveys, publications, conferences, research, and networking opportunities. An affiliate organization, WorldatWork Society of Certified Professionals, administers and issues the certification designations; Certified Compensation Professional (CCP®), Certified Benefits Professional (CBPTM), and Global Remuneration Professional (GRP®). The Canadian Compensation Association is affiliated with the ACA.

Worm
1. a rogue program that replicates itself and penetrates a valid computer system. It may spread within a network, penetrating all connected computers.
2. WORM (write once, read many), a storage medium that is loaded with software by the maker and can never be overwritten. An example is CD-ROM.

Wraparound Mortgage (Trust Deed) a mortgage (trust deed) that encompasses existing mortgages and is subordinate (junior) to them; also called *all inclusive trust deed (AITD)*. The existing mortgages stay on the property and the new mortgage wraps around them. The excising mortgage loan generally carries lower interest rates than the one on the new mortgage loan. This loan arrangement is a form of seller financing.

Writ a court order requiring the named individual to act or not act on something mentioned. An example is an order to a husband to make alimony payments to his ex-wife.

Write-Off (Down) a reduction of the value of an asset or writing-off of bad debts. The reason for a write-down is that some economic event has occurred indicating that the asset's value has diminished.

Wrongful Termination laws that allow an employee to sue an employer for a monetary award for causing her termination in violation of the law, such as termination due to age, race, or sex.

www *see* World Wide Web (www).

WYSIWYG (What You See Is What You Get) in word processing or desktop software, the term meaning that you will be able to print exactly what you see on the screen.

Yy

Yahoo a popular Internet search engine.

Yankee Bonds dollar-denominated bonds issued within the United States by a foreign corporation. These bonds are sold in the U.S. when market conditions are more conducive to them relative to the Eurobond market or in domestic markets overseas.

Yellow Page Advertising business advertising appearing in the non-residence section of phone books. It is printed on yellow paper.

Yellow-Dog Contract a document once required by management for workers to sign, in which the worker swore he was not a member of a labor union and would not become one.

Yield (Rate Of Return) Also called *Real Return*, *Real Rate of Return*, or *Effective Rate of Return*.
In General: The income earned on an investment, usually expressed as a percentage of the market price.
Stocks: Percentage return earned on a common stock or preferred stock in dividends. It is figured by dividing the total of dividends paid in the preceding 12 months by the current market price. For example, a stock with a current market value of $40 a share that has paid $2 in dividends in the preceding 12 months is said to return 5 percent ($2/$40). If an investor paid $20 for the stock five years earlier, the stock would be returning him/her 10 percent on his/her original investment. *See also* Dividend Yield.
Bonds: The Current Yield or Yield to Maturity (YTM). *See also* Bond Yields; Internal Rate Of Return (IRR); Yield to Call.

Note: Yield is not the same thing as the coupon interest rate. Actually, yield may be higher or lower than the bond's interest rate. If, for instance, a bond costs $1,000 and pays 8% interest, you'd receive $80 a year from this bond. So it would yield 8%. If, however, a year later, the bond loses value and it's sold for $800, the new buyers would still receive the $80 a year. However, because they only paid $800, the yield for them would be 10%. In contrast, should the bond be sold next year at a premium, say $1,200, the $80 a year interest would only be a yield of 6.67%.

Yield Curve a curve showing the relationship between yield (interest rate) and maturity for a set of similar securities; also called the *term structure of interest rates*. For example, the yield curve can be drawn for U.S. Treasuries. Other factors such as default risk and tax treatment are held constant. An understanding of this relationship is important to investors who must decide whether to buy long- or short-term bonds. A yield curve may take any number of shapes. It is an important measure of economic expectations. Because the shape of the yield curve influences investment strategies, it can provide a clue to the future pricing of all kinds of financial assets, from mortgages and "junk" bonds in the United States to South American sovereign debt and Hong Kong property. Flattening signals expectations of lower economic growth. In fact, if long-term end of the curve is lower than short-term rates, that's the signal of a possible recession in the near future. *See also* Term Structure Of Interest Rates.

Yield Differential *see* Yield Gap.

Yield Gap the difference between a yield on equities and a corresponding yield on fixed-income securities.

Yield Spread the difference between the yields received on two different types of bonds with different ratings (or risks); also called *yield differential* or *risk differential*. In times of economic uncertainty, the yield spread increases because investors demand higher premiums on risky issues to compensate for the increased chance of default. *See also* Bond Ratings.

Yield to Call the yield of a bond, if it is held until the call date. This yield is valid only if the security is called prior to maturity. The calculation of yield to call is based on the coupon rate, length of time to the call date, and the market price. In general, bonds are callable over several years and normally are called at a small premium.

Yield to Maturity (YTM) the annual rate of return that a bondholder purchasing a bond today and holding it to maturity would receive on his or her investment. It is the effective rate of return on a bond calculated from its market price, face value, coupon rate, and time remaining to maturity. The YTM incorporates the stated rate of interest on the bond as well as any discount or premium that may have been generated when bought.

Z Scale in statistics, the scale that standardizes a normal distribution by converting an x-scale to the standardized scale. The z-scale is computed by using the following formula:

$$z = \frac{\overline{x} - \mu}{\sigma}$$

where z is the standardized variable, or the number of standard deviations from the mean, $\overline{x}$ is the outcome of interest, and μ and σ are the mean and standard deviation of the distribution. This scale permits conversion of any set of observations of a variable into standard units with mean = 0 and standard deviation = 1, regardless of the mean and standard deviation of that set. This conversion allows the analyst to use a single table for the area under a normal curve for purposes of estimating probabilities and to directly compare sets of observations with different means and standard deviations. *See also* Normal Curves; Normal Distribution.

Z Score or Model

1. in statistics, the standard normal variate that standardizes a normal distribution by converting a x-scale to the z-scale. *See also* Z Scale.
2. a score produced by Altman's bankruptcy prediction model, which is as follows:
3. the "Z-score" equals:

$$\frac{\text{Working capital}}{\text{Total Assets}} \times 1.2 + \frac{\text{retained earnings}}{\text{total assets}} \times 1.4 + \frac{\text{operating income}}{\text{total assets}} \times 3.3$$

$$+$$

$$\frac{\text{market value of common stock and preferred stock}}{\text{(or net worth for private companies)}} \times .6$$
$$\frac{}{\text{total debt}}$$

$$+$$

$$\frac{\text{sales}}{\text{total assets}} \times 1$$

Altman's scoring chart follows:

Score	Probability of short-term illiquidity
1.80 or less	Very high
1.81 to 2.7	High
2.8 to 2.9	Possible
3.0 or higher	Not likely

The score is important to management in indicating whether capital expansion and dividends should be curtailed to keep needed funds within the business. The Z score is known to be about 90 percent accurate in forecasting business failure one year in the future and about 80 percent accurate in forecasting it two years in the future. Example; Company H provides the following relevant data:

Working capital	$250,000
Total assets	900,000
Total liabilities	300,000
Retained earnings	200,000
Sales	1,000,000
Operating income	150,000
Common stock	
Book value	210,000
Market value	300,000
Preferred stock	
Book value	100,000
Market value	160,000

The "Z-score" is:

$$\frac{\$250,000}{\$900,000} \times 1.2 + \frac{\$200,000}{\$900,000} \times 1.4 + \frac{\$150,000}{\$900,000} \times 3.3$$

$$+$$

$$\frac{\$460.000}{\$300,000} \times .6$$

$$+$$

$$\frac{\$1,000,000}{\$900,000} \times 1 = .333 + .312 + .550 + .920 + 1.11 = \underline{3.225}$$

The score indicates that the probability of failure is unlikely. *See also* Business Failure; Bankruptcy.

Zero Defects planned efforts emphasizing the importance and self-will of personnel to give high quality performance. It is the concept that no product is manufactured without any defects.

Zero-Balance Account an arrangement, agreed to in advance by a drawee bank, under which a customer issues checks on an account even though funds do not exist in that account to cover the items. When the checks are physically presented to the drawee and posted, creating a minus balance, the bank contacts the customer, reports the overdraft figure, and transfers funds from another account to eliminate it, thus restoring the account to a zero balance. Commonly used by corporations that have many disbursing points and by many agencies of government.

Zero-Based Budgeting (ZBB) a planning and budgeting tool that uses cost/benefit analysis of projects and functions to improve resource allocation in an organization. Traditional budgeting tends to concentrate on the incremental change from the previous year. It assumes that the previous year's activities and programs are essential and must be continued. Under zero-base budgeting, however, cost and benefit estimates are built up from scratch, from the zero level, and must be justified. The basic steps to effective zero-base budgeting are (1) describe each company activity in a "decision" package; (2) analyze, evaluate, and rank all these packages in priority on the basis of cost/benefit analysis; and (3) allocate resources accordingly.

Zero-Coupon Bond a bond sold at a deep discount and that accrues the interest semiannually. Both the principal and the accumulated interest are paid at maturity. Although a fixed rate is implicit in the discount and the specific maturity, they are not fixed income securities in the traditional sense because they provide for no periodic income. Although the interest on the bond is paid at maturity, accrued interest, though not received, is taxable yearly as ordinary income.

Zero-Sum Game the game in which the total gains of the winner exactly equal the total loss of the loser. For example, if two computer stores in a small town are competing for a share of a fixed market (i.e., a fixed number of customers) and one can increase a share of the market at the other's expense, the game is zero-sum. *See also* Non-zero Sum Game.

Zone Pricing a type of pricing under which the seller divides the economy into zones or regions and charges the same delivered price within each zone, but different prices between zones sufficient to cover average freight costs as a whole. In theory, the seller's average net is the same in every zone. If the seller's price zones are the same as the freight-rate zones, this type of pricing is the same as f.o.b. pricing, no legal problems are involved.

Zoning; Zoning Board; Zoning Ordinances laws designating how land will be used such as for residential, commercial, and industrial uses.

Zoning Board of Appeals a municipal or county local government board that resolves zoning disputes.

Zoning Laws local government ordinances originating from state police powers governing real estate development including structural and design requirements. Zoning ordinances normally define (1) various usage classifications ranging from agricultural to heavy industry, (2) building restrictions including minimum-square-footage building requirements as well as prohibitions, (3) the establishment of a zoning board of appeals to hear petitions for nonconforming uses, and (4) violation penalties and procedures.

Appendix
Acronyms

1. AAA — American Accounting Association
2. ABC — Activity-Based Costing
3. ABM — Activity-Based Management
4. ACA — American Compensation Association
5. ACRS — Accelerated Cost Recovery System
6. ACV — Actual Cash Value
7. ADA — Americans with Disabilities Act
8. ADB — Asian Development Bank
9. AD&D — Accidental Death and Dismemberment
10. ADEA — Age Discrimination in Employment Act
11. ADP — Automated Data Processing
12. ADR — American Depository Receipt
13. AFL — American Federation of Labor
14. AFL-CIO — American Federation of Labor-Congress of Industrial Organizations
15. AGI – Adjusted Gross Income
16. AGM — Annual General Meeting
17. AI — Artificial Intelligence
18. AICPA — American Institute of Certified Public Accountants
19. AID — Agency for International Development
20. AIMR — Association for Investment Management & Research
21. AIREA — American Institute of Real Estate Appraisers
22. AITD — All Inclusive Trust Deed
23. AKA — Also Known As
24. AMA — American Management Association/American Marketing Association
25. AMEX — American Stock Exchange
26. AMI — Alternative Mortgage Instrument
27. AML — Adjustable Mortgage Loan
28. AMT — Alternative Minimum Tax
29. AOL — America on Line
30. A/P — Accounts Payable

31. APB—Accounting Principles Board
32. APICS—American Production and Inventory Control Society
33. APM—Arbitrage Pricing Model
34. APR—Annual Percentage Rate
35. A/R—Accounts Receivable
36. ARM—Adjustable Rate Mortgage
37. ASCII—American Standard Code for Information Interchange
38. ASREC—American Society of Real Estate Counselors
39. ATAR—Awareness-Trial-Availability-Repeat
40. ATM—Automated Teller Machine
41. B2B—Business to Business
42. B2C—Business to Customer
43. BBB—Better Business Bureau
44. BBS—Bulletin Board System
45. BLS—Bureau of Labor Statistics
46. BOP—Balance of Payments
47. BOE—Board of Equalization
48. BPR—Business Process Reengineering
49. BOL—Bill of Landing
50. C2B—Consumer to Business
51. B2C—Business to Consumer
52. C++—Latest Program Language
53. CAD/CAM—Computer-Aided Design and Computer-Aided Manufacturing
54. CAI—Computer-Aided Instruction
55. CAPM—Capital Asset Pricing Model
56. CBOE—Chicago Board Options Exchange
57. CBOT–Chicago Board of Trade
58. cc—copy
59. CD—Compact Disc/ Certificate of Deposit
60. CDP—Certificate in Data Processing
61. CD-ROM—Compact Disc, Read-Only Memory
62. CEA—Council of Economic Advisors
63. CEBS—Certified Employee Benefits Specialist
64. CEO—Chief Executive Officer
65. CERN—Consel Europeen pour la Recherche Nucleaire
66. CFA—Chartered Financial Analyst
67. CFC—Chartered Financial Consultant
68. CFO- Chief Financial Officer
69. CFP—Certified Financial Planner
70. CFTC—Commodities Futures Trading Commission
71. CGA—Color Graphics Adapter
72. CGI—Common Gateway Interface
73. CI—Continuous Improvement
74. CIA—Certified Internal Auditor
75. CIF—Cost, Insurance, Freight

76. CIM—Computer Integrated Manufacturing
77. CIO—Chief Information Officer/Chief Investment Officer
78. CLU—Chartered Life Underwriter
79. CM—Contribution Margin
80. CMBS—Commercial Mortgage-Backed Securities
81. CME—Chicago Mercantile Exchange
82. CMFC—Chartered Mutual Fund Counselor
83. CMO—Collateralized Mortgage Obligation
84. CMS—Cost Management System
85. c/o—Care of
86. CO—Certificate of Occupancy
87. COBE—Chicago Board Options Exchange
88. COBOL—Common Business Oriented Language
89. COBRA—Consolidated Omnibus Budget Reconciliation Act of 1985
90. COLA—Cost of Living Adjustment
91. comps—Comparable Properties
92. COO—Chief Operating Officer
93. CO-OP—Cooperative Apartment
94. CPA—Certified Public Accountant
95. CPCU—Chartered Property and Casualty Underwriter/Certified Property and Casual Underwriter
96. CPI—Consumer Price Index/characters per inch
97. CPM—Cost Per Thousand/Certified Property Manager/Critical Path Method
98. CPS—characters per second
99. CPSC—Consumer product Safety Commission
100. CPU—Central Processing Unit
101. CRB—Certified Residential Broker or Commodity Research Bureau
102. CRE—Counselor of Real Estate
103. CRM—Customer Relationship Management
104. CRP—Capacity Requirements Planning
105. CRS—Certified Residential Specialist
106. CRT—Cathode Ray Tube
107. CRV—Certificate of Reasonable Value
108. CUSIP—Committee on Uniform Securities Identification Procedures
109. CV—Convertible Bond/Coefficient of Variation
110. CVP—Cost-Volume-Profit
111. CY—Current Yield
112. D&B—Dun & Bradstreet Report
113. DBA—Doing Business As
114. DBMS—Database Management System
115. DCA—Dollar Cost Averaging
116. DCF—Discounted Cash Flow
117. DCR—Debt Coverage Ratio
118. DDB—Double Declining Balance Depreciation

119. DF—Degree of Freedom
120. DFL—Degree of Financial Leverage
121. DIF—Discriminate Function System
122. DJIA—Dow Jones Industrial Average
123. DNS—Domain Name System
124. DOL—Department of Labor/Degree of Operating Leverage
125. DP—Data processing
126. DRIP—Divided Reinvestment Plan
127. DSL -- Digital Subscriber Line
128. DSS—Decision Support System
129. DTL—Degree of Total Leverage
130. EA—Enrolled Agent
131. EAFE—Europe, Australia, Far East
132. EAP—Employee Assistance Program
133. EC—European Community/Electronic Commerce
134. ECI—Employer Cost Index
135. ECOA—Equal Credit Opportunity Act
136. EDGAR—Electronic Data Gathering Analysis and Retrieval
137. EDI—Electronic Data Interchange
138. EEC—European Economic Community
139. EEOC—Equal Employment Opportunity Commission
140. EER—Energy Efficiency Ratio
141. EFT—Electronic Funds Transfer
142. EGA—Enhanced Graphic Adaptor
143. EIB—Export-Import Bank
144. EIS—Executive Information System
145. EMU—"European" Economic and Monetary Union
146. EOQ—Economic Order Quantity
147. EPA—Environmental Protection Agency
148. EPS—Earnings Per Share
149. ERA—Economic Recovery Act
150. ERISA—Employee Retirement Income Security Act
151. ERM—Enterprise Risk Management
152. ERP—Enterprise Resource Planning
153. ESOP—Employee Stock Ownership Plan
154. ETF—Electronic Transfer Funds/Equity Transfer Funds
155. EU—European Union
156. EVA—Economic Value Added
157. EX-IM BANK—Export-Import Bank
158. FAQ—Frequently Asked Questions
159. FASB—Financial Accounting Standards Board
160. FCBA—Fair Credit Billing Act
161. FCC—Federal Communication Commission
162. FCPA—Foreign Corrupt Practices Act
163. FCRA—Fair Credit Reporting Act

164. FDA—Food and Drug Administration
165. FDI—Foreign Direct Investment
166. FDIC—Federal Deposit Insurance Corporation
167. Fed—Federal Reserve System
168. FHA—Federal Housing Administration
169. FHLBB—Federal Home Loan Bank Board
170. FHLMC—Federal Home Loan Mortgage Corporation
171. FICA—Federal Insurance Contributions Act
172. FICO—Fair, Issac & Company
173. FIFO—First in, first out
174. FLSA—Fair Labor Standard Act
175. FMLA—Family and Medical Leave Act
176. FMS—Flexible Manufacturing System
177. FMV—Fair Market Value
178. FNMA—Federal National Mortgage Association
179. FOB—Free on Board
180. FOMC—Federal Open Market Committee
181. FOREX—Foreign Exchange
182. FORTRAN—Formula Translation
183. FRB—Federal Reserve Board
184. FSLIC—Federal Savings and Loan Insurance Corporation
185. FTC—Federal Trade Commission
186. FTP—File Transfer Protocol
187. FUTA—Federal Unemployment Tax Act
188. FV—Future Value
189. FY- Fiscal Year
190. FYI—For Your Information
191. G or GB—Gigabyte
192. G&A—General Administrative
193. G-13—Group of Thirteen Nations
194. GAAP—Generally Accepted Accounting Principles
195. GAO—General Accounting Office
196. GASB—Government Accounting Standard Board
197. GATT—General Agreement on Tariffs and Trade
198. GenX—Generation X
199. GB - Gigabyte
200. GC—General Contractor
201. GDP—Gross Domestic Product
202. Ghz—Gigahertz
203. GIC—Guaranteed Invest Contracts
204. GIF—Graphic Interchange Format
205. GIM—Gross Income Multiplier
206. GIGO—Garbage in, garbage out
207. GMAC—General Motors Acceptance Corporation
208. GNMA—Government National Mortgage Association

209. GO—General Obligation Bond
210. GPM—Graduated Payment Mortgage
211. GPO—Government Printing Office
212. GRM—Gross Rent Multiplier
213. GTC—Good Till Canceled
214. GUI—Graphical User Interface
215. HMO—Health Maintenance Organization
216. HOW—Home Owners Warranty
217. HPR—Holding Period Return
218. HR—Human Resources
219. HR-10 -- Keogh Pension Plan
220. HRM—Human Resource Management
221. HTML—Hypertext Markup Language
222. HTTP—Hypertext Transport Protocol
223. HUD—Housing and Urban Development
224. Hz—Hertz
225. IAS—International Accounting Standards
226. IASB—International Accounting Standards Board
227. IASC—International Accounting Standards Committee
228. IBES—Institutional Brokers Estimate System
229. IBF—International Banking Facility
230. IBRD—International Bank for Reconstruction and Development
231. IC—Integrated Circuit
232. ICC—Interstate Commerce Commission
233. ICCP—Institute of Computer Professionals
234. ICFA—Institute of Chartered Financial Analysts
235. IIA—Institute of Internal Auditors
236. ILO—International Labor Office
237. IMF—International Monetary Fund
238. Inc.—Incorporated
239. IOU—"I Owe You"
240. IP—Internet Protocol
241. IPO—Initial Public Offering
242. IPR—Intellectual Property Rights
243. IRA—Individual Retirement Account
244. IRC—Internet Relay Chat
245. IREM—Institute of Real Estate Management
246. IRR—Internal Rate of Return
247. IRS—Internal Revenue Service
248. IS—Information Systems
249. ISBN—International Standard Book Number
250. ISDN—Integrated Services Digital Network
251. ISO—Incentive Stock Option/International Organization for Standardization
252. ISP—Internet Service Provider

253. ISSN—International Standard Serial Number
254. IT—Information Technology
255. ITA—International Trade Association
256. ITC—Investment Tax Credit or International Trade Commission
257. ITO—International Trade Organization
258. JIT—Just-in-time inventory
259. K or KB—Kilobyte
260. LAN—Local Area Network
261. LAWN—Local Area Wireless Network
262. LBO—Leveraged Buyout
263. L/C—Letter of Credit
264. LDC—Less Developed Country
265. LEI—Leading Economic Indicators
266. LIFO—Last in, first out
267. LIBOR—London Interbank Offering Rate
268. LLC—Limited Liability Company
269. LP—Linear Programming
270. LTC—Less than Carload
271. LTD - Limited
272. LTV—Loan to Value Ratio
273. M1, M2, M3—Money Supply
274. MAC—Macintosh
275. MACRS—Modified Accelerated Cost Recovery System
276. MAI—Member, Appraisal Institute
277. MB—or Megs—Megabyte
278. MBA—Master of Business Administration/Mortgage Banking Association
279. MBO—Management by Objectives
280. MFN—Most-favored Nation
281. MGIC—Mortgage Guarantee Insurance Company
282. MHz—Megahertz
283. MICR—Magnetic Ink Character Recognition
284. MIPS—Million Instructions per Second
285. MIS—Management Information Systems
286. MMDA—Money Market Deposit Accounts
287. MLM—Multi-level Marketing
288. MLS—Multiple Listing Service
289. MPS—Master Production Schedule
290. MRP—Material Requirement Planning or Manufacturing Resource Planning (MRP II)
291. MS-DOS—Microsoft Disk Operating System
292. MSA—Medical Savings Accounts/Metropolitan Statistical Area
293. MNC—Multinational Corporation
294. MSCI—Morgan Stanly Capital International
295. MSN—Microsoft Network
296. MTM—Methods-Time Measurement

297. Munis—Municipal Bonds
298. NAA—National Apartment Association
299. NAFTA—North American Free-Trade Agreement
300. NAHB—National Association of Homebuilders
301. NAM—National Association of Manufacturers
302. NAR—National Association of Realtors
303. NASD—National Association of Securities Dealers
304. NASDAQ—National Association of Securities Dealers Automated Quotation
305. NAV—Net Asset Value
306. NBER—National Bureau of Economic Research
307. NFA—National Futures Association
308. NL—No-Load
309. NLRB—National Labor Relations Board
310. NOI—Net Operating Income
311. NOL—Net Operating Loss
312. NOW—Negotiable Order of Withdrawal
313. NPO—Non-Profit Organization
314. NPV—Net Present Value
315. NQSO—Non-qualified Stock Option
316. NR—Not Rated
317. Ns—Nanosecond
318. NSF—Not-Sufficient Funds
319. NTIS—National Technical Information Service
320. NYBOT—New York Board of Trade
321. NYSE—New York Stock Exchange
322. OASDHI—Old Age, Survivors, Disability, and Hospital Insurance
323. OB—Organizational Behavior
324. OCR—Optical Character Recognition
325. OECD—Organization for Economic Cooperation and Development
326. OJT—On-the-job Training
327. OM—Operations Management
328. OMB—Office of Management and Budget
329. OPEC—Organization of Petroleum Exporting Countries
330. OPM—Other People's Money/Option Pricing Model
331. OR—Operations Research
332. OSHA—Occupational Safety and Health Act
333. OTC—Over-the-counter
334. OWC—Owner Carrying
335. PCMCIA—Personal Computer Memory Card International Association
336. P&L—Profit and Loss Statement
337. PAC—Political Action Committee/Pre-Authorized Check
338. PAD—Pre-Authorized Debit
339. PCAOB—Public Company Accounting Oversight Board
340. PCEPI—Personal Consumption Expenditure Price Index

341. PDA—Personal Digital Assistant
342. PDCA—Plan-Do-Check Act Cycle
343. P/E—Price/Earnings Ratio
344. PERT—Program Evaluation Review Technique
345. PGIM—Potential Gross Income Multiplier
346. PIMS—Profit Impact Marketing Strategies
347. PIN—Personal Identification Number
348. PITI—Principal, Interest, Taxes and Interest Payment
349. PMI—Private Mortgage Insurance
350. PMS—Pantone Matching System
351. POP—Point-of-purchase Display
352. POS—Point of Sale
353. PPBS—Program Planning Budgeting System
354. PPI—Producer Price Index
355. PPO—Preferred Provider Organization
356. PPP—Point-to-Point Protocol/Purchasing Power Parity
357. PTN—Private Trading Networks
358. PUD—Planned Unit Development
359. PV—Present Value
360. QLF—Quality Loss Function
361. R&D—Research and Development
362. RAM—Random Access Memory/Reverse Annuity Mortgage
363. REIT—Real Estate Investment Trust
364. RFI—Request for Information
365. RFP—Request for Proposal
366. REPO—Repurchase Agreement
367. RI—Residual Income
368. RIF—Reduction in Force
369. ROA—Return on Assets
370. ROC—Rate of Change
371. ROE—Return on Equity
372. ROI—Return on Investment
373. ROM—Read-Only Memory
374. RSI—Relative Strength Indicators
375. RTC—Resolution Trust Company
376. S&L—Savings and Loan Association
377. S&P—Standard & Poor
378. SBA—Small business Administration
379. SBDC—Small Business Development Centers
380. SBIR—Small business Innovation Research Program
381. SBU—Strategic Business Unit
382. SCM—Supply Chain Management
383. SDR—Special Drawing Rights
384. SEC—Securities and Exchange Commission
385. SEM—Shared Equity Mortgage

386. SEP—Simplified Employee Pension
387. SERP—Supplementary Executive Retirement Plan
388. SIC—Standard Industrial Classification
389. SIG—Special Interest Group
390. SIPC—Securities Investor Protection Corporation
391. SKU—Stock-keeping Unit
392. SLIP—Serial Line Internet Protocol
393. SLMA—Student Loan Marketing Association
394. SMAs—Separated Managed Accounts
395. SML—Security Market Line
396. SMSA—Standard Metropolitan Statistical Area
397. SOHO—Small Office/Home Office
398. SOP—Standard Operating Procedure
399. SPE—Special Purpose Entity
400. SPDR—Spiders (Standard & Poor's Depository Receipt)
401. SPV—Special Purpose Vehicle
402. SSA—Social Security Administration
403. STRIPS—Separate Trading Registered Interest and Principal of Securities
404. SWOT—Strength Weaknesses Opportunity and Threats
405. SYD—Sum-of-the-year's-digits Depreciation
406. T or TB—Terabyte
407. TAB -- Tax Anticipation Bill
408. TAN -- Tax Anticipation Note
409. T-bills, T-notes, T-bonds—Treasury Securities
410. T&E—Travel and Entertainment Expense
411. TCP/IP—Transfer Control Protocol/Internet Protocol
412. TDA—Tax Deferred Annuity
413. TIGR—Treasury Investment Growth Receipt
414. TILA—Truth-In-Lending Act
415. TIPS—Treasury Inflation-Protected Securities
416. TIN—Taxpayer Identification Number
417. TOHO—Tiny Office/Home Office
418. TQM—Total Quality Management
419. TRA—Tax Reform Act
420. UIT—Unit Investment Trust
421. UGMA—Uniform Gifts to Minors Act
422. UCC—Uniform Commercial Code
423. UPC—Universal Product Code
424. UPS—United Parcel Service
425. URL—Uniform Resource Locator
426. USB—Universal Serial Bus
427. User ID—User Identification
428. VA—Veteran's Administration
429. VAT—Value Added Tax
430. VGA—Video Graphic Array

431. VMS—Vertical Marketing System
432. VP—Vice President
433. VRM—Variable Rate Mortgage
434. WAIS—Wide Area Information Server
435. WAN—Wide Area Network
436. WI-FI—Wireless Fidelity
437. WIP—Work in Process
438. WLAN—Wireless LAN
439. WORM—Write Once Read Many
440. WWW—World Wide Web
441. YTD—Year-to-date
442. YTM—Yield to Maturity
443. ZBA—Zero-Bracket Amount
444. ZBB—Zero-Based Budgeting

About TEXERE

Texere, a progressive and authoritative voice in business publishing, brings to the global business community the expertise and insights of leading thinkers. Our books educate, enlighten, and entertain, and provide an intersection where our authors and our readers share cutting edge ideas, practices, and innovative solutions. Texere seeks to cultivate, enhance, and disseminate information that illuminates the global business landscape.

www.thomson.com/learning/texere

About the typeface

This book was set in 10 point Times Roman. In 1931, The Times of London commissioned a new type design for the body copy of the paper. The design process was supervised by Stanley Morison. Times is actually a modernised version of the older typeface "Plantin", which Morison was instructed to use as the main basis for his new designs. Times font became the workhorse of the publishing industry and continues to be very popular, particularly for newspapers, magazines, and corporate communications such as proposals and annual reports. Due to its versatility, it remains a must-have typeface for today's designer.